ELTHAM PALACE

The west end of the interior of the great hall, c.1795, J.M.W. Turner.

ELTHAM PALACE

JOHN PRIESTLEY

First published in 2008 by Phillimore & Co Ltd
This edition 2013

The History Press
The Mill, Brimscombe Port
Stroud, Gloucestershire, GL5 2QG
www.thehistorypress.co.uk

British Library Cataloguing in Publication Data.
A catalogue record for this book is available from the British Library.

ISBN 978 0 7509 5554 6

Typesetting and origination by The History Press
Printed in Great Britain

Exeter:
> To Eltham will I, where the young king is,
> Being ordain'd his special governor;
> And for his safety there I'll best devise.

Winchester:
> Each hath his place and function to attend.
> I am left out; for me nothing remains.
> But long I will not be Jack-out-of-office:
> The king from Eltham I intend to steal,
> And sit at chiefest stern of public weal.

Gloucester:
> You have great reason to do Richard right;
> Especially for those occasions
> At Eltham Place I told your majesty.

King Henry:
> And these occasions, uncle, were of force;
> Therefore, my loving lords, our pleasure is
> That Richard be restored to his blood.
> … … … · ·
> Rise, Richard, like a true Plantagenet,
> And rise created princely Duke of York.

Henry VI Part 1, Act 1, Scene 1 & Act 3, Scene 1

CONTENTS

LIST OF ILLUSTRATIONS

ACKNOWLEDGEMENTS

I wish to acknowledge the information and assistance I have received in researching, writing and publishing this book from the following individuals and institutions:

F.W.W. Bernard; J. Birkbeck; Dr H. Booton; the late Professor A.L. Brown; the late Mrs D.M. Clarke; A. Emery; Professor A. Goodman; the Rt. Rev. S. Hawker; A. Hawkyard; J. Kennett; A.F. Kersting; J. Morgan; S. Mendelsohn; the late P. Paget; the late B. Skinner; D. Sleep; H. Stevenson; L. Taylor.

Art Institute of Chicago; Bibliotheque Nationale, Paris; Bodleian Library, Oxford; British Library; *Country Life*; Deck the Walls, Somerville, NJ, USA; English Heritage; Greenwich Local History Library; HQ DAE; National Gallery of Ireland; National Archives; Royal Commission on Historical Monuments (England); Smith College Museum of Art, MA, USA; Staatsbibliothek zu Berlin; Westminster Abbey Muniments; Yale Center for British Art Reference Library.

Illustrations are reproduced by kind permission of the following individuals and institutions, to whom any request for reproduction should be made:

Army Education: 12, 59, 64; The Art Institute of Chicago (Arthur Devis. Sir John Shaw and his family in the Park at Eltham Lodge, Kent. 1761. Oil on canvas. 134.3 by 199.1 cm. 1951.206. U.S.A): 13; Bibliotheque Nationale, Paris: 2, 4; J. Birkbeck: 63, 66; Bodleian Library, University of Oxford, MS.Top.Gen.d.14. fol.15v.: 16; Bridgeman Art Library: 43, 56; British Library: 5, 8–9; Bury Past and Present Society: 6; *Country Life*: 47–8, 58; William Davidson: 23; English Heritage: 32, 34–8, 60–1; English Heritage (NMR): 11, 33, 39–40, 50, 52, 57; Greenwich Museum: 7, 15, 22; the Rt Rev. Dennis Hawker: 25; J. Kennett: 24, 41, 44–5; A.F. Kersting: 62; J. Morgan: 49, 53–4; The National Archives. Reference MPF 1/228: 19; National Gallery of Ireland: 19; E.J. Priestley: 14, 17–18, 26, 30, 42, 51, 65; Private collection: frontispiece, 55; Smith College Museum of Art, Northampton, Massachusetts: 20; The Society of Antiquaries of London: 46; Staatsbibliothek zu Berlin – Preussischer Kultur Besitz: 1, 3; H. Stevenson: 27–9, 31; L. Taylor: 21.

PREFACE

Part of the history of a royal building consists of its links with royalty and national events, which in the case of Eltham Palace cover a period of three-and-a-half centuries. Its buildings, gardens, vineyards and parks and the staff responsible for their upkeep also feature while the effect on the local community of having a royal building in its midst should not be forgotten.

Like other royal buildings outside London, those at Eltham were, for most of the year, only inhabited by a few resident officials and occasionally visited by others concerned with future royal visits and the repairs and new buildings these entailed. Building works at Eltham sometimes involved the employment of considerable numbers of workmen. Records of royal itineraries and the dates of official correspondence sent from Eltham show that, in most years, court visits to the palace only occurred two or three times annually, although sometimes years seem to have elapsed between visits. Many of these lasted for about ten days; a few were longer and many were very brief. Easter and Christmas were favourite seasons for the court to come to Eltham.

While the court was at Eltham the palace was, for a few days, the centre of administration for the whole country as regards that part of the royal government that travelled with the monarch. During such visits a great many people came to Eltham on official and personal business, the largest numbers coming at Easter when alms were distributed to the poor.

Many medieval and Tudor chronicles mention Eltham in connection with court visits, the arrival there of foreign royalty and ambassadors, and the tournaments and festivities held there at Easter and Christmas. A large number of letters and official records coming from Eltham survive, as well as records concerning its staff, buildings, parks, gardens and home farm. From these sources, and from wills, court rolls, church registers and modern reports of excavations on the palace site, the earlier chapters of this history have been written. Other records have been used for the later history of the palace after most of its royal buildings were destroyed during the 17th century.

The royal buildings at Eltham while still complete were known as Eltham House, according to the manorial survey of 1649. The term 'palace' is used for them in a travel diary reference of 1609 and John Evelyn, who saw them in ruins in 1656, uses both 'house' and 'palace' in referring to them in his diary in that year. John Philipot, writing of them three years later, also calls them a palace, as does Harris, the Kentish historian, who mentions them in his early 18th-century history of Kent. The description of them as Eltham Palace seems to have arisen in the 1790s and has been generally used since that time.

1
ELTHAM BEFORE THE ROYAL PALACE

Bishop Antony Bek of Durham. ... Manerium de Eltham juxta Londoniam curiosissime aedificavit ...
(Robertus de Graystanes, *Historia Dunelmensis*, Surtees Society, 1839)

The modern dormitory suburb of Eltham is now part of the borough of Greenwich in south-east London. From it St Paul's can be seen on the horizon towards the north-west, six miles from the western end of the parish, while Greenwich Palace is two miles north of Eltham. Its neighbouring suburbs are Woolwich to the north, Bexley to the east, Mottingham to the south and Lewisham to the west, all former villages that, like Eltham, are now part of the conurbation of Greater London.

Eltham parish is situated on the north-west corner of the North Downs at the point where it slopes down towards the north-west. The old parish had its highest point, 425 feet above sea level, at its north-east corner where the boundary touched Watling Street as that highway crossed Shooter's Hill on its way from London to Dover. Lee Green, at the western end of the parish, was the lowest area, being just over fifty feet above sea level. Between Shooters's Hill and Eltham's high street there is a shallow valley, while to the south of that road the ground slopes downhill towards Mottingham. To the west of the high street those obscure streams the Quaggy and Kid Brook flow northwards across low-lying ground towards the Thames.

The high street of the old village of Eltham is part of the main road between Bexley and Lewisham, on its way towards London. It runs from east to west along the crest of a broad ridge, dropping some fifty feet in height over its length of three-quarters of a mile. Nearby, a short distance to the south-west of the old village and about 175 feet above sea level, there formerly existed the principal reason for the many references to Eltham in medieval and Tudor chronicles and official records: the ancient royal palace of Eltham, of whose former magnificence there now remains only its great hall, situated within a moat crossed by an old bridge, and a few buildings that have survived from its outer court. These are now the sole remnants of what was once one of the largest of the English royal homes, a building comparable in size with Windsor Castle, Hampton Court or Greenwich.

At some time in the mid–17th century, probably during the 1650s, the greater part of the old palace was pulled down. A surviving fragment became a farm, together with a new farm building, for which the former great hall, its roof stripped of lead and retiled, served as a barn. The palace parks became farmland and Eltham a quiet rural parish until, 200 years later, the provision of cheap and easy transport to London with the building of the Dartford Loop line in the 1860s, followed by the Bexleyheath line in the 1890s, began the process of turning the parish from a farming community into a dormitory suburb. The population greatly increased, especially in the present century, and new housing estates sprang up on land that in earlier times had formed the parks attached to the royal palace.[1] As houses multiplied, farms disappeared, until the recent closure of the last farm in the parish, situated near the south side of the moated site, which had been the inner palace court.

Prior to the appearance of the manor of Eltham in 1086 in Domesday Book, very little is known of the area's history. A find of Roman burial urns in 1913, on a site about a mile to the north of the palace moat,[2] and the discovery of Roman roof tiles in a rubbish pit during the palace excavations in the 1970s,[3] show that a Roman settlement or villa formerly existed in the area, but its exact location has not been discovered. The situation regarding the Anglo-Saxon settlement of the area is similar as no early sites for this occupation, believed to have taken place c.A.D. 600, have been found, although the excavations at the palace site previously mentioned uncovered Anglo-Saxon pottery and the foundations of a late 11th-century building within the moat.[4] These finds may perhaps be associated with Alwold, the last holder of the manor before the Norman Conquest. Domesday Book records that Alwold held the manor of Eltham from Edward the Confessor,[5] but it is not known when the Anglo-Saxon monarchy first acquired it.

The first written reference to Eltham is in Domesday Book.[6] The name is spelt 'Alteham' in 1086. Other spellings are found in later records and the present form of 'Eltham' is not recorded until 150 years later, and even then it was not invariably used until many years afterwards. The name probably dates from the time when the area was first settled by the Anglo-Saxons. The earliest effort to explain it is in Lysons' *Environs of London*, published at the end of the 18th century, in which Lysons suggests that the original spelling of the place-name was 'ealdham', with the meaning of 'old home or dwelling', although this particular spelling is not recorded among the early versions of the place-name that eventually became 'Eltham'.[7] It is more likely that its correct explanation is one of those suggested by two Swedish scholars who studied the origins of English place-names. One suggestion for its origin is that the original form of the name was 'Elta's ham', with 'Elta' being a personal Anglo-Saxon name and 'ham' meaning settlement. Other possibilities are that the first syllable might stand for a different personal name, that of Elfeta, or that this syllable refers to the Anglo-Saxon word 'elfetu', which means 'swan'.[8]

In Domesday Book the annual value of the manor before the Norman Conquest is given as £16 a year. By the time it had been acquired by its first Norman tenant-in-chief its annual value was £12, which rose to £20 by 1086.[9] These amounts are thought to be estimates of the yearly rent obtainable for the manor and suggest that the local effect of the Conquest, as in many other places, had been a loss of stock or other damage that was later made good and further improved by 1086. At that date Eltham was taxed on a valuation of one-and-a-half sulungs, or about 360 acres. A sulung was a Kentish land measure which dated back to an earlier time when the hundred, the Anglo–Saxon area of administration, was divided into sulungs for administrative purposes. In 1086 Eltham had about 180 acres of arable land. Of this, 30 acres formed the demesne, or home farm, of the lord of the manor, an area farmed for him by serfs with help from local peasant farmers who owed their lord services of ploughing, harrowing, sowing, reaping and carting. They also rented other land from him for which they paid rent.

By 1086 Eltham's farmers, who rented arable land for 12 plough teams, owned 11 teams of oxen. A further two teams were on the demesne of the lord of the manor. As each team would have had eight oxen the manor would have had about a hundred plough oxen to cultivate its arable land. The population of Eltham, as recorded in Domesday Book, consisted of 42 villein farmers, 12 lesser farmers, called bordars or cotters, and nine landless serfs. It is believed that villeins might have rented from 15 to 30 acres each and bordars about five acres, while the serfs worked for the lord of the manor on his home farm. Including their families, the population of Eltham at the end of the 11th century would have numbered from two to three hundred.

From what is known of other manors, Eltham's manorial livestock, apart from plough oxen, would have included horses, cows, pigs and sheep, all on record there in later centuries. Pigs were there by 1086 as the manor had a wood for which 50 pigs were given each year to the lord of the manor in return for the right, known as pannage, to feed them there.[10] Some of these animals would have been grazed on the manor's common land.

After the information recorded on Eltham in Domesday Book, nearly two centuries elapse for which very little indeed is known about the manor, although much is known about the successive tenants-in-chief who held it from the king. For most of them Eltham was only one of many manors that they held and, until the last years of the 13th century, there is no documentary evidence that any of them ever visited it. They included some notable personalities, some of them friends of royalty or marrying into the royal family, others rebels who were imprisoned or exiled. Two captured kings in battle, while a female tenant-in-chief married a future king, though her marriage was annulled before she could become queen.

As far as is known, Alwold's immediate successor at Eltham was Odo, or Eudes, Bishop of Bayeux, Earl of Kent and the younger half-brother of William I. Odo's representative in Eltham was Haimo, the Sheriff of Kent, a kinsman of the king who was the holder of the manor in 1086 from Bishop Odo.[11] Odo is recorded as holding 200 manors in Kent alone. He probably never visited Eltham but Haimo, who held only a few manors from him, probably would have been there.

Odo, more a baron than a churchman, became Bishop of Bayeux when he was about twenty. He took an active part in the preparations for the invasion of England and fought at the Battle of Hastings. His reward from his half-brother was larger than that given to any other of William's followers, consisting of 500 English manors and the title of Earl of Kent. In spite of this generosity these rewards were insufficient for him and he took, wrongfully, a number of further manors which he was later compelled to surrender.

Second in power only to the king, and a ruthless suppressor of rebellion, Odo had still greater ambitions. He sought, with the aid of other barons, to raise soldiers for an unauthorised expedition of his own overseas; he was also reputed to wish to become pope. His plans were, however, disrupted in 1082 when he was arrested at the king's command, William being the only person powerful enough to do this as, quite apart from his power based on his possessions, he was protected by his clerical status. Even the king was reported to have said that Odo was arrested 'Not as Bishop of Bayeux but as Earl of Kent'.

Kept in royal custody in Normandy for five years, Odo was only released in 1087, when his half-brother was on his deathbed. He returned to England, where he still held Eltham and his other manors, and in the following year led a rebellion against the new king, William II. During this revolt Odo was taken prisoner after a siege of Pevensey Castle from which he was taken to Rochester Castle, held by the rebels, to give its garrison his personal order to surrender, a plan disrupted when the castle garrison made a sortie and rescued him. After Rochester Castle's surrender Odo was banished from England and lost all his English manors. He went to Normandy where he became the principal advisor to Robert, Duke of Normandy, William II's elder brother. He died in 1097 while he and the duke were on their way to Palestine to take part in the First Crusade.[12]

When Bishop Odo lost his English manors in 1088, Haimo, who had held Eltham from Odo, became its new tenant-in-chief and was also presented with other manors. Haimo is believed to have died shortly before 1100, leaving two sons, Haimo and Robert, of whom one or both followed their father as tenant-in-chief of Eltham. Some years later the manor was held by Robert's daughter Mabel, the wife of Robert, Earl of Gloucester, an illegitimate son of Henry I. Eltham and many other manors held by the earl and his wife were to remain in the possession of their descendants for the next century-and-a-half.[13]

Robert was created Earl of Gloucester in 1122, a contemporary writing of him that he was given this title to make him of equal social status with his wife, a royal ward and a wealthy kinswoman of the royal family.[14] He was to play an important part in the civil war between Matilda, Henry I's daughter and former Empress of Germany, and her first cousin Stephen, son of William I's daughter Adela. Henry I had tried to ensure his daughter's succession to the throne by getting the barons to swear allegiance to her but, on his death in 1135, Stephen became king by obtaining the support of the senior royal officials and of the Londoners who preferred being ruled by a king. The Earl of Gloucester initially swore allegiance to Stephen in 1136 but two years later renounced this and in 1139 led an army from Normandy that escorted Matilda across the Channel, thus beginning the civil war.

The miseries that accompanied this war, as seen in East Anglia, are vividly described in the *Anglo-Saxon Chronicle*, which records that people 'said openly that Christ and his saints were asleep'. The soldiers of this war spared nobody.

'There had never been till then greater misery in the country … they respected neither church nor churchyard but they took all the property that was inside and then burnt the church … .'

A modern historian has paid tribute to Robert's chivalry, courage and intelligence, even though he allowed his army to burn Nottingham and sack Lincoln. Early chroniclers with differing allegiances in this civil war describe his character in very different ways. One wrote of him that he threatened much but did little, 'lionlike in his speech, but like a hare in his heart, great in eloquence but insignificant through laziness', while a more friendly chronicler wrote in praise of his magnanimity, generosity, prudence and the support he gave to scholars. His outstanding virtue was loyalty; unlike some of the other barons who took part in this civil war, he stayed loyal to one side, that of his half-sister.[15]

At the Battle of Lincoln in 1141 Robert captured Stephen but was himself taken prisoner later that year in a battle fought outside Winchester, after which the two were exchanged. In 1148 a temporary end to the civil war was reached, a year after Robert's death, but it later broke out again before ending finally in 1153 with the compromise that Stephen was to reign until his death, when he would be succeeded by Matilda's son Henry, who was crowned King Henry II on the death of Stephen in 1154.

William, the second Earl of Gloucester, was less formidable than his father. Initially a supporter of Henry II, he later aroused that king's suspicions and was imprisoned by him for a time. Very little is known of Eltham under the Earls of Gloucester, only the name of a local landowner and information that its tithes went to a prior and convent in Rochester, a grant agreed to by Henry I, confirmed by Richard I and later altered by Edward III.[16] William was one of the greatest of English landowners and had a son and three daughters. In 1167 the son died and nine years later the earl reached an agreement with Henry II about the future of his estates. These were to be inherited by his youngest daughter, Isabel, who was to marry Prince John, the king's youngest son, who later became king after the death in 1199 of his elder brother, Richard I.

On her father's death in 1183 Isabel became Countess of Gloucester in her own right but she did not marry John until 1189, soon after his father's death, as the Archbishop of Canterbury raised objections to the marriage on the grounds that John and Isabel were within the forbidden degrees of matrimony as they were second cousins. An appeal to the Pope, and the friendly intervention of a visiting papal legate, eventually allowed the marriage to take place, Isabel becoming the Countess of Mortain, but the marriage was flawed by the fact that a papal dispensation, which would have made it unquestionably legal, was never obtained.

On Richard I's death his younger brother John became king. Isabel, however, never became queen, as her husband, by whom she had no children, decided to repudiate her and, with the assistance of the bishops of his lands in France, obtained a decree of nullification of his marriage from the ecclesiastical courts, after which he married Isabel of Angoulême. This new marriage produced its own problems for John as his new queen had formerly been engaged to an influential French nobleman and the offence given to him had its effects on the war with France that broke out in 1202, during which the French captured Normandy.[17]

For most of John's reign Eltham, with Isabel's other lands, remained under the king's control as he kept his former wife a state prisoner until 1214, when he sold her marriage to Geoffrey de Mandeville, Earl of Essex, for the huge sum of 20,000 marks (about £16,000). By marrying Isabel the earl obtained a second earldom and control of his wife's fortune but he also went into debt to the Crown until the price of the marriage was fully paid up, a weapon that John could use against the earl if he so wished. By now Eltham had three different manors, Eltham, Eltham Mandeville and Eltham Albemarle, of which the latter two were possibly created in John's reign.

When, in 1215, the year of Magna Carta, the Earl of Essex and Gloucester joined the barons in arms against King John, his action once more placed Eltham and his other lands in the king's hands. In the following year both the king and the earl died, the latter while taking part in a tournament in London. Isabel then married Hubert de Burgh, Justiciar of England, in 1217, only to die herself very soon afterwards.[18] From these years a little information on Eltham survives in a fragmentary bailiff's account from 1216-19, which records the disposal of crops of wheat grown on two Kentish manors, of which one was Eltham. Some of this wheat was made into bread, some given in allowances (wages in kind) to ploughmen, harrowers and serfs, and some sown as seed grain, while most of the remainder was fed to animals, with an allowance of grain being given to a hermit living in Eltham.[19]

Some further information on Eltham in this period comes from excavations carried out within the moated area on the site of the future inner court of the palace in the 1970s. In the late 12th and early 13th centuries there were buildings on this site but from c.1250 to 1280 the area was under crops. New buildings were then erected, presumably for John, Isabel or William de Vescy, who held the manor between 1278 and c.1300, but these buildings were demolished when a manor house was built on the site for Bishop Antony Bek of Durham at the end of the 13th century.[20]

On the death of Isabel de Burgh in 1217, her possessions, including the manor of Eltham, were inherited by Gilbert, Earl of Hertford, the son of Isabel's elder sister Amice, second daughter of William, Earl of Gloucester. Both Gilbert and his father were among the 25 barons appointed in 1215 to be guardians for the observance of Magna Carta by King John. After the king's death Gilbert continued to be an opponent of royal power, now represented by John's young son Henry III. When the rebel barons were defeated by a royal army in 1217 at Lincoln, Gilbert was captured by the Earl of Pembroke, leader of the royal army. In the same year, besides inheriting his aunt's lands and being recognised as Earl of Gloucester, Gilbert married his captor's daughter, Isabel.[21]

When Gilbert died in 1230 his son Richard de Clare, the new Earl of Hertford and Gloucester, was only eight and he became a royal ward, his guardian being Hubert de Burgh, now Earl of Kent, the former husband of Richard's great-aunt Isabel. Some years later, apparently without the knowledge or consent of Hubert, Richard married his guardian's daughter, Margaret. Richard's lands were in wardship for 13 years, during which time they were said to have been 'marvellously and in various ways wasted', but we do not know how far this was true of his manor of Eltham.[22] On reaching the age of 21, in 1243, Richard was at last able to take possession of the lands he had inherited in 1230.[23]

Richard, Earl of Hertford and Gloucester, was an important nobleman in mid-13th-century England. His contemporaries described him as an intellectual and '… graceful, eloquent … and well skilled in the laws', but also as avaricious, deceitful and an unsuccessful soldier. He began his political career as a supporter of Henry III, who sent him on diplomatic missions, but he later went over to the king's opponents led by Simon de Montfort, Earl of Leicester, and was active in enforcing new conditions of government on the king at Oxford in 1258. By the time of his death in 1262 he had, however, changed sides again and was once more a supporter of Henry III.[24]

A survey carried out in 1262 of the holdings of the late Earl of Hertford and Gloucester includes the first detailed information on the manor of Eltham since the time of Domesday Book. The demesne or home farm contained 206 acres of arable land, 13 acres of pasture and two acres of meadow, the latter being valued at 3s. per acre per year whereas similar valuations for pasture were only 4d., while arable varied between 2½d. and 4d. An area of fenced woodland covering 200 acres was valued at 5d. per acre per year, including income from pasturage, pannage and the sale of underwood. Villeins farmed 216 acres and 245 acres of 'new land' were rented to villeins at 'the lord's will', indicating that this area was rented on different conditions to those applying to the other acreage. As 'new land' was land only recently reclaimed from the forest for the plough, or from common land, it would appear that Eltham's population was growing, as more land was being farmed within the manor than in the past.

In 1262 the manor was worth £20 13s. 4¾d. annually to its lord, a sum made up of the value of the produce of the demesne, rents paid on the lands mentioned above, further rents paid by free tenants who had not been recorded earlier and who owed no customary services, rents paid by others, the value of works carried out by villeins on the demesne and income from the manorial court.[25] The recorded acreage covers only half the area of the present-day parish and the rest would have been within Eltham's other two manors, land farmed by free tenants and others and common land.

When Richard de Clare died, his son was already 19 so he did not have to wait long before taking over his inheritance. He was already married by 1262 to Alice de Lusignan, a niece of Henry III, but this marriage broke down and was annulled in 1271. As the most powerful nobleman in England, Gilbert took an active part in politics and, unlike his father, he was a successful soldier. In the civil war between Henry III and the barons, led by Simon de Montfort, he initially supported the rebels and, at their victory of the Battle of Lewes in 1264, captured both Henry III and the king's brother, Richard, Earl of Cornwall. After this victory, however, Gilbert found that he was ignored by Simon, who took most of the business of government upon himself, so he changed sides. In the following year at the Battle of Evesham he led an army in support of the royalists, who were triumphant, and Simon was killed. Henry III, a prisoner of the rebel army, was released by this victory by the combined forces of Prince Edward, later to become Edward I, Gilbert, Earl of Hertford and Gloucester, and other barons.

Gilbert's support for Henry III depended upon his opinion of how royal policies affected himself and, two years after Evesham, in protest against the way in which the king had kept his promises about ruling the country, the earl raised an army that occupied London until a peaceful compromise was reached between the king and himself. This behaviour must have been later ignored, after Henry III's death in 1272 and while Prince Edward was crusading in Palestine, when Gilbert was one of those appointed as guardians of the realm to rule England until the return of the new king.

The earl became a close friend of Edward I, whose daughter Joan of Acre he married in 1290, although she was nearly thirty years younger than himself.[26] Twelve years earlier, probably shortly before January 1278, he had parted with his manor of Eltham by granting it to John de Vescy. Under the earl's ownership the manor had increased considerably in value since 1262,[27] but it is unknown whether this was the result of good management or due to the earl obtaining more Eltham land. When, in 1280, John de Vescy surrendered it to the king,[28] to be regranted to himself and his wife Isabel, its annual value was £33 6s. ¼d.[29]

John de Vescy, Eltham's new tenant-in-chief, was another former ally of Simon de Montfort. Captured at Evesham, he had been released but then became a rebel in the north of England until he was recaptured by Prince Edward, when Alnwick Castle was taken after a siege. Like Gilbert, he became a friend of Edward I, who employed him on diplomatic missions and whom he accompanied on a crusade.[30] He improved his manor of Eltham in 1284 by obtaining a grant of a weekly market and a three-day annual fair,[31] and two years later he enlarged his Eltham landholdings by an exchange of lands with another local landowner, Walter de Mandeville,[32] also acquiring land from other local landowners.[33] John appears to have died early in 1289 as in April of that year his lands in Eltham were ordered to be delivered to his widow Isabel,[34] another relative of Henry III. John's brother William also held land in Eltham.[35]

Like his brother and Gilbert de Clare, William de Vescy was another former supporter of Simon de Montfort. Apart from his lands in Eltham and elsewhere in England, he owned property and held official positions in Ireland, besides being an aspirant to the throne of Scotland after it became vacant in 1290 on the death of Margaret, the Maid of Norway and granddaughter of Alexander III. William, however, withdrew his claim to the Scottish throne just before Edward I gave his decision on which of the claimants had the best right to it.[36] Like his brother John, William did not hold possession of his lands in Eltham for long, in 1295 granting his estate there to Antony Bek, Bishop of Durham,[37] an action in which he was followed by his sister-in-law Isabel, who kept her life interest there until c.1300.[38] She then exchanged her rights in Eltham for property elsewhere held by the bishop, who thus obtained all the de Vescy lands in Eltham.

Antony Bek, last of the non-royal holders of the manor of Eltham, was a notable personality. Starting as a royal clerk, he later became a friend of both Edward I, with whom he went on crusade in 1270, and of Edward, Prince of Wales, later Edward II, to whom he was to give the manor of Eltham. Elected Bishop of Durham in 1283 and Patriarch of Jerusalem in 1305, his ability and influence with popes and kings was to raise his see of Durham to a position of autonomy from other ecclesiastical and secular jurisdictions that lasted until the Reformation. He was much admired by his contemporaries, of whom one referred to him as 'The noble Bishop of Durham the most valiant clerk in Christendom'.[39]

Bishop Antony Bek is the first holder of the manor of Eltham to leave a record of having visited it, mostly as a witness to documents sealed there during the 16 years that he owned the manor. He is recorded there on 10 occasions in nine different years.[40] He is also known to have had important building works carried out there, which are mentioned in his biography by Robert of Graystanes.[41] During the 1970s, archaeological excavations uncovered the foundations of some of Bishop Bek's buildings situated on the western side of the moated site, these consisting of a great hall with a tiled floor, a cellar and several towers. The hall, built c.1300, was 24 yards in length, north to south, and 9.6 yards in width, with a cellar on its northern side.[42] This hall was burnt down on 27 February 1450, by which date its tiles had become badly worn.[43]

In spite of having had these building works carried out at Eltham, the bishop presented the manor in 1305 to Edward, Prince of Wales, though he reserved his right to use it himself as long as he lived[44] and it was there that he died on 3 March 1311. His personality, achievements and high moral character, and perhaps most of all his success in upholding and extending the rights of his episcopal see, earned him the unprecedented honour of becoming the first bishop of Durham to be buried in Durham Cathedral, where St Cuthbert was buried.[45] He had been a valued royal councillor for a number of years under both Edward I and Edward II, of whom the latter showed his appreciation of his services by remitting all the bishop's debts to the Crown 'for the good and laudable service which the patriarch and bishop showed our father, and for the great affection he had towards us, and also for the immense gifts liberally given us by the said patriarch and bishop while he lived'.[46]

A record of the bishop's property, made just after his death, informs us that his manor of Eltham was valued at £31 16s. 10d. a year.[47] This valuation is below that for Eltham when it was possessed by John de Vesci in 1278 and 1280 but it is half as much again as when it had been held earlier by the Earl of Hertford and Gloucester in 1262. By 1311 the bishop held twice as much arable land and four times as much pasture in Eltham, in demesne, as the earl had held there 50 years earlier but, whereas the annual value per acre of his arable there had risen slightly, and of his meadowland substantially, the annual value of his pasture had fallen, per acre, by more than half.[48] The bishop's possessions in Eltham are listed as being a house and a garden, a dovecot, a windmill, a deer park, a wood, two acres of meadowland, 50 acres of pasture and 421 acres of arable.[49] The bishop's park in Eltham also appears in official records in 1309, when an inquiry was ordered into a raid that had been carried out upon it.[50]

While Eltham was still in the possession of Bishop Bek it received its first recorded royal visit on 2 August 1297, when Edward I sealed a convention there with some noblemen from Burgundy with both the Prince of Wales and Bishop Bek among the witnesses present.[51] The same day also witnessed the official end to a domestic drama within the royal family. On the death of the Earl of Hertford and Gloucester in 1295, his widow Joan of Acre was still under thirty and she was determined to choose her second husband herself before her father arranged to have her married off for reasons of state. She therefore made a clandestine marriage to Ralph de Monthermer[52] and her father was, understandably, very angry when he discovered what she had done. After two years, however, he must have realised that her marriage would have to be recognised and in 1297 Ralph de Monthermer was granted an official pardon.[53]

In November 1297 the king and his court, including once more both the Prince of Wales and Bishop Bek, returned to Eltham for a longer stay than the brief one of the previous August. During this visit a number of official records were sent which are briefly mentioned here as they are typical of the large numbers of documents sent from the palace in later years, showing also the variety of governmental matters attended to by royal officials during their travels with the court. One letter ordered the observation of the terms of Magna Carta and the Charter of Forests,[54] others that the heirs of deceased tenants-in-chief should take control of the estates they had inherited.[55] Further orders were concerned with the repair of certain buildings,[56] and that certain officials should receive their pay,[57] and the supply of hay and oats to the park deer at Windsor.[58] Other records include an agreement about a marriage,[59] an order to deliver land to a man who had lent 500 marks to the king,[60] the grant of a market and fair,[61] orders levying soldiers to serve against the Scots[62] with arrangements for the purchase of grain to feed these soldiers,[63] and orders to the exchequer about a debt to the king and to release from prison men accused of murder.[64] Such documents transmitted orders on subjects agreed between the king and his council, rewarded subjects and, while safeguarding royal rights and income, gave royal authority for the transfer of land and other matters. They also arranged royal finances, granted pardons and authorised secular and ecclesiastical appointments. Royal income was also raised from the fees paid for the grant of royal authority in certain of these matters such as appointments.

II

THE EARLY YEARS OF ROYAL ELTHAM

The Queen of England … went to Eltham … (and) sat solemnly at 'a table in the hall (with) all the knights and esquires of Hainault … and at the end of the dinner … there entered into the hall … twelve esquires … these … carried, two by two, each a great basket … all full of vessels of silver … shared out … to the knights and esquires.

(J. Froissart, *Oeuvres* (ed. K. de Lettenhove), Vol. ii, 1870, translated)

Once the manor of Eltham had been presented to the Prince of Wales in 1305, a knight and a clerk took official possession of it for the prince[1] who, like the bishop, occasionally visited the manor.[2] Later in that year he gave a great banquet there, with Bishop Bek and the Mayor and burgesses of London among his guests.[3] In 1307 he became king and in the following year he and his newly married queen, Isabella of Valois, visited Eltham while on their way back to London from France for his belated coronation.[4] They also came there in 1311,[5] six months after the death of Bishop Bek, and in the following year Edward II made a new grant to the manor of a market and a fair to be held there.[6]

With the manor and buildings in full royal ownership and possession, Eltham was soon regularly visited by the court. It so happens that only from these years does detailed information survive about food supplied to the court when it was there. In October 1311, when part of the queen's household moved to Eltham, bread, beer, cheese and flour were brought there by boat and cart for use by the pantry and buttery household departments, bread also being baked there in the palace ovens.[7] The larder, poultry and saucery departments purchased oysters, salt,[8] coal[9] and wood[10] for court use while beds were hired to be used by some visiting messengers of the King of France.[11] The hall and chamber household departments also appear in these Eltham accounts, which in addition mention the presence at the palace of the queen's chaplain[12] and physician,[13] and of a certain John the Organist, Frenchman.[14] Stable accounts record the wages of the grooms who looked after the queen's warhorses and palfreys there, as well as the cost of caring for a horse that had fallen sick at Eltham during this court visit.[15] Courtiers bought their own horses that they used while they were travelling with the court, but if these died the owners were compensated, as happened for two men during this Eltham visit.[16] Eleanor de Despencer, a lady with the court during this visit, must have remembered it later, as her husband took her sumpter horses and carriage and special arrangements had to be made to provide transport for her.[17] The palace chapel also appears in these accounts when a length of cloth of gold was issued to the queen's tailor in order that a chasuble be made for the priest serving the chapel.[18]

In November 1312 Prince Edward, the future Edward III, was born at Windsor.[19] In the following January the Queen came to Eltham, presumably with her child, travelling by way of London from whence she was escorted to Eltham by the Fishmongers' Company, described as wearing linen costumes embroidered in gold with the arms of England and France. These arms also appeared on 'a certain ship, worked with a certain marvellous cunning, with mast and sail erect', which preceded the queen's procession.[20]

Further royal household departments appear in accounts that refer to one or more court visits to Eltham in 1313-14.[21] These were the scullery[22] and great wardrobe departments,[23] and the accounts also mention the presence there of the queen's confessor,[24] ironmonger[25] and chandler.[26] Purchases during these visits included silk, used to line the roofs of the queen's carriages, and a cord with iron rings attached, used to make horses lie down.[27] Medieval medical science also appears in a list of ingredients bought by the queen's apothecary to treat Isabella's arm and hand. These were green wax, resin, oil of hempseed, quicksilver, verdigris, formalin, oils, 'aurilian rose leaves' and a plaster—certain items sound as if they would do more harm than good to Queen Isabella.[28]

John second son of Edward II and Queen Isabella, known as 'John of Eltham', was born at the palace in August 1316 and baptised in the chapel there with the font decorated with 'Turkey cloth' and cloth of gold.[29] Soon afterwards a churching service was held there, for which the queen wore a white velvet robe.[30] News of the birth of Prince John was sent to the king, then near York, who gave the fortunate messenger, a knight, a reward of £100.[31] Early in the 1320s Eltham may have been a royal nursery, as a companion from Eltham to Prince Edward is on record.[32] John of Eltham and his sister Joan shared the same nurse, Maude de Pirye, who was later given a royal pension by Edward III for her services.[33] Before that time, some twenty years later, John of Eltham died in Scotland in 1336. His tomb is in Westminster Abbey.[34]

When the court came to Eltham, official messengers were sent from there to all parts of the country. In one court visit during Edward II's reign they were sent from there to York, Canterbury, Holbeach, the Isle of Ely and Windsor. Full-time official messengers were not always used, as happened with the news of the birth of John of Eltham, and minor members of the court were sometimes employed for this purpose. In 1313-14 payments are recorded to message carriers from Eltham who were a porter, a cook, a clerk and a boy, the last of whom took letters to Windsor.[35] Visitors to the court while it was at Eltham in this reign are also sometimes recorded, such as the Earl of Warenne, with 11 Welsh archers;[36] the Bishop of Exeter's squire, with a sturgeon from the Thames; a sailor from Sandwich; squires and retainers.[37] Some visitors came seeking alms, given out by custom on Good Friday, and another form of charity recorded there in this reign was the feeding of 200 poor men at a cost of 1½d. a man.[38]

During the night of 26 June 1326, shortly after the end of a court visit to Eltham,[39] the French-born royal bailiff, Hervey de Forges, was killed in the course of a robbery on his Eltham home. Adam le Waferer, a leader of a gang of thieves and a murderer,[40] killed Hervey with a knife while he and his men were stealing Hervey's gold rings and brooches, silver cups, spoons, linen and woollen cloth valued at £20,[41] a valuation later increased to £100.[42] Hervey died in the arms of his wife Maud, who raised a hue and cry after the gang but without any immediate results.[43] Afterwards, four days after the murder, the coroner of the king's household held an inquiry,[44] this being followed on 6 July by the issue of orders to five men to 'follow and arrest Adam le Waferer and all in his company'.[45]

Before Adam's capture in the following year, dramatic events had taken place in England, the result of Edward II's unpopularity and of his estrangement from his queen. Isabella had gone on a visit to her French homeland and while she was there she arranged for Prince Edward to join her, ostensibly so the prince could do homage for Aquitaine to the King of France in the place of his father. Instead of returning to England, however, Isabella, in the company of her son and of Roger Mortimer, who had escaped from the Tower of London where he had been held for rebellion, went to Hainault in Flanders where she raised an army to invade England and depose her husband. The money to pay the rebel army came from the dowry of Philippa, daughter of the Count of Hainault, who, as arranged by Isabella and the Count, should marry Prince Edward. In September 1326 Isabella and her army landed in England, Edward II being captured by her supporters in Wales two months later. In January 1327 Edward II was deposed and succeeded by his son as Edward III. In the following September the former king was murdered in Berkeley Castle.[46]

At an unknown place and date early in the new reign Adam le Waferer was captured and by May 1327 he was held in Pontefract Castle in Yorkshire.[47] As Edward III twice gave orders that Adam was to be brought before him for trial[48] it would seem that he took a personal interest in this particular case and might have known Hervey de Forges at Eltham. On 9 May Adam was brought before Edward at York, where he was accused by Maud de Forges of the murder of her husband. In reply Adam denied committing either the murder or the robbery, saying that he was prepared to stand trial. This was to take place in York on 29 June.[49] A further inquiry was also ordered into the murder and robbery, to be held in Deptford before the Sheriff of Kent and two county coroners five days before the trial in York.[50]

The next information is the unexpected news of Adam's name being listed among a number of men accused of murder, with the names of those whom they were accused of killing. All were offered pardons on condition that they joined the English forces then serving against the Scots.[51] Adam did not take advantage of this offer but instead escaped from York Castle at some date before 20 July when fresh orders were issued for his arrest and of all others in his company 'as the king's rebels, dead or alive'. One man was given the task of capturing Adam and his associates.[52] At this point all information on this murder and robbery and the pursuit of Adam and his gang ends, so it is unknown whether these men were ever caught and brought to trial.

Within a month of his accession Edward III made a grant of the manor of Eltham to his mother, together with a great many other manors,[53] and soon afterwards he visited Eltham.[54] At this time he had the title of king but no personal power, all important decisions being taken by Roger Mortimer, created Earl of the March of Wales in 1328, and his mother.[55]

In August 1327 a farewell banquet was given at Eltham to the leaders of the Hainault forces who had served Isabella against her husband. Their departure from England was probably hastened by a clash that took place between them and the people of York the previous June, their presence in England now being unpopular. For this feast Isabella, accompanied by Edward III, her other children and the Earl of Kent, a half-brother of Edward II, arrived for 'a grand and large meal' held in the palace hall, probably the hall built earlier for Bishop Bek that would be burnt down in 1450. The meal ended with the arrival of trumpeters and minstrels to entertain the diners, followed by 12 richly dressed knights and 12 squires, of whom the latter carried, two by two, large baskets filled with silver cups, dishes, spoons and other items constituting a reward from Queen Isabella to the Hainault men. Having been carried round the tables, their contents were then shared out among the diners by two knights on a basis of 'to each according to his state', with a further £100, in cash, being shared out among the Hainaulter pages and grooms present. The guests then said farewell to the queen mother and the royal family and to their leader Count John, brother of their ruler, who was to stay on in England for several more months. The Hainaulters were then seen off from the palace courtyard where they mounted their horses and set off for Dover to embark for Flanders.[56]

The last part of the agreement between Queen Isabella and the Count of Hainault was completed with the arrival, in December 1327, of Philippa, the future queen of Edward III, at Dover. She was escorted from there to Eltham by her uncle Count John and other knights. At the palace she met a large number of lords and ladies of the court and said farewell to her uncle and her Hainault escort. She then set off for York where she was to marry Edward III in January 1328.[57]

The early years of Edward III's reign, while Queen Isabella and Roger Mortimer held power, witnessed frequent visits by the court to Eltham, the court being there in six different months in 1329.[58] Their rule was unpopular with many people, in part because they had failed to prevent Scottish raids into England and had followed this failure by making a humiliating peace with Scotland.[59] In 1330, the year after the death of Robert the Bruce, a delegation arrived at Eltham from Robert I's successor, David II, to discuss future relations between England and Scotland, to which Edward III would reply only after a council had met to advise him.[60] The same year also saw Parliament meeting at Eltham to discuss the war with France then in progress and to consider how to raise money to pay for it if peace was not achieved. A treaty was concluded with France that May but it left unsettled the disputed question of English royal homage to the French kings, for their lands in France. Homage saw a vassal acknowledge that he owed his right to land to his overlord, which was awkward when both overlord and vassal were kings. Aquitaine was held by English kings from the kings of France, with the former seeking full sovereignty, and such disputes on rights and boundaries could lead to war. In addition, Edward III had a claim through his mother to the French throne after the death in 1328 of the last king of the Capetian royal line, a claim he was to assert some years later.[61]

In October 1330 the question of who ruled England was resolved when, in Nottingham Castle, Edward III had the Earl of March taken by surprise and arrested. Tried by Parliament for usurping royal authority and other crimes, the earl was found guilty and executed, while the queen mother lost her former governing influence to her son.[62] Isabella still received an income from her son and apparently had the right not to pay taxes until she had received this allowance from her son, as she once protested to the Chancellor when Kentish tax collectors tried to get her to pay tax on her moveables in the manor of Eltham.[63]

In the early years of Edward III's reign, life at Eltham Palace is ill documented except for the dates of court visits and information in the many official letters and records sent from there on a wide variety of subjects concerning the king and his council in ruling England. Some records refer to individuals like Christina Scot, a murderess who had killed her husband and was granted a pardon at the request of the queen mother,[64] and Edmund, a chaplain pardoned for taking part in a riot at Bury St Edmunds.[65] More unusual were the orders to bring John le Rous and Master William de Dalby to the king at Eltham because they were 'said to be able to make silver by alchemy',[66] and to arrest those going to Leicester to take part in an unlicensed tournament in June 1329.[67]

Records with wider implications sent from Eltham included plans for marriages between the English and French royal families,[68] negotiations for peace between the two countries[69] and the still unsettled question of the homage owed for Aquitaine by Edward III to the King of France. On this last subject, a convention was ratified at Eltham in March 1331 after a council meeting.[70] Many of these documents sent from Eltham were concerned with finance and included the assignment of Crown revenues to Italian financiers who had lent money to the king,[71] loans they were to regret in the 1340s when part of them was not repaid.[72] Several letters also dealt with the unusual subject of Edward III's attempt to get his cousin Thomas, Earl of Lancaster, canonised. The earl had been executed for rebellion in 1322 and Edward hoped, by writing to Pope John XXII and certain cardinals, that he could get Thomas made a saint, an aim in which he was to be unsuccessful.[73]

After 1330, although Queen Isabella still kept Eltham manor, there would seem to have been fewer visits to it by the court than in the earlier part of Edward III's reign. Among later court visits, one in 1331 saw John of Eltham there[74] and another in 1337 witnessed the arrival of a deputation of Flemish burghers to discuss an agreement reached between the Count of Flanders and the King of France, to which both Edward III and the visitors were united in opposition.[75] In 1338 war broke out between France and England, with the English Channel ports being raided by the French while English forces were sent to Flanders. A French invasion fleet was also destroyed by English ships at Sluys in 1340.[76] Two years later William, Count of Hainault, Edward III's brother-in-law and occasional ally, visited England. A tournament was held at Eltham in his honour where the count received a wound in his arm.[77] In 1343, when the court came to Eltham for Easter, it was entertained there by Jean de la Motte, a Flemish poet and minstrel, given 40s. as a reward by the king.[78]

For reasons for which no documentary record survives it was decided in 1344 that the manor of Eltham should pass from the ownership of the queen mother to that of the king. For this loss Queen Isabella was compensated with £100 a year from the farm of the city of Norwich in the place of Eltham and another of her manors, Kings Langley.[79] It is possible that the reason for this change of ownership was simply Eltham's location. It was close to the route between London and Dover and, while England and France were at war, Edward III had to travel to Flanders and France via Dover, so a royal house on this route sited a few hours' travel outside London was a useful place to stop before making an entry into the capital, as later English kings were also to discover.

With one exception, there is no detailed information before 1350 on the building history of the palace under royal ownership, although it is known that building works or repairs were in progress there in 1317-18[80] and in the late 1320s.[81] The exception to this lack of detailed information occurs in 1315-16 when it was decided that the inner side of the moated area should be walled. It is, incidentally, not known exactly when the moat was dug, only that it was already in existence in 1315 and that buildings had existed on the site, with or without a moat, for at least two centuries before that date. The specifications for the new inner moat walls stated that they were to be built on piles where these were considered necessary to a height of 12 feet or more if this was essential. The new walls were to be five feet wide at the base, narrowing to four feet at the top, with buttresses along them at regular intervals and extra buttresses at the corners. The agreement between the queen's representatives and the masons mentions some earlier walls, referred to as 'the old work', along at least part of the moat's inner wall. This earlier work might perhaps have supported the outer foundations of Bishop Bek's buildings on the western side of the moated area. The type of stone to be used is specified and the work was to be carried out in two stages, one between May and September 1315, the other between April and September 1316.

The best-laid plans may go wrong and on this occasion the trouble arose from fraudulent practices by the masons, who made thinner walls than had been specified and used inferior stone. The result was that the order was given that the work already carried out was to be demolished, the masons were to be imprisoned and made to pay damages, and eight men were to stand surety for the correct carrying out of the work. The original masons were then released to undertake this.[82] It is possible that the rebuilding was not carried out thoroughly either, as further work had to be done on these walls in the mid-14th century[83] and recent archaeology has found subsidence on the western side of the moated area.[84]

In the early 14th century there were two recorded manors at Eltham, called Eltham and Eltham Mandeville, and no more is heard of Eltham Albemarle. The manor of Eltham has a straightforward history, being presented to Queen Isabella, with other lands in the area, by Edward II in November 1311,[85] a grant later improved by both her husband[86] and her son.[87] The history of Eltham Mandeville is very different. Absent from surviving records prior to its presentation to the queen by Edward II in 1314,[88] a further grant of this manor was made to her by the king two years later which includes information on its history. This 1316 grant states that the manor had formerly been in Bishop Bek's possession,[89] which is curious because it is not specifically mentioned in either Bek's 1305 grant to the future Edward II[90] or in the inquisition post mortem taken of the bishop's lands after his death.[91] After 1316 Eltham Mandeville seems to have passed from the possession of the queen to Gilbert de Aton in an unrecorded transaction, as in 1318 it was granted to Geoffrey le Scrope by Gilbert de Aton in a grant which does not refer to the former ownership of the manor by the queen or bishop but does state that Gilbert was the heir of William de Vescy.[92] This reference could be to either the former owner of lands in Eltham, who had died in 1297,[93] Gilbert being the husband of William's only daughter, Isabel, or possibly to Isabel's illegitimate half-brother William, who had been killed at the Battle of Bannockburn in 1314, leaving no direct heirs.[94]

Geoffrey le Scrope, the owner of Eltham Mandeville after 1318, held the manor for several years. A distinguished judge, diplomat and soldier, he became Chief Justice of the King's Bench in 1324.[95] After 1329 this manor was to change hands several times. It passed in that year from Geoffrey Le Scrope to the queen mother,[96] who granted it to Edward III in 1330.[97] Later in that year the king granted it to Geoffrey le Scrope,[98] who must have returned it to Edward III as in 1332 the king granted it to his mother.[99] At a later date, between 1346 and 1353, it became part of the manor of Eltham and was accounted for with it.[100]

The years between 1318 and 1325, while Geoffrey le Scrope held Eltham Mandeville, are illuminated for us by the survival of court rolls and bailiff's accounts which are of great interest, providing a most detailed record of many aspects of local life. During these years the manor was administered by an official called in different records bailiff, sergeant and keeper.[101] A junior official in the manor was the steward, who received rents and presided over manorial courts with the aid of a clerk, while another official, a sergeant, recorded the finances of the manor. The remaining manorial officials were elected annually at the manorial court, the most important being the borsholder or chief of the tithing, who presented offenders against the laws of the manor before the manorial court, carried out court orders and handed over taxes. The other elected officials were a bailiff, who compelled attendance at the manorial court; a bedell, who collected rents and fines with the help of two assistants; and a reap-reeve, who guarded the sheaves after the harvest and saw to their cartage into the manorial barn.

The manorial records provide many details of the daily lives of John Swyt, John le Shepherde, Robert le Parker, Agnes Martyn, Beatrice Webbe, Alice atte Holm and the other inhabitants of Eltham Mandeville.[102] Cottage rents ranged from 6d. to 3s. 4d. a quarter and could be paid either in cash or kind, in the latter case in rents of cocks, hens, eggs or pepper.[103] Information in the records shows us that cocks were valued at 1½d., hens at 2d. and 20 eggs had a value of 1d.[104] Rents for land varied between 4d. and 6d. per acre per year.[105]

The Eltham Mandeville farmers grew wheat, barley, oats, beans, peas, rye and vetch,[106] besides mixtures of these such as maslin, usually a mixture of rye and wheat,[107] and dredge, a mixture of oats and barley.[108] Grass is recorded when it was bought, sold[109] or made into hay[110] and there is a single reference to a field being left fallow.[111] From the records of seed sown and crops harvested it is sometimes possible to work out the return on the seed gain sown and the number of bushels harvested to the acre, information also available on the whole manor later in the century.[112] The records of Eltham Mandeville, but not the later ones, detail the fields in which crops were sown.[113]

By modern standards medieval Eltham's crop yields were extremely low. The highest rate of return on seed, for peas, was six-fold and most crop yields were much lower. Bushels harvested per acre vary from two to 16, the highest yields coming from barley, beans and peas, the lowest from oats, wheat and rye.[114]

References to individual fields show that the same crop was not grown in the same field year after year.[115] The areas sown on the manor vary considerably from one year to the next.[116]

The manor court rolls from Eltham Mandeville show the manorial court dealing with a variety of aspects of local life including debt,[117] trespass[118] and slander,[119] the last with reference to a man who objected to being told that he was a thief and a receiver of thieves. The court also arranged for the future livelihood of a widow, who was to be supported by her three sons after her husband's death.[120] Duties owed to the community by the people of the manor were regulated by the court, including the cleaning out of drainage ditches; those who neglected these duties were fined.[121]

Other expenses of local life in these records include the cost of house repairs,[122] the food given to ploughmen in return for their work[123] and information showing that the manor had an apple orchard,[124] a grange,[125] a stable,[126] a limekiln[127] and a room beneath a chapel where calves were kept.[128] One record lists the furnishings of the manorial court and kitchen, the former only having four trestle tables, three pairs of trestles, two forms and a chair; the latter a bronze pot and two tripods, all in bad condition.[129]

Information on the lord of the manor's livestock mentions draught animals (presumably oxen), carthorses, cows and pigs, all listed by types—for example the number of oxen, cows, steers, heifers and calves[130]—with their fate during the year. Records concerning chickens show that some were made into capons,[131] some had died,[132] one had been stolen[133] and several killed by foxes.[134] One of the functions of the manor for its lord was the fattening of geese and swans, these being bought in London, sent to Eltham to be fattened, and then returned to London for Geoffrey le Scrope's household there.[135] Grain, pigs, capons, hens and eggs are also recorded as being sent to London from Eltham.[136] Incidental references give the cost of sending a cart across London Bridge,[137] record the existence of serfs in Eltham[138] and show that the lord of the manor owned shops there.[139] One of these shops may have sold the six plates, dishes and salt cellars, costing 4d., mentioned in one record.[140]

The tasks carried out by local people for the lord of the manor are also recorded here. Apart from agricultural tasks, a smith is paid for making nails, horseshoes and ploughshares, shoeing horses and making and mending carts and ploughs;[141] a carpenter for making and repairing ploughs, doors and gates;[142] a roofer for thatching with straw;[143] a tilemaker for making tiles and tiling.[144] Brewing,[145] tanning,[146] woodcutting[147] and ditching[148] are also mentioned, while women were paid for planting beans,[149] winnowing corn[150] and cooking porridge[151] and a boy for looking after pigs feeding in the woods.[152] Payments to a housemaid[153] must refer to work in the manor house and to Agnes, 'the lady's maid', likewise.[154]

The first royal official recorded at Eltham was the unfortunate Hervey (or Herewek) de Forges, in charge of the manor in 1312.[155] He may have obtained his appointment, although he was French, as a favour from the French-born Queen Isabella. Other early royal officials were John de Henle, keeper of the manor in 1325;[156] Edmund de Kensyngton, appointed parker there in 1331;[157] Peter de Eltham (le Chapelyn), another Frenchman, keeper of both Eltham manors between 1330 and 1334[158] and chaplain there at a later date,[159] and Richard Caleware, who succeeded Peter de Eltham as keeper of Eltham Mandeville.[160]

III

BUILDING A ROYAL PALACE

Entre Eltem et Wesmoustier,
En une belle preorie,
Cuesci pastoureaus avant hier;
La avoit en la compagnie
Mainte faitice pastourelle,
Dont au son d'une canemalle
Cascuns et cascune dansoit.
(Jean Froissart, *Poesies* (ed. K. de Lettenhove), vol. ii, 1870)

The early years of Edward III's ownership of the manor of Eltham witnessed a number of court visits linked to the king's journeys to France and Flanders at the start of the Hundred Years War. One of these visits occurred in 1346 when Edward landed in France for the campaign that was to include both the Battle of Crecy and the taking of Calais, a town whose loss two centuries later was also to be associated with the history of the palace. During this 1346-7 campaign some royal councillors were left in England to rule the country while the king was overseas.[1] Their nominal head was Edward's nine-year-old son Lionel, who, on the day that his father landed in France for this campaign, witnessed a document at Eltham as 'Guardian of England'.[2]

A number of documents sent from the palace while this council was there are concerned with those who distinguished themselves in France or at the Battle of Neville's Cross, a victory won over an invading Scottish army outside Durham in October 1346. One of those rewarded was Robert de Coleville, who 'for good service in the war beyond the seas' was pardoned of the sum of 40 marks he owed the king;[3] another was Robert Bertram, given an annuity of 200 marks for giving up an important Scottish prisoner to the king, a grant later commuted for 800 marks.[4] A third man who benefited was William Hugate, a servant of the Archbishop of York, who received £10 for bringing the king 'news of the victory at Durham'.[5] The largest of these rewards went to John de Coupeland, who gained an annuity of £500 and a knighthood for capturing David II, King of Scotland, at Neville's Cross. He later became Warden of the March of Scotland and of the town, castle and county of Roxburgh, a Scottish shire then occupied by English forces.[6]

The council at Eltham also ordered the movement of the captured King David and other important Scottish prisoners to the greater security of the Tower of London, besides setting in motion inquiries into the escape or release of prisoners captured at Neville's Cross.[7] During these months while the council was at Eltham and Edward III overseas, an Eltham landowner complained to the royal council regarding an attack on his property, stating that 12 or more people had broken open his houses, felled his trees, stolen his goods and assaulted his servants, a matter into which the council ordered an inquiry.[8]

In October 1347 Edward III returned to England, a homecoming marked by a number of tournaments, of which one, apparently held in December, took place at Eltham, an occasion for which the king had a gown made for him ornamented with 12 blue garters of taffeta and camoca, the latter a type of silk, which bore the motto of the Order of the Garter, founded around this date.[9] During the following year, while the king was at Eltham, he learnt of a French plan to recapture Calais by treachery. Sir Walter Manny, a notable military commander, was sent to the threatened town to reinforce the garrison and with him went, incognito, both the king and his eldest son, the Black Prince. They successfully ambushed the French force that had hoped to recapture Calais.[10] The same year of 1348 saw the arrival in England of the Black Death, which is thought to have killed up to a third of the population, with both London, north-west of Eltham, and Rochester to the east being badly affected.[11] Its effect on the manor is unknown; no new officials were appointed there in 1348-9 and the court returned to the palace in the summer of 1349.[12]

Four years later, in 1353, the court was at Eltham both for Easter and Christmas.[13] For the former of these seasons Prince Lionel presented alms to the poor on Maundy Thursday while his father gave an offering of five shillings at the Cross during High Mass at the dawn service on Easter Day.[14] Chapel records also show that during a Christmas Day Mass the king had a gilded cloth called a 'rakemat' placed upon his head.[15] The Christmas festivities there the following year saw jousting taking place, with the Black Prince, Sir John Chandos and Sir James Audley among the competitors.[16] Two years later, at the Battle of Poitiers in 1356, all three distinguished themselves, besides being notable commanders in the wars in France and elsewhere.[17] Froissart mentions that Sir John Chandos was regarded as a pattern of chivalry and that his death in action in 1370 was felt as a great loss by all who had known him.[18]

Prince Lionel, the 'Guardian of England' at Eltham in 1346-7,[19] married a great heiress, Elizabeth de Burgh, and was created Earl of Ulster and later Duke of Clarence.[20] Their daughter, Philippa, was born at Eltham in 1355,[21] married the Earl of March and became an ancestress of Edward IV.[22] A building record from 1358-9[23] shows that the Countess of Ulster had a room at Eltham and it is therefore likely that Geoffrey Chaucer, a page in 1357,[24] visited the palace at about this time, as he was in her service until 1359.[25] The later 1350s saw extensive building works in progress at Eltham Palace, of which detailed records survive,[26] as they do for the same years regarding the manorial home farm.[27]

The first recorded visit to Eltham Palace by foreign royalty occurred in June 1360 when King John II of France, captured at Poitiers four years earlier, visited it briefly while on his way back to France, escorted by the Black Prince. He heard Mass at Eltham and said farewell there to Edward III.[28] He had been freed by the Treaty of Bretigny, sealed the previous month, but had to pay a large ransom and leave behind his three sons as sureties for its payment.[29] Their presence under English control was later to bring their father back to England.

Three-and-a-half years later, in January 1364, the palace witnessed the single best-known event in its history, the meeting there of John II and Edward III after

1 King John II of France enters London, 1364.

the voluntary return as a hostage of the French king. Louis, Duke of Anjou, had refused to return from parole to English captivity and his father, in spite of the opposition of his council, decided to take his son's place, feeling that he was under a chivalrous obligation to do so. In insisting on this he is said to have declared, 'If good faith and honour were to be banished from the rest of the world, they should be found in the hearts and words of princes'.[30] King John and his companions crossed from Boulogne to Dover where they arrived on 5 January and were met by knights sent from the English court. From there they were escorted by way of Canterbury to Eltham which was reached eight days after their arrival in England. At Eltham John II met Edward III and Philippa and stayed for two days of feasts, tournaments and entertainments. The last of these included songs and dances performed by members of the court, among whom, we are informed by Froissart, a French hostage, the Lord de Couci, particularly distinguished himself.[31] In 1365 this wealthy nobleman married Edward III's eldest and favourite daughter, Princess Isabella, and was also created Earl of Bedford.[32]

After King John's brief visit to Eltham Palace he travelled on to London, being entertained on the way as described in one of Froissart's poems. This entertainment took the form of dances by entertainers dressed as shepherds and shepherdesses, to the sound of horns, pipes, flutes and drums doing honour to 'the one that bears the fleurs de lys'. Crowds, including important Londoners and minstrels, accompanied the French king to London where he stayed at the Savoy Palace, his residence during his earlier captivity. The king did not live long after his return to England but died there unexpectedly the following April.[33]

Philippa, daughter of the Earl and Countess of Bedford, was born at Eltham Palace in August 1367.[34] Her baptism there in the palace chapel was attended by her royal grandparents, who presented her with a magnificent gift of gilt and silver bowls, cups, water pitchers, chargers, dishes, salt cellars, spoons and other pieces of plate costing almost £250.[35] Philippa later married the Earl of Oxford, created Duke of Ireland in 1386, only to be divorced the year after this creation, causing a great scandal. She did not marry again and so remained Duchess of Ireland until she died in 1411.[36]

Edward III revisited Eltham for the Christmas season of 1371 with Prince Thomas, his youngest son.[37] Both also came the following Easter when the prince presented Maundy Money there to 13 poor men, a number linked to his age; during his stay he also received a barrel of Gascon wine for use at Eltham and elsewhere.[38] Visits such as these kept royal messengers busy travelling on official business; in 1372-7 one sent from Eltham and other places was away from court for 220 days during the year.[39]

One of the wealthiest courtiers to visit Eltham was John, Duke of Lancaster, third son of Edward III and, at a later date, Shakespeare's 'Old John of Gaunt, time-honoured Lancaster'. In those days presents were customarily given not on Christmas Day but on New Year's Day. When the duke presented gifts on that day in 1374, he gave 'various cups of silver and gilded and various gold beads and gold clasps and gold rings and boxes and other jewels', costing him nearly £400, besides a further £65 worth of presents for heralds, minstrels and officials as well as to the squires and grooms of the lords and ladies at court, who presented the duke with their own 'new gifts'.[40] Court luxury can also be seen in the gold and silver vessels and chapel ornaments brought to Eltham for court visits[41] and in a gold ring set with a ruby and five diamonds found on the palace site early last century. Its French inscription can be translated as 'Who wears me shall perform exploits, And with great joy shall return'.[42] Another gift presented at Eltham in 1374 may not have been a New Year's Day present: 'an image of the Holy Mary, … taken by John de Ryngborne … upon the sea'.[43]

Edward III often came to Eltham in the last years of his reign when confidence in his government was shaken by military failure overseas and dissention at home. By 1376, the year before the king's death, the need for money to pay for essential government expenditure and for action on judicial matters made it imperative that a Parliament should be called. When it met it had many complaints and was reluctant to vote in new taxes, as well as demanding that Alice Perrers, the king's mistress, should leave the court. On its immediate wishes being met, this 'Good Parliament', as it was called, agreed to vote a small supply of money before the session ended.[44] Parliament then visited Eltham, where the king was presented with petitions for the redressing of grievances.[45] Various vessels were brought to Eltham from Westminster 'for the feast of parliament there',[46] so it would appear that the visitors were properly entertained, but they got little other satisfaction from their visit, as some replies to their petitions were evasive and others were given to the king's council to answer.[47] Worse still, months later, a council summoned by the Duke of Lancaster declared almost all the acts of the 'Good Parliament' to be null and void.[48]

Although Edward III acquired the manor of Eltham in 1344, it was not until the summer of 1350 that work began on the improvement of its buildings and two men were appointed to take carpenters and freemasons for building works at the palace.[49] The main early work, carried out in 1350-1, was the rebuilding of the wooden drawbridge which formed part of the old bridge, the principal entrance to the moated area that later became the inner court of Eltham Palace. Work was also carried out in these years on plasterwork, roofs and gutters; windows, doors and fireplaces were repaired and the moat was cleaned out.[50]

Between 1352 and 1355 new buildings were erected on the western side of the moated area, this work and further repairs being followed[51] by the building of a small new chapel for Queen Philippa besides a great kitchen, a 'rostynghous', the roof of a great hall and the erection of a new gate with a room above it.[52] In the 1360s a new bridge was constructed 'towards the park', which may have been on the site of the one in the centre of the south side where later, brick, foundations can still be seen.[53] The 1360s also saw the creation of a 'Queen's cross', sited between the palace and Eltham village, made of painted wainscot boards on a stone base with a crucifix and statues of the Virgin and St John the Evangelist.[54] The last years of Edward III's reign included more work on the great bridge and the erection of a new lodge in the park.[55] Repairs were also carried out on park and home farm buildings.[56]

The 1370s palace bore a very different appearance to that found in later centuries. The early palace was formed of an irregular group of buildings within the moat. All these, apart from the gatehouse and the towers built for Bishop Bek, seem to have had only a single storey.[57] The later palace had, at least on its western side, buildings two or three storeys in height; it was more regular in its layout and it had an outer court on the northern side of the moat.[58]

Building records have preserved many details of the early palace. Under Edward III some of Bishop Bek's towers, built c.1300, survived, and repairs to two of them refer to the turret of Master Jordan and to the Prince's tower.[59] Some rooms and buildings had lead roofs, including the king's chamber,[60] the pre-1358 great hall[61] and its successor,[62] the little hall,[63] and the great and small chapels.[64] Less important rooms and buildings had tiled roofs.[65] Straw was used for roofing[66] and may also have had other uses such as covering half-completed walls against winter frost, and bedding on floors and in stables.

The later 14th-century Eltham Palace buildings had stone walls,[67] covered inside with tiles,[68] plaster[69] or wainscoting;[70] with stone,[71] tiled[72] or plaster[73] fireplaces. Some walls were also of lath and plaster.[74] Floors were tiled[75] or stone,[76] while windows had iron frames[77] with plain[78] or decorated[79] glass. Manorial buildings are recorded as being wooden-framed, apparently those either on the home farm or in the park.[80] In 1358-9 a cable was bought for the purpose of 'raising houses',[81] presumably either wooden-framed houses or for raising the timbers used in roofs. Three building records mention the movement of wooden-framed buildings to Eltham. One came from Knockholt in 1367-8;[82] the others to Brandons in 1368-9 and 1371-2.[83]

Under both Edward III[84] and Richard II[85] records of building work at Eltham show that palace buildings there were joined to each other by passages with tiled roofs. Some palace rooms were for the personal use of the king and queen, others for courtiers. The chapel and great hall would have had a wider use, and the kitchens, storehouses and stables provided services for the whole court.

Edward III's Eltham rooms included a chamber with glass windows,[86] a garderobe with a paved floor and cupboard,[87] and a bathroom built in the 1360s with a tiled floor, iron-framed glazed windows, a chimney and a cistern, besides furnishings of 120 earthenware pots,[88] two buckets and four tin cans.[89] Less is known of Queen

Philippa's rooms at Eltham but during the 1350s they included a chamber with a fireplace, a chapel[90] and a new oratory or small chapel.[91] The king and queen may have had other rooms as well but these are the only ones in the building records. Four other individuals, Peter de Eltham in 1345,[92] the palace chaplain, the Countess of Ulster in 1358-9,[93] the Black Prince[94] and Master Jordan[95] are mentioned in building records, apart from the king and queen, as having rooms allotted to them at Eltham in the reign of Edward III. Later reigns show further members of the royal family, courtiers and officials with rooms allotted to them at the palace.

Rooms at Eltham Palace under Edward III included a great chamber[96] with tiled walls,[97] apparently sited above a cellar;[98] and a great hall, re-roofed with lead in 1358-61,[99] with a fireplace, two chimneys,[100] plastered walls[101] and glass windows.[102] Its new roof included the staves of 72 barrels which must have supported the lead roofing.[103] A small hall, also roofed with lead, is recorded in 1367[104] and 1372-3.[105] During the 1930s tiles from the 14th century were found beneath the western end of the 15th-century great hall that may have formed part of the flooring of one of these earlier halls.[106] Of Edward III's chapel at Eltham it is only known that it had organs encased in wood[107] and, apparently, a bell.[108]

Although the southern half of the inner court of Eltham Palace has never been professionally excavated, something of it is known from the 1603-4 inner court plan,[109] building records, the Tudor drains excavated there in 1833,[110] recorded with other underground passages in Brook's history,[111] and details shown on a plan made when Eltham Hall was under construction in the 1930s.[112] When the tunnel under the moat was made in 1528 or soon afterwards,[113] and during the early 17th century, the inner court kitchens were in the south-west corner of the moated area.[114] As no kitchens were traced to the north or west of the great hall in the 1970s excavations[115] it would seem that Edward III's royal kitchens within the moat were probably in the same area as those in use under the Tudors and Stuarts. The stone-walled great kitchen of 1358-61 had seven timber columns upholding a tiled roof surmounted by a weathercock.[116] A 'rostynghous' built at the same time as the kitchen was replaced, only nine years later, by a kitchen with walls 321 feet in length and 12 feet high.[117]

A wine cellar situated near the kitchens already existed by the 1360s when alterations were made to it.[118] Between 1344-6[119] and 1451[120] there are numerous references to the supply of wine to Eltham Palace, of which some was lost in transit by leakage[121] while other barrels, kept too long before they were drunk, became undrinkable while in the cellars.[122] Most of this wine was from Gascony,[123] some came from the Rhine,[124] Vernaccia[125] in Italy, and Greece,[126] which produced Malmsey and Romsey wine.

In 1367-8 other palace rooms included an armoury and a chandlery.[127] The palace had several latrines by 1368-9 when they cost 6s. 8d. for cleaning[128] and at least one well-equipped with a chain, a rope and two buckets.[129] Outside the moat there were two stables, one a 'great stable',[130] the other for the use of 'draught animals'.[131] The park, of which John Beverley was parker between 1369 and 1380,[132] included buildings to which a stable, pantry, buttery, kitchen and haystore were added in 1368-9[133] as well as a new lodge in 1375-6.[134]

Repairs and new buildings required the services of many craftsmen and labourers, with more than fifty at work there in 1358-9,[135] of whom about a third were labourers paid 3d. or 4d. a day.[136] Ordinary craftsmen received up to 6d. a day[137] and the most highly skilled craftsmen still higher rates, some being paid by the task rather than by the day.[138] The building accounts for 1358-9 are of particular interest, being the only ones for Eltham that record the dates men were paid, with, for certain craftsmen, the feast days or holidays for which they also received pay.[139] Building work continued during the winter when carpenters and plasterers received lower wages than in other seasons, presumably because of the shorter hours worked.[140]

The 1358-9 records show a succession of peaks of employment for workers when a new building was erected. The labourers first dug the foundations, followed by masons who built the walls, the carpenters who erected the roof and the tilers who covered it.[141] Some of these craftsmen had more than one skill, while others combined a craft with carting and the supply of building materials.[142] The carpenters were the most numerous craftsmen[143] and also worked the largest number of hours when a new building was erected. This can be seen when the new park lodge was built in 1375-6. In this case the carpenters were half the number of craftsmen involved and they worked over two-thirds of the work days required for the completion of this building.[144]

It was far more expensive to move goods by land than by water and the building materials needed at the palace site were transported as far as possible along the Thames before being unloaded at a riverside port, usually Woolwich, from where they went by cart uphill to Eltham.[145] It can be calculated that the carts used carried 0.7 tons of stone or 500 tiles.[146] Building records for 1358-9 show that it cost, per mile, between 12 and 13 times as much to move a ton of stone by road from Woolwich to Eltham as it had cost to move it by water from Maidstone to Woolwich.[147]

In Edward III's reign the stone used at Eltham Palace came from Merstham, near Reigate,[148] or Maidstone;[149] and chalk from Greenhithe or its vicinity.[150] Some timber came from Eltham Park[151] but most of it was from Croydon,[152] Merstham,[153] Knockholt[154] or Codeham Park.[155] Lead was brought by cart from London or Westminster.[156] Tiles came from either Woolwich[157] or Greenwich,[158] but may have been fired further afield before being sent by water to one or the other of these riverside ports. On one occasion it is recorded that the tiles used were made at Plumstead.[159] The total cost of the principal works carried out at Eltham between 1350 and 1359 amounted to over £2,237.[160]

Although the manor officially passed into the ownership of Edward III in May 1344,[161] it was already in the control of royal officials at Michaelmas (29 September) the previous year.[162] Three years after obtaining full ownership of the manor Edward must have decided that its parks were too small for him and a programme was begun to enlarge its area of parkland by the purchase of £400 worth of land[163] with the rights of Thomas de Apuldresfeld in the manor of Westhorne.[164] This was the area where Horn Park was to be created in the following century.[165] In 1348 further land was obtained for the new park from Robert de Corby, who received a manor in Rutland in exchange.[166] As far as is known, no more land was acquired for the new park for almost twenty years after these lands had been bought or exchanged. More land was obtained for the enlargement of the park in 1367 when Wrytel-mersshe was purchased from John Syme and John Richardes;[167] followed two years later by the manor of Henle and 32 acres in Eltham and Mottingham formerly owned by five men, together with an area of land of unspecified size owned by a sixth man.[168]

Two-and-a-half centuries later the 1605 survey refers to the Middle Park as the Old Park[169] and it therefore presumably included the area formerly possessed by Bishop Bek.[170] Horn Park only having been created in the 15th century,[171] the land acquired for inclusion in the park created for Edward III at Eltham in the 14th century must have gone in great measure towards making the third of the three parks at Eltham, the Great Park. Some of it paid tithes to the abbot and convent of Keynsham, near Bristol, who were compensated in the reign of Richard II for what they had lost to his grandfather Edward III.[172] The abbot and convent were also the patrons of Eltham church between the 12th and 16th centuries.[173] Edward III also acquired for the park tithes on land belonging to the prior and convent of St Andrew, Rochester, which were given in exchange lands and rents in London.[174]

Before the newly acquired land could be used as parkland some changes had to be made, old hedges being removed and new ones created. These, with ditches and palisades, enclosed the king's park. These alterations are recorded in accounts which date from 1354-5,[175] 1365-7,[176] 1367-9[177] and 1372-8,[178] when 3,334 perches (18,324 yards) of hedges and 92 perches (534 yards) of palisades were 'made anew' at Eltham. In 1367 ditchers and other workmen needed for this work were collected by John Spalding, keeper of the manor, with two other men who were empowered to take men for this task, put them to work at the king's wages as long as they were required and imprison those who were troublesome.[179] An agreement made in 1367-8, when labourers were 'making dykes of the enclosure of the park there, newly ordered', refers to ditches which were to be five feet deep and seven feet wide.[180]

One area enclosed in the park was separated from the rest, an eight-acre fenced meadow with the function of providing hay for the winter feeding of the deer, a practice first recorded at Eltham in 1325[181] and still carried on there in the 16th century.[182]

The garden of the manor, first recorded at Eltham in 1311,[183] was a kitchen garden in Edward III's reign, judging by the purchases made for it. Its location is unknown but seeds and plants of 12 herbs or vegetables were bought for it in 1367-8[184] and lesser amounts for the same purpose in other years.[185] Parsley and onion seeds are the most frequent purchases; other seeds bought less often were those of leeks, hyssop, savory, anise, clary, garlic, lettuce, rape, rue, spinach and hemp. A vineyard was begun in 1352-5 with the purchase of three cartloads of vine plants[186] and there are many later references in this reign to payments for digging, composting, watering, railing, pruning and tying up vines, as well as for hoeing and watering plants, besides the purchasing of stakes, rods, twigs, a pruning knife, bird scarers and dung for the vines and the garden.[187] Some workers in the garden and vineyard were women who are recorded as watering vines and plants during the 1370s. They received a lower rate of pay than the male workers.[188]

The latter half of the 14th century is the last period at Eltham for which detailed home farm records have survived. Royal bailiffs had to account for their income and expenditure but their records end when the home farm was leased out to farmers and from then on only the details of leases exist. Most of the manorial income came from the sale of grain, stock and wool, of which the first was always the largest sum and the second, except in one year, the smallest. Further income came from rents, the manorial court, sales from the dovecot, of fruit and of occasional other minor sources of income.[189] In the 1380s one record refers to an enclosed rabbit warren, but no income from it is recorded.[190]

Between the 1340s and 1380s, from when detailed records survive of Eltham's manorial income, certain changes are evident. As more land was rented out income from that source rose,[191] as it did also from renting out the cows that belonged to the manor, with a rate of 5s. per cow per year recorded in the 1350s.[192] This rise in renting out land foreshadowed, as in other places, the renting out of the whole manor later in the century.[193] Another consequence of renting out land was a decrease in the number of ploughmen, shepherds and drovers employed by the manor.[194] The largest element of manorial expenditure was that of the salaries paid to the manorial officials,[195] harvest expenses also being an important item.[196]

The yields and crops for the complete manor after 1344 are very similar to those recorded at Eltham Mandeville earlier in the century.[197] Oats and wheat were the principal crops. Some years, such as 1354-5, produced very poor crop yields, with less than a twofold return on the seed grain, while wheat, rye, barley and vetch had poor results in other years.[198] As seen earlier at Eltham Mandeville, the area of arable land varied widely from one year to the next, in the case of the whole manor from under a hundred acres to over four hundred.[199] The number of sheep kept on the demesne rose from 1345-6, when they numbered 117, to over four hundred in 1361, after which their numbers declined slightly until 1369-70 when 220 sheep died of disease and 162 had to be bought to replace this loss.[200] Pigs rarely appear in the Eltham records but they were evidently kept by the villeins, who were sometimes allowed to put them into the park and on manorial arable land after the harvest.[201] Part of the grain harvest was sold and part went to labourers as payment for their work. Oats were fed to carthorses, cattle and doves.[202]

Eltham's home-farm harvest is not recorded as going to feed the court when it visited the palace, though this may have happened. Food for the court was supplied by purveyors appointed to supply the bakehouse, poultry, kitchen, scullery and pastry departments of the royal household for various places including Eltham.[203] The provisions collected and the carts used to move food and other necessities were paid for at a low fixed price, below market value, and this payment was not always made in cash but instead could be offset against future royal taxes. Purveyance, as this system of supplying the needs of the court was called, was in effect a compulsory loan of food and services such as cartage at unfair prices. There were in addition various abuses to which the system was subject by purveyors and others – unpaid cartage, corruption, unjust grain measures and claims to purveyance by people with no legal right to it – and, not surprisingly, there were many complaints made on the subject in Parliament. New rules for purveyance were introduced late in the 14th century and may have done some good as, after their introduction, the number of complaints declined.[204]

Places like Eltham, frequently visited by the court with its 400 to 700 permanent officials and hundreds of horses, were much inconvenienced by purveyance and the requisitioning of lodgings.[205] A grant made to its inhabitants in 1348 of a remission of an increased grant on wool mentions these frequent visits by the court as one reason for the allowance as well as the acquisition of land by the king in the manor.[206]

Land added to the royal holdings in Eltham would be an indirect burden upon its inhabitants, as this land would no longer pay tax and would thus reduce the area of land within the manor from which royal taxes would have to be paid. A further concession, made to the inhabitants in 1374, was to the people of Mottingham and Woolwich when it was recorded that by ancient custom they were exempt from toll on the movement of goods,[207] a grant later repeated in Henry IV's reign.[208]

When the manor passed into Edward III's ownership, two of the officials appointed by his mother, Peter de Eltham, chaplain and keeper,[209] and Peter de Ellirker,[210] the parker, were confirmed in their positions by the king. The former, as chaplain, was entitled, apart from his salary, to a yearly robe, a chamber by the palace gate and brushwood from the park for his fire. New official positions were also created, including a 'keeper of the houses'[211] in the 1350s, later referred to as the 'warden of the king's houses',[212] porter[213] and janitor.[214] In the 1360s a gardener[215] and a steward[216] were appointed. The numerous records of these officials mention the pay to which they were entitled, but this was not always easy to obtain and from the 1370s to 1500 a series of orders require the payment of arrears of salary to holders of official positions at Eltham.[217]

In 1372 the first appointment was made of a farmer of the manor, still entitled keeper, who paid a yearly sum of £60 for his position.[218] This important change meant he replaced the salaried position of bailiff and kept the profits of farming the demesne. The demesne included the home farm but excluded the palace and its immediate precincts, the garden and the park.

As well as its manorial staff Eltham now had officials planning and supervising building works, giving orders to craftsmen and labourers, seeing to paying workmen, keeping accounts and arranging the purchase of building materials and their transport to the site. They had also to find workmen for the works, bring them back if they deserted and see that repairs were carried out in advance of court visits. They also arrested and punished trespassers, held courts and enquired into missing building materials.[219]

At a senior level a works official dealt with a number of other royal manors and buildings apart from Eltham. One such man was William of Wykeham, who rose from a clerk of works to being Chancellor of England and Bishop of Winchester. Such a senior official would only visit Eltham occasionally but officials such as the 'clerk of the king's works in the manor of Eltham' would have spent long periods there.[220] Above this clerk were two controllers and supervisors keeping a separate record of expenditure; below him were building purveyors arranging the purchase and transport of building materials to Eltham.[221]

By 1377 the new royal palace at Eltham had been enlarged by the erection of new buildings and its park had been increased in size. Royal officials controlled all aspects of life connected with the manor, park, garden and buildings. Many records survive detailing their appointment and list duties, wages and perquisites. Building accounts in listing expenditure at Eltham also record details of the men and women who worked there, with their names, skills and rates of pay, besides the sources of the materials they worked with to create and maintain this new royal home and its amenities.

IV
RICHARD II AND ELTHAM

And whan this book is maad, yive hit the quene,
On my behalfe, at Eltham or at Shene.
(G. Chaucer, *Complete Works* (ed. W.W. Skeat), vol. xx,
'The Legend of Good Women', 1951).

The early years of Richard II's reign, while he was still a child, saw few court visits to Eltham.[1] In the fourth year of his reign, in 1381, the Peasants' Revolt affected the manor,[2] after which 18 local people had to obtain pardons[3] and another man is known to have fled from the manor. Two items in the bailiff's manorial accounts for this year may also refer to the revolt, the theft of a carthorse and an unusual proportion of the manorial livestock being recorded as 'sold on the account'.[4] The occupations of 12 of those pardoned are known. Nine had been employed on works at the palace in the past or were to do so in the future, a proportion demonstrating the importance of these building works to the local economy. Two of those pardoned, William Warner and Simon Godard, were hedgers and labourers who were also carters; two others, Richard Barbour and John Holehurst, were labourers and carters, while Richard Pode was a carpenter whose wife Johanna also received a pardon. Both Pode and Holehurst had been employed on works at the palace as far back as 1358-9. Of the others, John Webbe was a smith and a labourer who also supplied iron for use in the palace works, William Pode was a hedger, Robert Webbe a farmer, and Adam Thresshere a labourer. John Blount, a carpenter, and John Watford, a tailor, are not recorded in the palace building accounts, nor were six others of unrecorded occupations, John Rande, William Forster, Walter Baret, John Wayte, John Bocher and John Smyth.[5] Richard Potys, who fled from Eltham, was another of unknown occupation.[6]

In June 1381 the revolt reached its climax.[7] By August, when it was being suppressed,[8] the court had returned to Eltham,[9] from where, in September, an order was sent to the guardians of the peace and justices in Kent to return to Chancery all indictments and records before them,[10] of which many must have been concerned with the revolt. An amnesty, with some exceptions, was given out to the rebels in November.[11] An individual pardon, from Eltham, is recorded three years later to a man involved in the revolt. It was one of those granted 'out of regard for Good Friday', a day on which it was traditional to grant mercy to offenders.[12]

Under Richard II Eltham was sometimes visited by the court at Easter and Christmas when festivities took place there. The 22 years of his reign saw the court at Eltham for six Easter and five Christmas seasons.[13] Several visits are on record in the early 1380s.[14] One of these, at Christmas 1383, was marked, as was the same season the following year, by jousts and games. These were embellished by the work of Gilbert Prince, a painter paid over £400 for his work at Eltham, Windsor and elsewhere during these two seasons.[15] Apart from these events, religious services are also recorded there. One, in mid- to late January 1384, during Epiphany, included the presentation in the chapel of gold, frankincense and myrrh by the king at the altar.[16] Later that month Richard left Eltham for Dover to appoint, in person, his former tutor Sir Simon Burley as Constable of Dover and Warden of the Cinque Ports, two of the several official posts held by Sir Simon.[17] The same year saw a visit to Eltham by the Duke of Lancaster, who came to inform his young nephew the king of the terms of a four-year truce arranged between England and France.[18]

Shortly before Christmas 1385 the palace was the scene of another visit by foreign royalty, the visitor being Leo VI, the exiled King of Armenia, whose former kingdom on the coast of Asia Minor, north of Cyprus, had been overrun 10 years earlier by the Mameluke Sultanate of Egypt. Leo came to Western Europe to seek help in raising a crusade against his enemies and, as this was not possible unless there was peace in the West, he first attempted to reconcile England and France. His visit had no permanent effect on Anglo-French relations, though Richard supported Leo by sending envoys to France and by giving him valuable gifts and an annuity of £1,000. Leo stayed at Eltham for a week before going to see the Duke of Gloucester, another of Richard's uncles, at Pleshey Castle in Essex. The duke was said to be interested in going on crusade but when he did, to East Prussia in 1391, he never got there as he was turned back by bad weather.[19]

In July 1386 the Duke of Lancaster, who might have mediated between Richard II and his opponents, left England for the Iberian Peninsula, where he had dynastic claims on the throne of Castile, not to return for three years. The following October saw a confrontation at Eltham between Richard and his political opponents, these being the Duke of Gloucester, discontented MPs and a faction among the London merchants. While the king was at Eltham that October, Parliament met at Westminster and speeches were made demanding the dismissal of the Chancellor, the Earl of Suffolk, and the Treasurer, John Fordham. Richard's reply was to send a message to Parliament stating that they should be quiet and proceed with Parliamentary business, adding that 'He was not willing, for them, to remove the least groom of his kitchen from his office'. Such a reply only fanned the flames of opposition and a Parliamentary declaration announced the removal of the Chancellor and stated that Parliament could not proceed with business unless the king was present. Richard replied that Parliament should send 40 knights to Eltham to inform him of the opinion of the Commons but this was met by the expression of fears by Parliament for the safety of the delegation. Another source of conflict at this time was Richard's favour to his friend Edward de Vere, who in 1385 had been created Marquess of Dublin and was now created Duke of Ireland, the first non-royal duke.

Instead of the delegation of knights requested by Richard there came in their place the Duke of Gloucester and the Bishop of Ely. No certain record is known of what was said at their meeting with the king at Eltham but it was reported that Richard was informed that he must hold Parliament every year and that any session he did not attend could go home after 40 days. His reply was said to have been that he would, if resisted, obtain help from the King of France, to which the retort was that the French king was his principal enemy. Five-and-a-half centuries later this confrontation at Eltham was to be dramatised in Gordon Daviot's play, *Richard of Bordeaux*.

The crisis ended with Richard giving way as he had few supporters and only Parliament could provide the taxes needed to pay for the expenditure of the government. He attended Parliament and allowed the Chancellor and Treasurer to be dismissed, the earl also being impeached, fined and imprisoned. New ministers were appointed who were nominees of the Duke of Gloucester and for the next year England was ruled by a commission of government that greatly reduced the powers of the king.[20]

The following summer, of 1387, witnessed Richard II's first attempt to break the restrictions placed upon him, failing disastrously late in the year when an army led by the Duke of Ireland was scattered ignominiously at Radcot Bridge, north-west of Oxford, by the forces of the Lords Appellant, the five principal noblemen opposing the king. The duke escaped, to die in exile, but other leading supporters of Richard, including Sir Simon Burley, were executed after trial by the 'Merciless Parliament' of 1388. Other supporters of the king were exiled.[21] In spite of these events the king continued with his usual royal progress round England, including a Christmas at Eltham 'with many tournaments and other entertainments'.[22] In May 1389 he became 21 and thus obtained the right to rule, which he asserted to his council and to which they agreed. He thus recovered most of the powers he had lost and discomforted his opponents, whose rule had not been a conspicuous success.[23] Richard did not take an immediate revenge on his opponents and ruled with moderation for the following eight years, avoiding trouble with his principal political enemies and leaving his exiled supporters overseas.[24]

The later 1380s are the years when Geoffrey Chaucer is particularly associated with Eltham, to which he refers in his poem *The Legend of Good Women*, probably written in 1385-6 in connection with Richard's queen, Anne of Bohemia, whom the king had married in 1382.[25] Later in that decade, in July 1389, he was appointed clerk of works for several of the royal manors, including Eltham,[26] where his only recorded activity in this post was to account for the sale of the croppings of over a hundred oaks blown down in Eltham Park by a storm.[27] This damage may have been caused by a terrible tempest in Kent, recorded by chroniclers as taking place on 13 July 1389.[28]

A series of events that affected Chaucer in 1390 have been supposed, though without direct evidence on the matter, to be connected with his post of clerk of works for royal manors, including Eltham. Chaucer was robbed early in September 1390 at the *Fowle Oak* at Hatcham, in Deptford, and also at Westminster. His official position and his responsibilities at Eltham, although there is no evidence about works taking place there in this year, have been linked to suggest that Chaucer was robbed while travelling towards Eltham to pay building workers. The records state that the robberies took place at Hatcham on 3 and 6 September, and at Westminster also on the latter day, but might in fact refer to fewer robberies being committed. Chaucer lost £40 of official funds, for which he later received a pardon, besides a horse and some of his own money.[29] In the following year he was replaced in his post of clerk of works but then received a non-official position[30] and retained royal favour as later in the decade he was given a new royal pension and royal protection in connection with a lawsuit.[31]

Royal charity at Eltham during the 1390s shows, in greater detail, the pattern of similar almsgiving at the palace in other reigns between those of Edward II[32] and Henry VIII.[33] In 1390 royal alms were distributed on Good Friday to no less than 4,718 poor men, who each received either 4d. from the king or 2d. from the royal almoner.[34] Three years later, for the same event, the number receiving alms there was 5,842.[35] Edward III's sons,[36] Richard II[37] and Henry IV,[38] also distributed alms at Eltham on Maundy Thursday. In 1390 Richard gave 6d. each to 96 poor men when he was aged 33[39] and the same amount to 99 poor men there when he was thirty-six.[40] Alms given on the same day by Henry IV,[41] like those presented by Richard II, and by Princes Lionel[42] and Thomas,[43] the later Duke of Gloucester, also seem to be related to their ages. In 1406, when Henry IV was 40, he gave alms at Eltham to 40 poor men.[44] More generous than Richard, he distributed in 1403[45] about three times as much as his predecessor had given 10 years earlier. A different royal form of charity is also found at Eltham in 1390[46] and 1393,[47] when Richard II offered a sum of money at the altar of the palace chapel, with the coins then being redeemed and exchanged for others. The original coins were later made into what were called 'cramp rings', believed to have the virtue of curing muscular ailments and epilepsy.[48]

In 1392 Richard II became involved in a new dispute, on this occasion with the merchants of London. In need of money for his administration, luxurious court and expensive diplomacy, Richard tried to borrow money from the Londoners, his usual source of loans, but was refused. Understandably he was furious when some Londoners assaulted a Lombard who lent him the money he needed and he took a comprehensive revenge. The City of London was fined £13,000 and placed under a royal official, the mayor and sheriffs were imprisoned, the liberties of London were cancelled, the law courts removed to York, and the mayor, sheriffs, aldermen and other important citizens were summoned to Nottingham to hear the above judgement from the king. Richard's response to what had happened was unwise, as he lost influential friends as a result and London was a major source of government revenue.[49] Late in the same year the quarrel was patched up through the friendly intervention of Queen Anne, who was well liked, and the Duke of Lancaster, a reconciliation marked by the arrival at Eltham, in January 1393, of a delegation of Londoners bearing gifts for the king and queen. Richard was presented with a camel, Anne with 'a great and wonderful bird, having a very broad throat', a description which would appear to refer to a pelican. The visit of this delegation was marked by dances and other festivities including a mumming, an early pageant-type play, for which the visitors provided the mummers.[50]

Richard II's reign saw Anglo-French peace negotiations taking place at Eltham in September 1391, with a lasting peace being finally reached four years later. In 1394 these conferences resulted in a four-year truce, confirmed at Eltham in June.[51] Four days after that event Queen Anne died at Sheen to the great grief of her husband.[52] They had no children and, although Richard had a presumptive heir, his cousin, the Earl of March, he would be expected to marry again and have a direct heir. Negotiations were begun with France for Richard to marry a French princess, an idea which was apparently the king's own contribution towards a peace treaty. The princess he was to marry, Isabella, was only eight years old; marrying her would give him time for Anne's memory to fade. The new truce was to last for 25 years,[53] a period extended to 28 years when the treaty was sealed in March 1396,[54] three days before a proxy betrothal between Richard and Isabella. Their marriage was celebrated at Calais the following October after which Richard II brought his new queen to England, stopping at Eltham for a fortnight after their arrival.[55]

While these peace and marriage negotiations were still incomplete, a royal council met at Eltham in July 1395 to discuss another matter, a meeting of which fuller details survive than of any other council meeting there because an account was recorded by the chronicler Jean Froissart.[56] Like Queen Philippa, he came from Hainault in Flanders and he served her as a clerk from 1361 until her death eight years later. He then left England, serving in the households of several important Flemish noblemen, and about the time of his departure from England he had begun his famous chronicle of medieval chivalry. His later years saw him take orders and hold various religious posts.[57] His visit to England in 1395, to a country he had not visited for some twenty-five years, was made for the purpose of presenting a book he had written to Richard II.

After arriving in England he came up with the court while it was at Leeds Castle, near Maidstone, but he then had the problem, because he had been away from England for so long, of finding a sponsor of suitable standing who knew him and could arrange for his meeting with the king. He found such a sponsor in Sir Richard Stury, who could arrange the presentation, but then discovered that the king would be too busy to meet him at that time. He therefore followed the court until the king was free to see him and arrived at Eltham, where the royal council was due to meet on 22 July.

On 20 July the court reached Eltham and the following day he witnessed the arrival, as he records in his chronicle, of the royal Dukes of York and Gloucester, the two archbishops, six bishops, six earls and many other important people with their followers. The meeting of the royal council on 22 July was attended by many of the notabilities whose arrival Froissart records. The subject, discussed over four hours, was the gift of Aquitaine in 1390 from the king to the Duke of Lancaster. Legally Aquitaine could only be held by the heir to the throne, and the Gascons of Aquitaine distrusted this separation of their duchy from the English crown. After the views of the Gascons had been heard, a compromise was reached. The 1390 grant was not revoked but a final decision on the matter was not made until the following year. The Duke of Gloucester, usually opposed to his brother, the Duke of Lancaster, supported him on this occasion, possibly with the aim of keeping

2   *Froissart presents his book to*
Richard II, 1395.

him overseas and out of England where he considered him to be 'over great …,
and to nere the kynge', according to Froissart.

   Once the council meeting had ended, dinner was served in the hall, the royal
dukes and the Earl of Derby, heir to the Duke of Lancaster, dining first. The Duke
of Gloucester was the first to part and took his leave of the king while Richard
was still sitting at the table. With the meal over, Froissart walked with Sir Richard
Stury in a gallery in front of the king's chamber, which was 'very pleasant and
shady for these galleries were than covered with vines', while Sir Richard described
to him the details of the council that had just ended.

   By 25 July most of the visiting lords, except the Duke of York, had left
Eltham, and Sir Richard Stury and Sir Thomas Percy, later the Earl of Worcester,
decided that the time had come to inform the king of Froissart's wish to present

3   *Froissart presents his book to Richard II, 1395.*

his book to him. This work had been specially prepared to be a suitable royal gift, having been given a cover of crimson velvet on which silver and gilt buttons and gold roses were scattered. It also had gilt clasps to keep the book closed when it was not being read. The presentation was made in the king's chamber, where Richard asked the author the subject of the book. Froissart replied, 'Love', 'whereof the kynge was gladde and loked in it, and reed it in many places, for he coulde speke and rede Frenche very well'.[58] It is not surprising that Richard appreciated this gift, as he was a cultured man and a patron of other writers. The first English king to sign his own letters, he also employed great architects, ordered a splendid tomb for himself and his first queen, had himself painted in the magnificent Wilton Diptych and had the first known English cookery book compiled for his use.[59]

With the presentation over, the book was taken to the king's private chamber. It is believed to have been a collected edition of Froissart's poetry. The only known surviving manuscript copy of his poems is in the Bibliothèque Nationale in Paris. Completed in 1394, it was formerly owned by Richard, Earl of Warwick, a godson of Richard II. This manuscript could be the only one given by the author to the king during Froissart's visit if it was later passed on the earl. If this is the case, however, it has lost its original cover and been divided into two volumes since its original presentation to Richard II in 1395.[60]

Later that day, Froissart talked at Eltham with a courtier, either a squire named Henry Castyde or a knight called Sir Henry Cristell. In his chronicle, his record of this conversation describes the unfamiliar subject to him of Ireland, where this courtier had campaigned and had been captured by an Irish chieftain, whose daughter he had later married. He was able to provide Froissart with an interesting account of life in Ireland and of Irish methods of warfare.[61] For the next three months the chronicler travelled round England with the court and would have revisited Eltham when the court returned there later in the year.[62] He finally left the court while it was at Windsor, where, in return for his book, he was presented with 100 nobles (about £33) in a silver gilt goblet, an object he says he 'valued greatly all my life since'.[63]

In the late 1390s the court came to Eltham on several occasions. One in 1396 saw in the preparations for its arrival the cleansing of the outer court and the setting up there of barriers, presumably for jousting.[64] One visit to the palace in this year witnessed an exchange of gifts between Queen Isabella and the Duke of Lancaster, the latter giving her a covered gold cup that, with other gifts to the young queen, was later taken to France in 1401 by the widowed Isabella. This particular cup may have resembled the covered gold cup of a slightly earlier date now in the British Museum. Other gifts received by Queen Isabella at Eltham were a cup covered with pearls from her husband, a large silver effigy of the Virgin from the Bishop of Chichester and a jewelled ladle from the Duke of Lancaster.[65]

Froissart (whose information on England after his 1395 visit is not thought to be accurate) states that two delegations from London visited Richard II and the Duke of Lancaster at Eltham in 1397 to complain about the policy and spending of the government. The first delegation was put off by the Duke of Lancaster until Parliament met, while a second one was told that a report claiming Calais was to be handed over to France was not true.[66] If these visits occurred they may have taken place either in late April[67] or late July[68] 1397 when the court was at Eltham. Froissart also reports that Richard was told in August of that year by the Earl Marshal at Eltham of a plot against him by the Duke of Gloucester and the Earl of Arundel, conceived by them at a meeting at Arundel in July at which the informant had been present.[69]

Richard II finally took his revenge on some of those responsible for the 1388 executions and exilings in the summer of 1397. One of the Lords Appellant, the Earl of Arundel, was executed; a second, the Earl of Warwick, was exiled; a third, the Duke of Gloucester, was arrested and taken to Calais where he died soon afterwards, probably as a result of an order from the king. Between the arrests in August and the Duke of Gloucester's death the following month, Richard, according to Froissart, was at Eltham. There he would have been in a good position to get in touch with the commanders of his archers stationed in Kent and Essex, who would have been needed if the arrests of the three lords had been met by armed resistance.[70]

Of the five Lords Appellant of 1387-9 only two were now left, the Dukes of Norfolk and Hereford. The former, Earl Marshal and former Earl of Nottingham, was understandably nervous; the latter, former Earl of Derby and heir to the Duke of Lancaster, was safe so long as his father lived, as he was a vital ally of the king. The Duke of Norfolk expressed his fears about the future to the Duke of Hereford, who safeguarded himself by reporting what he was told to his father, who passed on the Duke of Norfolk's words to the king. Both dukes then accused each other of treason and were placed under arrest, with the Duke of Hereford being allowed bail. Richard arranged for a trial by battle between the two dukes, to take place at Coventry, only to forbid it at the last moment. Most chroniclers of these events state that the announcement that the Duke of Norfolk was banished for life and the Duke of Hereford for 10 years was made at Coventry,[71] but Froissart states that this announcement was made at Eltham where a council had been assembled, also stating that councillors were sent to the two dukes, who were nearby, to make sure that they obeyed.[72] Froissart also states that late in September 1398 the Duke of Hereford came to Eltham to say farewell to Richard, who then reduced his sentence of banishment from 10 to six years.[73] An editor's dating of Richard's invitation to Lady Poynings to spend the Christmas season with him and his queen at Eltham also shows him there in 1398.[74] However, a recently compiled itinerary for Richard II shows him in the Midlands between late December 1398 and January 1399, and at Lichfield on Christmas Day, so Froissart and the editor must be incorrect and the invitation must refer to Christmas 1396, when Richard was at Eltham shortly after his second marriage.[75] As Froissart's account of events in England after his 1395 visit is believed to include many errors,[76] it would seem that Richard II did not visit Eltham during the last two years of his reign.

Richard II had now disposed of all his principal political opponents, either by death or exile, but one problem remained. The death of the Duke of Lancaster would mean that the duke's exiled son would succeed him as the wealthiest of the king's subjects and would eventually return home in an unfriendly frame of mind towards the king who had exiled him.[77] In February 1399 the Duke of Lancaster died and the following month Richard confiscated the inheritance that would have gone to the duke's exiled son. Richard also increased his sentence of exile from 10 years to life. The king's actions frightened and offended many, both noblemen and others, not only Lancastrian supporters, because it made them realise that if the royal will could deprive the wealthiest nobleman in England of his inheritance then no one's property was secure.[78]

In early July 1399 the exiled duke landed in England with a small force while Richard was in Ireland. He proclaimed that he had only come to claim his rightful inheritance and he was soon joined by many supporters.[79] The royal council left to rule England in the king's absence failed to take decisive action against the invasion,[80] while bad weather prevented the return of the king to England until late July. On his arrival in South Wales Richard found that his supporters had dispersed or had joined the exiled duke while some had been captured and executed.[81] Believing that he still had organised support in North Wales, the king made his way there only to find that he was too late and that most of his remaining supporters there had dispersed before his arrival.[82] He was betrayed into the hands of the Duke of Hereford in August[83] and taken to London where, in late September, Parliament met and decided that Richard had abdicated, not even allowing him to appear before them. The Duke of Hereford then claimed the throne by right of descent from Edward III and, his claim having been accepted by Parliament, he became King Henry IV while Richard was kept in safe custody.[84]

Surviving records of building works at Eltham during Richard II's reign[85] are few and, with rare exceptions, they do not refer to new building works but only to repairs and alterations to existing buildings. New glass 'stippled with deer' was placed in the windows of the hall[86] and a deer in a window of the king's chamber,[87] these being emblems of Richard's personal device of the chained deer, beautifully painted in the Wilton Diptych. The great north bridge was also rebuilt in stone late in his reign,[88] although later repairs to it show that, even after these works, it still incorporated a drawbridge made of wood.[89]

Richard II's reign is the first from which it is known that Eltham Palace had both an inner or lesser court and an outer court,[90] the inner court being enclosed by the moat. This division, however, may only formalise an earlier position as the existence of buildings outside the moat is recorded under Edward III.[91] The inner court buildings within the moat included royal apartments,[92] the chapel, with a bell,[93] the great hall,[94] a kitchen[95] and one or more cellars.[96] Outer court buildings included a great storehouse,[97] other storehouses for wood[98] and 'lead and nails'[99] besides one or two bakehouses.[100] Other recorded buildings, which may have been in either the inner or outer court, were a pantry,[101] poultery,[102] saucery,[103] two spiceries,[104] buttery,[105] wafery,[106] larder,[107] 'dressour'[108] and 'sethinghouse'[109] as well as lodging allocated to courtiers and officials.[110]

Among the royal apartments in the inner court in 1384-8 there was a tower used by Queen Anne on the western side of the court with an oriel window.[111] The queen also had one or more chambers there,[112] a hall[113] and both great[114] and small[115] chambers, the latter shared with the king. Richard's rooms included one or more chambers,[116] a wardrobe,[117] a closet,[118] a great chamber,[119] a bathhouse[120] and a private chapel,[121] which may be the small chapel or oratory which formed part of the great chapel.[122] A passage is also referred to as linking a great chamber, presumably the king's great chamber, to the chapel of the palace.[123] In the following reign this passage was hung with arras.[124] A garden fenced with a palisade was situated next to the king's chamber.[125]

Eltham, as a favourite resort for both Richard II and Henry IV for Christmas and Easter, was the scene of feasts, tournaments and entertainments. Other facilities emphasising its role as a place for relaxation included a new herb garden, created in 1384-8 on the south side of the palace, beyond the moat, which was made 'for the King and Queen to have dinner there in the summer time', with walls of earth and straw covered with reeds added in 1388-9.[126] The palace rooms included a dancing chamber, created in 1384-8 by the subdivision of a larger room next to the king's wardrobe, with which it shared a fireplace.[127] An additional amenity was fishing in the moat, a boat being provided for this purpose.[128] The palace also had a 'Watchchambre' for a personal royal bodyguard, Richard II being the first English king to have one.[129]

During the 1380s a number of senior courtiers had rooms allocated to them at Eltham, these being the Dukes of Lancaster[130] and Ireland,[131] the Earl of Nottingham,[132] Lord Nicholas Sharnesfeld[133] and the Dame de Luttrell, a lady in waiting to the queen.[134] In the following decade the parker of the manor, Baldwin Berford, also had a personal chamber.[135] A number of senior household officials are also recorded with their own palace rooms: the steward,[136] controller[137] and treasurer of the king's household;[138] the king's almoner[139] and chamberlain;[140] the rector[141] and clerk[142] of the king's chapel; the queen's esquire and groom;[143] the privy saucer[144] and the chandler;[145] this varied list of officials forming only a small part of the large and expensive royal household which visited Eltham during this reign. A kitchen is recorded 'in the inner court',[146] its position implying another kitchen in the outer court. The status of an official or courtier would no doubt determine which kitchen would be used by a member of the household travelling with the king. One of these kitchens is recorded as having a gutter or gutters with three iron grates leading into the park for the disposal of waste water.[147]

Although no more land is recorded as having been acquired for Eltham Park under Richard II, work continued during his reign on the fencing of parkland. In 1378 hedgers were ordered to be collected by the parker and another man to make a hedge 'round the king's park of Eltham'[148] in the same way as ditchers had been recruited in 1367. Between 1384 and 1389 1,583 perches (8,700 yards) of hedge were made for the park,[149] followed in 1397-9 by a further 1,945 perches (10,629 yards).[150] This extensive work implies either that the records of the purchase of further land for the park are lost or that work was continuing on the incorporation into the park of land acquired under Edward III.

Only one new senior official position at Eltham is recorded under Richard II, that of the keeper of the king's wardrobe there. This appointment is first recorded in 1396 when its holder, Hugh de Ellerbek, had died and his post was divided between a new keeper and Hugh's widow; with the new holder of the post having to find 'sufficient maintenance' for the widow while doing 'all things pertaining to the keepership'.[151] Another type of connection with an earlier holder of a position there is recorded in 1397[152] when, on the death of the gardener, his son took his place, a post which he held for over forty years.

Thoughtfulness for the interests of junior members of the royal household is recorded in this reign in several grants for life of houses and land in Eltham for royal servants, a type of grant first recorded there a few days before Richard II succeeded his grandfather Edward III as king.[153] A royal servant[154] and grooms and servants of the kitchen,[155] buttery,[156] scullery[157] and ewry[158] received these grants of houses with land attached in Eltham. In theory, wives of court servants were not allowed to travel with the court, so grants like these would give the recipients a permanent home to which they could expect to return several times a year. Similar grants are also found for Eltham in the reigns of Henry V[159] and Edward IV.[160]

The form of administration for Eltham's home farm was not settled until late in Richard II's reign. An earlier change in 1372 from a paid bailiff[161] to a farmer paying rent for his position[162] was reversed in 1381 when William Spalding, the farmer, was appointed as a paid bailiff.[163] His position was reversed again, in 1391, when he was once again appointed farmer of the manor, paying rent for his position.[164] He came to grief in 1395 when he lost his position for not having paid rent for two years and also for having illegally disposed of the stock belonging to the manor.[165] The livestock belonging to the manor in 1391 consisted of four carthorses, 16 oxen, a bull, 23 cows, 204 wethers and four horses, There were, in addition, a cart and the crops stored in the manorial barn.[166] A further accusation held against William Spalding was that he had levied illegal rents from tenants of the manor.[167] He was not the only Eltham official to get into trouble, others being under investigation in 1355[168] and 1402.[169] The system of a farmer paying rent for his position was not altered again after 1391.

V

ELTHAM AND THE EARLY LANCASTRIAN KINGS

The kyng from Eltham sone he cam,
Hyse presenors with hym dede brynge,
And to the Blak heth ful sone he cam,
He saw London withoughte lesynge …
(Anon, *The Battle of Agincourt* (ed. Sir N. Harris Nicolas), 1832)

Henry IV spent 10 of the 13 Christmases of his reign at Eltham,[1] where, early in his reign, he had new royal apartments built for himself and his queen.[2] It appears that he did not visit Eltham during his first months as king, except perhaps very briefly in November 1399 when a grant was dated from there.[3] However, both the king and his son, the future Henry V, were there between late February and mid-April 1400, Henry writing from Eltham on 1 March to the Pope to obtain the restitution to his office of his vital supporter Thomas Arundel, Archbishop of Canterbury, and the degradation of his clerical opponent the Bishop of Carlisle.[4] This visit occurred soon after the unsuccessful revolt in support of the imprisoned Richard II, who died in mysterious circumstances in February.[5]

During this Eltham visit Henry IV saw some French ambassadors regarding the future of Queen Isabella, Richard II's queen, then living at Sonning, north-east of Reading, in Berkshire. Having seen Henry, the ambassadors visited Isabella before returning to meet Henry a second time at Eltham, where he presented them with some jewels.[6] It was decided that Isabella should return to France but, as the large sum needed to send her back in suitable state was not available, Isabella had to wait until the money was raised. She finally returned home in the summer of 1401,[7] a few months before the birth of her sister Catherine who, nearly twenty years later, married Henry V and came to Eltham in 1421.[8]

While the court was at Eltham for the Christmas season of 1400 there came with it the third overseas ruler to visit the manor.[9] Manuel II Palaeologus, Emperor of Byzantium, was, like an earlier royal visitor from the East, Leo of Armenia, visiting England to seek English assistance against his enemies. These were, in his case, the Ottoman Turks who had, with other Muslim armies over the previous two centuries, conquered most of the once great Byzantine Empire.[10] During this visit the court was entertained by a mumming performed by 12 London aldermen and their sons, 'for whiche they hadde gret thanke',[11] while Manuel presented Henry with a tunic said to have been made for Jesus by the Virgin.[12]

This Christmas season at the palace also witnessed a tournament held in the outer court, which was cleaned, sanded and decorated for the occasion with banners, standards, pennons and horses' harnesses, all displaying the royal arms.[13] The fortunate survival of copies of a number of letters referring to this tournament has preserved many details of this day and of the chivalrous imagery involved.[14] The recipient of these letters was Princess Blanche, the eight-year-old eldest daughter of the widowed Henry IV, who presided over the tournament. She was to have a brief life. In 1402 she married Louis, son of the King of the Romans and grandson of the Holy Roman Emperor, only to die four years later.[15] A relic of her short life, a magnificent crown of gold and pearls, was on display in London in 1987 as part of an exhibition on 'The Age of Chivalry'.[16]

The letters include much high-flown rhetoric on the subject of chivalry. Henry IV appears in them not as King of England but as King of Albion and Gaul,[17] King of Great Britain[18] and as 'King of the Isle of Giants'.[19] His guest from the East is mentioned as Emperor of Constantinople,[20] while heroic figures appearing from the past include Alexander,[21] Arthur,[22] Charlemagne,[23] William the Conqueror[24] and Saint Louis, King of France.[25] Certain places considered to be of chivalrous and romantic interest are also mentioned, such as Troy,[26] India[27] and the Kingdom of Jerusalem.[28] Perhaps the most unusual aspect of the letters is to be found in the places from where they are said to have been sent, including 'our marvellous mansion of the firmament in a full court of stars',[29] 'our palace of pleasure, full of delights'[30] and 'our noble keep of Perfect Diligence, free from evil'.[31]

The tournament took place on New Year's Day, 1401.[32] From the letters we learn the romantic names assumed by the jousters taking part and in some cases details of their opponents,[33] described either by their coats of arms or by their personal histories. In most cases the letters take the form of the bearer of a feminine romantic, allegorical or classical name greeting the princess and introducing a knight to her. The ladies of the court who would have carried out these introductions are given such names as Penolose (Penelope), 'wife of Prince Ulysses',[34] Cleopatra, 'Queen of Mesopotamia',[35] Gobosse, 'eldest daughter of the most high emperor Dynde la Maior, called Prester John',[36] Phebus (Phoebus),[37] Venus,[38] Naturo[39] and Vertu;[40] while the jousters took such names as Ferombras,[41] Feresbar,[42] Le Poer Perdu,[43] Ardent Desirous,[44] Joesrue le Amerues,[45] Tolet Detollide[46] and Nonsaichart.[47]

Several letters mention the rules of the tournament. Low saddles were to be used in most cases,[48] although three jousters were allowed high saddles,[49] and the contestants were not permitted to be bound into them.[50] The lances were all to be of the same length, with lawful blunt standard lance heads.[51] Most jousters were to run six courses,[52] though some were allowed 12,[53] and the prize for the best jouster was to be a rod of gold.[54] The jousts themselves were not the only event of the day. A 'parade of your royal court' is mentioned in one letter, something which must have preceded the jousting. The knights and esquires taking part in this 'will do wonders, riding dragons, others carrying serpents on their heads throwing out flames of fire', which would seem to refer to the use of stage fire on the armour of the participants. Dancing and a feast are also mentioned and must have concluded the day's festivities.[55]

The sum of £2,000 presented to the emperor by Henry IV may have been, as far as the former was concerned, the only practical result of his visit to England. After staying almost two months, Manuel returned to France in February,[56] to remain there until, 18 months later, he learnt that his enemy, Bayezid, had been defeated in June 1402 at the Battle of Ankara by Timur, also called Tamburlane, ruler of the Mongol state to the east of the Ottoman Turks. Manuel then returned to his capital of Constantinople, the main surviving part of his empire, which Timur, unlike Bayezid, did not wish to capture. This fortuitous victory over the Ottoman Turks was to preserve the last fragments of the Byzantine Empire from its enemies for another half-century until its final destruction in 1453 under Manuel II's son, Constantine XI Palaeologus.[57]

Under Henry IV, visits by the court to Eltham normally occurred two or three times a year.[58] In the intervals between these visits the palace was left partially furnished and, when a court visit was about to take place, extra furnishings were forwarded to it from the Tower of London. Preparations for Christmas visits in 1400, 1401,[59] 1406 and 1407[60] to Eltham included the sending there of beds and arras from the Tower, to where they were returned after the visits were over. Other preparations included, in 1406, the washing of the king's sheets[61] and, on a later occasion, the cleaning of the palisade in the outer court and the setting up there of a pair of beams for tilting.[62] Similar visits between the reigns of Edward III and Elizabeth I witnessed, prior to the arrival of the court, the forwarding there of gold and silver vessels and chapel furnishings,[63] table silver,[64] beds,[65] arras[66] and the king's clothing.[67] The fullest details of these preparations come from Henry VIII's reign, from March–April 1534, when new furniture was made there, the water conduit repaired, repairs carried out on windows, doors and roofs, lavatories cleansed and rubbish removed from the precincts of the palace.[68]

In April 1402 Henry IV, whose first wife, Mary Bohun, had died in 1394,[69] went through a proxy marriage at Eltham with Johanna, Duchess of Brittany, sister of the King of Navarre and widow, as his third wife, of the elderly Duke of Brittany, who had died in 1399. Henry was then 35 and his new bride about thirty. The proxy marriage ceremony was performed at the palace by the Bishop of Bath and Wells; the duchess was represented for the occasion by her envoy Antoine Ricze, on whose finger Henry placed a ring, while Ricze, on Johanna's behalf, took the king for her husband. Only a few courtiers were present at this event, including the Earls of Somerset, Worcester and Northumberland, together with the latter's son Sir Henry Percy, known as Hotspur.[70] Johanna herself finally arrived in person in England the following January under the escort of the king's half-brothers, the Bishop of Lincoln and the Earl of Somerset, and the Earl of Worcester, who, 18 months earlier, had escorted Queen Isabella back to France.[71] The marriage was celebrated at Winchester in February 1403.[72] Soon afterwards Henry and Johanna, with three of Henry's sons and his daughter Philippa, paid a visit to Eltham which was interrupted by a journey to Westminster for the ceremony of Johanna's coronation.[73] During this visit to Eltham the new queen was granted a large yearly income from the exchequer until she received an equivalent sum as dowry in the form of rent, land or other income.[74]

In July 1403 two of the courtiers present at the proxy wedding at Eltham, the Earl of Worcester and his nephew, Sir Henry Percy, rose in revolt against the king whom they had helped place on the throne in 1399. Both died when Henry IV defeated the rebels outside Shrewsbury late that month. The Earl of Northumberland, brother of one rebel leader and father of the other, was to be killed in battle five years later leading another rebellion against Henry IV.[75]

During Henry IV's reign the court was at Eltham for Easter on three occasions.[76] This was a season when royal pardons were traditionally granted 'out of reverence for … Good Friday', either on that day or with reference to it,[77] as occurred at Eltham in 1404.[78] One such pardon, granted from Windsor, illustrates an aspect of court luxury at Eltham, as it was given to a sergeant of the table silver, held responsible for the loss of 17 silver ladles, each weighing a little over a pound, that had been stolen while being taken by road from London to Eltham.[79] In spite of his victory at Shrewsbury, the threatening aspects of the times for Henry IV appear later in 1404 in connection with a Christmas visit by the court to Eltham. Two months after this ended, after the failure of an attempt to abduct the young Earl of March and his brother, potential claimants to the throne, it was claimed that the Duke of York had plotted to kill Henry during this Christmas visit.[80] Other aspects of court life at Eltham are seen in April 1406, when French ambassadors seem to have visited the king there,[81] and at the following Christmas when jousts were held[82] and expensive brooches purchased for the king to present to his courtiers as gifts on New Year's Day. The sum of £1,000 was set aside to pay for that Christmas at Eltham, part of which would have gone towards the cost of these New Year gifts.[83]

While Henry IV was at the palace during the winter of 1408 he became seriously ill, though he later made a partial recovery.[84] A later visit for the Christmas season of 1409[85] witnessed the arrival there of envoys from three foreign countries. Those from the Hanse towns had come to see Henry regarding a long drawn-out commercial dispute, but the others, from the Order of Teutonic Knights and Poland, were rivals and enemies, each seeking the king's aid against the other side. The knights' envoys arrived first, with the Polish envoy, a herald, a few days later with a present for the king of four stallions. Before he became king, Henry had visited East Prussia, in 1390-1 and again in 1392, on the first occasion serving with the Teutonic Knights against the Lithuanians, who, being pagans until 1386, were regarded as suitable foes for Christian knights wishing to take part in a crusade against the heathen. As a result of his earlier service in East Prussia Henry probably favoured the knights, and he told their envoys that he would help them in person if he had peace with France, though in the end he did nothing to assist either side. In the following July the Poles and their allies won a famous victory at Tannenberg, during which the knights were almost annihilated.[86]

Two further Christmases were spent by Henry IV at Eltham where, early in 1412, he received envoys from the Armagnac faction in France, who were then engaged in a civil war with their Burgundian rivals. The Dukes of Berri, Bourbon, Alençon and Orleans, the leaders of the Armagnacs, offered through their envoys to recognise Henry as their feudal lord, surrender a large part of south-western France and arrange marriages between their children and the Lancastrian royal family, in return for military assistance. An agreement on these lines was agreed in May.[87] The Burgundian faction had no higher patriotic principles; in 1411 they gained English help in return for promises including a marriage between Anne, daughter of the Duke of Burgundy, and the Prince of Wales. Preparations began in 1411 for an English invasion of France, but this was not launched until July 1412, when a force commanded by Henry's second son, Thomas, newly created Duke of Clarence, was sent to assist the Armagnacs.[88] In October of the same year orders were issued for the cutting down of 80 oaks in Eltham Park to build three galleys, probably in connection with this campaign in France.[89] At the end of 1412 Henry IV revisited Eltham once again but for the last time, as by now he was gravely ill. He only lived a few months longer, dying at Westminster in March 1413.[90] His son, the Duke of Clarence, was still in France when his father died and, on hearing the news, he returned to England.[91]

The new king, Henry V, was to spend much less time than his father at Eltham as for a large part of his reign he was campaigning in France. In preparation for his campaign there in 1414, which was to continue into the following year when the Battle of Agincourt was fought, vast preparations were made, including the cutting down of more oaks in Eltham Park for shipbuilding.[92] The court came to Eltham for the Christmas of 1413, when Henry and his brothers were the subject of a plot by the Lollards, who wished for changes in religion. In connection with their plot the Lollards planned to capture the king and his brothers at Eltham, intending to gain access disguised as mummers for a performance at court. Their plan was, however, betrayed to the king who, with his brothers and many courtiers, left the palace for London on 8 January 1414 before the Lollard plot could be put into effect. Arrests were made of some suspicious characters found near the palace, who were fettered and imprisoned, and on the following day a Lollard assembly in St Giles' Field outside the walls of London was broken up by a force led by the king himself.[93]

Nearly two years passed after the failure of this Lollard plot before Henry V revisited Eltham, for a single day on 22 November 1415, while returning to London after the Battle of Agincourt, bringing with him the most important of the French prisoners.[94] The following day he was welcomed ceremonially on Blackheath by the Londoners before entering his capital, which had been decorated in his honour.[95] This notable victory, and the king's return to London, were celebrated in the ballad 'The Battle of Agincourt', in which Eltham makes a brief appearance. One version of the ballad describes the final stages of the king's return to London as follows:

To Caunterbury full fair he past,
And offered at Seynt Thomas shryne;
Fro thens sone he rod in hast,
To Eltham he cam in good tyme.
Wot ye right well that thus it was,
Gloria tibi Trinitas. …

The kyng from Eltham sone he cam,
Hyse presenors with hym dede brynge,
And to the Blak heth ful sone he cam,
He saw London withoughte lesynge;
Heil, ryall London, seyde oure kyng,
Crist the kepe evere from care;
And thanne gaf it his blessyng,
And praied to Crist that it well fare.[96]

Henry V is next known to have visited Eltham in July and August 1416, when he was visited there by Sigismund, King of the Romans, Emperor Elect of Germany and brother of Anne of Bohemia, the first queen of Richard II.[97] His stay lasted for two weeks and Henry presented his household with £200 towards their expenses.[98] This royal visit had as its aim the obtainment of peace between England and France from Henry V, thus assisting Sigismund's plans to reunify the Church, then divided by the Great Schism, in which England and France supported rival popes. Although his plans as regards peace were unsuccessful, agreement was reached on a treaty between Henry V and Sigismund on mutual help and assistance.[99] During the visit Henry's prisoners taken at Agincourt were present at court because, as had previously occurred there in 1364 during the visit of John II of France, knights of all countries, even if prisoners or hostages, were still considered to be an international brotherhood. Suitable provision was made for their welfare at court during this visit, with beds, coverlets and other necessities being provided for them.[100]

After Sigismund's visit Henry V did not return to Eltham for over four years, a period he spent campaigning in France, where he captured Normandy. This, and his alliance with the Burgundians, who controlled the mentally unstable King Charles VI of France enabled Henry to obtain very favourable terms in a peace treaty with France at Troyes in May 1420. By this treaty Henry V was recognised both as Regent of France and as Charles VI's successor, and was also betrothed to Charles VI's daughter Princess Catherine, whom he married at Troyes in June, a few days after the sealing of the treaty of peace between the two countries.[101]

With peace achieved Henry could return to England. He and Catherine landed at Dover in February 1421 and, after visiting Canterbury, Henry went on to London without his wife to make arrangements for their reception and Catherine's coronation in London. Catherine followed his route towards London more slowly as far as Eltham, where she awaited her husband's return. When all was ready in the capital, three weeks after their arrival in England, Henry retraced his route to Eltham and they both set out together for London on 21 February. Their reception on Blackheath, and triumphal entry into a capital decorated in their honour, resembled Henry's arrival there after Agincourt five years earlier. Two days after their entry, Catherine was crowned in Westminster Abbey,[102] some of the scaffolding put up for the occasion coming from trees cut down in Eltham Park.[103]

In June 1421 Henry V returned to France, Queen Catherine following him the following May, some months after the birth of their son, the future Henry VI.[104] The month following her departure saw an official appointed to collect stone cutters, carpenters and other craftsmen for new building works to be carried out at Eltham and other royal manors,[105] but it is not known if these were completed before Henry's death late in August 1422, a month before the death of his father-in-law, Charles VI. At the age of nine months Henry VI thus became King of England and, a month later, by Charles VI's death, King of France, the latter title claimed also by the Dauphin, Charles VI's eldest son, with Armagnac support.[106]

The early years of Henry IV's reign saw much of the western side of the inner court at Eltham rebuilt, including the erection between 1400 and 1403 of a new building for the personal use of the king.[107] Thirty-eight feet long and 18ft wide,[108] it had wainscoted ceilings,[109] a roof partially made of lead but mostly tiled,[110] and was sited 'on the west side of the great chapel and the moat'.[111] Its first floor included the king's chamber,[112] study[113] and latrine[114] and was reached by a staircase lit by a window displaying 'images of the Holy Trinity and the Salutation of St Mary'.[115] Its ground-floor rooms were a parlour with a fireplace,[116] a wainscoted ceiling[117] and a tiled floor,[118] and a buttery.[119]

The king's chamber on the first floor had two tiled fireplaces and four doors.[120] Its floor[121] and walls were plastered[122] and its wainscoted ceiling was embellished with '44 angels with escutcheons and 12 archangels with scrolls in their hands' and 24 demi-keys.[123] The only furniture recorded for this room consisted of two tables and a screen, the latter made of painted boards.[124] The glass in this room was more expensive than that used in the ground-floor windows of the building.[125] A lead-covered timber bay window, of four lights of 80 square feet, was a principal feature of the room, displaying escutcheons, crowns and flowers, together with the king's motto 'soveignez vous de moy' ('Remember me').[126] Four further windows, of 102 square feet and 8 inches, held escutcheons, garters and colours of the king's badges,[127] with two smaller windows, one displaying royal badges and the other birds and the arms of St George.[128] Work on this building probably had to be hurried to be ready for the king's arrival as the masons and carpenters used up 96 pounds of candles working on it at night.[129]

Henry IV's study, next to his chamber,[130] had its own tiled fireplace[131] and held a large two-stage desk to hold his books,[132] a smaller desk and two forms.[133] Its windows had more expensive glass than that in the king's chamber next door.[134] There were seven windows, containing 78 square feet of glass, displaying in single windows portraits of St John the Baptist, St Thomas, St George, the Trinity and St Thomas the Evangelist,[135] and, in two central windows, a display of the 'Salutation of the Virgin Mary'.[136] 'Various images of birds and beasts' also appeared in the windows of the study,[137] while a later purchase of glass for this room, describing it as the 'sovereign's scriptorium', shows it had three bay windows and four side windows.[138] This glass, of 91 square feet, was diapered (patterned) with images of broom, eagles and scrolls.[139] Another glass purchase, of 42 square feet, for the ground-floor parlour windows, included 'birds and other grotesques'.[140] Glass was also bought for a new oratory for the king, its 54 square feet 'worked with images and canopies, the background … cloth of gold'.[141] The glass used at Eltham came from a London glazier, William Burgh, and was despatched to the palace by cart, packed in straw.[142] A new palace kitchen, a larder and a saucery were sited to the north of the king's new building, the kitchen being presumably the king's privy kitchen.[143] This kitchen was 51 feet long and 13 feet wide.[144]

Between 1400 and 1404 four suppliers of new furniture to Eltham are recorded, John Joyner of Lombard Street supplying a table, forms and stools;[145] Roger Joyner, the great desk for the king's study;[146] John Wygmore, an 18-feet-long varnished table on trestles,[147] and John Deken, a small desk for the king's study, a screen, two hanging cupboards for the queen's parlour and two chairs 'off state'.[148] Some of this could have replaced stolen furniture, as in February 1404 an inquiry was ordered into the theft of tables, forms, trestles and other furniture from several royal residences including Eltham.[149]

The king's new building completed, a new one was built for Queen Johanna between 1404 and 1407.[150] Two-storeyed and 35 feet long,[151] it had a parlour[152] and drawing chamber[153] on the ground floor, and a chamber,[154] drawing chamber[155] and latrine[156] on the first floor. The queen also had her own kitchen,[157] chapel[158] and hall[159] at Eltham.

Apart from the new royal apartments, a number of other buildings and rooms were erected at Eltham between 1400 and 1403. These were two drawing chambers 30 feet by 22½ feet,[160] an oratory 16½ feet by 13 feet;[161] a kitchen 60 feet by 21 feet[162] that had a great fireplace[163] and two ranges,[164] a dresser 37½ feet by 18 feet,[165] a larder 16 feet by 9 feet[166] and a 12-feet-square latrine.[167] Another new building erected for the king, of unstated purpose, was sited to the north of the great chapel and was 60 feet long and 20 feet wide.[168] An unusual feature of these particular records is the specification of the sizes of these rooms and buildings. Two other buildings mentioned in the records which were not new and were for royal use were rooms situated in one case over a cellar near the great hall,[169] and in the other case close to the bridge to the park.[170] The other rooms of the king at Eltham in this reign included a wardrobe with a press for his clothes and two partitions,[171] a bathroom[172] and a latrine near the bathhouse.[173] In this period the palace is recorded as having 25 latrines.[174] Certain walls had rails fixed to them on which arras[175] or cloth of gold hangings could be hung, arras being used on secular walls, cloth of gold on chapel walls.[176] In this reign the chapel was also provided with a roodloft, reached by a winding stair.[177]

The Eltham building accounts for Henry IV's reign are the first to record the positions of some of these new buildings in relation to each other, which makes it possible to work out part of the inner court's layout. The king's new building on the western side of this court had its kitchen and larder to the north and the queen's new building to the south. Its latrine was to the east with, beyond it, the chapel, which had a new oratory attached to it. North of the chapel there was an enclosure and a further building of the king's.[178]

Apart from the king and queen, other members of the new Lancastrian royal family had rooms at Eltham. The Prince of Wales,[179] his brother Thomas[180] and sister Philippa (later Queen of Denmark)[181] had their own rooms, while a reference in 1402-3 to a room called the 'Blaunchechambr'[182] may refer to a room formerly used by Philippa's elder sister Blanche before she left England for her marriage, mentioned earlier. The two royal brothers also shared a bedroom at the palace.[183] Individual courtiers with allotted rooms at Eltham in Henry IV's reign were the

Duke of York, uncle of the king and one of Edward III's sons, whose windows had 'flowered' glass,[184] the Earl[185] and Countess[186] of Somerset, Sir Thomas Erpingham, whose windows had 'flourished' (ornamental) glass,[187] John Cressey,[188] John Norbury,[189] and Margaret Hervy.[190] Sir Thomas Erpingham and John Norbury had been followers of the new king from long before he ascended the throne. The latter became Treasurer of England in 1399-1401. Both had been with Henry on his East Prussian crusade in 1390-1 and the former, as Shakespeare reminds us in *Henry V*, was later to fight for the king's son at Agincourt in 1415.[191] A year before that battle, as steward of the king's household, Sir Thomas took charge of the prisoners taken near Eltham Palace at the time of the Lollard plot.[192]

Both household officers and courtiers are recorded in building accounts as having allotted rooms at Eltham in this period. The officials were the Treasurer of England;[193] the treasurer,[194] controller[195] and steward[196] of the king's household; the king's confessor[197] and almoner;[198] the dean of the king's chapel;[199] John Burton, 'one of the king's cooks';[200] the clerk of the jewels,[201] and, in shared rooms, the esquires[202] and grooms[203] of the king's chamber. The Pope's collectors of papal revenue in England also had their own room at the palace.[204]

Building accounts preserve information on the layout of the palace. Two entrances into the inner court are mentioned, a great gate over the great bridge to the north and another gate over the bridge to the park, both provided with drawbridges and portcullises.[205] A 'storegate'[206] and a 'wodhousgate'[207] could be different names for the same gate; they entered the outer court that included the palace's storehouses.[208] Somewhere in this area was the storeyard,[209] with a 'framing place' for the assembly of timbers used in building works.[210] The main outer court included houses in which courtiers were presumably lodged, as was the case there two centuries later.[211] The storerooms at the palace in Henry IV's reign included ones for holding 'rushes for strewing',[212] wood[213] and coal.[214]

Information on the kitchen building at Eltham in Henry IV's reign is particularly full. The new kitchen previously mentioned may have replaced an earlier one. Its features were a tiled roof, a door banded with iron and fitted with a great lock, a reredos, a great window, a great fireplace covered with white Flanders tiles, a hearth, two ranges, a paved floor and plastered walls. A dresser, a circular room and a well, the last with a gibbet for drawing water, were near this kitchen.[215] The palace also had two other kitchens, one a privy kitchen[216] presumably for the king's use as the second kitchen was for the use of the queen.[217] There were, in addition, two bakehouses, one of which had two boards for kneading and two for moulding bread,[218] and an 'oven for Franchebred'.[219] Other kitchen rooms were a larder,[220] a saucery[221] and a privy saucery.[222]

The palace buildings included a great stable,[223] probably outside the outer court as was the case, 200 years later, in the reign of James I.[224] Other features of the palace were its vines, recorded in the 'garden outside the mansion' (1399-1400),[225] on the banks of the moat (1399-1407),[226] and in the great garden (1399-1401).[227] They are last mentioned in surviving accounts in 1413-14.[228]

Under the first two Lancastrian kings the parks attached to the palace have a similar history to that under Richard II. There are no known records of the acquisition of land for the parks but work was still in progress to create parkland, including an area, in 1399–1400, called 'Le Westland'.[229] A timber lodge taken from a place called Joydon to the park, near Maundevylesmede, was no doubt for use in newly enclosed parkland[230] and could be 'Le Westlog', whose walls were daubed in 1400-1.[231] A will made in 1403 referring to the sale of the manor of 'Hourne'[232] would seem to refer to land added to the park, as later that century it was within its boundaries.[233]

Between 1399 and 1407 2,187 perches (12,730 yards) of enclosures were created, a figure which does not include repairs to hedges and palisades or the few perches of palisades made to enclose the palace garden.[234] Some of these enclosures were palisades made of posts, strengthened with braces, to which paling boards were fixed. On two occasions the sizes of the posts and braces are given, in one case the posts were 9½ feet long and the braces 7½ feet in length;[235] in the other, for the great garden, the posts were 12 feet in length and the braces 8½ feet.[236]

No new official positions are known to have been created at Eltham under either Henry IV or Henry V. The position of keeper of the king's wardrobe at the palace, granted by Richard II to John de Carleton, was continued by Henry IV.[237] Apart from this post, there were six other senior officials at Eltham in this period: the farmer,[238] steward,[239] keeper of the houses,[240] chaplain,[241] parker[242] and gardener.[243] The farmer, as in the past, paid a yearly sum for his position for a fixed term, made what he could from it and was allowed expenses for feeding the park deer in winter. The other positions were paid and were for life. The steward was presumably paid from the receipts of the manorial court, whose records have not survived, and the other four received annual salaries. Of these, the highest paid was the keeper of the houses with 6d. a day. The chaplain received 10 marks a year, equivalent to about 4½d. a day, and the parker and gardener 3d. a day.

Besides their salaries, these officials had in some cases official perquisites. The parker and the chaplain had official quarters, a lodge, presumably as in later centuries, in the case of the parker,[244] and a house and garden for the chaplain who, under Henry IV, was allowed 'from all time' 'Le Presthous' and 'le preste gardyn'.[245] In addition, judging by the rights of earlier and later holders of these posts, they would have been allowed firewood from the park.[246] The status of these chaplains may not have been high as the recorded fees paid to preachers to the court when it was at Eltham, which range from a noble (3s. 4d.) up to 40s., are never recorded as going to the official palace chaplains.[247] It is not known if these palace and manorial officials were always in residence but in 1406 one of them, the parker Thomas Bruge, was granted legal protection against lawsuits as he was then employed on royal service in Ireland.[248]

The building works officials at Eltham, who in some cases also had duties at other royal manors, received higher salaries than the manorial and palace officials. In 1378 the clerk of works at Eltham was entitled to 2s. a day,[249] while the more senior official, the controller, would have been paid a higher salary. However, the junior officials, the purveyors who had the task of organising building materials for the works, had much lower salaries; one in 1399–1400 was only entitled to 4d. a day.[250]

The earliest surviving local will dates from 1403 and is that of William Reynewell, a citizen and merchant of London living at Mottingham. He left a bequest for the repair of the highway 'near Mottingham under the king's park at Eltham' and ordered the sale of his 'manor of Hourne', with some of the proceeds going to the church in Eltham.[251]

VI

LANCASTRIANS AND YORKISTS

I had enough, I held me not content,
Without remembrance that I should die,
…
I made Nottingham a place full royall,
Windsor, Eltham and many other mo:
Yet, at the last, I went from them all,
Et, ecce, nunc in pulvere dormio!
('On the Death of the Noble Prince, King Edward the Fourth',
Complete Poems of John Skelton, ed. P. Henderson, 1948)

By comparison with the preceding century, the 63 years of the reigns of Henry VI and his three Yorkist successors are poorly documented as regards Eltham, with reference both to its buildings and to events taking place there. This lack of information compared to the earlier period is particularly frustrating as the major surviving parts of the palace, the great hall and the bridge, date from Edward IV's reign.

Henry VI is not known to have visited Eltham in the first three years of his reign and is first recorded there in 1425-6, in connection with a quarrel between two of his relatives. These were his uncle Humphrey, Duke of Gloucester, his father's youngest brother, who held the position of Protector of England, and his great-uncle Henry, Bishop of Winchester, half-brother of the king's grandfather Henry IV and Chancellor of England. The bishop shared the responsibility of being in charge of the king's person with his younger brother, Thomas, Duke of Exeter, and is best known by his later title of Cardinal Beaufort. The rivalry between the two may have been in a clash of personalities, but it also involved money. The bishop, with the income of his wealthy see, was able to lend money to the government at a high rate of interest on good security, with guaranteed terms of repayment, increasing his wealth and gaining him an important position in the government. This was resented by those like the duke who were ambitious and less fortunately situated financially.

The dispute between the Duke of Gloucester and the Bishop of Winchester began in October 1425, when the duke ordered the Mayor of London to see that the city was well guarded, on which the latter set an armed guard at the northern end of London Bridge. The bishop, who lived in Southwark immediately to the south of the bridge, took this action to be directed against himself and countered it by collecting an armed force of his own in Southwark. This attacked, unsuccessfully, the gate on the bridge and by its presence prevented the duke, with his escort of 300 horsemen, from visiting the young Henry VI at Eltham.

Mediation by the Archbishop of Canterbury and Peter, Duke of Coimbra, son of King John I of Portugal and of Philippa, sister of Henry IV, prevented further fighting, and the rival guards on London Bridge were disbanded. On 5 November the Dukes of Gloucester and Coimbra, accompanied by many lords and the mayor and alderman of London, escorted Henry VI from Eltham to London, where he stayed for a few days before returning to Eltham Palace. Before these journeys, however, the bishop had extended the dispute by involving his nephew John, Duke of Bedford and regent of both France and England, in the quarrel. The bishop asked his nephew to return from France to settle the dispute and prevent violence, knowing that the presence of the regent would supersede the authority of his younger brother, the Duke of Gloucester, as protector. This move, the bishop no doubt felt, would frustrate the ambitions of his rival.

The Duke of Bedford returned to England in December 1425, first going to Eltham where he presented his nephew the young king with a gold and ruby ring. Early in January the duke wrote to his brother from London to ask the Duke of Gloucester to attend either a council due to meet at Northampton on 13 January or the Parliament that was to sit at Leicester five days later. The Duke of Gloucester preferred the Parliament at Leicester and appeared before it to make a series of charges against the bishop. One of these was that the latter had tried to remove the king from Eltham, another that he had blocked the duke's access to the king by his guard on London Bridge. To these charges the bishop replied that he had not planned to remove Henry from Eltham Palace and that his placing of a guard on the bridge had been an action taken in self-defence. Parliament appointed a committee of lords to mediate in the dispute and in March 1426 the two rivals both swore to keep the peace, though as the bishop also had to make a public apology to the duke he seems to have felt that he had got the worst of the quarrel. Soon afterwards he resigned his position as chancellor, though in his other career in the Church he obtained a notable promotion by becoming a cardinal. His hat, the symbol of his appointment, was presented to him by the Duke of Bedford at Calais in March 1427.[1]

Shakespeare's only references to Eltham in his plays occur in *Henry VI Part 1* and refer to the dispute just described and to another event six years later. The play is not a reliable guide to what actually occurred as Shakespeare compresses, omits and transposes events to obtain dramatic effects, besides giving his own interpretation of the real people who appear in his plays. He foreshadows the quarrel of 1425–6 in the opening scene of *Henry VI Part I*, set at the funeral of Henry V in 1422. It ends with the words:

Exeter.	To Eltham will I, where the young king is,
	Being ordain'd his special governor;
	And for his safety there I'll best devise.
Winchester.	Each hath his place and function to attend:
	I am left out; for me nothing remains.
	But long I will not be Jack-out-of-office:
	The king from Eltham I intend to steal,
	And sit at chiefest stern of public weal.

The lines here allotted to the bishop misrepresent both his actual situation regarding his own position and his intentions towards Henry VI. The quarrel occurs in the third scene of the first act and the third act has a reconciliation between the rivals in Parliament at Westminster, although in fact the actual Parliament in question had met at Leicester. The following scene, set in 1432, has an incidental reference to Eltham when it refers to the creation of Richard Plantagenet as Duke of York, a title that he, by that date, had in fact been using for several years. The real event that occurred in 1432 was that the duke, on becoming 21, had been put into the possession of his estates.[2] Two years later he became the father of the future King Edward IV.

After 1425 Henry VI visited Eltham at the following three Christmases. During one of these, though which one is not known, the court was entertained there by a mumming of which the words, by John Lydgate, have survived. It has 12 verses, of which the first seven are addressed to the young king and the four following to his mother Queen Catherine. The final verse is addressed to both of them. These verses explain the action in the silent allegorical events shown on the stage. The first verse reads:

> Bachus, which is god of the glade vyne,
> Juno and Ceres, acorded alle theos three,
> Thorughe theyre power, which that is devyne,
> Sende nowe theyre gifftes vn-to Your Magestee:
> Wyne, whete and oyle by marchandes that here be,
> Wheeche represent vn-to Youre Hye Noblesse
> Pees with your lieges, plente and gladnesse.

The six verses that follow amplify the message of the first, the next four offer courtly tributes to the queen, wishing her joy and gladness, 'care and sorowe for ever sette asyde'—a reference to the death of her husband—and a gift of the love and loyalty of her people. The final verse combines the themes of the earlier ones.[3]

During both the 1426[4] and 1427[5] Christmas seasons at Eltham, plays were performed before the court by 'Jakke Travaill & ses compaignons'. One of these performances may have been the mumming written by John Lydgate. In 1428[6] music was provided by the king's portable organs, brought from Windsor for the festivities, and four boys performed interludes, these being light dramatic pieces put on between the acts of more serious morality plays. Another company of players, 'The Jews of Abingdon', also performed at Eltham that Christmas. One of those present at Eltham in 1428 that Christmas was the Duke of Bourbon, a French nobleman captured at Agincourt and brought to Eltham later in 1415 by Henry V. Now, 13 years later, he came again and was 'sworne Englysche in the Kyngys manyr of Eltam besyde Grenewyche'.[7] In the same year there is a rare glimpse of the transport used by female members of the court when visiting Eltham, a reference to a wagon drawn by two horses and used by the queen and her ladies.[8] After these visits for Christmas in the 1420s, Henry VI's court is only recorded there for this season in 1436, 1441 and 1451.[9]

After 1428 Henry VI next came to Eltham in February 1430,[10] three months after his coronation at Westminster, while on his way to France, where he was to remain for the next two years and where, in December 1431, he was crowned as King of France in Paris by Cardinal Beaufort. Not long after that ceremony he returned to England, travelling again by way of Eltham, with a company of 'dukes, earls, barons ... magnates ... knights and squires'. On 20 February 1432 he and his escort were met on Blackheath by the mayor and aldermen of London, with 12,000 citizens, who accompanied them to London.[11]

Henry VI is not recorded as visiting Eltham again after this 1432 occasion for nearly five years, returning at Christmas 1436,[12] but after that visit he came there on many occasions during the following 15 years.[13] Very little, however, is known of most of these visits except their dates, the exception being in the early 1440s in the detailed records of two Privy Council meetings held at Eltham.[14] These frequent visits caused inconvenience to local inhabitants from purveyance, the requisitioning of carts for transport and the quartering of the court, and this must have inspired the royal grant of March 1439, which included the concession that those who attended Eltham's market would be exempt from paying dues or of being attached for debt or crime, treason and felony excepted.[15] This grant was otherwise similar to those made in 1284 to John de Vescy[16] and later in 1312,[17] which included a weekly market and a three-day annual fair. In 1450 a further grant was made to a number of manors, including Eltham, which ordered regular payment for what was taken for the use of the court, these places being 'charged, with continuell takyng of theire goodes and Catell for ... his honourable Housbold'.[18]

The subjects discussed in the Great, 'Innest' or Secret rooms at Eltham by privy councillors are recorded in the minutes of the Privy Council for meetings held there in October 1442 and March 1443. Some of these meetings were attended by Henry VI. The number of councillors present varied from three to 10, the usual attendance being about eight. The councillors were either noblemen, like the Duke of Gloucester, or clergy, including Cardinal Beaufort and the Bishop of Salisbury. The business under consideration included foreign policy and the wool trade, these being interconnected subjects when wool was both England's principal export and a major source of government income. Anything affecting the free movement of the export of wool was therefore a matter of concern and when the Burgundians, by now no longer English allies, refused to allow money to enter Burgundy from the English staple port of Calais, the council at Eltham had to decide on the action they should take. Other subjects discussed included a tax on wheat entering Bordeaux and aid for both Bordeaux and Bayonne, towns now in their last decade of English rule, rioting in England and the appointment of a new commander of the English-held castle of Roxburgh in Scotland.[19]

Although Henry attended some of these Privy Council meetings, his interests are usually considered to have been more concerned with religion with state affairs. When Henry was being put forward as a candidate for canonisation as a saint, John Blacman, author of a biography of the king, refers to him at Eltham in a way that supports this view of his character. His account is reported on the authority of Henry's household chamberlain, Sir Richard Tunstall, who is mentioned as stating:

The Lord King himself complained heavily to me in his chamber at Eltham, when I was
alone there with him employed together with him upon his holy books, and giving ear to
his wholesome advice and the sighs of his most deep devotion. There came all at once a
knock at the King's door from a certain mighty duke of the realm, and the King said 'They
do so interrupt me that by day and night I can hardly snatch a moment to be refreshed by
reading any holy teaching without disturbance'.

Blacman may, however, be unreliable concerning this story, as it and others
showing Henry as an unworldly person are not backed by any strictly contemporary
evidence.[20] Both worldly and religious concerns can be seen in letters Henry VI
sent from Eltham. In August 1443 he ordered that money owed to the English
commander in France, John Talbot, Earl of Shrewsbury, should be paid to him,[21]
while in March 1442 he wrote from there to the Bishop of Hereford to order
prayers and processions for the success of the war in France[22] and in September
1446 his interest in his foundation of King's College, Cambridge, can be seen in
a letter from Eltham. In this he regrets that 'ye aier and ye pestelence' made it
unwise of him to go in person to lay the foundation stone of the college chapel
and so he was sending the Marquess of Suffolk in his place for the ceremony.[23]

In 1444 negotiations began for the marriage of Henry VI to Margaret
of Anjou, niece of the late King of France, Charles VI. By January 1445 the
arrangements for the marriage were so far advanced that it was safe to assume that
the marriage would take place and orders were therefore given for improvements
to some royal buildings, including Eltham, so the new queen would be fittingly
housed. Eltham Palace was given a new hall for the queen, kitchen improvements[24]
and, soon afterwards, changes to the queen's closet.[25]

Margaret of Anjou arrived in England in April 1445 and married Henry VI that
same month. In May she travelled from Eltham to Blackheath, where she was
officially welcomed by the Lord Mayor of London with the aldermen, sheriffs and
guildsmen and then escorted by the Duke of Gloucester to Placentia, the future
Greenwich Palace. From there she went upriver to her coronation at Westminster
the following day.[26] She may have revisited Eltham again later that year.[27] Two of
her letters from Eltham, sent in the early years of her marriage, show her promoting
the personal interests of her friends and retainers. One, to the Marchioness of Este,
recommends a certain Reynold Chicheley to her and refers to a present she is
sending her of, 'to use the native tongue, an ambling hobby', in modern terms a
small horse used for riding.[28] In another letter she tried, in vain, to assist the suit
of Thomas Burneby, one of her gentlemen servants, who wished to marry a young
and wealthy widow, Dame Jane Carew.[29]

After Henry VI's marriage, until 1450, the king and queen were usually
together, but late in February of that year the queen was on her own at Eltham
when, during a thunderstorm, lightning set fire to part of the west front, destroying
a hall, kitchen and storehouse and part of a chamber.[30] In the 1970s, excavations
revealed that the hall destroyed was the one originally built for Bishop Bek in
c.1300. After the fire, lead was collected in pits dug into the hall floor, and a worn
coin of Henry VI's reign was found among the debris from the fire.[31] The building
records for Eltham from the 1450s also refer to the collection of lead from 'ashes
and lead of the great hall, burnt there'.[32]

War with France broke out again in 1449, to end in 1453 with the loss of the last English-held lands in south-western France. These years also saw, with one exception, the last known visits of Henry VI to Eltham, in late 1451 and early 1452;[33] the following year also witnessed the fall of Constantinople to the Turks. The first battle of the Wars of the Roses was fought in 1455, followed by three others before Henry VI's last visit to Eltham, in October 1460, when he was a Yorkist prisoner, having been captured three months earlier at the Battle of Northampton. This visit to both Eltham and Greenwich was so he could go hunting there.[34] In the following March, just before the Yorkist victory at Towton confirmed the defeat of the Lancastrians, the new Yorkist King, Edward IV, succeeded to the throne.

In the three years that preceded Edward IV's accession, some building work took place at Eltham. Very large numbers of bricks were delivered to the site[35] but where these were used is not known. Five months after Edward IV became king, orders were sent out for the collection of workmen to repair the royal palaces, including Eltham.[36] Some years later, between 1463 and 1466, a building record includes a reference to '16 panels of glass placed in the great hall'[37] which is of interest, showing that such a hall existed at Eltham after the fire in 1450 but before work had begun on the present hall in the 1470s.

Edward IV is first recorded as visiting Eltham for the Christmas season of 1464,[38] seven months after his clandestine marriage to Lady Elizabeth Grey and two months after his disclosure of his marriage to the Privy Council. It is possible that the new queen may have visited Eltham at some earlier date when she was a lady of the bedchamber to Henry VI's Queen Margaret. During the festivities for this Christmas season Edward IV distributed gifts of rings to his courtiers as New Year's Day gifts, at a cost of over £200, while the expenses of the queen's chamber, wardrobe and stable during this season amounted to over £400.[39] These seasonal expenses concerned both the royal family and their visitors, as one of those present at Eltham, Sir John Howard, later to become Duke of Norfolk, kept accounts which show him paying his barber and launderer there and buying shoes for a servant and fodder for his horses. This is the only record to survive that shows the trade brought to Eltham by court visits. These were not the only expenses incurred by Sir John as, although he and Lady Howard were given gifts by the king, they also presented him with a courser worth £40, besides a horse worth £8 that was given to the queen. He also presented seasonal gifts to various departments of the royal household, officers of the cellar, pantry and buttery receiving 20s. each, with a further 10s. being given to the heralds, minstrels and trumpeters. In addition, other expenses were incurred at court for the Howards' personal attendants.[40] In May 1465 Queen Elizabeth revisited Eltham shortly before her coronation. By this visit she continued, perhaps inadvertently, visits recorded to Eltham shortly before their coronations by Elizabeth's three Lancastrian predecessors.[41]

In April 1467 Edward IV was once more at Eltham Palace and while he was there he took part in a tournament recorded in a letter by Sir John Paston. The latter, with the king and two others of the court, formed a team that jousted with four other courtiers. Although Sir John injured his hand during the jousting, he evidently enjoyed himself as he wrote that this event was 'the goodliest sight that was sene in Inglande this forty yeares'.[42] Two years later, in late May 1469, another member of the Yorkist royal family visited Eltham when Princess Margaret, the King's sister, stayed there prior to her embarkation for Burgundy where she married Charles, Duke of Burgundy, the following month. Edward IV paid a very large dowry for his sister's marriage in order to gain Burgundy as an ally against France and thus prevent the two countries combining against England.[43]

After Princess Margaret's visit nothing is known of any visits by the court to Eltham for the next eventful years, during which Henry VI was briefly restored to the throne in 1470-1 and Edward IV won victories over the Lancastrians at Barnet and Tewkesbury. Not until December 1477 and January 1478, when Lord Stanley was there paying the expenses of the royal household, is there any link between the court and Eltham.[44] The palace had not been forgotten, however, as it was during this blank period regarding court visits there that the building of the great hall, and apparently the rebuilding of the north bridge, was begun.

The last years of the reign of Edward IV included several recorded court visits and it would have been during these years that the king would have seen building in progress for the work that has survived to the present day. Edward was there at some time between November 1478 and the following February, a visit possibly prompted by an outbreak of plague in London during these months,[45] and Elizabeth gave birth there to her sixth daughter, Princess Catherine, in August 1479.[46] The King would also have been there in 1480 when his personal library was sent to Eltham, his books including bibles, religious books, 'Le Gouvernement of Kinges and Princes … thre smalle bookes of Franche … La Forteresse de Foy' and works by Josephus and Froissart.[47] The last of these may have been the latter's chronicles but conceivably might have been the book of poetry presented to Richard II at Eltham in 1395. Princess Bridget, Edward and Elizabeth's seventh daughter, was born at the palace in November 1480 and was christened in the palace chapel the day after her birth.[48] Details of this ceremony were recorded by a herald who was present[49] and this event is also mentioned in a letter written by Richard Cely, a merchant who saw it before going on to London.[50] Princess Catherine, who married the Earl of Devon, lived until 1527; her sister Bridget became a nun and predeceased her sister by 10 years.[51]

The herald's description of this christening, made perhaps to provide a record of precedents for use when similar ceremonies were held in the future, has preserved a detailed record of this ceremony. He began by noting that the Bishop of Chichester officiated, and the day, time and place, before going on to list the order in which the participants entered the chapel. The first to do so were a hundred 'Knightes, Esquires and other honneste Parsonnes' carrying unlit torches. These were followed by named courtiers, of whom the first three carried a basin and towel, an unlit taper and a salt. Next came three knights and a baron, upholding a canopy that must have been held over the infant princess, as the next two persons mentioned were a lady carrying the 'crysom', or christening robe, and the Countess of Richmond who held the child. The countess, although a member of the Yorkist court, was by an earlier marriage the mother of the Lancastrian claimant to the throne, Henry of Richmond, later Henry VII. She was the wife of Lord Stanley, steward of the king's household, and by custom used the higher title held by her during her earlier marriage. Three relatives of the infant princess followed, these being her eldest half-brother, the Marquess of Dorset, her eldest sister, Princess Elizabeth, later to marry Henry VII, and her grandmother on her father's side, Cecily, Duchess of York. The godparents were the last two members of the Yorkist royal family and the Bishop of Chichester.

When the christening ceremony had been completed, the torches were lit and the heralds put on their tabards. The child was then taken up to the high altar and afterwards to a partitioned-off part of the chapel where the gifts of the godparents were presented. The infant princess was then taken back in procession to the queen's chamber. The herald then records the presence in the chapel of four important courtiers who had not taken part in the ceremony, these being the king's second son, Richard, Duke of York, the Lords Hastings and Stanley, the former holding the position of chamberlain of the household of the king, and Lord Dacre, chamberlain to the queen.[52] It is a pity that so few detailed records of events and ceremonies held at Eltham have survived.

The last visits of Edward IV to Eltham occurred in April[53] and December 1482. On the latter of these visits the queen was also present when Edward IV kept 'his estate all thole feast in his greate Chambre and the quene in her Chambre' with over two thousand people present at court each day. The herald who recorded this also listed the sums the heralds received as 'largesse' at this season and the names of the donors. These seasonal gifts ranged upwards from the single mark (13s. 4d.) given by some courtiers to the five marks (£3 6s. 8d.) from the queen and the six pounds presented by the king. The listed donors were all important courtiers and included Edward, Prince of Wales, who was to reign briefly the following year as Edward V.[54]

The destinies of the courtiers recorded as visiting Eltham under Edward IV were to differ greatly. The fate of the king's two sons is still debated.[55] Lord Hastings was to be executed in 1483 by order of Richard III,[56] Lord Dacre,[57] Sir John Paston[58] and Sir William Parr[59] were to die natural deaths. The Duke of Norfolk was to die at Bosworth fighting for Richard III,[60] where the Earl of Northumberland[61] and Lord Stanley, later Earl of Derby,[62] were to betray him. The Marquess of Dorset joined Henry Tudor[63] but was not present at Bosworth. Viscount Berkeley[64] and Lords Fitzhugh,[65] Welles[66] and Matrevers[67] survived the change of dynasty to become Lancastrians in their later years, Sir John Elrington lost his position at court and his estates in 1485 but survived and later became a JP.[68] The Earl of Lincoln[69] and Viscount Lovel,[70] after fighting for Richard III at Bosworth, remained loyal to the Yorkists and went overseas, to return in 1487 with an army of mercenaries to fight and lose the Battle of Stoke, in which the earl died. Viscount Lovel, of whose fate differing stories are told, was never seen again after that battle.[71]

Edward IV, still a comparatively young man, died after a short illness in April 1483 and neither his son nor his brother are known to have visited Eltham while they reigned. Edward IV was later to be commemorated in the poem *On the Death of the Noble Prince, King Edward the Fourth*,[72] sometimes wrongly attributed to John Skelton. The fifth of its eight stanzas lists the royal buildings improved by the late king, including work carried out on the walls of London during his reign.[73] Edward IV had the Tower of London repaired,[74] Tattershall Castle had been forfeited to the Crown during his reign,[75] Dover Castle had been repaired,[76] Nottingham Castle had been given a new tower,[77] Windsor Castle had gained St George's Chapel, where the King was buried,[78] and Eltham had a new great hall. The stanza in question reads:

> I had enough, I held me not content,
> Without remembrance that I should die,
> And more ever to increase was mine intent,
> I knew not how longe I should it occupy.
> I made the Tower stronge, I wist not why;
> I knew not to(for) whom I purchased Tattershall;
> I amended Dover on the mountain high,
> And London I provoked to fortify the wall,
> I made Nottingham a place full royall,
> Windsor, Eltham, and many other mo:
> Yet, at the last, I went from them all,
> Et, ecce, nunc in pulvere dormio.[79]

Under Henry VI and Edward IV the principal recorded Eltham building works were, under Henry VI, those on which over £1,000 was spent up to 1437, including a new outer ward gatehouse,[80] later repairs[81] followed by new works for Queen Margaret in 1445[82] and 1447,[83] the repairs that replaced the buildings destroyed by fire early in 1450,[84] and further works carried out in the 1440s and 1450s.[85] Under Edward IV repairs were made in the early 1460s,[86] and the new great hall, a water conduit and the rebuilding of the north bridge, with, apparently, other buildings, were all undertaken between 1475 and 1483.[87] Brick is first mentioned as used at Eltham in 1439-40[88] and in 1451 no less than 100,000 bricks were sent there, of which the whole lot had been used up by 1469.[89] The place where these bricks were used at Eltham is uncertain. Some might have been used for an intermediate great hall of 1463-6, with 16 glass panels,[90] which must have replaced the hall burnt down in 1451, or the other buildings also destroyed in that fire.[91] Bricks were used on the inner sides of the later great hall completed in 1480 or soon afterwards.[92] The north bridge, built of stone with a later brick parapet, has been attributed on stylistic grounds to the reign of Edward IV.[93] Further Eltham building works in this reign, mentioned in the next chapter, included a number of fireplaces.[94]

The existing Eltham great hall is dated to Edward IV's reign by the survival of a number of records referring to its creation[95] and by the incorporation into the frame of the north door of the hall, and also into the ceilings of the oriels, of the emblems of Edward IV. Only in 1823 was the hall correctly dated to his reign when the use of the *rose en soleil*, Edward IV's emblem, was noted by a visitor in the hall's stonework.[96] Roger Appulton's appointment as surveyor of the works at Eltham in November 1475 may mark the start of work on the new great hall.[97] The hall, however, is not directly mentioned in surviving records until May 1479.[98] It is of interest that in August 1475 Edward IV obtained a large annual subsidy from Louis XI of France by the Treaty of Picquigny and this new source of income could have supplied the funds that allowed Edward IV to spend money on new and expensive royal buildings at Eltham and elsewhere.[99] By 1478, when the roof timbers had been brought to the palace site for seasoning,[100] the walls of the hall, of Reigate ashlar on the north side and squared ragstone on the south side, must have been nearly complete.[101] The hall roof was being given its lead covering in 1479[102] and for the months of September and October of this year there survives the only detailed building record of the creation of the hall, first printed in 1886.[103] The hall's designer was Thomas Jurdan, who held the official position of king's master mason,[104] while the outstanding feature of the great hall, its magnificent timber roof, was created by the king's chief carpenter, Edmund Graveley.[105] James Hatefield supervised the erection of the roof,[106] which, for the period of two months for which records survive, employed 51 masons, 48 carpenters, 32 labourers, two plumbers and two smiths as well as a clerk and a purveyor, all concerned in 'the bilding of the newe halle withyn the manour of Eltham'.[107]

No records have survived that record the precise date of the completion of the great hall, or the wainscoting of its walls and other woodwork or the glazing of its windows. Work on the great bridge in this reign is also unmentioned in surviving records. The appearance of the hall, especially the magnificence of its timber roof, has attracted praise from a number of writers.[108] On this the only dissentients are two architectural writers, of whom one states that its poor construction was 'cloaked by the finely finished detail'[109] and the other comments that the roof is 'lush' and an example of 'ornate heartlessness'.[110] It has been suggested that the hall is one of those that inspired the construction of the great hall of Stirling Castle, nearing completion in 1503. The great hall at Stirling (46 by 16 yards) is larger than that at Eltham. It has a similar ground plan with two oriel windows at the dais end and similarly grouped windows along the body of the hall. Little is known of its roof plan but it appears to have been less elaborate than that at Eltham. It is perhaps relevant that Scottish ambassadors sent from James III to Henry VII were at Eltham in 1485 and that James IV's queen, Margaret, was at Eltham in 1499 prior to her marriage to James in 1503.[111]

One development in the history of the palace, though perhaps one rather of words than of new buildings, is first found in 1456-61, the last years of Henry VI's first reign. A record from these years describes the rooms of the palace as divided into three sets of apartments, referred to as the great, privy and prince's palaces,[112] while an earlier reference to the prince' s ward is found in 1439-40.[113] A similar tripartite division, using the terms King's, Queen's and Prince's sides, is recorded in 1649.[114] Another development of the palace buildings dates from 1482 when a water conduit was constructed[115] that would have replaced the earlier supply drawn from wells.[116] An earlier water supply, created in 1399-1400 for a different purpose, was 'a watering place for the king's horses at the end of Eltham town near the park'.[117]

There are a number of differences between the great hall we see today and the hall as it was originally built, changes arising principally from damage and repairs during the 500 years since the hall was first erected. Prior to c.1650 its roof covering was lead[118] and it was surmounted by a louvre or turret, removed before 1724,[119] very probably at the time when the roof received a covering of tiles after the lead had been removed. Roof repairs carried out in 1952[120] revealed that the roof timbers had been cut in order to insert the louvre, showing that the turret was not an original feature of the roof's design.[121] The turret might have been added pre-1560, when the palace was still frequently visited by the whole court. Missing original features include, therefore, the hall's lead covering[122] and the stonework of the south oriel windows.[123] Further alterations are the window glazing,[124] the pitched roofs over the oriels,[125] the crenellated parapet of the north front of the hall,[126] the outer woodwork of the roof pendants[127] and their colouring,[128] besides almost all the interior woodwork[129] of the hall except the main screen beams[130] and the roof.[131] Some present features, the tracery on the screen beams, the outer woodwork of the pendants and the roof bosses of the oriels are copies of earlier work.[132] The reredos at the west end of the hall is new work in keeping with the age of the building.[133] The hall was also formerly wainscoted,[134] a feature now replaced by tapestry on the side walls, with iron torches above.[135]

The interior dimensions of the hall, excluding the oriels, are a length of 101 feet 3 inches, a breadth of 36 feet 3 inches, and a height to the apex of the roof of 54 feet. The oriels are 9 feet 5 inches wide, north to south, and 14 feet 4 inches long, east to west, by internal measurements.[136] By comparison with other great halls it is smaller than those of Westminster and Hampton Court. Its roof, and that of the hall at Beddington, in Surrey, are the earliest to combine pendants with hammerbeams.[137] The roof is oak and is technically known as a false or archbraced hammerbeam roof[138] and is an outstanding example of the work of medieval carpenters. The hall's position, in relation to the entrance bridge into the inner court, is similar to that at Herstmonceux Castle in Sussex, a building begun in 1441.[139] Eltham's example of a hall with oriel windows flanking its dais is also to be seen at Stirling Castle and, formerly, in a since demolished hall at Oxburgh.[140]

More land may have been added to the parkland attached to the palace when in 1446-7 an estate including the manor of East Horne was escheated to the king by John Tatershall.[141] Yet before this event some land in that area was already within the park, as a record dated 1441-3 refers to the cutting down of timber 'at le Horne in the park there'.[142] Prior to 1481 the parkland was under the control of a single parker until in that year the new post was created of parker of 'the king's new park of Horne within … Eltham'. The man appointed to this position had formerly been parker of the king's great park at Eltham.[143]

Early records with references to officials dealing with the manor and its buildings mention the salaries attached to these posts but give few details of the perquisites attached to the positions. From Henry VI's reign onwards, however, more details are recorded and, as occurred in 1401, some of the Eltham official positions were made in reversion to take effect when the post became vacant.[144] As for perquisites, a parker is found to be entitled to 'herbage and pannage … trees dry and thrown down by the wind and branches of trees given within the park',[145] keepers of the manor to reasonable 'fyrebote', 'cartebote', 'ploughbote' and 'heggebote',[146] a principal clerk of works to 'clothing, fur and lining of tartan' each year,[147] and a clerk and surveyor of works to a travelling allowance of 4s. a day in 1461.[148] Another benefit of officeholding, received by William Cleve when he became clerk of works for Eltham and other royal manors, was exemption from quartering by the court for the buildings for which he was responsible.[149] Similar grants are recorded at Eltham regarding quartering in 1333,[150] and 1401,[151] the latter recipient not being the holder of an official post.

As might have been expected, the political changes from Lancaster to York and back occurring in 1461,[152] 1471[153] and 1485[154] are reflected in new appointments being made to official positions at Eltham. In all three years, within a few months of the accession of a king from a different dynasty, new officeholders at Eltham were appointed. In one case, in 1485, the new official is specifically stated to have been appointed as a reward, John Browne being given the post of purveyor at Eltham for his services to the new king, Henry VII, 'as well in the parties beyonde the see as … at our late victorious felde'.[155] In the same year the Yorkist officeholder James Pemberton was dispossessed of his positions of keeper of the manor, of the park, of the new park[156] and as gardener[157] by new men.[158] The only senior official appointed under the Yorkists to keep his position was the chaplain Henry Brocas.[159] Although a new man was put into his post,[160] Henry replaced him the following year[161] and continued as chaplain for almost twenty years.[162] Works officials were also affected by a new dynasty, as can be seen at Eltham in 1461.[163]

Surviving wills of this period from Eltham are few, plain and brief. Apart from church bequests, the donors leave all their property to their widows and relatives.[164] In 1466 John Hooman ordered in his will that his widow Lucy should give his mother Emma, then living in a newly built cottage, 20s. in silver, six cartloads of wood for her fire and pasture for two cows each year.[165] A later testament from 1477 sees John Fraunceis leave cattle, money and household goods to his wife, daughters, brother, kinsmen, godchildren, servants and to the church. His brother received a 'plain cup of silver with a rose depicted at the bottom'.[166]

VII

THE EARLY TUDORS AT ELTHAM PALACE

The king kept a solēpne Christmas at his maner of Elthā … in the hall was made a goodly
castel … & when the kyng and quene were set, in came … knights, & assailed the castel …
And issued out knightes and ladies out of the castel … And when the daunsing was done,
the banquet was serued in of ii C dyshes, with great plēty to euery body.

(Hall's Chronicle, 1809 edn)

Under the early Tudors the palace of Eltham remained in royal favour
until the mid–1530s, frequently visited by the court and brought up to
date regarding its buildings and facilities for royal sports. Henry VII is
not recorded there before 1490 but some of his courtiers probably came in 1485,
a few months after the Battle of Bosworth, escorting Scottish ambassadors from
James III to Henry VII's coronation on 30 October. The latter were provided with
bows and arrows to hunt in the parks at Eltham.[1]

In the 1490s, and into the opening decade of the 16th century, the palace was
sometimes recorded as a home or nursery for the children of Henry VII. The
king's second son, Henry, the future Henry VIII, was there in October 1494 when
he travelled from Eltham to London to be created Duke of York,[2] and it was also
at Eltham that Henry VII's daughter Elizabeth died late in 1495. Her tomb is still
to be seen in Westminster Abbey.[3]

Erasmus, writing to a friend in 1523, described a visit he had made many years
earlier to the children of Henry VII during his stay in England in the autumn of 1499,
apparently to Eltham Palace.[4] While staying with Lord Mountjoy, Thomas More
called and took him to see the royal children in 'the next village' to Lord Mountjoy's
home. As that home was probably in Greenwich, where Mountjoy's daughter is
later found in the possession of an estate, the reference to 'the next village', with the
others referred to here, make it probable that the children were then at Eltham.[5] The
royal children were probably also at Eltham in 1501 when Henry, Duke of York, was
presented that August with a book written by the poet John Skelton, his tutor at
that time.[6] More's visit would appear to show that he was already in good standing
at court to have been given permission to make this visit.

In describing the visit, which Erasmus seems to have recollected in considerable
detail considering the years that had elapsed since, he mentions that Henry, aged
eight at the time, had impressed him by his dignity and courtesy. The other
children present were Margaret, aged nine; Mary, who was three; and Edmund,
an infant not yet a year old. Henry VII's eldest son, Arthur, Prince of Wales,

was not present. The children met their visitors in
the hall, presumably the present great hall, where
the palace staff and Lord Mountjoy's retinue were
also assembled, and after More had given Henry
something which he had written, the visitors dined
with the royal children.[7] This presentation by More
must have dismayed Erasmus, who had not been
warned of it in advance, and had nothing of his
own ready to present. His discomfort must have
been increased when the young Henry, who must
have been informed of the fame of Erasmus as an
author, sent him a note during the meal requesting
something from his pen.[8]

Three days after his visit Erasmus completed
a Latin poem for Henry and was able to send this
hastily written work entitled *Prosopopoeia Britannia*
(*Britain Personified*) to the young prince. Erasmus
comments that it had taken him some hard work as
he had not written poetry for some time. In its 150
lines, which Erasmus published the following year,
he praised Henry VII, his children and his kingdom
in flattering terms. The five children of the king are
referred to in allegorical terms as roses, red in the case
of the three boys for vigour, and white for the two
girls for innocence. The praise given to each child is
linked to that child's name, with Henry's referring to
his having the same name as his father. John Skelton
was apparently present during this visit as, although
the letter does not mention him, he is mentioned
both in the poem and in a covering letter sent with
it. Erasmus also wrote another Latin poem, 30 lines
in length, in honour of John Skelton, praising his
poetry very highly.[9] In 1910, four centuries after this
meeting, it became the subject of a historical painting
by F.C. Cowper, in fresco, on a wall in the House
of Commons. It is shown in the picture, however,
as taking place at Greenwich Palace and this caused
a protest on the matter in the local paper.[10] The
meeting is also depicted in a stained glass window in
St Mary's Church, Bury St Edmunds, where Princess
Mary, later Duchess of Suffolk, is buried.[11]

While Eltham was in use as a nursery for the
children of Henry VII, it was also visited by the
court.[12] During one visit in 1498 an acrobat, described
as 'one that tumblet at Eltham', was rewarded with
£1 from the king's privy purse for his performance.[13]

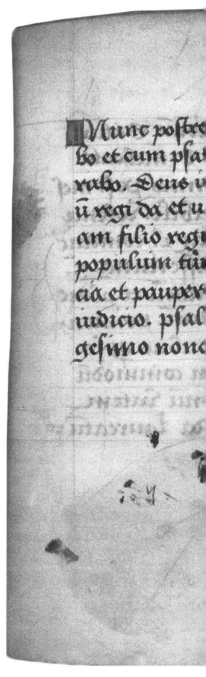

5 *John Skelton's book dedicated at
Eltham to his pupil Henry, Duke of
York (later Henry VIII), 1501.*

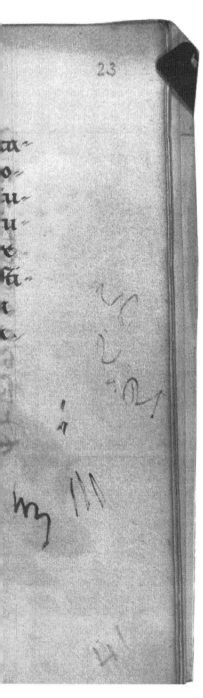

Further court visits are recorded in 1501, when the king spent Easter there,[14] 1506, when Katherine of Aragon, then widow of Arthur, Prince of Wales, and not yet married to the future Henry VIII, was present,[15] and 1508, after which Lord Daubeny, the Lord Chamberlain, fell from his horse while riding from Eltham to Greenwich, dying soon afterwards.[16] Later in that year Henry VII came to Eltham again in order to hunt in its parks.[17]

In 1492 Henry VII granted the inhabitants of Eltham 38 acres of royal land there, later called the 15 penny lands, from which the income went to pay the annual royal tax of one-fifteenth of the annual value of their possessions. The reason this grant was made was similar to those made on other occasions, the burden placed on Eltham's inhabitants by royal visits and, as mentioned earlier, the area owned by the Crown in Eltham.[18]

According to William Lambarde, writing in the 1570s, after Henry VII's reign Eltham Palace was 'not … so greatly esteemed' as in earlier times while Greenwich Palace was more readily accessible by water than Eltham, whose parks could be visited for hunting as readily from Greenwich as from Eltham.

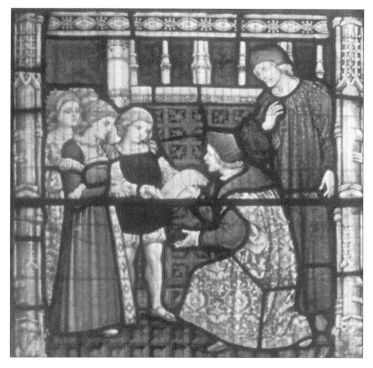

6   *The children of Henry VII, with More and Erasmus, at Eltham. A detail from a window presented by Queen Victoria to St Mary's Church, Bury St Edmunds, where Queen Mary of France (later Duchess of Suffolk), a daughter of Henry VII, is buried (1881).*

Henry VIII, however, visited Eltham Palace frequently up to the mid–1530s and Lambarde seems to have antedated by some years the date of the palace's decline in royal favour.[19]

After Henry VII's death, in April 1509, he was succeeded by his son Henry, who, two months later, unexpectedly married his elder brother's widow, Katherine of Aragon, five years older than himself. They had been betrothed in 1503, soon after Arthur's death, but this marriage contract was later broken off, though Katherine remained in England after this event.[20] Henry VIII was to visit Eltham frequently in the earlier part of his reign and came more often than his father.[21] Early visitors who saw him there included five gentlemen whom he knighted,[22] his sister Mary, then known as the Princess of Castile as she was betrothed to Charles, Prince of Castile (later to become the Emperor Charles V), whom she ultimately did not marry,[23] and the masters of several of the king's ships, who visited the king concerning the laying up of their ships in the winter.[24]

The best-documented years of Henry VIII's reign, as regards Eltham, are from 1514 to 1516. In 1514 the royal court was there for part of seven months, an unusually long usage of the palace for a single year.[25] During one of these visits, in May, only a small royal household came to Eltham for fear of the 'great sickness' then present in the neighbourhood, though among those present were the members of the royal chapel and the heralds.[26] Accounts of the history of the palace often include a story that it was at Eltham, in May, that Sir Edward Stanley was proclaimed Lord Monteagle 'for his valiant acts at the battle of Branxton (Flodden) where the King of Scots was slain'.[27] Heraldic records, however, show that although the court was at Eltham in this month, this proclamation was made after it had left and that this event actually took place at the Bishop of London's palace in London.[28]

Routine business transacted at Eltham in 1514, during the court's presence there, included the appointment of Lord Mountjoy, the host of Erasmus 15 years earlier, to be Lieutenant of Tournai,[29] a town in Flanders taken from the French in 1513 and to whom it was returned six years later.[30] Other appointments made there in this year included that of purveyor of building materials at Eltham[31] and that of the marshal of the king's minstrels.[32]

Foreign envoys to come to Eltham in this year included one from the Marquess of Mantua, bringing a gift of four mares,[33] and two deputations of ambassadors from the Holy Roman Empire.[34] One of these ambassadors, writing to the Emperor Maximilian, described Eltham Palace as 'a castle situated between two parks'.[35] In either June or July Erasmus may have revisited Eltham to say farewell before departing from England after another visit.[36] The latter month also saw orders given for the refurnishing of the palace chapel, which was given new altarcloths and other furnishings, a new vestment for the priest for holy days and a chest with locks and keys to keep these items safe.[37] These would have been used when the court was not at Eltham; when it was there the furnishings of the Chapel Royal would have been used. Five months later the chapel clock was repaired,[38] the only record of its existence. A few years later this chapel was to be demolished and replaced by a new one sited slightly nearer to the main entrance to the inner court.[39] Further Imperial ambassadors met Henry at Eltham in September, coming from Margaret of Savoy, Regent of Flanders and deputy for her nephew Charles, later the Emperor Charles V.[40]

In October 1514 both Henry VIII and his principal advisor, Thomas Wolsey, were at Eltham writing to Louis XII of France who, earlier that month, had married Henry's younger sister, Mary.[41] Louis died only three months later and Henry decided to send his friend the Duke of Suffolk on a diplomatic mission to the new King of France, Francis I. Knowing that the duke and Mary had formed an attachment before her marriage, Henry made the duke come to Eltham before his departure for France in order that he might swear, with Wolsey present, that he would not marry the widowed queen.[42]

In spite of this promise, at Mary's insistence and without her brothers consent, Mary and the duke were married secretly in France, an act that, as Wolsey wrote to the duke, Henry took 'grievously and displeasantly', putting the forsworn duke 'in the greatest danger that ever man was in'.[43] Mary and the duke both wrote from France to Henry begging forgiveness, Mary reminding her brother that she had only consented to marry Louis (she was his third wife), 'though he was very aged and sickly', on the condition that if she survived him she was to be allowed to marry whom she chose afterwards.[44] With Wolsey's help, the two were eventually pardoned and married publicly the following May. Nevertheless, they had to pay a heavy financial penalty, Mary surrendering to her brother all the part of her dowry restored to her by Francis I as well as her plate and jewels.[45]

The last months of 1515 saw Wolsey rise to the summit of his career in both Church and State. In September he was created a cardinal,[46] and on Christmas Eve in the chapel at Eltham, in the king's presence, he took the oath of office as Lord Chancellor.[47]

The Christmas visit by the court to Eltham that saw Wolsey become Lord Chancellor also witnessed seasonal festivities there, of which full details have survived. The entertainment at court on Twelfth Night, 5 January 1516, when several different festivities followed each other in the great hall, began with a comedy or interlude entitled 'The Story of Troylous and Pandor', written by William Cornish, master of the children of the Chapel Royal. Its text has unfortunately not survived but it is known that 15 players took part in it, mostly royal choristers, and that they included six named parts, these being Troylous, Pandor, Kallkas, Kryssyd, Dyomed and Eulyxes. Accounts of the master of the revels show that Troylous's costume included a satin doublet, a double or reversible cloak, velvet shoes and a cap or bonnet with a feather. The heroine, Kryssyd, was a 'wedow of onour, in blake sarsenet', the latter a silken material used in all the costumes unless some other material is specified in the records. Kryssyd's surcoat, mantle, widow's hood and wimple were all of Florentine cotton. The part of Kallkas, a Trojan priest, was played by Cornish, who wore a yellow bishop's surcoat with a mantle, long girdle and bonnet. Dyomed and the players in Greek parts wore 'Grekkyche' costumes of red and yellow as 'men of Warre'. Their dress included wide, short sleeves of linen or Holland cloth. The players in the Trojan parts wore white and green costumes, the Tudor colours, a courtly allusion to the legendary descent of the Kings of England from Brutus, first King of Albion and great-grandson of Aeneas, of the royal family of Troy. This ancestry, invented by Geoffrey of

Monmouth in the 12th century, was to be exposed as legendary by Polydore Vergil, an Italian working in England, in his *Anglica Historia* a few years after this performance at court, annoying those English writers, like John Leland, who had studied English history and cherished even its legends.

The latter part of this Twelfth Night's entertainment was centred around a timber castle in the hall. This part of the festivities began with Cornish, now dressed in black as a herald, announcing the arrival of three strange knights wearing red and yellow costumes, who had come to challenge the knights within the castle. Three knights wearing green and white satin costumes came out of the castle and fought the strange knights, first with spears and then with swords, finally driving them away. The knights in these mock battles were played by men-at-arms.

This clash was followed by the entry from the castle of a crowned queen, apparently named Faythe, attended by six ladies in yellow satin dresses adorned with 'braydes of gold, fret with mouing spangels, sylver and gilt'. They declaimed speeches written for them by Cornish and were followed by seven minstrels, standing on the walls and towers of the castle in long green and white robes, who sang a 'melodyus song'. Next came dances, performed by six lords and gentlemen and six ladies of the court, to the sound of tambourines. These dancers also entered the hall from the castle and they wore the most elaborate costumes, the men in green and white satin with crimson satin bonnets, a form of dress said to be like that worn by Hungarian Jews; the ladies' dresses, of the same materials and colours as those worn by the men, were 'after the fassion of Amsterdam', which meant headdresses of crimson satin and loose and woven gold damask, and short satin jackets or stomachers, also crimson, bearing the letters 'H' and 'K' in yellow satin in compliment to King Henry and Queen Katherine. The end of these festivities was a banquet, during which 200 dishes were served to the diners 'with great plenty to euery body'[48]—altogether, a diverse and colourful entertainment.

A few months later, in April that year, there was another visit by the court to Eltham when a chapter of the Order of the Garter was held there as the result of the death of Julian di Medici, a brother of the reigning Pope Leo X who had been elected to the order at an earlier date but died before he could be installed. Five years later Leo X was the pope who gave Henry VII the title of 'Fidei Defensor' ('Defender of the Faith'), the title later reconferred on the king by Parliament after Henry's break with papal supremacy and still in use on our coinage.[49]

Palace recreations at this date included tilting, for which a new tilting ground was laid out in 1517[50] and where, two years later, the Earl of Devon is recorded as practising.[51] This new ground may have been laid out to avoid the inconvenience of using the outer court, where earlier tournaments had been held. September 1518 witnessed a visit to Eltham by Sebastian Giustinian, the Venetian ambassador, who met Henry VIII, Thomas More ('newly made councillor, who is a great friend of his') and Cardinal Wolsey at the palace.[52] Two years later the parks at Eltham, which provided recreation for the king and his court, were among those from which bucks were taken for the feasting that accompanied the meeting of Henry VIII and Francis I at Guisnes, near Calais, at the famous Field of the Cloth of Gold.[53]

December 1522 saw Eltham as the scene of Cardinal Wolsey's second attempt at reducing waste in the royal household,[54] which he had previously tried to do in

1519[55] and which he finally dealt with at the palace in January 1526 when he there produced the 'Statutes of Eltham', his last effort at reorganising the establishment and rules of the court. The statutes included a list of courtiers who were entitled, with their servants, to 'bouche of court' or free board and lodging there, a record of the number of servants allowed to each rank of the nobility at court, an account of the salaries, wages and duties of court officials, and a list of the courtiers with the right to enter the apartments of the king and queen. These reforms resulted in some courtiers losing the right to come to court and the statutes gave the level of compensation they were to receive, this depending on the positions they had held.[56] It has been suggested that some of those excluded lost their positions not because their departure would reduce waste but instead because Wolsey wished to see no more of them at court.[57] Some orders also regulated the behaviour of courtiers, forbidding gossip about the king's movements but allowing moderate play at dice, cards and tables (backgammon) in the king's privy chamber when the king was not present, though this had to cease when he entered the room.

The Statutes of Eltham also covered the subjects of payment for food and fodder supplied to the court, the times of meals there, the administration of the hall and chapel, fuel economies, the prevention of theft, arrangements concerning visitors with petitions and the exclusion from court of boys, 'vile persons', dogs and hawks.[58] In spite of Wolsey's efforts these statutes were not wholly successful in limiting waste, as they got in the way of Henry's wish to maintain great state at court and those excluded by the statutes tried to return.[59] Further attempts at court reform were to be made in the 1530s, by Thomas Cromwell, and in 1558 after the accession of Elizabeth I.[60]

The last years of Cardinal Wolsey's supremacy witnessed his plans taking shape for his new college at the University of Oxford and for a school at Ipswich, where he was born. While Henry was at Eltham for the Christmas season of 1524 he asked the Bishop of Lincoln to explain to the queen the cardinal's plans for his new Oxford college, which was to be called Cardinal's College.[61] The following July, after a royal patent had been granted for the foundation, Wolsey laid its first stone. After his fall from power four years later, even his college was taken from him. Twice refounded by Henry, in 1532 and 1545, on the latter occasion it was given its present name of Christ Church.[62] Henry VIII also came to Eltham for the Christmas season of 1525, which was affected by an outbreak of plague, the season being called the 'Still Christmas' as, for fear of infection, only a small household summoned by name accompanied the king.[63] During this particular visit the practice of presenting gifts on New Year's Day, recorded at Eltham in the 14th and 16th centuries, is found there again in a list of gifts presented to the king. This, drawn up early in 1526, includes shirts from ladies of the court, jewels, hat ornaments and collars set with jewels.[64] The king also made gifts to others, including bucks he had killed. One of these, from Eltham Park, was presented to Cardinal Wolsey in June 1528.[65]

The later 1520s saw the royal household at Eltham on at least two occasions.[66] Extensive building works, costing £2,030, were carried out there between November 1528 and February 1531[67] which included finishing the king's chapel and glazing both the hall and a gallery between the king's and princesses' lodgings.[68]

The amounts involved are beyond the costs of annual repairs, and the chapel reference indicates that the undated record ordering a new chapel 'made of tymbre worke sett upon a vawte with a fowndacon of stone', though dated to 1519–22 by one authority, must date from the late 1520s. The chapel was excavated by archaeologists in the 1970s.[69]

Between May and July[70] and September and November[71] of 1532 the court was at Eltham, the king's privy purse accounts recording for these months both his recreations there and the names of some of his visitors.[72] Archery,[73] hunting,[74] coursing[75] and bowling in a newly made bowling alley[76] are all mentioned, together with the bets that Henry lost on matches in which he took part or witnessed.[77] His rewards to the huntsmen and parkers who provided his sport also appear.[78] On one occasion his love of hunting even appears in an ambassador's dispatch, when Eustace Chapuys, the Imperial ambassador, mentions to Charles V in November 1532 that he had just had an interview with the king at Eltham when Henry was in hunting dress and on the point of setting out to hunt. The ambassador's reception there is also described. He first went to his lodgings, where he met the dean of the chapel, who took him to the first hall. There he met the Earl of Wiltshire, incidentally Anne Boleyn's father, who led him to the dining room to meet the Duke of Norfolk, who discussed official business with him over dinner. When the meal ended Chapuys went to see the king. Chapuys refers to the recent presence at Eltham of the French ambassador[79] but does not mention Thomas Cromwell, who was probably also present there.[80] The Venetian ambassador had come with Chapuys to Eltham.[81] This court visit in November took place just after Henry and Anne's visit to France to see Francis I.[82]

Visitors to Eltham the previous June had included three gardeners, two from the royal palaces at Greenwich[83] and Hampton Court[84] and another from Beaulieu,[85] who came to bring the king cherries, lettuces, artichokes and strawberries. Two visitors were Frenchmen, of whom one, Vincent Annys, sold jewels to Henry,[86] while the other, who is not named, brought a gift of a brace of greyhounds for Francis I.[87] Other visitors were Ambros, painter to the Queen of Navarre, with the gift of a picture,[88] and Andrew Mancyon, who brought the king two 'antikes' or pieces of classical art.[89] The privy purse accounts also list a stream of gifts to Henry from donors like Henry Norres,[90] who presented a horse and a greyhound, and Thomas Cromwell, who gave him some 'sucado', a kind of fruit syrup, and 'marmelado'.[91] Gifts such as these were brought to Eltham by servants and were not personally presented by the donors. Others bringing gifts to Henry, presumably in the hope of royal favour, were the Abbot of Glastonbury, with the gift of two horses,[92] and the Mayor of London, who presented the king with a sturgeon.[93] Some donors and visitors are unnamed in these privy purse accounts, such as a man bringing furniture,[94] an Eltham priest who bred pheasants[95] and a woman with a gift of beans and chickens.[96] These records display the great variety among the visitors to Eltham Palace when the court was in residence.

Although Henry's marriage to Katherine of Aragon was not annulled until several months later,[97] the king married Anne Boleyn in January 1533[98] and she was crowned as queen in June.[99] Princess Elizabeth was born at Greenwich Palace in September of the same year.[100] In April 1534 the infant princess was brought to

Eltham where Henry and Anne came to see her, Elizabeth being described then as 'as goodly a child as hath been seen'.[101] Before this visit some work had been carried out at the palace, including the purchase of two bands of iron and an iron brace for a cradle[102] and the redecoration of one of the rooms.[103] Anne Boleyn's personal badge and coat of arms were also placed in the palace windows.[104] Both Elizabeth and her much older half-sister Mary came to Eltham in July 1534 when their father also arrived there. On this occasion Mary, being out of favour with her father, had to retire to her room before Henry's arrival 'for fear of her seeing him'.[105]

One of these 1534 court visits to Eltham was probably the occasion when Anne Boleyn and Princess Mary quarrelled there. This event is described in a biography, written long afterwards, of Jane Dormer, who later became one of Mary's ladies in waiting and married the Spanish Duke of Feria, an advisor to King Philip of Spain, husband of Queen Mary. Jane Dormer was not born when the quarrel took place at Eltham and so its details must have been repeated to her, some twenty years later, by some much older member of the court. It is possible, incidentally, that the recorded account of the incident shows Mary as more hostile to Anne than she actually was at that time.

The quarrel occurred after Anne and Mary had heard Mass in the same room. When it ended Mary made a low curtsy and the two left to return to their own rooms. One of Anne's ladies then told her that Mary had curtsied, upon which news Anne, who had been trying to improve relations between herself and her stepdaughter, sent one of her ladies to Mary to excuse herself for not having noticed and returned this act of courtesy. She added a friendly message to Mary. The lady in waiting with this message found Mary at dinner and passed on what she had been told to say. The unfriendly reply she received from Mary was that the message could not have come from the queen as ' ... You would (should) have said (it was from) the Lady Anne Boleyn, for I can acknowledge no other queen but my mother ... And for the reverence that I made, it was to the altar ...', a reply which, when passed on, not surprisingly maddened Anne, making her say that she would pull down this high spirit.[106]

During 1535 the queen's lodgings were damaged by both fire[107] and storm.[108] Despite this, the court returned there, though it enforced some changes in the accommodation that was used, with Princess Mary moving into the queen's lodgings[109] and the king's privy chamber being temporarily moved into the outer court there.[110] Both princesses were at Eltham that September and October but Mary was kept out of sight during a visit by some French ambassadors, who came there with the intention of asking Mary whether she was prepared to marry the Dauphin, heir to the French throne. This meeting was prevented by royal instructions that the princess was not to be allowed to see or talk with these envoys.[111] Mary is also mentioned as being popular locally, as women had cheered her while she was passing between Greenwich and Eltham in April of this year.[112] At Christmas the court came to Eltham, both Henry and Anne being present, and the king was visited there by both the French and the Imperial ambassadors.[113]

The fateful year of 1536 witnessed both the suppression of the smaller monasteries and the Catholic rebellion, known as the Pilgrimage of Grace, which followed. It also saw the fall of Anne Boleyn[114] who was arrested, put on trial and executed in the Tower of London all in the same month of May.[115] One of those accused with her, and also convicted and executed, was Henry Norres, a courtier who was master of game and holder of the fee farm of the lordship of Eltham.[116] Anne's successor as queen was Jane Seymour, who died in 1537 after giving birth to Henry's long-desired son and heir, the future Edward VI.[117] The latter years of Henry VIII's reign rarely saw visits to Eltham by the court, although it came there in 1538, when both Thomas Cromwell and the Duke of Norfolk were present,[118] in the following year, when the king was entertained there by three minstrels,[119] and possibly also in the summer of 1541.[120]

The last visit by the court to Eltham in Henry VIII's reign took place in September–October 1544,[121] although the king himself was not there but at the siege of Boulogne.[122] Preparations for this visit are fully recorded and included a three-day search for signs of sickness which might affect the court before it came to Eltham, searches being made in Greenwich, Otford, Dartford and Knole. Other preparations for this particular visit included carrying 'the Queen's coffers' (baggage) from Oking to Eltham, making everything ready at the palace, the repairing of local roads and arrangements for lodgings and guides. Purchases of 'pins, starch and other necessaries' were also made in London for use during the visit,[123] during which 26 horses were stabled at Eltham. Eleven of these were the queen's palfreys for her use and for the use of her ladies.[124] The visiting queen was Catherine Parr, the sixth and last of Henry VIII's wives, who came to Eltham with Princess Elizabeth, aged 11, and the 'Queen's Highnesse's Council', which governed England during the absence overseas of the king.[125]

The years between 1545 and 1555 included the last years of Henry VIII's reign, the reign of his son Edward VI, and part of the five years when Mary I was queen, first on her own and then with her husband Philip of Spain. The court is not known to have visited Eltham during these years, but under Edward VI the cost of repairs to the buildings at Eltham amounted to £952,[126] a larger sum than that spent there during any comparable period of time during the long reign of Edward's half-sister Elizabeth I.[127] On Edward VI's death in 1553 Mary succeeded him after the failure of the attempt to place her cousin Lady Jane Grey on the throne,[128] an attempt with fatal consequences for Sir John Gates, who held a number of official posts at Eltham.[129]

In 1554–6 the sum of £250 was spent on repairs to the palace[130] and in July 1556 the first recorded visit of Mary I, as queen, took place. She was accompanied by many courtiers, including Cardinal Pole, the Earl of Pembroke and Viscount Montagu, and some courtiers' wives, a procession that moved from St James' Palace to Whitehall Palace, where Mary embarked on a barge, crossing the Thames to Cardinal Pole's home, Lambeth Palace. There the queen 'toke her charett' on the way towards St George's Fields and Newington before taking the road into Kent and Eltham that led from London Bridge. The contemporary diarist Henry Machyn recorded that the court procession on this occasion was watched by 10,000 people.[131]

Mary I's 1556 visit to Eltham lasted for almost a month and is a tribute to the good condition of the palace buildings after repairs, although, as far as is known, it had not been visited by the court for 10 years. The Privy Council met there during this visit almost every day from 22 July to 18 August, with five to 11 councillors attending each of these council meetings. Two councillors are recorded attending every one of these meetings, while one was only absent on a single occasion. The queen did not attend these council meetings. The subjects discussed and on which decisions were reached included the security and fortifications of Berwick and Calais, of which the latter was to be captured by the French 18 months later in January 1558. Other topics dealt with were the Scottish border, the ports, escapes from prison, the torture of an embezzler held in prison and the reception in England of Philip of Spain, who had married Mary I in 1554.[132] Official correspondence sent from Eltham during this visit covered further matters of governmental concern at the time, such as leases,[133] clerical presentations,[134] the refounding of a religious fraternity,[135] the pardoning of two heretics who had been converted and had abjured their heresies,[136] licences to keep retainers,[137] grants[138] and pardons.[139] The council also sent an order to Sir Thomas Pope, the official custodian of Princess Elizabeth, to tell him to inform 'the Lady Elizabeth's Grace' of the failure of an attempted revolt on her behalf.[140] In the reign of Mary I, her half-sister Elizabeth was the focus of the hopes of the Protestants and of those who disliked Spanish influence in England, resulting in a number of plots against the government, of which the best known was Wyatt's revolt, defeated in 1554.[141] One grant made during this visit was connected with an earlier rebellion, in 1549 under Edward VI, as the lands in question had formerly been in the possession of the leader of that revolt, Robert Kett, after whom the uprising was named.[142]

A further brief visit by Mary I's court to Eltham took place in July 1557, when grants were made to four of the queen's servants. Of these, two were gentlemen ushers who were given official posts formerly held by Sir Nicholas Throckmorton, who had been tried for treason but acquitted after Wyatt's revolt.[143] Mary I died in November 1558, to be succeeded by Elizabeth I, who briefly visited Eltham Palace in August 1559,[144] where she signed a warrant for the delivery of some secret service money,[145] while her council wrote from there on official business to the Council of Ireland.[146] These were to be the last known official royal and court records written at the palace for, although Eltham was to receive occasional royal visits during the following 80 years, its function as an occasional centre of government activity when the court was there seems to have ended, after two-and-a-half centuries, in 1559.

Detailed building records for Eltham surviving from this early Tudor period are principally from the earlier part of Henry VIII's reign. They show, in greater detail than is available from earlier years for the palace, the number of different rooms used by members of the royal family and by their principal advisor, Cardinal Wolsey. On the first floor these were arraying,[147] bed,[148] breakfast,[149] dining,[150] great (or presence)[151] and privy[152] chambers as well as closets.[153] Cardinal Wolsey had similar apartments, though in his case great and arraying chambers are not recorded but he had little and withdrawing chambers[154] and in c.1528 his closet was ordered to be altered to make it into a withdrawing chamber.[155] Henry VIII had a breakfast chamber,[156] a study[157] and a watching chamber,[158] with a privy gallery.[159] Princess Mary had a chamber, arraying chamber, bedchamber, second chamber, wardrobe and uttermost chamber.[160] In 1535-6 the palace had the Lady Princess's apartments for Princess Elizabeth with a closet, kitchen and buttery.[161] The king,[162] queen[163] and Princess Elizabeth[164] had privy galleries, the king a chamber of state,[165] the queen a chamber, or great chamber, of presence,[166] and the queen[167] and Cardinal Wolsey[168] withdrawing chambers. There may have been other personal rooms not recorded in surviving building records.[169]

The descriptions given to rooms and galleries may alter between one record and another, with the result that rooms are wrongly duplicated. An example is the new gallery of c.1528 'from our new lodgings to our old bedchamber',[170] which may be the king's privy gallery. Another gallery from the king's great chamber up to the chapel was ordered in c.1528 to be widened by five feet.[171] This last gallery may be the one shown in the mid-17th-century 'Stent' print on the outer side of the western front of the palace. There are also further references to galleries, one being described as by the closets,[172] another between the lodgings of the prince and the king,[173] and another in 1535-6 as a privy gallery by the queen's bedchamber, perhaps another description for the queens privy gallery.[174]

In the late 1520s a new study was ordered to be made at Eltham for the king. It was to have, besides a wainscot ceiling and partitions, coffers (chests), almoryes (cupboards) and desks.[175] Other furniture recorded there in Henry VIII's reign included tables, trestles, forms and stools.[176] Some of this was made at the palace by local men in 1533-4[177] and 1542-3[178] but the furniture intended for use in the privy chambers of the king and queen, consisting of joined tables, trestles and stools, was supplied by Thomas Bonyvaute of Southwark.[179] At a later date, in 1583-4, the same situation is recorded regarding palace furniture, some being made at the palace and some supplied by outsiders.[180]

As occurred in earlier reigns, some courtiers are recorded at Eltham with rooms allocated to them by their names. In 1535-6 this was the case with the Duke of Norfolk,[181] the Earl of Wiltshire[182] and the unfortunate Henry Norres, who had rooms outside the moat, possibly those known at a later date as the Chancellor's Lodgings, which had a great chamber, parlour, closet, bedchamber, kitchen and buttery.[183] Court officials with rooms allotted to them were the steward, with a chamber and a counting house,[184] the Lady Princesse's steward,[185] the clerk comptroller,[186] the clerk of the kitchen[187] and the 'Lady Maistres' in charge of the young Princess Elizabeth.[188] A waiting chamber called the 'kynges watchyng Chamber' is also found, which would have been used by the yeomen of the guard.[189]

The date of building of the royal apartments used by the Tudor royal family at Eltham is uncertain. William Lambarde, in his book on Kent published in 1576, states that 'the fair front ouer the mote there', by which he presumably refers to the west front, which included the royal apartments, was built for Henry VII.[190] Along this front there still survive Tudor bricks, some at ground level and others in patterns of light and dark bricks on the outer face of the moat walls.[191] Henry VII certainly carried out some building at Eltham but surviving documentary evidence concerning it is scanty. An official was appointed in 1488 to collect workmen for building there and at other royal houses,[192] and there are some surviving, uninformative, building accounts for Eltham in this reign.[193] It is possible that Lambarde was misinformed and that the royal apartments on the west front were built under either Edward IV[194] or Henry VIII,[195] or perhaps by both, they having spent money at Eltham on important works apparently situated among the royal apartments on the west front.

In Edward IV's case, an undated works account from his reign records the purchase of stone for 11 chimneys for 'the logyng over the newe Seler', also mentioned as 'newe Chamberes over the Seler', and work upon a library,[196] showing that major works apart from the great hall were carried out at Eltham in this reign. The ground-floor plan from the early 17th century depicts spaces on the eastern, inner side of the west front, which might be the fireplaces sited beneath the chimneys mentioned in this record.[197]

Under Henry VIII, between 1511 and 1523 almost £4,400 was spent on works at Greenwich, Eltham and Richmond, besides some expenditure on the Tower of London. Of this amount £650, and perhaps more, was spent at Eltham,[198] although part of this amount might have been spent on the enlargement of Eltham's parks in c.1514.[199] A further record mentions recent expenditure at Eltham in 1517.[200] No building accounts survive for Eltham for 1524-7, although a reference to lead being sent from Tonbridge Castle to Eltham in 1525 suggests that building works were then in progress.[201] An interesting but undated record, apparently of the late 1520s,[202] refers to 'baye wyndowes in our new lodginges', 'lodgings under our new Lodging', 'three Closettes oon standing above a nother at the South West Corner of our newe Lodginges' and the embattlement of 'Our new Lodginges'.[203] These references, especially the third, show that new work had recently been erected that included new apartments for the king's use at Eltham. Between 1528 and 1531 a further £2,030 was spent on buildings at Eltham,[204] including money spent on 'fynyshing of the kinges chapell' in November 1530.[205]

Two wainscot panels, each six feet by three feet and six inches, now in Plumstead Museum, were discovered in a farm 'adjoining' the palace site in the late 19th century, probably at Middle Park Farm, situated half a mile from the palace.[206] As in the survey of the manor in 1649, only the chapel and the great hall are described as 'garnished with wainscote'[207] and, as one panel is of early 16th-century date,[208] it would appear that this panel is from the chapel completed late in 1530.[209]

Two of the works ordered at Eltham for Henry VIII can still be seen there today, although one of these can only be visited with some difficulty, except in dry weather, this being the 'Synk that goeth from our kechyn under our Mote'.[210] This tunnel, 179 yards long, has short branches situated beneath the lawn to the south of the great hall, the area formerly occupied by the palace kitchens. Its entrance is close to the moat wall to the west of the present south bridge.[211] The cleaning of tunnels at Eltham and other royal buildings was contracted in 1536 to John Wylkynson, 'scowrer of synkes', a Londoner, who received 26s. 8d. annually as well as a red cloth coat each year valued at 5s. 8d.[212]

The second surviving work at Eltham from Henry VIII's reign is the 'brick wall round the orchard'.[213] This wall, completed in 1517,[214] adjoined the garden and is the one with a Tudor archway at the north-east end of the former outer court.[215]

The same undated building record previously mentioned shows Henry VIII's appreciation of personal privacy at Eltham. An alley was to run from the south

7 *Two wainscot panels purchased in the late 19th century from a farm, apparently Middle Park Farm, adjoining the remains of the palace. The uppermost, a), has been dated to the 1530s and may be from the palace chapel completed in 1530.*
a) Continental workmanship, possibly Flemish or Italian.
b) English traditional workmanship.

bridge along the outer side of the moat, first eastwards and then north to the garden gate, with plank walls and banks set with 'quyk settes of Thornes' so the king could 'goo oute of our lodging that waye into our Gardeyn … secrete'.[216]

The buildings erected at Eltham under the Tudors were quite different to those built there for Edward III and Henry IV. No longer made of stone, they used more brick and timber. The new chapel, built for Henry VIII, was to be made 'of Tymbr' worke sett upon a vawte with a fowndacion of Stone', with 'a Flat Ruf inbatelled' and 'commely wyndowes most Chapellyke as well as the higher aulter as oon boeth sydes'.[217]

Buildings little mentioned in records, although much in use, were the stables. Not shown in the late 16th-century outer-court plans, they were enlarged in c.1512,[218] probably as part of the 1511-12 building works there.[219] Horsebreeding was also carried on in the Eltham parks under Henry VIII, a stud house being completed there in 1517.[220] Its precise location, like that of the stables, is unknown. When the Statutes of Eltham were drawn up in the 1520s the court had an establishment of 160 horses and 25 mules, as well as a further 120 horses required for the yeomen of the guard.[221] Some stabling also existed at the park lodges.[222] When, after the mid-1530s,[223] the palace was less frequently visited by the court, it is also possible to see a decline in the amount spent on its buildings.[224]

Under both Henry VII, in 1493-4,[225] and Henry VIII, in 1522-3,[226] surveys were made of the manor. These have not survived but they are mentioned in the later 1605 survey. The later of these Tudor surveys included the names of tenants, the types of land leased by them and field names. Henry VIII's reign saw the parks at Eltham slightly enlarged in 1512[227] and in c.1532[228] by the purchase or exchange of land with local landowners. Under Edward VI, in July 1549, during a year of widespread peasant revolts, Kentish rebels destroyed the fences or hedges round one of the parks at Eltham.[229]

Until the mid-1530s, appointments of officials to administer the manor, parks, buildings and gardens, and to be chaplain there, continued as in the past.[230] Among these appointments one, of Robert Palmer as gardener in 1485, is interesting, as he lost his position two years later for non-attendance, thus showing that at that time such appointments were not sinecures.[231] After 1535, however, the decline in visits by the court, and in the amount spent on its buildings, is paralleled among its officials. After two centuries of these appointments 1528 saw the last chaplain appointed[232] and 1534 the last appointment of a gardener holding no other manorial position.[233] The holding, at the same time, of several official posts at Eltham by one man is known at an earlier date but this was now carried to greater heights. On 6 July 1553, the last day of Edward VI's reign, Sir John Gates was appointed keeper of the houses, parker of two of the parks and steward of Eltham, with the reversion of the posts of gardener, purveyor, keeper and surveyor of woods there.[234] Fatally for himself, he supported the Duke of Northumberland's attempt to place Lady Jane Grey on the throne in place of Princess Mary. He and the duke were both found guilty of treason and executed in August 1553.[235] His successor at Eltham was Henry Jerningham, a prominent supporter of Mary I.[236] Both Gates[237] and Jerningham[238] were important courtiers who held a number of other official positions.

Nearly seventy local wills, mostly left by men from the wealthier part of the local community, survive from early Tudor days. A number of these wills came from men who held minor positions at court such as Christopher Segryg (1520),[239] chamber yeoman, Thomas Parkar (1523),[240] footman, Willyam Atkynson (1533),[241] a yeoman holding court office who bequeathed 'my second cote of my lyvery of the kyng', and John Rolte (1535),[242] a yeoman of the guard who left a bequest to John Brickett,[243] a local man holding the office of master cook to the king. Rolte was also keeper of Eltham parks and, with Henry Skylman, mentioned below,[244] was keeper of the houses at the palace, executor for John Colenson,[245] and surveyor and paymaster of the palace's building works between 1528 and 1532.[246] Other local officeholders were John Plom (1535),[247] yeoman of the catery, John Wyllesdon (1541),[248] yeoman usher, John Plume (1547),[249] 'late mayster Cooke to the quenes hyghnes', and Robert Hordron (1547),[250] 'yoman of the male', who bequeathed 'two

Cootes of the kinges lyvery' in his will. Further local court officeholders were Henry Berde,[251] yeoman of the guard, who is named in the wills of Christopher Segryg, mentioned above, and Thomas Sybson (1525),[252] John Browne (1533),[253] a wealthy man and probably appointed purveyor at Eltham in 1485, and John Pasley or Passy, yeoman and porter to the king (1509), whose damaged brass survives in Eltham church.[254] Henry Skylman (1526), keeper of the king's houses at Eltham from 1486 and later keeper both of the manor and of two of its parks,[255] was executor of one local will,[256] supervisor of two others[257] and both supervisor and witness of another local will.[258] The only local female known to have held office at court was Margery Roper, of the well-known family linked by marriage to Sir Thomas More, who was lady of the bedchamber to Queen Katherine. She died in 1578 and was buried in Eltham church.[259]

Until the 1530s, wills made in Eltham always included bequests to the church,[260] but in later years, except under Mary I, these are uncommon.[261] Three wills of Mary I's reign show local Catholic sympathies. One of these is that of Thomas Huxley (1557),[262] vicar of Eltham. He bequeathed vestments and church goods to Eltham church and bequests to the friars of Greenwich, the black friars of London, the monks of the Charterhouse of Sheen and the nuns of Syon, all of which were religious orders suppressed under Henry VIII and re-established under Mary I. Another Eltham priest, Christopher Wymyngton (1557),[263] bequeathed money for a light in Eltham church, a common pre-Reformation bequest, while Richard Maynard (1556),[264] parish clerk, left money to buy vestments for Eltham church. Bequests of books were uncommon in this period, but one Eltham layman bequeathed 'a prymer to serve God with all' in 1494[265] and two Eltham priests left bequests of books in 1557, one 'a masse book',[266] the other 'all my bookes'.[267]

Non-church bequests are found before and after the Reformation. Some, for road repairs, are recorded in 1509,[268] 1529,[269] 1534,[270] 1541[271] and 1556,[272] and bequests for bread and ale for the poor, after funerals, are to be found in 1509,[273] 1529,[274] twice in 1533,[275] three times in 1556[276] and once in 1557.[277] A careful bequest of this latter type is made in the will of Henry Stewunson (1549),[278] where his donation was to be 'gyven in no open doole, but at poore howses wher nede requireth at the discretion of myn Executours'. Two wills also provide bequests of money towards a dowry for 'maiden' marriages'.[279]

Many of these early Tudor Eltham wills bequeath items of dress, those worn by the wealthier section of the Eltham community. Gowns, coats and doublets are listed, coloured tawny,[280] black[281] and russet,[282] the most colourful item being a crimson velvet doublet.[283] Materials used in these garments were worsted,[284] velvet[285] and camlet,[286] the last of these being a mixture of wool and silk. Wills left by priests refer to black,[287] russet[288] and blue[289] gowns, and coats and vestments made of camlet[290] or friese,[291] the last material being a coarse woollen cloth. Seventeen materials,[292] ten types of male dress[293] and nine colours[294] are mentioned in these early Tudor Eltham wills. Some garments are described as trimmed with fur, usually fox,[295] and some as faced with a material different to that making up the body of the garment, for example a cloak guarded with velvet and a gown faced with damask.[296]

The outstanding dress bequest among these early Tudor Eltham wills is in Henry Stewunson's will (1549), a gentleman who bequeathed boots, shoes, boothose, hose and caps besides two nightgowns, one faced with black lamb, black and tawny gowns trimmed with fox and rabbit fur, coats of freeseadow, a fine variety of woollen friese, and velvet, and doublets made of leather, black and tawny worsted and satin.[297] At a lower level of society Christopher Nicholson (1541),[298] a husbandman or small farmer, was only able to bequeath a fustian doublet and a tawny jacket. Early Tudor womens' wills from Eltham number less than a tenth of those left by men.[299] Their clothing bequests include black and tawny gowns[300] and one coloured mellay, a mixture of colours,[301] girdles,[302] kirtles,[303] corletts[304] and a petticoat.[305] Kirtles were womens' gowns and corletts were tight-fitting garments. One man's will, that of William Dygon (1494),[306] bequeaths gowns to his daughter Al(i)son and his cousin (H)elen. The former was to receive a violet-coloured gown trimmed with squirrel fur, the latter a murray (purple-red) gown ornamented with marten fur, strongly suggesting that the legatees had chosen the details of the types of gown they were to receive.

The bequests that appear most often in these wills other than those already mentioned, and aside from land, animals, grain and hay, are those associated with beds. All parts of the bed and its furnishings are found in these wills, the frame,[307] ceiling,[308] curtains,[309] mattress,[310] feather bed,[311] down pillow,[312] bolster,[313] coverlet,[314] blankets[315] and sheets, the commonest bedroom bequest being a pair of sheets.[316] Some wills bequeath beds with all their furnishings,[317] while Nicholas Priour (1535)[318] left five beds, each with a bolster, blanket and feather bed, to different legatees. Towels were also bequeathed.[319] Among kitchen items the commonest bequests were pots[320] and pans,[321] of brass[322] or pewter[323] and, in one case, silver.[324] Kettles,[325] mortars,[326] iron spits,[327] a cauldron,[328] a chaffer,[329] a chafing dish[330] and a bason[331] also appear in these wills.

Dining room bequests show that they were furnished with table cloths,[332] platters,[333] dishes,[334] saucers[335] and napkins.[336] Table cloths may have been uncommon as they are only mentioned in two wills.[337] Silver spoons were the only cutlery items bequeathed,[338] some being more fully described as plain[339] or with maidenhead tops[340] or gold knops.[341] A few wills include grander items. These are chargers,[342] mazers or shallow bowls,[343] a silver cup,[344] silver[345] and gilt[346] salts and ewers.[347] Only one will, that of John Browne (1533),[348] has more than a few such pieces. He was able to bequeath two flat pieces of silver (salvers), three goblets, three mazers, four cups, a great salt, a silver pot and 30 silver spoons, some of these items being described as silver, gilt, parcel gilt and new fashion parcel gilt. He also bequeathed armour, church vestments and church furniture, the latter two suggesting his house included a private chapel.

Furniture apart from beds and chests[349] is rarely mentioned in these early Tudor Eltham wills. Only two include tables and chairs[350] and only one a settle.[351] Minor furnishings, such as andirons[352] and candlesticks,[353] are mentioned in several wills. Unusual bequests include swords,[354] one with a buckler[355] and another said to have belonged to Henry VII,[356] a pece, or gun,[357] a gold chain,[358] and a saddle, bridle and harness.[359]

The fullest record of household furniture in these wills is to be found in the will of Margret Breckett, 'wedow'.[360] A son-in-law received her bedstead 'of Joyned and carved worke standing hole in the parlour', with its 'valence or Seling' and five red and green curtains, besides other items of bedding. A daughter was bequeathed three 'Trustinge Bedsteddles', or truckle beds, which were slid under bedsteads during the day. These truckle beds, used by servants, were all provided with feather beds, bolsters, pillows and coverlets. The parlour was also hung with hangings made of say, a fine serge cloth, and other hangings are mentioned in the hall and upper chamber.

Margret Breckett also bequested three chests. Of these, one was a standard chest, another 'one great Standard Cheste covered with ledder and bound with Iron' and a third one described as a 'gret chest of waynscott'. Further bequests by her were her 'best carpett of Tapistree' and, in her hall, a long settle of 'Joyned worke' and two great andirons 'standing in the hall Chymney'. Another bequest in the parlour was 'a presse of Joyned work' and, from elsewhere in the house, 'my bell candilstickes'. Her pewter was bequeathed in two half-garnishes, a garnish consisting of a set of vessels for use at table. The whole pewter garnish bequeathed numbered a basin and ewer, three more basins, a charger, two salt cellers, 12 voiders or trays, 12 porringers, four wine pots, of which two were quart pots and two pint pots, four bow pots, four drinking pots and one pottell or small pot. Her kitchen bequests included some items that do not appear in other Eltham wills, these being 'a pair of Rackes', a skimmer, a pair of tongs, a gridiron, a bread grate and a frying pan.

VIII

DECLINE AND CIVIL WAR

I went to see his Majesty's house at Eltham, both palace and chapel in miserable
ruins, the noble woods and park destroyed by Rich, the rebel.
(J. Evelyn, *Diary* (ed. E.S. de Beer), vol. iii, 1956, entry for 26 April 1656)

After her accession to the throne in 1558, Elizabeth I is only recorded as visiting
or passing through Eltham 13 times during the course of her 45-year-long
reign. Six of these visits, all in either July or August, occurred between 1596
and 1602.[1] Some of her visits, and others by James I, are only known from entries in
the accounts of the Eltham churchwardens, when church bellringers were paid for
ringing the bells to celebrate a royal visit to the parish.[2] It is not unlikely that other
visits by Elizabeth I to Eltham passed unrecorded. Apart from the August 1559 visit,[3]
very little is recorded of these except that she dined at the palace in November 1559[4]
and in 1576[5] and hunted in Eltham's parks with her courtiers in 1581[6] and 1601.[7]
Hunting was probably the principal attraction of Eltham for Elizabeth I, as its parks
could be easily reached from Greenwich Palace, one of her favourite residences.[8]
The queen spent little on her palaces except for essential repairs and very little on
Eltham Palace[9] so, by early 1603, when James I visited the palace, it was 'so farre in
decay, as it was not fitt for our aboad'.[10]

Sir Christopher Hatton, one of Elizabeth I's favourites and Lord Chancellor
from 1587 until his death in 1591,[11] was appointed keeper of the houses and parks
of Eltham, with other minor appointments, in 1568.[12] He entertained a Spanish
ambassador from Flanders there in 1576 with hunting and a concert;[13] five years
later he was present when the queen hunted at Eltham,[14] and in 1590 he wrote from
there to Elizabeth on official business.[15] His official lodgings were on the north
side of the outer court, next to the moat, a building which survives today and is still
known as 'The Chancellor's Lodgings'.[16] It was repaired and altered in 1586-7 and
appears in building records under his official title,[17] or as 'Master Hatton's lodgings'[18]
or 'Sir Christopher Hattons Lodgings'.[19] In the outer court plan of 1590 it is labelled
as 'my Lo. Channceler: his Lodginge'.[20] Hatton's relations with the parishioners of
Eltham seem to have been friendly, judging by his presentation to them of a buck
in 1572-3,[21] a year which also saw the five men of the parish who wore the parish
armour mustering in the outer palace courtyard near his lodgings.[22]

The first book to include information on the history of Eltham Palace was published in 1576, William Lambarde's *Perambulation of Kent*,[23] followed shortly afterwards in 1590 by another account of its history in William Camden's *Britannia*.[24] Fifty years later, in 1640, William Habington's *History of Edward IV* mentions the palace as being one of the buildings repaired or altered by order of that king.[25] A further brief reference to its history appears in John Philipot's *Villare Cantianum*, written by a local man but published under the name of his son.[26]

After a visit to the palace by James I, soon after his accession to the English throne,[27] an expensive two-year programme of repairs was begun in 1603.[28] Despite this, royal usage of the palace did not increase, as far as is known,[29] and later in that decade a foreign visitor who saw the buildings recorded in his travel journal, no doubt repeating what he had been told by a guide, that the king rarely visited it.[30] One of James I's visits to its parks took place in 1606 when he came with his eldest son, Henry, Prince of Wales, and his brother-in-law, King Christian IV of Denmark. The royal visitors, then staying at Greenwich Palace, are recorded as killing two stags in the park attached to that palace in the morning, and three more in Eltham's parks during the afternoon, while being watched at their sport by a large crowd of spectators.[31]

In 1609-10 the Eltham Palace buildings housed a display of mechanical inventions created by a Dutchman, Cornelis Drebbel, which attracted fashionable interest in London[32] and visitors from overseas.[33] Among these inventions the best known was called the 'Eltham Motion', mentioned by Ben Jonson both in an epigram[34] and in his play *Epicoene, or The Silent Woman*, first performed in 1609.[35] A further reference to it appears among the mock laudatory poems preceding Henry Peacham's *Coryat's Crudities*, published in 1611.[36]

Two German visitors, one in September 1609, the other the following May, include brief descriptions of their visits to Drebbel's display of inventions in their travel journals. The earlier visitor, a companion of Georg von Schwartzestat, Baron of Offenbach, says the palace was built very beautifully on a gentle slope in an elegant and pleasant park,[37] while the later visitor, travelling with Lewis Frederick, Duke of Wurttemberg, mentions that Drebbel was in attendance on the visitors and says of him that he was a 'very fair and handsome man, and of very gentle manners, altogether different from such-like characters'.[38] The machines they saw included a model of a maiden that sang to the music of a clavichord when the sun shone on it and virginals that played of themselves without the touch of a human performer, but the principal attraction of the display was the elaborate 'Eltham Motion'.

The fullest description of this invention appears in a book written by Thomas Tymme and published in 1612. The Eltham Motion is here described as displaying the time of day, the hours when the sun rose and set, the sign of the zodiac in which the sun was, the degrees of distance between the sun, moon and earth, the distance of the sun from the moon, the increase and decrease of the brightness of the moon, and the rise and fall of the tides. The last feature was displayed by water rising or falling within a glass globe the size of a man's head that enclosed a brass globe representing the earth. The device is illustrated in Tymme's book under a roof supported by four pillars and would appear to have been driven partly by clockwork and partly by an air thermometer.[39] By September 1610 Drebbel had left England for Prague, where he worked for the Emperor Rudolf II until the emperor was deposed, an event which nearly led to Drebbel losing his life.[40] By May 1612 he was back in England petitioning James I for employment.[41] In later years he worked for both James I and Charles I, for whom his inventions included mines and a submarine, and he received a royal pension before his death in 1633.[42]

James I came to Eltham on four or five occasions between 1612 and 1624 in order to hunt in the palace's parks.[43] On one of these visits, in 1619, he killed a buck and, in a gruesome attempt to cure his gout, bathed his legs and feet in its blood.[44] Charles I is only once recorded as visiting Eltham, in 1629,[45] a few months after he had granted the manor to his queen, Henrietta Maria, as part of her dower.[46] Four years later the palace was refurnished and offered as a residence to the recently widowed sister of the king, Elizabeth of Bohemia, an exile, but she preferred to live in the Netherlands.[47] Another person associated with Eltham in the decade prior to the Civil War was Sir Anthony van Dyck, the painter, who was stated in the following century to have lived in an old house in Eltham where he left behind several sketches, in two colours, depicting stories by Ovid.[48]

In 1643, when the First Civil War had been in progress for 18 months, the revenues of the manor of Eltham, with those from other crown lands, were sequestrated by order of Parliament,[49] an order later cancelled, for some unknown reason, as regards Eltham.[50] The Earl of Essex, commander of the Parliamentarian army from 1642 to 1644, lived in Eltham for a time[51] and is said by a writer later in the century to have died there,[52] though contemporary sources show that the earl died at his London home, Essex House, in 1646.[53] During the Second Civil War, in 1648, when a Royalist army advanced on London from Kent, Parliamentarian forces under General Fairfax spent a night in Eltham[54] while on their way to defeat the Royalists at Maidstone on 2 June. In that battle the Royalist forces included a man from Eltham who, after the Restoration, put in a claim for relief for the injuries he had suffered in it, followed by a year's imprisonment.[55] The divided loyalties of the time can be seen in 1651 when another local man was excused from taking up parochial office as borsholder of Woolwich 'for that hee was then imployed in the service of the Common-wealth'.[56]

After Charles I's execution in January 1649, local people began to kill the deer in Eltham's parks, joined by the soldiers[57] who had been sent to stop them,[58] a crime for which several were court-martialled in September.[59] Between mid-summer and October all the deer in the parks at Eltham were killed,[60] about eighty being slaughtered in less than a week in early September.[61]

The manor was surveyed by commissioners appointed by Parliament between October and December 1649 in accordance with an act passed by the House of Commons for 'the sale of the houses, manors and lands of the late King, Queen and Prince'.[62]

8   *The 'Eltham Motion' of Cornelis Drebbel, 1612.*

The survey recorded the value of the manor and its buildings, to be sold to pay arrears owed to the Parliamentarian forces. The manor was to be the security for arrears owed to the cavalry regiment of Colonel Nathaniel Rich, which, in this year, was stationed there.[63] The colonel and four of his officers are on record as buying and selling land in Eltham during the 1650s,[64] and they were not the only Parliamentarian purchasers of land in Eltham, as Captain Thomas French, not a member of Colonel Rich's regiment, owned land in Eltham in 1650,[65] was Lord of the Manor there in 1651-2[66] and sold land there in 1653-7.[67] Colonel Rich purchased a lot of Eltham land in 1653[68] and was its lord of the manor in 1655-6.[69] He also sold land there,[70] in one sale reserving for himself an underground lead pipe, no doubt the one that had formerly supplied the palace with its water.[71] In 1656 John Evelyn, a Royalist sympathiser, visited the palace, by now in ruins, and in his diary blames Rich for the cutting down of the park trees, calling him 'Rich, the rebel'.[72] The demolition of most of the palace, and part of the blame for the destruction of the park trees, seems to have been the work of Colonel Rich.[73]

The early military service of Colonel Nathaniel Rich had been in the armies of the Earls of Essex and Manchester but he later served in Cromwell's New Model Army, fought at Naseby and was a commissioner for the surrender of Oxford in 1646.[74] During the Second Civil War of 1648-9 his regiment fought at Kingston and, under Fairfax, at Maidstone, after which it recovered some Kentish castles taken earlier by the Royalists.[75] In spite of all this military service, the eminent Royalist the Earl of Clarendon wrote of Rich in his history of the rebellion that he was 'eminent for praying but of no fame for fighting'.[76] In the later years of the Commonwealth Rich became a political opponent of Oliver Cromwell, for which in 1655 he lost the command of his regiment and was imprisoned.[77] When Cromwell died, late in 1658, Rich regained his former command,[78] though in the following year he was first confined to his Eltham home on political grounds,[79] but then informed in July of that year of a Royalist rising about to take place and ordered to secure suspected persons in Kent, with their horses and arms, and send two troops of his regiment to a rendezvous at Blackheath with infantry and militia cavalry from London.[80] He was an opponent of the Restoration in 1660, lost his regiment and was arrested,[81] only to be released soon afterwards as he had not been a member of the regicide court that had tried and condemned Charles I.[82] The Restoration resulted in Rich losing his Eltham lands, which returned to Henrietta Maria, and some land in Eltham has remained part of the Crown Estates ever since.[83] In January 1661 Nathaniel Rich was arrested again, on suspicion of complicity in Venner's Fifth Monarchy rising, not to be released until 1665.[84] He died in 1701.[85]

Soon after the Restoration, Captain Edward Morgan petitioned for a grant of the house, park and gardens of Eltham[86] but received instead an annuity for his services to Charles II when he was in exile.[87] This grant was later allowed to fall into arrears.[88] The future of the manor was left unsettled until 1663, when the queen mother's trustees granted a lease of its lands to Sir John Shaw and others.[89]

Although this long period of declining royal usage of the palace and its parks saw, apart from the 1603-5 building works,[90] little beyond routine and insufficient maintenance of the palace buildings, it is from these years that there survive the only plans, at ground-floor level, of the old palace,[91] the only view of the palace buildings while they were still complete,[92] and the two manorial surveys of 1605[93] and 1649,[94] all adding very considerably to our knowledge of the manor and palace. In 1605 seven commissioners surveyed the manor, one of them being Sir Francis Bacon,[95] when 27 jurors were summoned to appear before them. Only 15 appeared and the others were each fined 10s. for non-attendance. Among the jurors only one, Thomas Barneham 'generosus', came from Eltham.[96]

The earlier of the ground-floor plans mentioned above is dated 1590 and shows the outer court. Signed by John Thorpe, it shows the court on a scale of 20 feet to an inch and records the uses to which the outer court buildings were being put as well as, in some cases, their condition. Some of the lodgings were in need of repair though this was not the case with those formerly used by the late Sir Christopher Hatton,[97] which, as mentioned earlier, had been repaired and altered in 1586-7.[98] The other outer court buildings, the kitchens and privy bakehouse on the eastern side of the court and the spicery, pastry, coal house and slaughterhouse on the western side, were still in good order.[99] The Chancellor's lodgings next to the moat, with his buttery next door and the spicery and pastry on the western side of the former outer court, still survive today as nos 32, 34 and 36 Court Yard. The date of the destruction of the eastern side of the outer court and other nearby buildings is unknown, the only surviving parts of them being the Tudor wall and arch just outside the former enclosed outer-court buildings.[100]

Beyond the continuous line of buildings that formed the three-sided outer court, with its open side facing the moat bridge and the inner court, there formerly existed to the south-east a works storehouse, a second coal house and a scalding house. Two further buildings, the great bakehouse to the north-east and the chaundry or candlery to the north-west, were linked by walls to the outer court.[101] A number of other buildings are mentioned in works accounts but do not appear on the inner- and outer-court plans. These buildings are the stables,[102] coach houses[103] and barns,[104] the conduit head, which still survives, though incomplete,[105] and the lodges and their associated buildings in the three parks.[106]

Although the plan of the inner court is undated it can be ascribed to 1603-4 by an entry in the Eltham building accounts for that period[107] referring to payments to 'Mazons imployed in helping to measure all the Rooms about the Mannour of Eltham for a plott to be made thereof to be given to the Lord Threasurer for thalteracion of the same'. Unfortunately this plan, unlike that for the outer court, with which it shares the same scale of 20 feet to an inch,[108] does not record the uses of the inner court ground-floor rooms. This plan, evidently made in connection with the alterations and repairs begun in 1603 and completed in 1605, was discovered among the Hatfield manuscripts by A.W. Clapham and W.H. Godfrey, who published a redrawn version of the two plans combined as one in 1909.[109] The Lord Treasurer in 1603-4 was the Earl of Dorset but the plan survived among the papers of his successor, Robert, Earl of Salisbury.[110]

The view of the palace previously mentioned only shows the inner court of the palace. Known as the 'Stent' print, it dates from c.1653 and is 2.5 inches square. It is ascribed to Peter Stent, a London printseller who offered for sale in a catalogue, c.1653, a set of prints of named royal palaces including Eltham. Two copies of the print are known, one cut from the sheet of prints,[111] the other in a

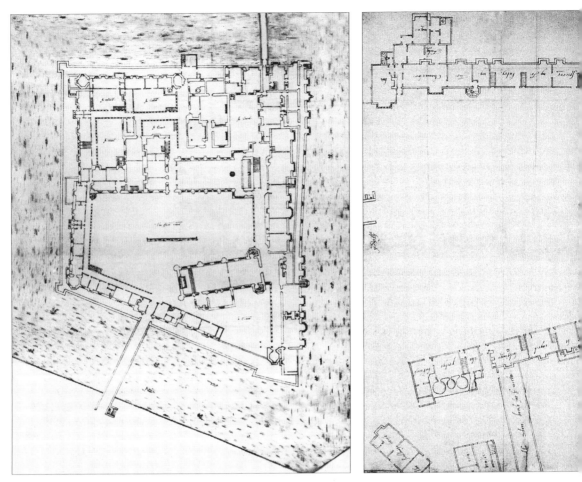

Clockwise from top left: **9** *The ground floor of the inner court of Eltham Palace, 1603-4;* **10** *The ground floor of the outer court of Eltham Palace, 1590, John Thorpe;* **11** *The ground floor of Eltham Palace based on the 1590 and 1603-4 plans;* **12** *The 'Stent' view of the west front of Eltham Palace, c.1653.*

sheet of 12 named palaces all listed in Stent's catalogue. The sheet is, however, incomplete and does not include the publisher's name.[112] No artist would have visited all these buildings to draw them for such insignificant prints and they must be copied from earlier views. A few of these, though not the original view of Eltham, can be identified. Another view of the palace, long since vanished, is also known to have existed. Painted by George Portman, it was produced in 1637 as one of a set of views of 'all the late Queen's joynture houses'[113] drawn 'in Landskipp in oyle' on the walls of a gallery in Oatlands Palace in Surrey. Its existence is known from a Parliamentary survey made of that palace in 1650.[114]

The 'Stent' view of Eltham Palace shows the most impressive side of the buildings, the western side with the three-storeyed royal apartments at each end of that front and a long two-storeyed building in the centre.[115] The great hall, then surmounted by a turret or lantern with the effigy of a lion above the lantern,[116] appears above the lower roof with, to its left, the western end of the palace

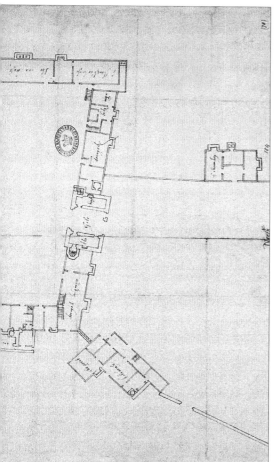

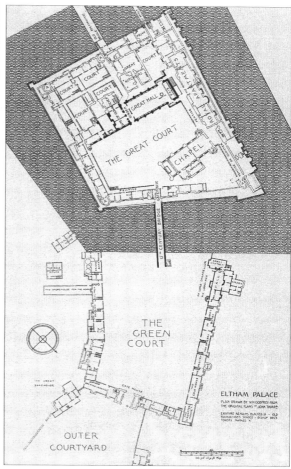

ELTHAM PALACE

PLAN DRAWN BY WM.GODFREY FROM
THE ORIGINAL PLANS BY JOHN THORPE

EXISTING REMAINS BLACKED IN – OLD
FOUNDATIONS SHADED · BISHOP BEC'S
TOWERS MARKED 'X'

THE GREAT COURT

THE GREEN COURT

OUTER COURTYARD

ELTHAM

chapel's roof.[117] The undated building record of Henry VIII's reign mentions an exit used by the king to leave the inner court, pointing to his apartments being at the south end of the western front of the palace, with the queen's apartments being at the north end of this front.[118] A comparison of the print with the inner court plan shows some features of the print, in particular the simultaneous view of both the north front and the bridge at the south-west corner, do not fit in with the close-up view of the buildings. The print view would appear to be a composite picture incorporating views of the buildings from several angles, views which did not include the north bridge as this is incorrectly depicted.[119] Also, although the palace was much out of repair by 1649,[120] this c.1653[121] print does not show disrepair. Either this aspect has been omitted or the views on which the print was based were made when the palace was still in good repair.

The bridge crossing the moat at its south-west corner appears in both the 1603-4 inner court plan and in the 'Stent' print[122] of 50 years later. It was probably the bridge built in the 1580s.[123] Another bridge 'towards the park'[124] had a drawbridge[125] and its foundations can still be seen in the centre of the south front of the inner court.[126] This particular bridge is not shown on the 1603-4 plan and it must therefore have been demolished after the 1520s when it was last recorded in a building account.[127] A new timber bridge was built on its site during the 1930s.[128]

The 1605 survey has a detailed record of the manorial lands in Eltham, but of the palace only records the area it covered, the area of the outer courtyard and that of the outer courtyard buildings, in one measurement.[129] The survey of 1649 is much more detailed as regards the palace buildings, these being referred to as 'comonly called Eltham howse'. The number of rooms in the main buildings is given, as well as those in the park lodges, distinguishing in the palace between those 'below stayres' on the ground floor and those 'above stayres' on the first and upper floors. The full description reads:

> one Faire Chappell, one greate Hall, thirty six Roomes and offices below stayres, with two large Cellers, and above stayres, in Lodgeings called the Kinges side, seaventeene, in Lodgeings called the Queenes side, Twlve, and in Lodgeings called the Princes side, Nine. In all Thirtie eight, with other necessary small Roomes, as Clossettes and the like, None garnished within (except only the said Chappell and Hall, both which are garnished with wainescote) but all covered with Lead and tiles; with one Greene outward Court ... incompassed with out howses erected on three sides of the said Court, consisting of about Thirtie five Bayes of Buildinges conteineinge in two stories seaventy eight Roomes or ther aboutes, formerly employed as Offices to the said Manour, Mansion or Court house ... [130]

The survey also records, 'The said Messuage, Mansion, Manour or Courthouse is much out of repaire, and soe not Tenentable ... '.[131] The palace buildings were valued, for their materials, in 1649 at £2,753.[132] In comparison Nonsuch Palace, another large building, was valued similarly a few months later at £7,020.[133]

Although the 1649 survey[134] does not record the names of the ground-floor rooms in the inner court, many of the rooms in the upper floors, above stairs, appear in earlier building accounts. Some of these were probably on second or third floors. The 17 rooms on the king's side would have included the king's closet,[135] privy closet[136] and study,[137] unless the first two were too small to count, with three further closets[138] with the arraying,[139] bed,[140] great chamber of state,[141] breakfast,[142] privy,[143] watching,[144] dining,[145] withdrawing[146] and presence[147] chambers. On the queen's side her 12 rooms[148] would have included her great and presence chambers,[149] and arraying,[150] bed,[151] privy,[152] dining[153] and withdrawing[154] chambers, besides a closet,[155] which may not be included in her 12 rooms. On the prince's side seven of his nine rooms[156] would have been his arraying,[157] bed,[158] dining,[159] great,[160] presence,[161] privy[162] and withdrawing[163] chambers with, in 1603–4, 'two little Clozetts'.[164]

The money spent in a single year on the maintenance or alteration of the buildings of Eltham Palace between 1559 and 1640 varied from under £2 to nearly £4,000,[165] the latter cost, in 1603–4,[166] including a new brick and stone frontage to the royal apartments on the western front of the inner court. Other years of above-average expenditure were 1565–74,[167] 1586–7,[168] 1622–5,[169] 1627–8[170] and 1631–3.[171] The gables of the great hall were replaced in brick in 1573–4,[172] while the 1586–7 repairs[173] included work on the queen's lodgings, perhaps carried out before an unrecorded visit by Elizabeth I. The repairs confirm the king's side apartments were at the south end of the west front and the queen's side apartments at the north end of this front[174] and show that the prince's side apartments were south-east of the great hall.[175] Other work included repairs to the palace kitchens in the 1580s and '90s.[176]

Out of doors a new timber bridge was built in 1583–5[177] and 1586–7,[178] while in 1583–5 seats were placed in the great arbour,[179] a feature presumably situated in the garden or park. The new bridge would have been at the south-west corner of the moat, allowing ready access to the park, and work on the kitchens suggests that hunting visits included meals at the palace. The building accounts show that prior to the last recorded repairs of 1639–40 the Eltham buildings were deteriorating, some decayed, others falling down, even after the expensive repairs of 1603–4.[180]

The buildings at Eltham that received particular attention after 1559 were those of the lodgings of the courtiers who were keepers of the houses, Sir Christopher Hatton,[181] Lord North,[182] Sir John Stanhope[183] and the Earl of Dorset,[184] some of whom are mentioned by their more important official posts of Lord Chancellor and Vice-Chamberlain. The other lodgings were not repaired, thus showing the court no longer stayed at Eltham as it had done in the past.

Other buildings at Eltham kept in repair during these years were the park lodges. In 1607–9 Sir Roger Aston's lodge, in the Little Park, was given a water supply,[185] while in 1623–6 a new lodge was built in the Great Park for the chief ranger, Patrick Maule.[186] Each park had a lodge, with the Great Park having both a lodge and an 'old Lodge'. This park covered 612 acres, surrounded by paling and the brick orchard wall; in 1605 the two totalled 1,457 perches (26,290 yards) in length. In that year the Great Park had 50 oak trees and 510 deer, of which 150 were stags.[187] By 1649 the park was slightly smaller, with 596 acres, and had 1,200 trees fit for Navy use and 1,062 others described as 'for the most part old Dottrelles and Decayed trees, good for Little save the fyre'. In 1605 it had between three and four trees to the acre and grazing for slightly over one deer to the acre. The Old, Middle or Little Park, with 308 acres in 1605 (333 in 1649), was surrounded by 948 perches (17,216 yards) of paling and held 250 oak trees and 240 deer, including 47 stags. In 1649 this park had 1,000 trees suitable for use by the Navy and 324 inferior trees, figures very similar for both trees and deer per acre to the Great Park. Horne, Lee or New Park was different. Though comparable in size to Middle Park (345 acres in 1605, 336 in 1649), with paling

988 perches (17,828 yards) long, it had many more trees than either of the other two parks, 2,740 oak trees in 1605, and 1,700 fit for Navy use and 2,620 old trees in 1649. The 1605 survey shows it then had 240 deer, of which 55 were stags. Its deer figures per acre are similar to the other two parks, but it was much more heavily forested, with between 12 and 13 trees to the acre.[188] The parks in 1649, as in earlier days, still included enclosed meadows and paddocks to provide winter feed for the deer.[189]

Orders, presumably at royal instigation, were issued under Mary I in 1556,[190] Elizabeth I in 1559,[191] James I in 1605,[192] 1608[193] and 1620,[194] and Charles I in 1637,[195] 1638[196] and 1639[197] for the better preservation of the deer and game at Eltham. The parks were also slightly enlarged as late as 1604-5.[198] Both Elizabeth I[199] and James I[200] hunted in the parks at Eltham but no hunting visits to Eltham by Charles I are recorded.

Both the game and the trees in Eltham's parks were coveted by the less law-abiding members of the local community, who committed a number of crimes in the parks. In 1578 a tree was cut down, besides 'other unlawful acts'.[201] Eighteen years later Robert Whirret was caught taking partridges near the palace,[202] while at an unrecorded date Michael Leigh and William Blood were inprisoned in the Fleet prison in London for killing a stag in the Great Park.[203] Other recorded crimes there were, in 1620, the stealing of fawns[204] and the beating down of beech mast to provide food for pigs.[205] Unspecified 'wasts and spoils' were also committed there in c.1644.[206] The orders, issued in 1620 by the Privy Council, that no one was to enter the parks at Eltham when the deer were fawning must have been a response to the stealing of fawns mentioned in the same year. Such orders were sent to the local justices, who had to pass them on to the clergy in Eltham to declare to their congregations.[207]

Although some wood was cut down in the parks for sale in 1644-5,[208] the major part of the destruction of the trees there, noted in 1656 by John Evelyn,[209] must have occurred under the Commonwealth in and after 1649. From these years local folk memory recalled nearly a century later that 'for many months the Roads were fill'd with the Carriage of Timber that the Collonnel cutt down and sold'.[210] Details, however, were not always remembered correctly in later years, and in 1731 a visitor was told that General Ireton had pulled down the palace and cut down the woods.[211] Colonel Rich was not responsible for all the destruction, for some cutting down of mature trees was the work of the commissioners of the Commonwealth navy in the early 1650s and trees were also cut down in the early 1670s after the Restoration.[212]

After 1559 the Eltham officials were in a similar position to those holding these positions in earlier times. The senior posts were held by influential courtiers like Sir Christopher Hatton, holding several official positions there at the same time.[213] Another pluralist office holder at Eltham was Roger, Lord North, who in 1597 was steward, purveyor of woods, purveyor and keeper of the houses, gardens, Corby Hall and all three Eltham parks.[214] These positions were not always held by the same person, as in 1649 Sir Thomas Walsingham was high steward there,[215] Patrick Maule chief ranger and master of game for the Great Park,[216] with Sir Theodore de Mayerne holding the same two posts for Horne Park.[217]

The actual duties of these offices were carried out by deputies appointed by the office holders, in 1649 by Thomas Maule, a cousin of Patrick Maule, for the Great Park,[218] and by Thomas Slyn, underkeeper, for Horne Park.[219] During the 1640s and 1650s Parliament raised money by fining Royalists, including some who were officeholders at Eltham. Patrick Maule was fortunate as he was let off a composition or fine,[220] but Edward Panton, the keeper of the palace, was unlucky as, in spite of his having carried out 'a particular service to Parliament', he had to compound for his estate,[221] as had the Earl of Dorset, keeper of the manor.[222] Patrick Maule's office was valued at £80 a year,[223] Edward Panton's at only £20.[224]

Court rolls survive for Eltham for the early and mid-17th century and show that the manor then included parts of Woolwich, Mottingham and Foots Cray as well as Eltham itself. The manorial court then met once a year and in 1611–16, the years covered by the earliest surviving court rolls, it was presided over by the deputy steward, William Wideson. The court appointed the manorial officials for the forthcoming year, these being borsholders, constables and ale or beer tasters for Eltham and Woolwich and borsholders only for Mottingham and Foots Cray.[225] Anyone who refused to take up the position to which he was appointed was fined £1, as occurred in 1655.[226] The court passed regulations concerning roads, common land, animals, food and travellers, throwing some light on the realities of 17th-century Eltham life.[227]

Among the regulations are some that order the regular scouring of ditches, those who neglected this duty being fined,[228] the removal of encroachments on common land,[229] the cutting back of hedges overhanging the roads[230] and the removal of rubbish which had accumulated on the roads outside private houses.[231] Those who left diseased horses on common land,[232] or allowed animals to feed on roadside verges,[233] were also to be fined, as were those who kept unringed pigs.[234] Concern for public health can also be seen in regulations, and fines, for those selling unwholesome meat[235] and underweight bread.[236]

As a main road between London and Kent passed through Eltham, travellers on it were a subject of concern lest they become a burden on the parish. One manorial court regulation with this in mind, though perhaps impractical, laid down in 1611 that householders were not to harbour subtenants, travellers or unknown men without the permission of the steward of the manor and six of the 'principal homage men' of the manor. For a month's transgression of this order there was a fine of 10s.,[237] a sum increased in 1655 to 12d. a night, when it was added that if the person harboured was a woman with child the fine was 10s. a night, an inhumane attempt to avoid a possible burden on the parish.[238]

Nearly one hundred and sixty wills of Eltham inhabitants dying between 1559 and 1663 are known and these, with the parish burial register beginning in 1583, throw light on further aspects of local life. As in earlier times most wills were left by the wealthier part of the community but, compared to early Tudor Eltham, they include a much higher proportion of women's wills, forming about one third of the total. Another comparison, of the wills with the post-1583 burial register, shows that wills are available for about one in six of the deceased adult male population. The largest number of recorded burials took place in March and October, the smallest number in July, and of the 1,500 burials recorded, no fewer than 600 were of children, a reminder of the high child death rate in Britain until very recent years. Incidentally, not all the children buried in Eltham were from the parish, so some must have been sent out of London to avoid plague outbreaks, as Pepys records during the Great Plague of 1665. The burial register also confirms, in an unusual way, the prominent local position of the Roper family, as it includes the burials of 16 of their servants, while no other local family is represented by more than two servants' deaths.[239]

The decline in the use of Eltham Palace by royalty and the court in this period compared to early Tudor times is not reflected in the number of wills and burials of local people holding minor offices at court. Under Elizabeth I and her two Stuart successors, Eltham wills include Hughe Tenche, 'one of the yeoman Usshers of the Quenes majestyes chamber' (1562),[240] John (1599)[241] and Thomas (1601) Reston,[242] brothers and queen's trumpeters, John Phillips, yeoman of the King's household (1609),[243] William Bull, 'Master gunner of Win(d)sor Castle' (1618),[244] and John Philipott, Norroy King of Arms (1645).[245] Two others with court connections were Katherine Flower, 'widowe (of) Frauncis Flower, Esquier, one of her Majestes gentlemen pencioner(s)' (1598),[246] and John Stobes, king's yeoman, who is mentioned in a will left by another local man (1612)[247] as coming from Eltham. Francis Flower was a follower of Sir Christopher Hatton and owned a house in Eltham, where he was keeper of the Great Park. He was also an MP.[248] Another of the queen's pensioners with a house in Eltham was George Gifford, arrested in 1586 on suspicion of involvement in Babington's plot against Elizabeth I. Later released, he may have been a double agent as, in spite of being the head of a Catholic family in Hampshire, he held a court position. A man of doubtful character, he was suspected of a series of crimes but prospered in later life, changed his religion and was knighted by James I.[249]

Other royal servants in Eltham were John Smythson, alias Taylor (1585),[250] first recorded as a yeoman of the queen's privy kitchen and who, by 1585 when he made his will, had become chief master cook to the queen. His son-in-law, Hughe Miller, was a royal footman in 1585,[251] later keeper of the Little Park[252] and by the time of his death in 1615 a local gentleman farmer.[253] Two others connected with John Smythson were Henry Smythson and John Poste, who in 1585 were children of the queen's kitchen.[254] Eltham's burial records also include Simon May, park keeper (1575),[255] Cornelius Orts, a Dutch 'servaunte unto the King for providing haukes under Sir Anthony Pell' (1621),[256] and Anne Twiste, 'formerly laundress to Queen Elizabeth' (1624).[257] Another resident of Eltham with this surname was Thomas Twiste, a gentleman who was 'one of H.M. ordinary servants' and is mentioned in the will of another Eltham man (1577).[258] Thomas Sampson, of the Chapel Royal, was a further local royal servant. Living in the parish in 1581,[259] he died in 1615[260] and would seem to have been wealthy as when his house was burgled in 1603 he lost a parcel-gilt basin and ewer, two gilt bowls, a gilt salt, 10 silver spoons and £59 in money.[261]

After 1559 religion is rarely mentioned in these wills. Exceptions are, in 1593, 20s. left for 'three sermons to be made after my deathe' in the parish church,[262] a bequest in 1612 of £6 to be spent at 10s. a year 'to hyre a preacher at Midsomer Daye … to instructe youthe in the feare of God',[263] and a 1642 bequest of 8s. to the vicar of Eltham to preach a sermon on 5 November 'as long as pleases him'.[264] These bequests show Protestant sentiments, unlike the Catholic ones mentioned earlier from before the Reformation and then from Mary I's reign. Charity of a non–religious kind mostly took the form of bequests to the poor of sums ranging from 4d. up to £10.[265] Bequests were also given in kind,[266] as in the case of 'three dossone of brede and astand of all' to be distributed at a 1569 funeral.[267] A later bequest of bread stated that only this should be given out, 'not … money for the most of them will be Drunken' (1635).[268]

A number of Eltham wills, particularly those made between 1590 and 1630, are very informative concerning dress bequests. Women's wills often list what must have been favourite dresses,[269] as in the case of 'my newe silke Grograin gowne … my best hatt with the pearle band … and my petticote of Stammelle garded with velvett and a foreparte of Tuffe Taffatie' (1608).[270] Men's bequests are less descriptive[271] but one mentions 'my Cloake laide with two gould galone lace' (1624)[272] and others bequeath hose[273] and even a pair of breeches.[274] Hats, both men's and women's,[275] ruffs[276] and handkerchiefs[277] are also mentioned. Women's dress first mentioned in this period are aprons,[278] cross clothes (linen cloths worn across the forehead),[279] smokes,[280] unrecorded in the *OED*, and a scarf.[281] Comparison with early Tudor Eltham wills shows a striking increase in the number of materials mentioned in wills, these including silk, grogram, watchet and stammelle, some being used in dress and others in furnishings.[282]

Wall furnishings first appearing in Eltham wills in these years are 'paynted Clothes' (1600)[283] and 'Tapestrie or Arras' (1606).[284] Overseas items are French (1608)[285] and Danish (1616)[286] chests, Italian tables (1607)[287] and cypress chests (1607 and 1608).[288] The single most interesting will is Lucy Rooper's. Widow of Thomas Roper, of the local Catholic gentry family previously mentioned, her dress bequests include a 'Gowne of Tufted Taffata … wroughte velvett kirtle … Petticoate of crymosyn damaske … (with a) Gowne of sylke mockadoe and a kirtle of stitched Taffata with Stomacher and Sleeves to the same'. Her other bequests include two family portraits, one of her late husband, the other of her father, Sir Anthony Browne, and a 'Cupboard with divers drawinge Boxes in the same' (1606).[289] Her son, Sir William Rooper, was the only Eltham man wealthy enough in this period to bequeath a coach and horses and mourning dress for 38 mourners who were family members, friends and servants. The family link with Sir Thomas More is mentioned in a bequest to his widow of a book by Sir Thomas (1628).[290]

Strife in two Eltham families appears in two wills, one left by John Forde, vicar of Eltham, who states in his will that it was made after 'the departure of my wife Mary Ford Maie 10 1626'.[291] The other will was left by Hughe Edwardes, who bequeathed to his 'daughter Barberie, because shee thinkes that I have lived too long … twelve pence in monie and nothing els' (1627).[292] A grant of letters of administration in the same year interestingly refers to the estate of Ingram Frizer, remembered in English literary history as the man who killed Christopher Marlowe in 1595 during a brawl in a public house in Deptford.[293]

The best surviving information concerning an Eltham house during this period, one belonging to a prosperous local man, is to be seen in the 1615 inventory of the home of Hughe Miller, previously mentioned for his court connections.

His home was a two-storeyed farm building with 20 rooms, a cellar and precincts including a farmyard, a barn, a stable and a building that had formerly housed a bull. The 11 ground-floor rooms were a hall, two parlours, a nursery, a kitchen with two associated rooms, further rooms used for pastry, milk and cheese, and a great chamber. Upstairs rooms included a study and a gallery. Four of the ground-floor rooms, the hall, the two parlours and the nursery, were wainscoted.

Hughe Miller's property included nine bedsteads. Of these, six were on the upper floor, two in the great chamber on the ground floor and one was stored in the building that had formerly housed a bull. The beds for these bedsteads had fillings of wool, flock and, in one bed, straw. Some of the walls of the house were hung with painted cloths and painted leather hangings, while seating consisted of settles, chairs, benches, stools and a form. The two parlours had five framed tables between them, a broken round table stood in the nursery and another round table at the head of the stairs. In the great chamber the furnishings included a 'paire of playing tables' (a backgammon board) and six pictures. A similar number of pictures and four escutcheons of arms decorated the great parlour. Hughe Miller's books were kept in a chamber on the first floor, above the cellar, and consisted of an old bible, an old service book and 11 other books. Storage was provided by court cupboards, a trunk, a chest and some shelves.

Hughe Miller's inventory provides information on his farming as well as his furnishings. One room held his seed corn and the inventory shows that his servants made butter and cheese, operated a still and beat hemp, from which some of his sheets were made. His farm livestock consisted of a yoke of oxen, a pair of steers, three milking cows, a bullock, two yearling heifers, two mares and five pigs.[294] Hughe Miller's will also survives but, unfortunately, it is not particularly informative.[295] The 1605 survey of the manor, however, records that in that year he leased about fifty acres of crown land on which, judging by his seed corn, he would have grown oats, barley, flax and hemp. Part of the land he farmed would have been under grass on which he would have grazed his livestock.[296] Another form of agriculture practised on a small scale in Eltham was that of Sir Theodore de Mayerne, who was keeper, chief ranger and master of game of Horn Park, as well as being chief physician to both James I and Charles I. In 1647 he grew herbs for medicinal use 'in vivario meo Horne Park', presumably in the garden attached to Horn Park lodge, recorded in 1649 as covering three rods, including houses, a garden and an orchard.[297]

IX

ELTHAM AND THE SHAW CROWN TENANCY

I ... bring (to) notice the intended demolition of the once splendid hall of Eltham-palace. ...
This venerable relic, beautiful as a specimen of art, and doubly interesting for its historical
associations, is doomed ... To the architectural antiquary its loss is irreparable.

(Letter by E.I.C. in the *Gentleman's Magazine*, May 1828)

It is probable that most of Eltham Palace was demolished under the
Commonwealth during the 1650s. The ruins seen by John Evelyn in 1656[1]
were to be described in the 1663 lease of the palace site as 'all that the scite of
the Capitall Messuage, Mansion house or Pallace comonly Called ... by the name
of Eltham Courthouse dureinge the late troubles ... ruinated and almost quite
Demolished' and also as 'the Scite of the Mansion House called Eltham Court,
now ruined'. At that time the outer court buildings consisted of 24 'tenements in
the ... occupation of severall tenants', while the Great Park had been 'during the
late troubles Disparked and distroyed and converted into Arrable, meadow and
pasture ground',[2] a fate which a later 1699 lease shows us had also overtaken the
other two parks.[3]

From this destruction the great hall was to survive, becoming a barn, though
without its turret, while its lead roofing was replaced by tiles.[4] Some years seem to
have elapsed between the removal of the lead from its roof and its replacement by
tiles, as 'distinct signs of weathering' were noted on the roof timbers when repairs
were made to the great hall during the present century.[5] The years between 1653,
when Colonel Rich bought the palace site,[6] and 1663, when the Restoration lease
was granted,[7] are the likely years when the great hall roof was without its covering.
Other changes made to the hall were the removal of the southern side of the south
oriel, replaced by tall doors to allow farm carts to enter,[8] the blocking-up of the
windows with bricks in place of glass,[9] and the removal of the wainscoting and
most of the other woodwork within the building.[10] Apart from the hall, a building
situated to the east of it[11] and another building at the entrance to the former inner
court also survived,[12] as did the western side of the outer court[13] and the great
bridge to the north of the former inner court.[14]

A new farm building was erected within the moat, apparently soon after
the Restoration, according to mid-18th-century information.[15] This was sited
between the great hall and the north bridge and can be seen from the north in
the 1735 Buck print[16] and in more detail from the south in the 1741 Robinson

13 *Sir John Shaw, 4th Bt, and his family at Eltham Lodge, 1767, Arthur Devis.*

plan. The latter also shows the causeway across the moat to the south, part of a road between Eltham and Mottingham that passed between the great hall and the surviving fragment of the palace situated to the east of the hall.[17] The earliest view of the hall in use as a barn dates from 1724.[18]

When the Restoration settlement returned Crown property to its former owners, Henrietta Maria, now queen dowager, recovered her manor of Eltham which was controlled by her trustees. The immediate post-1660 tenant was Thomas Panton, lord of the manor in 1663 and 1666-7.[19] New leases of the manor were granted in 1663 by the queen dowager's trustees, who divided it up, the Great Park and the site of the former palace going to Sir John Shaw, Sir Nicholas Crisp, Ellys Crisp and Randolph Isaakson, the Little Park and the manor to Thomas Panton, Horn Park to Sir William Swanne and William Swanne, and other land in Eltham to Ellys Crisp and Randolph Isaakson.[20] By 1667-8, however, Sir John Shaw held a Crown lease of the whole manor[21] and in the latter year was lord of the manor.[22] In 1672 he was paying rent for the whole manor including its three parks.[23]

Under the Commonwealth John Shaw was a banker in Flanders, where he advanced money to the Royalists for the purchase of arms and for the use of the exiled Charles II. On good authority he has been described as 'the principal channel of communication between the English Royalists and the exiled Court'.[24] The principal adviser to Charles II, the future Earl of Clarendon, wrote of him in a letter written shortly before the Restoration that he was someone 'without whom at this time the King could not get bread'.[25] Reference to his services in these years are also to be found in an Eltham lease signed by the King in 1679 as 'many … performed unto us in the time of our Exile togeither with his Greate Loyaltie and suffereinge for us'.[26] Knighted in July 1660,[27] three months after the Restoration, it is not surprising that for his services he was given the Eltham lease on advantageous terms, besides his other rewards and official positions.[28]

The terms of the 1663 Great Park lease included the repair and maintenance of its houses[29] and Sir John must have begun work on the replacement or improvement of one of its lodges soon after the grant, for by the time John Evelyn visited Eltham Lodge in July 1664 the house is described by him as 'now building'.[30] Its name reflects the fact that the new house was either on or very close to the site of one of the two Great Park lodges. Designed in English Renaissance style by Hugh May, who also designed new state apartments at Windsor Castle, it was the home of the Shaw family for over a century before being leased to tenants.[31] After the succession of crown leases to the Shaw family[32] ended in 1838,[33] the Crown found other tenants for the house, firstly private ones, then the Eltham Golf Club[34] and most recently the Royal Blackheath Golf Club, who use Eltham Lodge as a clubhouse and the former Great Park as their golf course.[35]

Sir John, apart from his knighthood,[36] received an annuity of £500 in 1660[37] and was created a baronet five years later,[38] an honour still borne by his descendants, the Best-Shaw family, today.[39] He was also given several official appointments, including those of a trusteee of the queen's lands, surveyor of the king's woods and farmer of the customs, besides being MP for Lyme Regis.[40] Samuel Pepys, who knew Sir John slightly during his diary-keeping years in the 1660s,[41] mentions that his friend Sir William Coventry commented sarcastically of Sir John that he was 'a miracle of a man for ... he executes more places than any man in England ... the most inconsistent (with each other) in the world'.[42]

The second, third and fourth Shaw baronets, all with the same name as Sir John, followed him in the baronetcy in 1680, 1721 and 1739, succeeded in 1779 and 1831 by the fifth and sixth baronets, Sir John Gregory Shaw and Sir John Kenward Shaw, a father-to-son succession for six generations.[43] The Eltham estate lease was renewed to the family on varying terms until 1810, when the last lease renewal, to expire in 1838, was granted to the family.[44] The last link between Eltham and the Shaw family broke in 1840 with the death of the Rev. J.K. Shaw Brooke, son of the fourth baronet, vicar of Eltham for over fifty years and well-regarded there. Seven years before his death a Jubilee dinner was arranged to celebrate his service, the parishioners assembling in the Court Yard before marching in procession to the vicarage field for a dinner followed by sports and a fireworks display.[45]

The ending of the succession of renewals of the Eltham crown lease to the Shaw family can be attributed to the acts of the fifth baronet after the lease had been renewed to him in 1810.[46] Taking the maximum advantage of his new lease and the exceptionally high prices given for agricultural produce at the time, he put the farm tenancies in Eltham up to public auction, obtaining £25,000 in fines from tenants who promised to pay high rents in the expectation of continuing high prices for their produce. Former tenants who had recently improved their farms, relying as in the past on having their leases renewed, had expected more considerate treatment from their landlord. Sir John Gregory Shaw had lost the vital goodwill of the Crown officials concerned with leases by his acts and the Shaw family, 'entitled to claim the first offer of a new lease of the estate', had forfeited this goodwill by failing to consider the interests of their former tenants. After 1822, following the end of the wars with France that had kept farm produce prices high, prices were depressed and the new Eltham tenants found themselves unable to pay the high rents. They asked their landlord for an abatement off their rents, he in turn asked the Woods and Forests officials for a reduction in his own Crown rent. Reminded of the high profits he had made by putting the Eltham farm leases up to auction, his request was refused, it being thought that he had breached the covenant made with the Crown and had also let the estate get into a poor condition. When the Eltham Crown lease came up for renewal in 1838 it was not renewed to the Shaw family.[47]

During the 175 years that the Shaw family held the Crown lease of Eltham manor, its manorial court, as happened in other places, gradually ceased to function. It met annually until 1719 but after that year, except in the early 1730s, it met at longer intervals of up to 10 years. The court records show the gradual disappearance of subjects seen in earlier records such as the brewing of beer, the keeping of pigs, flyblown meat and false weights. The later courts, of which the last met in 1869, were mostly concerned with the reliefs that had to be paid when tenants died and with fining those who encroached upon common land.[48] The court of the manor was no longer concerned with the welfare of the local community but only with the court as a source of income.

The appearance of the great hall and its immediate surroundings can be seen in some detail in the 1741 Samuel Robinson plan of the moated site[49] and in a large number of watercolours, drawings and prints.[50] The 1741 plan is of particular interest in that it shows, unlike later views, the moat and northern part of the moated area as planted with trees, which appear to be an orchard. It also depicts the farmhouse, mentioned earlier, a shed and summerhouse, these last two at the north-west and north-east corners of the moated area, and a cartshed to the south of the hall.[51] Shortly before 1749 a year's rent was spent on repairs, which must have removed the Charles II farmhouse, whose function passed to the surviving palace building east of the great hall, and built the cottage next to the north door of the hall. The outer courtyard is also found to have its own farmhouse.[52] The cottage, seen in many later views,[53] had occupants who, in the next century, acted as guides to the hall, though one visitor comments that the information they provided was very inaccurate.[54] A further alteration to the moated area, dating from about the mid-18th century, was damage to the moat wall on its south-east side. Undamaged in the 1741 plan,[55] a 1787 print by Paul Sandby shows this part of the wall as supported by the buttresses still found there today.[56]

The great hall, once it had been altered for use as a barn, may have changed little (apart from the delapidation caused by lack of maintenance and by vandalism that damaged the screen at the east end of the hall),[57] until storm damage to the roof in the winter of 1827 was followed by the repairs carried out in 1828.[58] The area within the moat was tidied up early in the 19th century. On the other hand, a row of pigsties was placed along the outer wall of the south side of the hall in the early 1820s.[59]

It is impossible to place full reliance on the accuracy of the many views of the hall and its immediate surroundings. Comparison of two views of the hall from about the same date makes it impossible to say which is correct. Grimm's watercolours of the interior of the hall show it empty and tidy,[60] other views of a few years later show the hall cluttered with carts and hay.[61] The latter may be more correct, as a letter written in 1828 describes the east end of the hall as containing cow stalls with a granary floor above them, the centre of the hall occupied by a threshing machine and a horse wheel and another threshing machine at the

14 *The east end of the interior of the great hall, 1779, S.H. Grimm.*

west end of the hall.[62] As regards the exterior, two Paul Sandby views of the west frontage of the moat in the 1780s differ in that one shows the moat as under grass while the other shows the same area under water.[63] A striking example of the unreliability of pictures can be seen in the contrast between the desolate appearance of the area round the hall in a drawing made in 1827 by Joseph Nash;[64] and the picturesquely romantic view of the same area in a print published in 1830 based on Nash's drawing.[65] Views of what may be part of the old palace at the south end of the north bridge can be seen in the 1735 Buck view, an altered version in a Sandby view of the 1780s and in 1811 but not in Robinson's much earlier 1741 plan.[66] A small modern building seen in Buck's print at the north-west corner of the moat is also omitted from Robinson's plan of the site in 1741.[67]

After the destruction of most of the palace in the mid–17th century, interest in what remained, and in the history of the palace, seems to have been at a very low ebb for many years as no visitors' descriptions, official records, local history accounts, prints or drawings are known of the palace site after 1663 until it is mentioned in a history of Kent published in 1719.[68] During this blank period of its history some treasure hunting and removal of building materials from the site

Clockwise from top: 15 *West end of the great hall, early 19th century, T. Baynes;* **16** *The great hall from the south, 1724, W. Stukeley;* **17** *The great hall from the north, 1787, attributed to P. Sandby;* **18** *West end of the great hall, 1779, S.H. Grimm.*

seems to have occurred. An antiquarian diarist recorded in 1722 that a jewelled crozier had been found underground at Eltham 'some time since',[69] and a local public house has a fireplace thought to have been removed from the palace.[70] Defoe, in his description of his travels around Britain published in the late 1720s, says that little or nothing had survived of the palace, showing that he could hardly have visited the site where the bridge and hall, as well as the moat walls and part of the outer court, still survived.[71]

During the 1720s some antiquarian interest in the palace remains and its history was expressed in accounts in Harris's *History of Kent*, published in 1719,[72] and in a survey of British antiquities by Cox that appeared in 1720.[73] Five artists whose drawings have survived also visited the palace site between 1724 and 1741. The first of these was William Stukeley, later well-known for his interests in prehistoric and Roman antiquities and in the Druids, who came in 1724,[74] followed by others in 1727,[75] 1733,[76] 1735[77] and 1741.[78] Visitors with a different purpose were Charles Wesley and some of his local followers, to whom he preached an outspoken sermon in the hall on 16 June 1740.[79]

The ancient links between Eltham and the royal family were, at least nominally, renewed in 1726 when Frederick Lewis, grandson of George I, was created Earl of Eltham, a title that passed to his son, the future George III, on his father's death in 1751. The title was absorbed in the Crown on the accession of George III in 1760,[80] not to be revived until 1917 when HSH Adolphus, Prince of Teck, was created Marquess of Cambridge and Earl of Eltham as part of the

creation of the House of Windsor in that year.[81] On the Earl's death 10 years later the title passed to his son George, only to become extinct in 1981 when the latter died without leaving male heirs.[82]

Harris, in describing the history of Eltham Palace in his history of Kent, mentions the use of the hall as a barn, its roof and the appearance of the moated site of the former palace, thus showing that he, or someone on his behalf, had actually visited the site. His description, and that by Cox,[83] may have stimulated antiquarian interest in Eltham and visits by artists, but only one description of a visit to the hall is known from the years immediately following the publication of these books. Viscount Percival, in his diary for July 1731, records being taken there by a cousin living in Eltham. He compares the hall to the one at Westminster, describing it as 'a very noble lofty building … about two thirds as long, large and high' as the other. He also states that General Ireton, a name given erroneously in place of Colonel Rich, had pulled down most of the palace buildings besides selling the lead from the hall roof and cutting down the park trees. The tenant farmer, acting as their guide, told them that he had travelled for a quarter of a mile along a tunnel leading from the palace site towards Greenwich, and was also presumably the source of the diary statements that the building to the east of the hall was called King John's bedchamber apartment and that Charles I was supposed to have lived at the palace as a child, the last assertion perhaps based on the visits to Eltham, as children, of Henry VIII and Elizabeth I.[84]

Another visitor to record local traditions about the history of the palace was Samuel Robinson, in 1741. In a brief history of the palace, attached to his plan of the site, he mentions the destruction of the park woods by Colonel Panton (another error for the name of Colonel Rich), the approximate date of the new farmhouse within the moat, and the name of the farm tenant, Thomas Newland.[85] His immediate predecessor as tenant had been William Forty.[86] A third visitor to record his impressions of the site was the antiquary John Loveday who came there in April 1746, noting the outer court, the porter's lodge that appears in the 1735 Buck print and the 'curious' roof of the great hall, which, he states, was made of Irish oak.[87] Another record showing that the hall was still being visited is one of 1782, which states that vandals had damaged the hall screen earlier that century.[88]

A second and longer period of interest in the hall and the history of the palace began around 1775 and lasted until at least the 1840s. During these years there was a growing interest in all aspects of English history, especially in its ancient buildings, of which Eltham's great hall was a magnificent specimen in a state of fashionably romantic decay. Interest in the hall may perhaps have been stimulated by the recent publication of histories of Kent and of the environs of London, which included accounts of the surviving buildings at Eltham and of the history of the palace. Two county histories, by Seymour[89] and Hasted, appeared in 1776 and 1778, the latter including Thorpe's plan of the outer court at Eltham.[90] The latter year also witnessed the exhibition of a view of the great hall by John Feary at the Royal Academy,[91] the first of a number of views of it to be shown there or at other art exhibitions over the following century-and-a-half.[92] Another visiting artist, in 1779, was Samuel Grimm, who produced several watercolours of the hall, three of which were engraved to illustrate a 1782 article on the palace in the newly founded

publication of the Society of Antiquaries, *Archaeologia*.[93] Another competent artist
to draw the great hall at about this date was Thomas Hearne, whose views of it
were sold at auction early in the following century.[94] Their present location, like
that of the hall view by Feary, is at present unknown.

Paul Sandby, drawing master at the Royal Military Academy, Woolwich,
and an accomplished topographical artist, visited and drew the great hall from
several different viewpoints. Three of his aquatints depict it, and two of these
were published in 1782 and 1787.[95] Two younger artists to visit the hall, Thomas
Girtin and J.M.W. Turner, produced what are probably the finest watercolours of
the hall.[96] A number of writers also produced brief accounts of the history of the
palace, one being Daniel Lysons, who wrote the *Environs of London*.[97] Many artists
now little known also drew the hall and bridge as well as those already mentioned.
Some of their work was reproduced as prints.[98]

Late in 1827 Jeffry Wyatt, knighted a year later for his work at Windsor Castle,
visited Eltham's great hall and had drawings made of it to show George IV, with
the aim of moving the great hall roof to Windsor. This proved to be impossible
as the roof was too decayed to be moved,[99] in spite of temporary repairs carried
out on it in 1824. By now, as an official report stated in 1823, the hall was 'in
a very ruinous state arising from its great age, its exposed position on elevated
ground, and the little attention ... paid (to it) for many years past'.[100] Age and
neglect were soon afterwards to be nearly fatal for the future of the hall, when a
gale in October 1827 damaged the roof[101] and, as a result, the Treasury informed
the Department of Woods and Forests, responsible for Eltham and other Crown
estates, in December 'that this building should be taken down'. Plans were then
begun to replace the great hall with a barn and a modern farm building.[102] Its
appearance as a barn early in 1828 is described as follows: 'The interior is now
fitted up at the east end with a range of cow stalls and a granary floor over; in the
centre is a thrashing machine & horse wheel firmly fixed in the ground; at the
west end is a boarded thrashing floor ...'.[103]

When the news of the Treasury decision reached those with an interest
in ancient buildings it caused an outcry in the press and expressions of support
for its preservation in Parliament.[104] Echoes of this controversy appear in a letter
written to the Department of Woods and Forests in February 1828 by Robert
Saunders, the tenant of Court House Farm on the site of the old palace. He
informed the department that several artists were then at work on 'Architectural
and Picturesque Drawings for Publication' of the hall and 'they were anxious for
a few more weeks in order to complete their work'. His letter also refers to an
unnamed 'gentleman [who] has been down today who was very urgent with me
to suggest some plan which may obviate the necessity of its immediate removal'.
The writer himself also expresses his concern for the hall, referring to 'the great
interest I feel in this most beautiful specimen of Gothic Architecture' and to
his hope that its 'proportions and ornaments may yet be preserved in a uniform
and complete detached Publication of all its parts ... which some draftsmen are
now employed about'.[105] In mid-July 1828 the subject of the preservation of the
hall was raised in a debate in the House of Lords by the Marquess of Lansdowne
and Viscount Darnley.[106] This intervention and the letters in the press must have

19 *Eltham Palace from the south-east, 1787, P. Sandby.*

turned the scale and altered the Treasury's decision, although there is no official record of the reasons for the change of heart. On 7 August the Woods and Forests Department wrote to their architect, Robert Smirke, to inform him that the hall was to be preserved, although with a minimum expenditure of government funds. The first campaign to preserve an ancient building had been successful.[107]

Repairs to the hall, costing a little under £800, were carried out at Eltham late in 1828, with the hall continuing to be used as a barn.[108] Though these repairs preserved the building, including its magnificent roof, the work had certain unfortunate effects, some permanent and others temporary. Perhaps the most important permanent effect on the hall was the removal of the peaked roofs over the two oriels, these being replaced by flat roofs. The crenellated north parapet of the hall was also altered, becoming a plain parapet.[109] A more obtrusive alteration, which, though temporary, lasted into the opening years of the 20th century, was the placement of huge timber beams in the hall to support the roof.[110] To fix these in position, small sections of the original beams were cut into to hold these temporary supports. The insertion of these beams into the hall obscured the view of the roof from below and it is possible that this reduced public interest in the hall, its principal beauty being in the design and craftsmanship of its timber roof.[111]

The threat to the hall and the consequent publicity must have provided the impetus for the publication in 1828 of two books concerned with the great hall and the history of the palace. J.C. Buckler, a topographical artist like his father, John, had drawn the great hall some years before 1828 and he now revisited it to make further drawings. His architectural knowledge of the hall and similar buildings elsewhere enabled him to make valuable comparisons between them, including the location of the hall within the moat as compared to others.[112] The other book, by Dunnage and Laver, is a detailed record of all aspects of the architecture of the hall and, if it had been demolished, this work would have provided an invaluable source of information which would otherwise have been lost.[113] Both books also

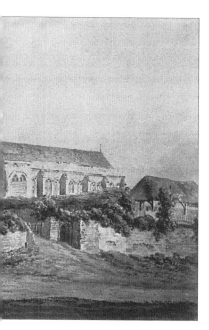

20 *Eltham Palace from the south-west, c.1785, P. Sandby.*

21 *The great hall from the north, 1791, J.M.W. Turner.*

used chronicle evidence to record something of the history of the palace. A third book, A.G. Pugin's *Examples of Gothic Architecture*, also includes detailed views of the architecture of the hall.[114] Published in 1831, it was supplemented by a book of views of his 'Examples', these including prints of the hall based on drawings made of it by Joseph Nash in 1827.[115] Three further books by Pugin also mention or illustrate different aspects of the great hall at Eltham.[116]

Some years before the repair of the hall, it was correctly dated for the first time, when in 1823 Joseph Gayfree, writing to Robert Saunders, mentioned that he had identified the personal emblems of Edward IV carved in stone both inside and outside the great hall.[117] Four years later, in 1827, another aspect of the palace was given publicity, the bargeboarding of the gables on the surviving palace building to the east of the hall. This, with aspects of other ancient buildings elsewhere, was illustrated in a book by John Hunt, who thought that copies of these ancient features could be incorporated in new 'Gothic style' buildings erected for the use of the clergy.[118] It would be interesting to learn if parsonages exist that include copies of the Eltham bargeboarding. A further aspect of the remains of the palace to be studied, by two amateur archaeologists in 1833, consisted of the

22   *Excavations in progress to the south of the great hall, 1833.*

old kitchen tunnels. These, to the south of the great hall, were dug out and put on show for a small fee. The booklet the archaeologists wrote about their discoveries includes some fanciful speculations about the purpose of these tunnels,[119] a matter on which a better-informed critic was able to put them right.[120]

A 'Gothic' great hall with a royal history, in a state of romantic decay, could not be expected to escape the attentions of early 19th-century poets, of whom at least two wrote poetry about the great hall. The earlier of these, A.J. Kempe, produced 'On the Remains of the Palace at Eltham', published in 1816. In this poem the hall appears as:

> One grey old pile in Gothic majesty,
> Her pointed windows and her rich-wrought roof
> Still giving of her antient grandeur proof;

It ends with a suitable period moral on the transitory nature of pride and pomp when 'To worth alone is fair duration given'.[121] Both Kempe and the other poet, the Rev. S.J. Allen, of whose poem 'Eltham' only part survives, linger on the theme of departed grandeur and refer to the hall, which they date to the reign of Edward III, as the scene of 'baronial councils'. Allen's poem says of the hall that it:

> Now echoes but the thresher's song,
> Or the sad flail's incessant stroke.[122]

X

REPAIR AND RESTORATION

There is no approach to a palace comparable to that of Eltham, nor any hall standing
throughout England, save Westminster Hall, to vie with the great hall of Eltham Palace.
(B. Fletcher, *Royal Homes near London*, 1930)

Until the early 1840s the great hall at Eltham was still in use as a barn.[1] By
1845 the farm had become a private home, with the hall being used as
a storeroom,[2] where, two years later, carriages were housed.[3] Owls and
starlings are mentioned as nesting in the roof in 1857 when the floor of the hall
is described as covered with 'broken carts, old wheels and all sorts of rubbish'.[4]
Pigeons had lived on the palace buildings as far back as 1535, when they caused
damage to the queen's lodgings,[5] and a visitor recorded in 1893 that they made
'this ruin their home'.[6] They still nest in quiet corners of the oriel roofs.[7] The
appearance of the interior of the hall had been improved by 1878 when it was
in use as an indoor tennis court[8] and in 1881 it was described as 'clear and clean,
carefully under lock and key, but open to every applicant'.[9]

Robert Saunders, tenant farmer of Court House Farm, left it in 1850[10] and
was succeeded as tenant of the site by a lawyer, Richard Bloxam of the Court of
Chancery. The farm, now renamed Eltham Court, was enlarged in 1859 by a new
building that filled the gap between the former farm and the hall, thus closing the
road between Eltham and Mottingham that had formerly passed between them.[11]
Moat Cottage, the other principal residence within the moat, sited to the east of
the southern end of the great bridge, had been tenanted since 1818 by Richard
Mills,[12] a lawyer colleague of Richard Bloxam. This house was rebuilt and enlarged
before 1860[13] and, by the end of the century, was a substantial building renamed
Moat House, further altered about 1880 by a later tenant, Thomas Crundwell.[14]
The Bloxam and Mills families lived in some comfort: in the 1861 census Richard
Bloxam, his wife and five children had a living-in staff of a butler, housekeeper,
cook, nurse, two housemaids and a nursemaid, while Richard Mills, a widower
with two unmarried daughters at home, had a cook, lady's maid, nurse, parlour
maid and kitchen maid living in.[15]

During the late 19th-century Bloxam tenancy of Eltham Court, another
new use was found for the great hall. A visitor in 1860 recorded that a board
outside the hall proclaimed that 'the 23rd Company of the 'North Kent Rifles'

24   *Eltham Court, the great hall and the Moat House seen from the east, c.1910.*

23   *The west end of the interior of the great hall, c.1795, R.P. Cuff.*

drilled there,[16] a statement partially incorrect as it was the 32nd, not the 23rd company, that was based in Eltham.[17] This usage of the hall is recorded down to the 1890s.[18] A fête is also known to have been held in the grounds surrounding the hall during the early 1860s to raise funds for this company.[19] Its first captain was Frederick Saunders, son of Robert Saunders of Court House Farm, who in 1862 was succeeded in this position by Richard Bloxam.[20]

By 1878 the hall was lit by gas for its other use as an indoor tennis court[21] and a photograph taken in 1909 shows the hall floor still marked out for this purpose.[22] Sadly, the hall had lost much of its former appeal for artists and there are few views of it between 1840 and 1900[23] compared with the half-century before 1840.[24] The hall and bridge were, however, both mentioned and illustrated in publications about medieval architecture appearing in the latter half of the century, and the roof was used as a model for a new school hall roof at Wilson's Grammar School,

26   *East end of the great hall, 1847, from* Summer
          Excursions in the County of Kent.

25   *The palace bridge from the east, 1886,*
R. T. Hawker.

Camberwell, built in 1887, although the result
is not a close copy.[25] Richard Jefferies, then
living in Eltham, also refers to the hall in a
essay published in 1885.[26]

In about 1860 Mary Cull, a local poetess,
visited the hall and wrote a poem about it
entitled 'On viewing the ancient royal grounds
at Eltham'. In the poem the hall appears as
'this ancient, mouldering pile' and the writer
seems to have taken the hall's local name of
'King John's Barn' literally when she contrasts
the sufferings of the nobility under this king
with the very different scene in 'our lov'd
Victoria's reign'.[27] Another female visitor,
probably during the 1880s, was the exiled
Empress Eugenie of France, who arrived
unannounced and was shown round by an
unmarried Bloxam daughter, the only member
of the family at home, a visit recalled some 70
years later by the daughter of the guide.[28]

27 A group of elderly people from London on a visit to the great hall, 1903.

The first recorded visit to the hall by a society interested in its architecture and history occurred in 1878 when it was visited by the Kent Archaeological Society,[29] the first of many similar visits.[30] Between 1883 and 1913 the hall and grounds were the scene, in early June, of the Eltham Flower Show, held with a band in attendance and described at length in the local paper.[31] In the 1880s the grounds were also open to the public for a day when the 2,000 rose bushes growing there were at their best.[32] The hall was also used as the scene for an old folks' tea in 1911, part of Eltham's celebrations for the coronation of George V.[33]

The advent of Bank Holidays in the 1880s allowed large numbers of people to travel and visit places of interest during their newly gained free time. One of the places Londoners came to see was the great hall at Eltham, where the local press records about a thousand visitors to the hall on Bank Holidays in August 1895 and May 1898, and smaller numbers in other years.[34] Other uses for the hall and grounds were for a garden party given by the Bloxam family,[35] bazaars[36] and school treats.[37] In 1891 schoolchildren are reported as running races in the great hall[38] and attending Sunday School there.[39] When, during the 1890s, cycling became fashionable, a ladies' magazine mentioned the hall as a place for cyclists to visit and gave directions on how to reach it from London Bridge.[40] In the following decade, when motoring was growing rapidly, the *Motor Car Journal*, in describing a trip into Kent, mentions Eltham's great hall as a place worth visiting.[41]

The only history of the local area to include Eltham and be fully provided with references to the sources used by the author was published in 1886. This was H.H. Drake's *History of the Hundred of Blackheath*, a tombstone of a book which weighs nine pounds. Eltham's palace and manorial history are described in great detail[42] and the book was later used as a source for a booklet on Eltham Palace by A.G. Milne, a local historian, in 1900.[43] It is surprising to find, from a letter written by Milne to Drake in 1881,[44] that both knew the 'Stent' palace print, as neither mention it in their publications on local history published after this date. In 1881 the only known copy of the print was owned by a local resident, Mr A. Brookes, from whom it passed to the Bloxam family until, in the 1930s, the Misses Bloxam presented it to Stephen Courtauld.[45]

28 *The great hall, seen from the south, under repair, with J.C. Stevenson, tenant of Eltham Court, in the foreground, 1903.*

   The Mills family tenancy of the Moat House ended in 1880 with the death of Richard Mills, tenant of the house for over sixty years,[46] and the tenancy of the Bloxams at Eltham Court in 1899 on the death of Mrs Bloxam, three years after the death of her husband.[47] At the Moat House the Mills' tenancy was followed by that of the Crundwells[48] and then the Dunns[49] until, in 1921, the house became a residential hotel.[50] Eltham Court's new tenant in 1900 was J.C. Stevenson, a northern industrialist and former Liberal MP. He lived there until his death in 1905, followed by that of his wife in 1908.[51] The tenants to succeed them, in 1909, were the Wilsons.[52] G.D. Wilson died on active service in France in 1916;[53] his widow and family remained at Eltham Court until 1933.[54] Two members of the Bloxam family, a pair of unmarried sisters, stayed on in Eltham during the Second World War after the end of their Eltham Court tenancy, living in the Chancellor's Lodging until their deaths.[55]

   After the hall had been rescued from demolition in 1828 and had then been repaired, the next work to be carried out on its fabric took place in 1856. Details of this work are unrecorded but they would appear to have included the removal of the barn doors attached to the south oriel as, in their place, a wooden brace can be seen upholding the oriel roof in an 1880s view of the hall from the south.[56] This brace was

29 *James and Elizabeth Stevenson, tenants of Eltham Court, 1900-8.*

30 *The Chancellor's Lodgings on the west side of the outer court, c.1960.*

31 *Croquet in progress on the south lawn of Eltham Court, c.1905.*

changed to a brick pillar in 1894–5, work paid for by the Society for the Protection of Ancient Buildings.[57] In 1903 the beams placed in the hall in 1828 to uphold the roof were finally removed, with the timber roof beams being unobstrusively strengthened with iron.[58] Major repairs followed in 1912–14 when, at a cost of £7,771, the whole building was both strengthened and repaired. This work included taking down the roof, treating the timber for decay and then replacing the beams strengthened by an iron framework that could not be seen from below.

This work was all the more necessary as the roof timbers at the east end were bowed out, probably from the 1827 gale damage, moving the south parapet outwards as can be seen from the south oriel roof.

The major restoration of 1912–14 included retiling the roof and the opening up of six windows on the north side, previously blocked up with bricks. The framework of the windows was restored and the hall windows reglazed, including those of the south oriel, where missing stonework was replaced by a copy of the north oriel stonework. Other repairs to time–eroded stonework included the north

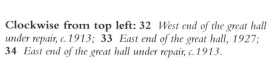

Clockwise from top left: 32 *West end of the great hall under repair, c.1913;* **33** *East end of the great hall, 1927;* **34** *East end of the great hall under repair, c.1913.*

35   *The great hall from the north, 1913.*

36   *The great hall, seen from the south, under repair, 1910.*

37   *The north bridge seen from the east, c.1933.*

38   *The north bridge and part of the west side of the outer court, c. 1913.*

39   *The north bridge seen from the west, 1937.*

40   *The north bridge seen from the east, 1923.*

41 *Local souvenir china showing the great hall from the north, c.1903-13.*

bridge, which was also strengthened and restored, more restoration being carried out on the brickwork on the inner side of the west front of the moated area.[59] This work had safeguarded the structure of the hall but had done little to improve the general appearance of its interior, apart from the reglazing of the windows and the replacement of the missing stonework of the south oriel. It was not until a further 20 years had elapsed that the hall interior was to receive a full restoration.

Apart from safeguarding the structure of the great hall, the early years of the century also witnessed increasing interest in the history of the palace and of Eltham. The hall was depicted on souvenir china of this date[60] and three books appeared between 1904 and 1910 about Eltham and the palace. The authors, the Rev. Elphinstone Rivers,[61] R.R.C. Gregory[62] and Edith Anderson (E.A.),[63] the last a member of the Stevenson family, tenants of Eltham Court, reprinted much from earlier histories, adding new information on Eltham but little concerning the palace. Gregory's book, the most substantial of the three, first appeared in instalments in the local paper in 1907-9[64] before it was reprinted, by subscription, in the latter year with a supplement in 1910 of the newly discovered early 17th-century plan of the inner court of the palace.[65] This plan was discovered by A.W. Clapham and W.H. Godfrey among the archives of the Marquess of Salisbury, to be published, redrawn with the outer court plan,

1937.

43 *The herbaceous garden in the south-east corner of the moat, c. 1910, Lillian Standard.*

as an article in 1910[66] and more fully in 1911,[67] an account later reused as a chapter in their book on various ancient buildings published in 1913.[68] Another poem on the palace, 'The Ruins of Eltham Palace' by J.B., appeared in the local paper in 1911, probably the worst poem to be written on this subject.[69]

Professional interest in publishing details of the remains of the palace began in 1930 with the inclusion of Eltham in a book on East London published by the Royal Commission on Historical Monuments.[70] This was followed after the Second World War by a further description in Pevsner's *Buildings of England* series, of which a revised version appeared in 1983.[71] The building history of the palace site, based on archaeological excavations and surviving works accounts relating to Eltham, is included in two volumes of *The History of the Kings' Works*, published in 1963 and 1982.[72] Information from these sources was used in the first official guide to the palace, by Dr D.E. Strong, which was published in 1958,[73] and in Captain Roy Brook's history of the palace, published in 1960.[74] A later edition of the palace guide, in 1983, was able to use information from the excavations carried out to the north of the great hall during the 1970s, published in detail in the *Transactions of the London and Middlesex Archaeological Society* in 1982.[75]

During the First World War, in January 1917, the great hall was slightly damaged, a window being broken, by the Silvertown explosion in East London, which destroyed an armaments factory over six miles away to the north, with heavy casualties.[76] The hall and grounds were used during

Anti-clockwise from top left: 44 *The court of Elizabeth I, from 'Merrie England', at the north bridge, 1924;* **45** *The cast of 'Merrie England', with Mrs Baldwin, outside the great hall, 1924;* **46** *14th-century gold ring, set with a ruby and five diamonds, found on palace site in the early 19th century. Inscription in French;* **47** *East end of the great hall after restoration,*

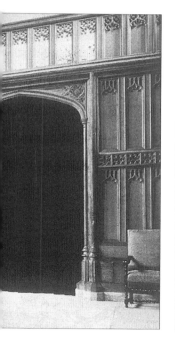

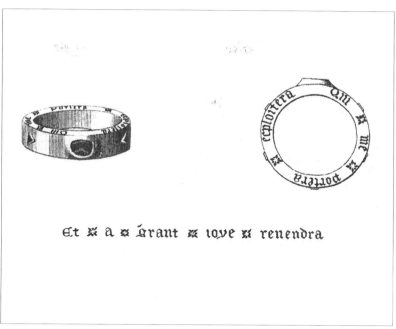

Et ✠ a ✠ grant ✠ love ✠ renendra

the war for charity and hospital events[77] and in 1918 as the headquarters, in the hall, of a unit of Royal Engineer cadets.[78] After the war the hall and grounds were occasionally used for fêtes and garden parties[79] but the Eltham Flower Show ceased to be held there after 1919.[80] Among the events held at Eltham Court in the post-war decade the outstanding one was 'Ye Olde Eltham Fayre', a two-day Conservative garden fête in 1924, opened by Mrs Baldwin, whose husband became Prime Minister for the second time later that year. It included Sir Edward German's *Merrie England*, set in Elizabethan England, which was performed on the lawn to the south of the great hall.[81]

Great changes to the palace site were to result from a visit to the hall on 18 June 1933 by Henry Paget, former Bishop of Chester, who had preached in the parish church earlier in the day before being taken by his hosts to see the great hall. The knowledge that the estate was available for a new lease from the Crown Lands Commissioners, and the importance and associations of the site, was of especial interest to the bishop as his son Paul, an architect, was looking for a suitable site in or near London where a new house could be built for his client Stephen Courtauld. Paul Paget, of Seely and Paget, was told about Eltham Palace,[82] his client was informed and on 26 June a request was made to Cluttons, agents for the Eltham estate, for full particulars and an order to view.[83] Four days later Seely and Paget sent full details of the estate to Stephen Courtauld.[84] Agreement on a new lease was reached and this was signed to date from 10 October 1933. A 99-year lease was obtained for a rent of £300 a year, with a premium or fine of £3,750 and permission to build a new house on the moated site of the former palace.[85]

Since 1860 the area within the moat had hardly altered,[86] a situation that changed greatly with the erection of Eltham Hall, the initial name of the new

42   *Collage of programmes of events
held at Eltham Palace, 1924-89.*

house, built between 1934 and 1936,[87] which involved the demolition of most of
Eltham Court, its gables, cellars and some internal structures excepted, as well as
the Moat House, the 18th–century cottage by the door of the great hall and some
minor structures.[88] At the same time the great hall was restored and embellished,[89]
new gardens were laid out[90] and the moat was widened and extended. Previously
the water in the moat extended along just under a third of the moat walls; this was
now lengthened to half of these walls including the whole north front, most of the
east front and a little of the west front. On the north side the moat was widened
so the water enclosed the two central arches of the bridge.[91] A new timber bridge
was also erected to cross the moat in the centre of the dry south front where a
medieval bridge had stood, whose foundations were left exposed.[92]

Eltham Hall was completed at a cost of a little over £100,000 excluding
furnishings, of which part came from the Courtauld's former home in London.[93]

51   *Eltham Palace seen from the south,
c.1960.*

48 *Eltham Hall seen from the south, 1937.*

50 *The dining room of Eltham Hall, 1936.*

Built of brick, concrete and Clipsham stone in English Renaissance style,[94] its exterior included modern sculpture by Gilbert Ledward and E. Carleton Attwood referring to hospitality and the sporting and other interests of Stephen and Virginia Courtauld.[95] The house has two wings, a southern one joined at its western end to the east end of the great hall, its northern side in line with the north front of the hall. The northern wing, starting from a point just east of the north bridge, joins the southern wing at nearly a right angle, with a curved wall, including the front door and enclosing a triangular entrance hall, joining the two wings.[96] There are eight bedrooms. A squash court and an orangery are situated to the west of the great hall and an underground billiard room lies just to the east of the great hall.[97]

The south wing of the house looks on to the south lawn and provides family living rooms on the ground floor with family and guest bedrooms on the first floor. The north wing contains the dining room and kitchen, with associated kitchen and staff rooms, on the ground floor, with guest and staff rooms above them.[98] The entrance hall between the two wings is lit from above by a cupola. It has striking intarsia wall decorations on each side of the front door, depicting buildings in Venice on the south side and buildings in Stockholm on the north side of the entrance, These were designed by Rolf Engstromer and created by Jerk Werkmaster, both from Sweden.[99] The dining room, the principal living rooms and some of the bedrooms were planned by Peter Malacrida and decorated by the firm of White Allom in a variety of 1930s styles described in the latest, 1999, edition of the house guide.[100]

The restoration and embellishment of the great hall, previously a bleak and empty space, was approved by the Crown Lands Advisory Committee and carried out, for the most part, at Stephen Courtauld's expense.[101] This work was supervised by Sir Charles Peers, a former Chief Inspector of Ancient Monuments,[102] who had been in charge in 1912-14 of the earlier repair and restoration of the great hall.[103] The work both strengthened and beautified the roof, the latter in particular by the restoration to the roof pendants of their missing tracery, of which the last original

49 *Virginia Courtauld, with her dogs, at Eltham Hall, c. 1937.*

54 *The badges of Edward IV in the windows of the great hall, 1936.*
53 *The coats of arms and standards of Edward IV and his Queen in the*

fragment had been lost for over a century. Their replacement was made possible by the survival of a drawing, made in 1817 by J.C. Buckler, of the last pendant to have retained its tracery, shortly before that too disappeared.[104] These pendants retained traces of yellow pigment on their undersides, showing they had originally been gilded.[105]

Further restoration work replaced decayed stone ceiling bosses in the oriels with others made of wood, with new themes including the Courtaulds' pet lemur;[106] restored window surrounds[107] and Edward IV's personal badge in the framework of the north door.[108] New stained glass, designed by George Kruger Gray, was placed in the windows of the great hall,[109] displaying, in the body of the hall, the personal badges used by Edward IV, the sun, the white rose of York, the *rose en soleil* and the falcon and fetterlock.[110] Edward IV and his queen were shown in the north oriel windows with their coats of arms and standards. Here, although the white rose was the Yorkist emblem, Queen Elizabeth is shown with

52 *The entrance hall of Eltham Hall, 1936.*

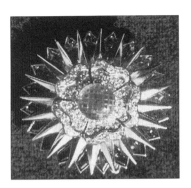

great hall windows designed by George Kruger Gray, 1936.
55 *Brooches by Cartier of the badges of Edward IV, designed by George Kruger Gray for the windows of the restored great hall. Presented to Virginia Courtauld by her husband, 1937.*

a red rose in her hand, a reference to the fact that her first husband had been a Lancastrian. In the south oriel, Bishops Odo of Bayeux and Bek of Durham are depicted together with the coats of arms of Edward I, Edward III, Richard II and Henry VIII, all monarchs associated with the history of the palace.[111] A pleasant personal touch relating to Edward IV's badges was that copies of two of them, the falcon and fetterlock and the *rose en soleil*, were made as brooches by Cartier in gold, diamonds and enamel for Stephen Courtauld to present to his wife.[112]

The restoration of the hall included plastering part of the formerly bare brick walls. Tapestry was hung along the side walls and also high up at the west end of the hall.[113] At the east end, where time and vandalism had reduced the screen to its main beams, the screen was restored and panelled. Here, although the tracery formerly applied to the beams was long since lost, the pattern remained,

bleached by the sun on to the beams and now revealed by washing. This tracery was now replaced, including some details copied from the tracery of the roof.[114] A new addition to this end of the hall was a minstrels' gallery placed above the screen against the east wall, an appropriate feature, although one for which there was no architectural evidence.[115]

At the west end of the hall a low dais was placed. Behind it, against the wall, a reredos or canopied screen was placed, based on a medieval rood screen in Attleborough church in Norfolk.[116] A line of carved heraldic beasts, each holding a shield, runs along the top of the canopy, the shields displaying the badges of the Plantagenet, Lancastrian and Tudor rulers who had lived at Eltham. A half-shield on the left has Edward II's badge, then the seven full

a) Falcon and fetterlock
b) Rose en soleil.
56 *Stephen and Virginia Courtauld at 47 Grosvenor*

Square, London. Shown at the Royal Academy exhibition, 1934. Leonard Campbell Taylor, 1945.

shields show the sunburst of Edward III, the chained white hart of Richard II, the feather, beacon and chained swan of the Lancastrians Henry IV, V and VI, and the dragon and phoenix of the Tudors Henry VII and VIII, the line ending with a half-shield of St George.[117] Between the canopy and the panelling, a line of wooden bosses commemorates the names of those involved in the restoration of the great hall. The four central bosses record the date of the work (1935), the others, from the left, refer to J.W. Hopkins, the clerk of works, unidentified, Seely (the firm of Seely and Paget, the architects), Stephen Courtauld, Virginia Courtauld, Sir Charles Peers, who supervised the restoration, the Hon. John Seely, Paul Paget and Winifred Monnington, consultant.[118]

On the east wall of the south oriel a Latin inscription commemorates the part played by the Courtaulds in the restoration of the great hall, the wording reads:

Haec avla qvam rex splendidvs angliae
Edwardvs olim strvxerat in dies
sqvalore labens nvnc refrecta est
Virginiae Stephaniqve cvris
[This hall which the magnificent King Edward built, having fallen into disrepair, is restored by the care of Virginia and Stephen][119]

By his generosity and thoughtfulness for the great hall and its surroundings, Stephen Courtauld had restored them, after three centuries of decay, to a condition worthy of the craftsmanship of the building and its historic associations. When the work was complete the hall was opened once again to visits from the public.

The work on the hall included a new floor and, while this was

57 *West end of the great hall, 1927.*

under construction, tiles were discovered from an earlier building on the same site, apparently of Edward III's reign.[120] These tiles and other objects of interest discovered during the construction of the house were placed on show in the dining room of the new building,[121] and a plan of the foundations of earlier buildings found within the moated site was sent to the Commissioners for Crown Lands.[122] Ancient cellars below the new building were incorporated into the basement of the new house.[123] Another cellar, situated to the north-west of the great hall, was found during the archaeological excavations carried out in the 1970s.[124]

The restored hall was furnished with a mixture of ancient and modern furniture, mostly antique, which included an old hall table placed on the dais at the western end of the hall. The metal torches above the tapestries on the side walls were later removed but have been replaced during the restoration completed in 1999.[125]

The building of Eltham Hall, a modern house in a style considered to be suitable to its proximity to the great hall, led to a correspondence in *The Times* on the suitability of this juxtaposition, This controversy was begun by G.M. Young,[126] later supported by Sir Herbert Baker and others,[127] and, while no one took exception to the work carried out on the restoration of the great hall, the new house was unkindly described by G.M. Young as 'an admirably designed but unfortunately sited cigarette factory',[128] while Sir Herbert Baker listed examples of architects who had, in his opinion, shown 'admirable taste in adding to old buildings',[129] implying that this had not taken place at Eltham. Such remarks could not pass unchallenged by the architects of Eltham Hall and their supporters,[130] and criticism and counter-criticism flew back and forth on the subject in the press for over three weeks. Seely and Paget, and those who agreed with them, were able to point to the recent destruction of both the Old Bank of England building and Old Waterloo Bridge, where 'really beautiful work' had been destroyed, whereas at Eltham everything of real historical value had been preserved.[131] In the end it was a matter of taste. New work had replaced a scene that had seen almost no alteration for three-quarters of a century, and lovers of the traditional surroundings of the hall mourned what had been a familiar scene to them. As one headline on the subject put it, 'Romance Dies at Eltham'.[132]

Apart from this correspondence in *The Times* and elsewhere, additional publicity was given to Eltham Hall and the restoration of the great hall by letters and articles in the local,[133] national[134] and technical press[135] and in exhibitions of views of the house and its interior decorations in the Royal Academy and of the gardens at the Chelsea Flower Show.[136] Three articles in *Country Life*, by Christopher Hussey, were particularly well informed[137] and, with a booklet on the palace by Stephen Courtauld, were the first publications to reproduce the 'Stent' view of the old palace as it had been in the mid-17th century.[138]

The Courtaulds were to have only three years in which they could fully enjoy the amenities of their new home, into which they moved on 25 March 1936. Initially the house was called Eltham Palace, a name altered to Eltham Hall when it was found that their post was going to the local cinema with the same name.[139] The Courtaulds' hospitality to their friends included a ball held in the great hall in July 1937, with a fireworks display in the grounds.[140] Apart from the hall being

open to the public once a week, other functions open to the general public were held in the grounds during these three years prior to the outbreak of the Second World War. A Conservative fête took place there[141] and Scouting events, Stephen Courtauld having become president of the local Scouting Association, with Virginia Courtauld president of the local Girl Guides.[142]

In the 20th century the former royal home of Eltham has been revisited by royalty on a number of occasions, the first such visitor being Queen Mary, who came in 1931[143] and revisited it twice after its restoration, in 1935[144] and 1938.[145] The Duke and Duchess of York, who became king and queen a few months later, visited it in the summer of 1936[146] and our present queen came to Eltham Palace for a royal garden party there that commemorated the 50th anniversary of the founding of the Royal Army Educational Corps, then tenants of the estate.[147] The Duchess of Gloucester, Colonel-in-Chief of the R.A.E.C., came to see their Corps HQ there on four occasions in the 1970s and '80s.[148] Other royal visitors have been Princess Margaret, who visited Eltham with friends on several occasions in the summer during the early 1980s,[149] and the Prince of Wales, who came to the palace late in 1995, soon after the estate had come into the tenancy of English Heritage.[150]

After the Second World War had broken out in September 1939, a new function was found for the great hall as an air-raid wardens' reporting point, with the underground billiard room next to the hall becoming an air-raid shelter for both the family at Eltham Hall and others. Stephen Courtauld became a head air-raid warden[151] and his wife a leader of Eltham's Women's Voluntary Service.[152] The great hall was twice damaged by air raids during the war. The first occasion was at the height of the Battle of Britain, on 13 September 1940, when over

58   *West end of the great hall after restoration, 1937.*
     59   *HM Queen Elizabeth II in the entrance hall of Eltham Palace, 1970.*

a hundred incendiary bombs fell on the Courtauld estate. Two of these struck Eltham Hall and were extinguished, little damage being done, but four hit the great hall. Of these, three were quickly extinguished by Stephen Courtauld and another warden but the fourth broke through the tiles of the roof and stuck in the hall rafters, where it was hard to extinguish. Before the fire brigade was able to put it out, damage had been done to the eastern end of the hall roof, with more damage done by the dislodgement of tiles and by the water from the hoses of the fire brigade. The marks of burns from this fire can still be seen on the gallery.[153]

After this bomb damage, temporary repairs were carried out, but only seven months later, on 20 April 1941, a parachute mine explosion a quarter of a mile to the south of the house blew off the temporary covering placed over the roof of the great hall, displaced many tiles and broke much of the glass on the south side of the building.[154] Full repairs to this wartime damage were not completed until 1954.[155] Work was also carried out, between 1952 and 1954, on restoring the surviving buildings on the western side of the former outer court.[156] Since then, only routine work has been required for the roof of the great hall, to deal with death watch beetles in the beams of the roof.[157] When the repairs were complete, the hall was opened to the public twice a week; since 1999 the hall and house have both been open to visitors four days a week.[158]

During the Second World War the Eltham Hall grounds were used for WVS garden parties[159] and for Eltham's War Weapons Week.[160] Life in Eltham Hall in wartime was, however, uncomfortable. More staff were needed than were available during the war,[161] while fuel rationing made it hard to keep such

60 *The western end of the great hall roof, c.1950.*

a large house warm in winter.[162] Pre-war living-in staff had numbered eight,[163] while about fifteen gardeners had been employed in the gardens,[164] but in the war years the grounds and garden only had the services of two old men, assisted by Mrs Courtauld.[165] Despite the pleasure that Eltham Hall had given them, the Courtaulds decided, by late 1944, that they would surrender the Eltham lease.[166]

Negotiations concerning the future of the remaining part of the lease granted in 1933 went on during late 1944 and early 1945 between the tenants, the Commissioners for Crown Lands and different government departments, with several options for the future tenancy of Eltham Hall being considered.[167] In March 1945 a decision was finally reached on the advice of R.A. Butler (later Lord Butler), who was Stephen Courtauld's brother-in-law, that the remainder of the lease should be offered to the War Department for the use of the Army Educational Corps (who became the Royal Army Educational Corps in 1946).[168] Early in 1945 the Courtaulds left Eltham Hall for a brief stay at Taynuilt in Argyll[169] before a move to Umtali in Southern Rhodesia (now Zimbabwe), where a new house was built for them. Stephen Courtauld was knighted for public services to that country in 1958[170] and died there in 1967,[171] Virginia dying four years later in 1971.[172]

61 *An aerial view of Eltham Palace with the great hall roof under repair,*

1953.

The army lease of Eltham Hall, now known as Eltham Palace, began in April 1945 and the Army School of Education opened there the following October,[173] running short courses in connection with the post-war resettlement of the army. These courses for officers, on teaching methods, educational theory and staff duties, were held there for three years until October 1948 when the unit moved to Bodmin, in Cornwall,[174] being replaced by the Institute of Army Education, which was there for 34 years, administering the executive elements of army education. These altered from time to time but included research, the inspection of army schools, the recruitment of civilian teachers for army childrens' schools overseas, language training, setting First Class Army Certificate of Education examination papers and the production of visual aids, current affairs leaflets and information concerning correspondence courses.[175]

During the 1960s the need for more office space than was available in Eltham Palace, which was also used as an officers' mess, and the closure of two small outlying camps used by the institute, led to the building of a small office block half a mile south-east of Eltham Palace. Completed in May 1963, it left the Courtauld building free for use as an officers' mess and for army educational conferences.[176] Later army reorganisation led to the combining of the functions of the institute with those of the Directorate of Army Education, which had been housed at Stanmore and in central London. After a year during which the buildings were shared by the two units,[177] a new unit HQ Director of Army Education took over at Eltham from September 1983[178] and used the buildings for nine years. This unit's office block was damaged by an IRA bomb on 14 May 1990, seven of HQ DAE's civilian office staff being injured.[179] When the Cold War ended, further changes in the army brought

65   *The great hall from the south-east,*
c.*1985.*

1950.
62   *The south front of Eltham Lodge,*

63   *The great hall from the south in*
winter, c.1985.

about an end to the tenancy of army education at Eltham Palace, in December 1992, some months after the R.A.E.C. had been absorbed into the new Adjutant General's Corps as its Education and Training Section.[180]

During the years when the R.A.E.C. were at Eltham Palace, it was the Corps HQ Mess and the scene of many Corps activities, including the annual Corps Conference and other army educational meetings.[181] It also witnessed social events like the garden parties from 1946 onwards,[182] R.A.E.C. annual dinners in the great hall from 1950,[183] and officers' balls in the same hall.[184] These events brought many guests and visitors associated with education and the services to the palace, where they were shown the great hall and told the history of the hall and the former royal palace.[185] The R.A.E.C. also provided information displays on the palace's history in the great hall,[186] and in 1960, in conjunction with a firm of publishers, helped to finance a new history of the palace written by Captain (later Major) Roy Brook of the Corps.[187]

Between 1945 and 1992 the commanders of the army educational units at Eltham Palace gave permission for the holding of a variety of events open to the public in the great hall and palace grounds. One of the earliest of these was a Victory Day fête held in June 1946.[188] The largest event in terms of numbers was either a Coronation Ball held in the appropriate setting of the great hall in 1953[189] or a Scouting event in the palace grounds in the same year.[190] Other functions held in the hall have been fêtes, galas and fairs,[191] plays and pageants,[192] concerts,[193] operas,[194] dinners,[195] TV's *Mastermind*,[196] radio's *Any Questions?*,[197] exhibitions,[198] and festivities for the Eltham Society,[199] founded in 1965. A memorable outdoor event was a week of *Son et Lumière* displays in 1960 on the history of the palace, with the hall appropriately lit up for audiences seated on the outer bank of the south side of the moat.[200] Outdoor functions were probably fewer than those held in the great hall. Some events used both the hall and the grounds. Bazaars, dances and fêtes were held in the grounds for the Royal British Legion[201] as well as Scouting events.[202] The palace has also been used as a theme for poems by an Eltham Society member.[203]

The Crown lease passed from the Ministry of Defence to English Heritage in September 1995, when the latter already controlled the great hall. It now opened the Courtauld building to the public, Eltham Palace becoming their first 20th-century building to be put on show. Guided tours of it were arranged for the public and copies of the architects' house plans and photographs of rooms as they were in the 1930s were displayed. Initially, however, the rooms were shown unfurnished.[204] The house was also available for functions including a memorable birthday party, with a medieval banquet, in 1996.[205] After being shut for redecoration, it reopened in June 1999 furnished with reproductions of the Courtaulds' furniture, assisted with a grant by the Heritage Lottery Fund, with a new guidebook by Michael Turner appearing at the same time. Unlike earlier guides this one was principally devoted to the 1930s building, its design, interior decorations and facilities, the life lived there by the Courtaulds, and the history of Stephen and Virginia Courtauld.[206]

APPENDICES

APPENDIX A

LETTERS TO PRINCESS BLANCHE CONCERNING THE 1401 TOURNAMENT AT ELTHAM
These letters, translated from French by Mrs D.M. Clarke and the author, exist in
five copies, all slightly different from each other. The translation below is from the
copy in Bodleian Douce 271 ff 40r-47r. The other four copies are College of Arms
Arundel xxvi ff 33-40v and MS L. 6 ff 145v-50v, and British Library Cotton MS
Nero D.ii ff 260v-262r and Add. MS 34801 ff 36-42v.

The presence at the tournament of Manuel II Palaeologus, Emperor of Byzan-
tium, is mentioned in two of these letters and his visit to Eltham for the Christmas of
1400 is referred to in four printed chronicles:
Chronicon Adae de Usk, ed. Sir E.M. Thompson (1904).
A Chronicle of London from 1089 to 1483, eds. E. Tyrrell and Sir N.H. Nicolas (1827).
Duo Rerum Anglicarum (Otterbourne's Chronicle), ed. T. Hearne (1732).
Chronica et Annales Johannis de Trokelowe et Henrici de Blaneforde, ed. H.T. Riley, R.S.
    (1866).
The emperor's presence at Eltham is also mentioned in two chronicles still in MS:
British Library Harl. 565 f 66, and Cotton Titus D.xv f 49v.

Letter 1
To the most excellent and noble princess Lady Blanche daughter to the most
powerful prince the King of Albion. Phoebus, the principal planet of the
firmament, to the most excellent princess, daughter to the most powerful prince,
King of Albion, greetings and sincere friendship. As we, in our constant travels
encompassing the high circle of the firmament, seeing clearly the government of
all earthly things, know for certain that everything on the moon receives its course
and light direct from us so does the splendour of this world receive nourishment
and glory from your royal court which is the fountain of nobility. We, desiring the
improvement of our dearly beloved child Ferombras by this fountain of honour
send him to your highness to see your royal court and learn the profession of
arms; requesting you that you would order one of your honourable knights at
your feast to run six jousts with the lance against our said child, with weapons
of the same length, in high saddles to which they must not be bound, so our said
child may return to us better experienced in arms as we trust in your kindness.
And if there is anything that we can do for your pleasure or comfort please let us
know by our child and we will do it with the greatest pleasure. May the Creator

of all creatures preserve your excellent and honourable estate in honour, joy and full prosperity. Given at our marvellous mansion of the firmament in a full court of stars.

Letter 2
To the excellent and most noble princess Lady Blanche, daughter of the most powerful prince, King of Great Britain, a young and ignorant squire, bringer of these letters, wishes for entry to your royal court in order to learn the profession of arms requesting of your highness that you will be pleased to order the most valiant bachelor or squire under 32 at your feast to meet the said suppliant in low saddles with twelve jousts with the lance, using standard blunt lance points, and not bound into the saddle.

Letter 3
Jenneste, by the grace of the god of love queen of joy and of all pleasures, to the high and mighty princess and our dearest and famous sister Blanche, eldest daughter of the most high and powerful prince, King of Great Britain, lord of the land of wonders and true successor of the powerful emperor Arthur whose honour and reputation for chivalry is greater than any prince living, of great reputation for high chivalry in many foreign countries and renowned throughout the world, greetings and sincere friendship. Our very dear and much loved sister, know that in our court we have brought up a young knight, by his right name called Nonsaichart, who has suffered in the cause of love and has undergone many travails and dangers to alleviate his pain. He is engaged in a quest searching for a lady of great renown called Grace of whom he has no information or other news. Since he has heard that there will be a magnificent assembly of ladies, maidens and valiant knights and squires before your presence at this forthcoming feast of Christmas, in this journey and progress towards this part of the world to look and learn our son wishes to obtain assistance in his quest and also because it is usual for knights seeking adventure to visit the courts of kings and princes for practice with arms. We have learnt that at that solemn feast and noble assembly among the other valiant knights and squires there is a knight who has lately fought in the Kingdom of France so valiantly that he has gained great praise and prizes in the said Kingdom of France and in other countries. We request that our protégé, the said Nonsaichart be taught the profession of arms by the deeds of those noble knights. We heartily request that at the said display that our protégé be allowed to run six jousts with the lance in low saddles with the said noble knight who bears on his shield arms of which the field is azure with three cinquefoils of gold and a crescent of silver, jousting unbound in hand or saddle. In doing this you will do us a great service if that is your wish. If you wish anything in our kingdom we will do it gladly. Praying Him who has power over all to keep you in prosperity, honour and happiness. Written in our castle of pleasure, the day of the present month. Also, our very dear and much loved sister, know that our above-said protégé is coming to your presence to meet a maiden who has come from the Kingdom of Panthaluce who he accompanies into your presence.

Letter 4
Dalida, by the grace of Mahomet, god of all true infidels and saracens, Sultan of Babylon and King of Alexandria, to the high and powerful princess and our

very dear and much loved cousin etc. By the grace of Him to whom the three kings offered gold, incense and myrrh, eldest daughter of the most noble King of Albion, heir and successor of the most noble emperor Charlemagne, Soundanal and Alexander greetings. Our very dear and much loved cousin there is in your court a lady of great reputation called Plaisance who has long held prisoner in her prisons a knight of the king of love known as Le Pouer Perdu who cannot be released without six jousts with the lance riding in low saddles, unbound in saddle or hand. It appears he must travel to many countries, castles, towns and cities, over mountains, valleys, woods and rivers, before he can discover someone from whom he can obtain good advice that would shorten his journey. And since we have heard that our very dear and much loved cousin the king your father will hold a solemn festivity at Christmas, a very solemn and notable court of such great splendour that an emperor of great renown, noble ladies and maidens, valiant knights and squires will be there. Some will do wonders riding dragons, others carrying serpents on their heads throwing out fire and flame. Others who are so ardent in love that their shields throw flames of fire, with many other adventurous knights who come before you both from the Empress Penthesilea and from the Queen of Carthage. We have advised him to present himself before your tender and youthful presence, and bring also Poure Perdu, our very dear and much loved nephew Feresbar of Damascus the young governor general of our Kingdom of Alexandria in order that he does not escape from his prison and, so he does not escape, he is bound by a chain round his neck. We affectionately petition that you allow our said knight Poure Perdu to meet the knight from your court who is the most desirous of taking part in the conquest of the Kingdom of Jerusalem, be he king, prince, duke or earl, knight or squire, in six jousts with the lance which will give us very great pleasure. Praying to Alpha first that your reign endures. Given in our city of Jerico the day of the Translation of Appolin.

Letter 5

Naturo, nurse of life, executor of the most powerful King of Kings, to the most excellent princess, eldest daughter of the most powerful King of Albion, greetings and deepest love. We, who ordain to man and beast their lives according to the high commandments of the Creator of all creatures, know for certain that as our subject Priapus, the god of gardens, grasses and flowers, renews and refreshes the face of the earth in the noble season of April which was bare and without grass from the terrible winter which is the king of cold, a region and area covering the whole earth now takes once more its fine covering of sweetness and flowers so truly all states of the living world await the honour of being clothed and adorned by the knowledge of the gracious rule and content of your excellent, noble and royal heart, as the true model of all honour, goodness and gentility, at this your noble festivities to see the government of your excellent estate and to learn the profession of arms. We, desiring the improvement of our much loved protégé Ferrant de Ferieres, bringer of these letters, pray that by the advice of the nobles at your feast you would please to order the knight or squire present at your festivities who has spoken most of love to different maidens, and who has most frequently changed his dress of loyal suitor, to meet our said squire in six jousts with the lance in high or low saddles with standard blunt lance points and not bound to the saddle so our said protégé can, in his Jenneste, avoid being double-faced or false in love, which God forbid. As we trust most fully in your goodness and nobility. Most excellent princess we pray to the god of love to grant you honour, perfect health and joyous life, long to endure. Given in our palace of pleasure, full of delights.

Letter 6

Vertu, mother and nurse of honour, lady of perfect pleasure, to the most excellent princess, our very dear and much loved cousin and lady of this high and honourable feast, lady and daughter of the most powerful prince, King of the Isle of Giants, greetings and love. We, with full intent, have ordained and deputed your noble person as general executrix of all things concerned with the nobility of our office granted to us by the King of Kings, as the most noble lady destined by God to fulfil it loyally and honourably. We send before your nobility a knight of our chamber called Jenne la Prenant who has a great wish and particular desire to see the noble plan and display of our mandate of which you have been told by our provident care besides learning the honourable profession of arms, praying you to command the most honourable and noble knight of reputation or account, who has long been of arms against the wicked and present at your royal feast, to teach our said knight of our chamber the profession of arms. And, excellent princess, we have heard that two of the most excellent princes of all Christendom are at your high and honourable feast, the most noble Emperor of Constantinople, and the most powerful prince the King of Albion and Gaul, we send to them, not as a gift but for remembrance, for New Year's Day two small tokens for our said knight. Praying to you that our letter commends us to the high and honourable consideration of the excellent above-mentioned princes, like us in your perfect and honourable kindness. Most excellent and noble princess, the especial cause of our creation keep and govern you in perfect health and give you joyous life, long to endure. Given in our noble keep of Perfect Diligence, free from evil.

Letter 7

To the most excellent and noble princess, lady and daughter of the most powerful King of Great Britain. Shows most humbly a young knight named Ardent Desirous who has come from distant parts of the land of India to this your noble feast to see the splendour of your excellence and learn the profession of arms humbly requests that you should be pleased to order the knight at this feast who has most often travelled into foreign lands between the ages of twenty and twenty-four to meet your suppliant in six jousts with the lance without unlawful lance heads, not being bound into the saddle, on New Year's Day in your hall, in low saddles, and he who jousted the best course in your most noble judgement and in that of his companion in that course shall have a rod of gold as a good reward. This wish we pray you to grant and accomplish and inform me of the name of the knight who will meet me in the way of kindness and nobility.

Letter 8

To the most excellent princess, lady and daughter of the most powerful King of Albion. Penolose, wife of the most noble prince Ulysses, greetings and sincerest love. Since common report has shown and informed us that you are about to hold shortly a royal feast at which at which you are normally accustomed to have many good knights and squires to joust, dance and lead a joyous life we send to your highness our well-loved child Palaundes the loyal bringer of these letters who has a great desire to learn the profession of arms, begging of your kindness that your highness order a noble knight present at your festivities who wears as his device three different leaves in the form of a trefoil to meet our said child in six jousts with the lance, not using unlawful lance-points, in low saddles, so our said child may return to us well instructed in the profession of arms. We will inform us through him of the pleasure to your highness of the true news of your high and honourable estate for particular solace to our heart, as we trust most sincerely in you. Most excellent princess the true god of love give you honour, joy and perfect health and a good life, long to endure.

Letter 9

Venus, mother of Cupid, god of love, to the most excellent princess lady of this high feast, daughter of the most powerful prince King of Great Britain greetings and sincerest love. Since we have full information by the statement of our faithful messenger called Loyal Rapport that in your noble court are the best knights in the world at your royal feast to joust, dance and lead a joyous existence we of your great goodness desire advancement for our little child called Joesrue le Amerues bringer of these letters. We send him to your highness for nourishing and to learn the profession of arms. We pray you to order some knight at your festival to meet our said child in six jousts with the lance without unlawful lance-points, in high saddles, so our said child can return to us with news of your honourable estate and perfect health, better after the training already mentioned. Most excellent princess the high and powerful King of Kings safeguard you and give you perfect health, honour and joyous life long to endure. Given in our wondrous mansion of Monsicheroun the year of our building five thousand five hundred and sixteen.

Letter 10

Cleopatra, by the grace of Saturn and all the other planets, Queen of Mesopotamia, and Gobosse, eldest daughter of the most high emperor Dynde la Maiour, called Prester John, captain of the lower courts of the terrestrial paradise. To the high and powerful princess and our very dear and much loved cousin Blanche, by the grace of Him by whom birds fly in the air, eldest daughter of the most noble king, true successor of the king Saint Louis and of the valiant William the Conqueror forgiveness, greeting and womanly love. Our dear and well-loved cousin we have heard that many knights and squires from a number of foreign kingdoms are coming to your presence to learn and witness the feats of arms that the valiant knights and squires of your court will do this Christmas. Therefore we send you our much beloved eldest knight called Pert Sapeine, lieutenant to the captain of our city of Troy to learn the science of the profession of arms with the other mounted knights and squires above said. Wherefore we request of you most affectionately that you will send to our knight the officer of your court who bears as his arms a shield of silver with a chief of azure with two balm flowers of gold to meet him in six jousts with the lance, seated in low saddles, neither fixed or bound to the saddle, and do not keep him too long remembering the long journey he has to make to return. Given in our city of Troy within the temple of Jupiter on the day of the descent. He who makes bread and wine give you a reign without end.

Letter 11

To the most excellent and noble princess, lady of this high feast, lady and goddaughter we most humbly inform you that a little youth called Toret Detollide, bringer of these letters, has come from foreign lands to see the splendour of your royal court and to learn good upbringing and the profession of arms, humbly begging of your highness that it may please you to order the best knight at your feast aged between sixteen and twenty who has been longest or his age the servant of love, without any reward, to meet your suppliant in six jousts with the regular lance, without unauthorised lance-heads, in your excellency's presence in your hall when it pleases your highness, in order that the poor little suppliant can return to the foreign country from which he came well-taught in the contest aforesaid through your highness' goodness and nobility.

Letter 12

To the most excellent and noble princess, lady and godchild. Humbly presents a young man called Lancelot de Libre who has come from distant parts to seek the bright star of good understanding and love having good information that your royal court is the true university of all excellent virtue. Wishing from your high authority to learn good upbringing and the profession of arms begs of your high nobility that you will be pleased to order the knight living in your court who bears on his shield a device in the form of a kind of beast called a foliart (unidentified, possibly a foumart, also known as a marten or polecat) to meet your said child in six jousts with the lance, in low saddles, with standard lance-points and not bound or attached to the saddle, to teach the young suppliant in the said contest. This truly of your kind courtesy.

Letter 13

To the most excellent princess, lady of this high feast, godchild etc. Shows most humbly that a little young child called Voulente Dapprend, bringer of these letters, coming from distant parts to see the noble splendour of your royal court and learn the profession of arms humbly requests of your excellent highness that you would be pleased to command the best knight and finest jouster at your feast, true cousin of the redoubtable prince, the King of the Isle of Giants, to meet the first jouster in six jousts with blunt lance-points, not bound or attached to the saddle … (unfinished).

APPENDIX B

BRITIAIN PERSONIFIED BY ERASMUS

Translated by Dr Harold Booton. The text is taken from *The Poems of Desiderius Erasmus*, trans. & ed. Dr C. Reedijk (1956). Erasmus presented this ode in Latin to Henry, Duke of York (later Henry VIII) after a visit in 1499 by Erasmus, More and Arnold to Henry VII's children at an unnamed palace, considered by most writers on Erasmus and More to have been Eltham Palace, which was used as a royal nursery before and after this date in Henry VII's reign. The royal children in 1499 were Arthur (1486-1502), who was not present at Eltham on this occasion, Margaret (1489-1541), Henry (1491-1547), Mary (1496-1533) and Edmund (1498-d. very young). Britain is speaking of itself.

Britain speaks[*]

If one is allowed to boast of the gifts of the great gods and it is right for true merits to please, why should I not think of myself as a most blessed land? It is wrong to think too little of one's good fortune. Distant India is proud of her wool-bearing groves,[1] the Arab of his rich perfumes, Panchaia[2] rejoices in her incense-bearing sands, the land of Iberia[3] boasts of her golden river, the seven mouths of the Nile give pride to the Egyptian, their much praised mine exalts those who live by the Rhine, fertile Africa does not displease with its rich soil, this place will be superior with its harbours and that with its merchandise, but I am not lacking in springs and rich rivers, or fertile furrows and smiling meadows. Productive of man, rich in wild animals and metals. Let me not boast that the ocean surrounds more bountiful wealth and that heaven is not more friendly to any region, nor does the wind blow more sweetly on any place. Phoebus[4] sets late in my western waters, and his charming sister[5] induces clear nights. I am able to praise, not to condemn, the fleeces of much praised Boetus,[3] where is the fleece of a sheep softer and whiter? And I do not intend to scorn your miracles, Memphis, but that glory is greater and deserved because I, Britain, am celebrated among Latins and Greeks because antiquity called me another world. I do not boast of this however, for these are ancient things, but I carry my head high and triumph in truth over this, that the king is the most splendid part of the beautiful kingdom, the king is the unique miracle of this age. Specially trained in the arms of Mars[6] and Pallas,[7] he is skilled in war but fonder of peace. Indulging others he permits himself nothing, relaxing the reins for his own citizens he draws them tight for himself. This is the monarchy he believes in, to be very dear to his country, pleasing to the good, to be feared only by the wicked. Their Rome was not more valued by the Decii[8] or Attica by its Codrus,[9] both saved by a common sacrifice. His respect for the will of heaven is as great as Metellus[10] had or Aegeria's husband.[11] The eloquence of the king of Pylos[12] was not more honey sweet nor the mind of Caesar greater or more lofty, nor Moecena's[13] right hand ever more kind or his reluctance to shed blood so great. Aeneas was believed to be descended from the seed of Venus, Scipio said to be born of father Jupiter. What if former ages had seen my king, with his lordly countenance and such a heart? Surely they would have believed that Jupiter himself concealed in a body like ours was coming to help human affairs? And he to me will always be an immortal, my Apollo father of a golden age. When he arose the age of iron withdrew from my shores, Astrea[14] returned and scattered evil just as the stars vanish all over the sky as soon as the Titan[4] shines forth with fiery countenance. It is right now to shut the doors of Janus[15] and enjoy long peace now with so powerful a guardian of events. Ah me! Why Jupiter did you not add eternal years to him, when you gave him so much? The gods do not wish our kingdom to be made equal to theirs. But if any prayers can reach the great dwellers in heaven may he at any rate be carried back late to the citadels of the stars, may Atropos[16] be late to cut the thread on which his fate depends. Alcides[17] ended his splendid labours by death, the heaven on high is owed to good kings. May the gods above take him back, but at a time when he has surpassed the lifetime of Nestor[12] and the old age of Tithonus.[18] And yet he will live on for me while the royal children are endowed with their father's name, face and talents. Five of them are now growing up at the royal court, three the future fathers and two the future mothers of kings. Nothing unpleasing is seen in the colourful gardens of

---

[*]   See p.141 for Notes.

verdant Paestum[19] where the most beautiful roses grow with the kindly dew, a flower most welcome to lovely Venus, than which no other breathes or is more charmingly bright, nor has such beauty in its woven garlands worthy to encircle a king's hair alone. Here when the joyous industry of the learned gardener enjoys uniting the red with the white[20] and on many a thorn one rose is red and white as if you were joining milky ivory to a purple dye, all have the same scent, the same dew feeds them all, the same youth, the same appearance, the same stem and the same earth support them with the same moisture, that are caressed by the same breezes and the same climate. There are two things that distinguish them from one another, bringing about a beautiful contrast between neighbouring buds, their age and their colour. This one newly born lies almost hidden by its green cover[21] and its tender crimson shines through a thin crack. This one has just put forth the tip of its snowy face but gradually opening breaks its swollen curves. This one tearing its dress stretches out its point, now threatening to unfold its confined hair. That one has not yet emptied its milky cloak, it scarcely trusts its riches still unripe to the winds, but its white face is suffused with a gentle red, whether this is the colour of a brother or of a star, when full grown it rejoices in the honour of twelve petals, unfolding its shining hair with Tyrian purple. Not like this is the wool red when dyed with the sea shell, not like this in Phoebus[4] emerging from the waters of the dawn. Not only does he smile with graceful face to those to come but he now promises yellow seeds. Here my Arcturus[22] who lucky in the omen of his name will recall you with his courage whom he recalls with his name. Look at what an example of a high born appearance there is in him, how the lively vigour of his mind shines in his eyes. Precocious wisdom does not wait for slow adulthood, his eager nature outstrips his years. Such was Jesse's son[23] and his offspring very like him when this boy slew terrible wild beasts, since this boy could defeat danger from any direction and skilfully face evil and deceit. Next comes the nymph who draws her name from the pearl, the offspring of the Persian sea. I am pleased by the omen, the gem delights with its pleasing purity, Margaret with her milk-white gentleness. It is smooth, nor is its orb marked with roughness, in Margaret's character there is nothing unpleasing. The gem has a strange relationship with the clear sky; it is light when the sky is clear and pale when it is cloudy. But my maiden is very devoted to the holy gods and prefers to follow the sky rather than the restless sea. When he saw her play with her attendant nymphs and her brother using his weapons with skilful hands: he is golden Phoebus[4], she Phoebus' silver sister,[5] let her trust by the very kindly eye of Phoebus. Now the boy Henry happy in his father's name, with the poet Skelton explaining the sacred spring and meditating on the art of Pallas[7] with all his young heart. How much his father shines in his face! Such in Ascanius was reflected the image of his father,[24] like this did Achilles resemble the beautiful Thetis[25] in his face. Mary promises something from the very name of the famous star that never sets. But in what poem, Edmund, shall I tell of your cradle? Be present here sisters[26] with your golden plectrum and summon calm sleep for the boy with your lyre, and ring out the Fescennine verses. Strew, nymphs, his cradle with delightful plants. There are delightful ambrosia, lavender and marigold, thyme, saffron and Syrian balsam with pleasant marjoram. Then a thousand kinds of flowers and a thousand colours, but let the rose shine most numerous among them all, mingle the red and the white[20] in beautiful garlands, the little child delights in his father's flowers. Ye fates I pray that your thumbs pluck for the boy a soft, white and fortunate thread.

NOTES

1. Cotton. 2. A mythical country in South Arabia. 3. Spain. 4. The sun. 5. The moon. 6. War. 7. The arts. 8. A Roman family who fought to the death for Rome. 9. A king of Athens who sacrificed his life to gain victory for Athens. 10. Caecilius Metellus who saved the palladium from the burning Temple of Vesta in Rome in 241 B.C. The palladium was a statue of Pallas reputed to have fallen from heaven on Troy from which it was taken first to Greece and later to Rome. The fate of the city was said to depend on this statue. 11. Numa Pompilius, the Roman king who succeeded its founder Romulus and was notable for his study of the gods. 12. Nestor, famous for his wisdom. 13. Maecenas, celebrated for his patronage of the arts. 14. Goddess of justice. 15. Symbolic of peace. 16. One of the Fates who determined the length of men's lives. 17. Hercules. 18. Tithonus, given immortality by the gods, was not granted eternal youth. 19. Paestum was famous for its roses. 20. The red and white Tudor rose. 21. Sheath. 22. Arthur. 23. David. 24. Aeneas. 25. Thetis was the mother of Achilles. 26. The Muses.

APPENDIX C

IN PRAISE OF JOHN SKELTON, AN IMPROMPTU SONG

Translated by Dr Harold Booton. A Latin ode by Erasmus written in honour of John Skelton soon after the writers visit to Henry VII's children.

Why did it please you to give the spring of eloquence to pour on thy name, Skelton bard most worthy of the eternal laurel and glory of the Muses? We have not frequented the caves of the sister Muses, nor drunk from the Aonian spring[1] the waters which enrich the life of poets. But Apollo[2] has given you a golden lyre[3] and the sisters the plectrum, inspiring song, and on your lips rests persuasion sweeter than Hyblean liquid.[4] Calliope[5] has imparted herself wholly to you, you surpass the swan[6] in song. Rhodopeian Orpheus[7] himself also yields to you, voluntarily offering his lute and you with the playing of the lyre can sooth wild beasts and soften solid oaks, you can also halt the rapid course of rivers with your persuasive lyre; you can move rocks aside. As much as Greece owed to Lydian Homer and Mantua to Vergil so much does the land of Britain confess she owes to her Skelton. He was the first to bring the Muses from the world of Latium to this region, the first to teach people here how to speak properly, perfectly and purely. Under your leadership Skelton England nay in no way fear to vie with Roman poets in poetry. Live long and farewell.

NOTES

1. Connected with the Muses. 2. God of poetry and music. 3. Literally tortoiseshell, used in legend to make the first lyre. 4. Honey. 5. The chief Muse, Muse of Epic Poetry. 6. A reference to the fable that a swan sang sweetly when about to die. 7. Orpheus was associated with Mount Rhodopeia in Thrace, a district in Greece.

APPENDIX D

SURVIVING RECORDS OF THE BUILDING OF ELTHAM'S GREAT HALL

A) CPR 1467-77 555. 8 November 1475. Westminster. m 17.

Appointment, during pleasure, of Roger Appulton, esquire, as master and surveyor of the repair and building of the king's manor of Eltham, co. Kent, receiving daily as the king shall please, with power to take stone cutters, plumbers, carpenters, masons and other officers and labourers for the works and stones, timber, tiles, glass, iron, lead and other necessaries and carriage for the same, rendering his account before certain persons appointed by the king.

By p.s.

B) E. 405/80 m 28. Easter 18 Edw. IV (after 7 April 1478).

To Roger Apulton and James Hatfeld for the King's works and repairs at Eltham, by the hands of Hugh Brice—£300.

C) E. 403/847 m 10, Wednesday 26 August 18 Edw. IV (1478).

To Roger Apulton and James Hatfeld in moneys paid to them by the hands of Hugh Brice on account of works at the King's manor of Eltham, by writ of Privy Seal among the mandates of this term—£300, wherefor he will answer.

D) E. 101/329/2. unnumbered membrane, tied up in two bundles back to back.

In the pell of issues of Michaelmas term year 18 of King Edward IV (1478) among other things is contained thus, videlicet 12 October.

To Thomas Hunt, clerk of the King's works, in moneys delivered to him at different times, videlicet once by the hands of Hugh Brice, citizen of London, £100, and another time by the hands of the aforesaid Hugh Brice, £64, on account of the works of the King's manor of Eltham ... £164, wherefor he will answer.

E) E. 405/66. Michelmas 18 Edw. IV (after 6 October 1478).

m.2d. To James Hatfield for the King's works of his manor of Eltham, by the hands of Peter Courteys—£66.13.4.

m.3. To Roger Apulton, master and overseer of various works of the King of the manor of Eltham, on the works aforesaid, by the hands of John Dounham, his servant—£19.2.7.

To the same Roger on the works of the manor aforesaid, by the hands of the said John Dounham—£9.17.10½.

To the same Roger on the works of the manor aforesaid, by the hands of the said John Dounham—£21.2.9½.

m.4. To Roger Apulton and James Hatfeld for works and repairs of the King's manor at Eltham, by the hands of Hugh Brice—£66.13.4.

F) E. 403/848. Issues of Michaelmas Term 18 Edw. IV (after 6 October 1478).

m.2. Friday 23 Oct. To Roger Apulton, esq., and James Hatfeld, in moneys paid to them by the hands of Hugh Brice, on account of the works of the King's manor of Eltham, by writ of Privy Seal among the orders of this term—£66.13.4.

m.6. Tuesday 26 Jan.

m.7. To James Hatfeld in moneys delivered to him by his own hands, receiving money from Peter Curteys, on account of the works of the King's manor of Eltham, by writ of Privy Seal ... £66.13.4.

m.11. Thursday 1 April. To Roger Appulton, master and overseer of various works of the King within his manor of Eltham, in moneys delivered to him by the hands of John Dounham, his servant, at times, namely once £19.2.7, another time £9.17.10½, and another time £21.2.9½, on account of the works of the manor aforesaid, by writ £50.3.3.

G) E. 403/850. Issues of Easter Term 19 Edw. IV (after 28 April 1479).

m.1. Friday 7 May.

m.2. To the same James (Hatfeld) ... by his own hands, on account of the works of the King's new hall within his manor of Eltham, by writ of Privy Seal—£33.6.8.

... To Roger Appulton, esq. ... by the hands of John Dounham, on account of the repair of the King's manor of Eltham, by writ—£54.21½ ...

To James Hatfeld ... by his own hands, on account of the making and building of the new hall within the King's manor of Eltham—£46.14.2.

Monday 10 May.

m.3. To Roger Appulton, esq., master and overseer of various works of the King within the manor of Eltham, by the hands of John Dounham, servant of the said Roger, on account of the works aforesaid, by writ of Privy Seal ... £14.19.3. ...

To the same Roger ... at times, namely once by the hands of John Goder 60s., another time by the hands of William Bere, servant of the said Roger, £7, and another time by the hands of the aforesaid John Dounham £41.12.11, on account of the works of the manor aforesaid, by writ—£51.12.11 ...

To the same Roger ... at times, namely once by the hands of John Dounham £30.10.3½, another time by the hands of the said John £33.2.9., and another time by the hands of the said John £62.6.3., on account of the works of the aforesaid manor, by writ—£125.19.3½ ...

To James Hatfeld ... by his own hands at times, namely once £13, another time £6, another time £28.9.3, another time £36.14.1, and another time £31.15.0½, on account of the works of the new hall within the manor of Eltham, by writ of Privy Seal—£115.18.4½ ...

To James Hatfefd ... by his own hands, on account of the works of the new hall within the King's manor of Eltham, by writ of Privy Seal—£18.3.1 ...

To James Hatfeld ... by his own hands, on account of the works of the King's new hall within his manor of Eltham, by writ of Privy Seal—£31.17.4 ...

To Roger Appulton, esq. ... by the hands of John Dounham, on account of various repairs to be made by him in the manor of Eltham, by writ of Privy Seal—£63.18.3 ...

After the feast of Trinity (after 21 June 1479).

m.6. Tuesday 6 July.

m.7. To Roger Appulton, overseer of the King's repairs in his manor of Eltham ... by the hands of John Dounham ... once £63.13.2, another time £37.10d., another time £58.19.5½, another time £56.8.6, and another time £60.3.5½ on account of repairs aforesaid, by writ of Privy Seal—£276.5.5 ...

To James Hatfeld, purveyor of the King's manor of Eltham, and overseer of the works and buildings of the new hall in the same manor ... by his own hands ... once £36.16.6½, another time £40.13.1, another time £40.11.7, and another time £45.2d., on account of the works aforesaid, by writ of Privy Seal ... £163.16½d.

H) E. 405/67. Easter 19 Edw. IV (after 28 April 1479).

m.1. To Roger Appelton, overseer of the repairs and building of the King's manor at Eltham, receiving money at various times, as is fully shown by the indentures and bills of account made by him, namely once £63.13.2, another time £37.10d., another time £58.19.5½, another time £56.8.6, another time £60.3.5½. Receiving the money by the hands of John Dounham ... £276.5.5.

To James Hatfeld, overseer of the works and building of the new hall of the King's said manor of Eltham, receiving the money at various times, as is fully shown by the indentures and bills of account made by him, namely once £36.16.6½, another time £40.13.1, another time £40.11.7, and another time £45.2d, by his own hands—£163.16d.

m.3d. To Roger Appulton on the repairs of the manor of Eltham, by the hands of John Dounham, by writ—£54.21½d.

To James Hatfeld on the building of the hall of the manor of Eltham aforesaid, by his own hands—£46.14.2.

m.4. To Roger Appulton, master and overseer of various works of the King of his manor of Eltham, on the works aforesaid, by the hands of John Dounham—£14.19.3. To the same Roger on the works aforesaid, by the hands of the said John Dounham—£30.10.3½.

To the same Roger on the works aforesaid ... by the hands of John Goder, 60s ... by the hands of William Bere, servant of the said Roger Apulton, £7 ... by the hands of the said John Dounham, £41.12.11—£51.12.11.

To the same Roger on the works aforesaid, by the hands of the said John Dounham—£33.2.9.

To James Hatfield on the works of he King's new hall within his manor of Eltham, by his own hands—£13.

To the same James on the works of the hall aforesaid ... £6 ... £28.9.3, by his own hands £34.9.3.

To the same James on the works of the hall aforesaid, by his own hands—£36.14.1.

To the same James on the works of the hall aforesaid, by his own hands—£31.15.0½. ...

To Roger Appulton, master and overseer of various works of the King of his manor of Eltham, by the hands of John Dounham—£62.6.3.

To James Hatfeld on the works of the King's new hall within his manor of Eltham aforesaid, by his own hands—£18.3.1. ...

To James Hatfeld on the works of the King's new hall within his manor of Eltham aforesaid, by his own hands—£31.17.4.

m.4d. To Roger Appulton, master and overseer of various works of the King of his manor of Eltham, by the hands of John Dounham—£63.18.1. ...

To the same James on the works of the King's new hall within his manor of Eltham aforesaid, by his own hands—£33.6.8.

I) E. 101/496/21 f.1. (1479).

Costes and expenses don' upon' the bildyng of the newe halle withyn the manour of Eltham in the charge of James Hatefeld from Sonday the xixth day of Septembr' the xixth yere of the reigne of oure sovereyn lord kyng Edward the iiijth unto Sonday the iijd of Octobre the yere aforeseid.

Fremasons   To the warden for xij dayes ad xd by the day -x.s.
             xliij Fremasons every of them at vj.d by the day
             for iiijᶜiiiˣjˣxj dayes among them—xij.li,v.s.vj.d   (xij.li.xviij.s.ijd.)
             And iiij Setters every of them at iiij.d. by the
             weke for viij wekes betwene them ijs. viij.

Hardehewers To a hardehewer at vij.d by the day for vj dayes—
             iij.s.vjd. And ij othire hardhewers every of them   (xv.s.vj.d.)
             at vj.d. by the day for xxiiij dayes betwene them
             xij.s.

Carpenters	To the chef warden at x.d. by the day for x dayes— viij.s.iiij.d ij undrewardens every of them at viij.d. by the day for xx dayes betwene them— xiij.s .iiij.d. xliij Carpenters every of them at vj.d. by the day for iij^ciii^xj^xx dayes among them— ix.1i.xv.s. And ij Prenteyces every of them at iiij.d by the day for xx dayes betwene them— vj.s.viij.d.	(xj.li.iij.s.iiij.d)
Plommers	To ij plommers every of them at vj.d. by the day for xviij dayes betwene them	(ix.s.)
Smythes	To ij Smythes every of them at vj.d. by the day for xx. dayes betwen' them	(x.s.)
Laborars	To xxxij laborars every of them at iiij.d. by the day for iij^cxiij dayes among them all	(ciiij.s.viij.d.)
Clerk and Purvyour	To the Clerk for xiiij dayes at vj.d. by the day —vij.s. And to the Purvyour for xiiij dayes at iiij.d. by the day – iiij.s.viij.d.	(xj.s.viij.d)
Ironwerke bought	To Jhon Croucherd for xxx grete spykyngges for the halle roofe weyng xxviij lb. price the lb. at London—ij.d.	(iiij.s.viij.d.)
	Item for x grete clampes of yron for the bynddyng of the princyples weyng Ciii^{xx}jxvj lb. price the lb. at London, ij.d	(xxxv.s.iiij.d.)
Nayle bought	To John Croucherd for iij^C broddes bought for the garneshyng of the seid roofe price the C. xvj.d.	(iiij.s.)
	To Robert Inkersale for m¹ of xpenynayle price at London	(vj.s.iiij.d.)
	Item for m¹ of vjpenynayle price at London	(iij.s.viij.d.)
	Item for v m¹ of iiijpenynayle bought for the boordyng of the halle roofe price the m¹ at London ij.s,iiij.d.	(xj.s.viij.d.)
	Item for iiij m¹ of ledenayle bought for the seid roofe price the m¹, ij.s.iiij.d. (ix.s.iiij.d.)	
Stone bought	To Willyam Ropkyns for vj lod' of Raygateston' price the lod' at the seid manour iiij.s.	(xxiiij.s.)
	To Robert Goore for xij tonne of Ragg price the tonne at Grenewych xiiij.d	(xiiij.s.)
Lymme bought	To John Waller for ij^c lyme bought price the C at the seid manour vj.s.	(xij.s)
Neccessaries bought	To Stevyn Tawyer for iij calvesskynnes bought for the keweveryng of the robynnettes (hoisting tackle) and the xfoldtaklyng (gear or ropes) for the reyne price	(xv.d.)
f.2.		
	To John Claver' for iij qayers of papire bought for the chek rolles and billes price the quayere at London, iij.d.	(ix.d.)
	Item for iij.lb of Candell bought for the plummers price the lb., j.d.	(iij.d)

Cariage from Grenewyche	To Thomas Gillot for cariage of xij tons of Rag to the said manour price of cariage every tonne vj.d.	(vj.s)
	Item for cariage of the seid Ironwerk nayles and neccessaries to the seid manour	(vj.d.)
Cariage from Eltham Park	To John Manwar' for cariage of ix lod' Sande to the seid manour price the lod' j.d.	(ix.d.)
Cariage by day	To Joone Fraunces, Edward Nicolas, Willyam Henley and John Volet for cariage of the framed tymbre from the storeyard to the newe halle by xvij dayes among them all at xvj.d. by the day.	(xxij.s.viij.d.)
Taskwerk	To Robert Goodesole for sawyng of xiij^C fote of Saylyng peces of the hall price the sawyng of every C, xij.d.	(xiij.s.)
Conductions	To ij Cookes servyng the foreseid Fremasons and Carpenters at xviij.d. by the weke for ij wekes betwene them	(iij.s.)
Rentt payed	To James Pembreton for the rent of a close called Withefeld whereyn the tymbre lyeth for a hole yere endyng at the feste of Seynt Mighell the Archangell the xix yere of the reigne of ouerre seid sovereyn lord kyng Edward the iiijth.	(viij.s.)

The hole Summe commeth to xl.li.xiij.s.vj.d.

Examinatur per Castelton.

J) E. 405/68. Easter 20 Edw. IV (19 April 1480).

m.1d. To Roger Appulton on the repair of the manor of Eltham, receiving the money from John Barker, one of the collectors of the King's Customs and Subsidies in the port of the town of Sandwich—£100 ...

To James Hatfeld on the repair of the manor of Eltham, by the hands of Robert Raby—£13.4.10.

m.2. To James Hatfeld over the new building of the hall of Eltham ... first time, 15 April, by the hands of Robert Raby, Purveyor of the King's works, £25.17.8., second time, 13 May, by the hands of the said Robert, £24.13.11., third time, 20 May, by the hands of the said Robert, £23.16.0., fourth time, 16 Sept., by the hands of the said Robert, £14.18.0—£89.5.7.

To Roger Appulton over the repairs of the manor of Eltham ... first time, 15 April, by the hands of John Dounham ... £19, second time 30 April, by the hands of the said John, £28.15.1., third time, 13 May, by the hands of the said John, £25.5.11., fourth time, 20 May, by the hands of the said John £39.13.5., fifth time, 17 July, by the hands of the said John, £62.13.5., sixth time, 2 Aug., by his own hands, £25.18., seventh time, 17 Aug., by his own hands, £21.10.3., eighth time, 26 Aug., by the hands of the said John Dounham, £24.6.1., ninth time, 10 Sept., by the hands of the said John, £24.15.3.—£271.12d.

m.3. To Roger Appulton over the repairs of the manor of Eltham, by his own hands—10 marks. ...

To Roger Appulton over the repairs of the manor of Eltham, as is shown by a bill of particulars of the said Roger, by the hands of John Dounham—£34.10.9.

To James Hatfeld over the new building of the manor of Eltham, by the hands of Robert Raby -£14.15.0.

m.4. To James Hatfeld over the works of the King's new hall within his manor of

Eltham, by the hands of Robert Raby—£53.9.7. …

To Richard Langton for 5 fothers 3 cwt 3 quarters of lead, price le fodr' £4.13.4., thus bought from him to the King's use, delivered to James Hatfeld over the building of the King's new hall within his manor of Eltham, by the hands of John Brychalt, the lord King's plumber—£24.4.2. …

To the same Roger (Apulton) for like red stones (Brykkes) likewise made and provided for the King's manor of Eltham, by the hands of the said William Elles—£8.

To James Hatfeld over the works of the King's new hall within his manor of Eltham by the hands of Robert Raby—£17.11.0.

To Roger Apulton over the King's works within his manor of Eltham, done by the hands of John Dounham—£34.11.1. …

To the same Roger over the King's works of his manor of Eltham, for similar brykkes provided and made for the same works, by the hands of Willlam Elles—£8.

To James Hatfeld over the works of the King's new hall within his manor of Eltham, by the hands of Robert Raby—£27.17.1.

m.5. To James Hatfeld over the works of the King's new hall within his manor of Eltham, by the hands of Robert Raby—£16.12.8.

To the same James over the works, by the hands of Robert Raby—£21.19.3.

K) E. 28/92. 26 May 20 Edw. IV (1480).

Parcelles and sommes of money paid and delyvered by the kinges high Commaundment by John Fitzherbert and other the kinges Tellers in his Receipt of the kinges Tresoury Remaynyng in ther keping. …

Also delyvered to James Hatfeld upon the building of the new hall within the kinges Manour of Eltham at divers tymes—Ciiij^{li}. xiiij^{d}.

Also paid to Roger Appelton for Diverse Reparcions made within the kinges Manoir of Eltham—lxxiij^{li}.xiij^{d}.

verso …

Also delivered to William Ellis for making of Brike for the kinges Castell of Dovor and his Manoir of Eltham—xxiiij^{li}. …

Also paid to Richard Langton for v foulders iij^{c} iij quarters of lede, every foulder at iiij^{li}.xiij^{s}.iiij^{d}., bought to the kinges use for this Manoir of Eltham—xxiiij^{li}.iiij^{s}.iiij^{d}. 29 Sept. 20 Edw. IV (1480).

Parcelles and sommes of money paid and delivered by the kinges high Commaundment by John Fitzherbert and other the kinges Tellers in his Receipt of the kinges Tresoury Remaynyng in ther keping. …

Also paid to Roger Appelton for Reparcions of the kinges Manour of Eltham at diverse tymes—Ciiij^{xx}xix^{li}.x^{s}.vij^{d}quad.

Also paid to the said Roger upon the said Reparcions, that is to wite for vj^{C} tonne tight of Ragg ston at xx^{d}. the tonne – 1^{li}. – for v foulder of lead, price the foulder with the cariage, iiij^{li}.viij^{s}.iiij^{d}. for Clx Wayne scottes, price the C, lxvj^{s}.viij^{d}., and for cariage of the same, iiij^{s}.viij^{d}. - xxxj tonne di' of plaister of Pareys, x^{li}., and for cariage of the same, xvj^{s}.- ij lodes of lathes, price the lode, xiij^{s}.ij.^{d}., and for boltes of Iren, for lockes, bondis and Dogges of Iren and of brasse and nayles of diverse sortes, x^{li}. And upon the Reparacions of the same place, xjs .iiij^{d}. - C^{li}.

Also paid to James Hatfeld upon Reparacions of the said Manour of Eltham ad diverse tymes—iiij^{xx} ^{li}.ix^{s}.ix^{d}.

L) E. 405/69. Michaelmas 20 Edw. IV (after 6 Oct. 1480).

m.4d. To James Hatfeld over the works of the King's new hall within his manor of

Eltham, from 1 Oct. to the 15th of the same month, done by the hands of Robert Raby—£14.7.0. ...

To the aforesaid James Hatfeld over the King's works within his manor of Eltham, as is shown by a bill of parcels (particulars) made from 15 Oct. year 20 to 5 Nov. then next following—£43.13.5½. ...

To James Hatfeld over the King's works within his manor of Eltham, by the hands of Robert Lyndesey, brekmaker—7s. ...

To the same James over repairs done within the King's manor of Eltham, by his own hands—£21.20½d.

m.5.To Roger Appulton over the repair of the manor of Eltham, by the hands of John Dounham ... 8 Oct., £32.14.11. ... 20 Oct., by his own hands, £8, ... 14 Nov., by the hands of the said John Dounhan, £67.3.10½—£107.18.9½. ...

To Roger Appulton for a great boilyng led weight 1477 lb., price the lb. ¾d., and 3 scoops of brasse, weight 66 lb., price of a lb. 4½d. , thus bought by him for the scullery and saucery within the manor of Eltham, by the King's order, also for carriage of the same from the parish of St Sepulcre, London to the said manor, by the hands of John Tyler, his servant—£6.7.6¾.

To William Elys, Brykmaker, for making various brikkes for repairing the Castle of Dover and the manor of Eltham, besides 50 marks paid to him therefor, by his own hands—£33.6.8.

REFERENCES

References in letters and numbers without an identified source refer to records in The National Archives.

1. ELTHAM BEFORE THE ROYAL PALACE

1. 1801 Census, *Abstract of the Answers and Returns ... for Taking an Account of the Population of Great Britain*, 41, George III (1802), p.155.
Census of England and Wales 1901, County of London, table 9, p.22.
Census of England and Wales 1931, County of London, tables 3 and 4, pp.9, 10.
Census of England and Wales 1951, London, table 3, p.7.
Simmons, R. (ed.), *Eltham in the Making*, vol. 1 (1990), pp.67, 77.
2. Vincent, W.T., 'The Romans in Eltham', *Transactions of the Woolwich and District Archaeological Society*, vol. xix (1914), pp.55-7.
Victoria County History, Kent, vol. iii (1932), p.153.
3. Woods, H., 'Excavations at Eltham Palace', *Torch*, vol. xi, no. 2 (1977), p.18.
4. Woods, H., 'Excavations at Eltham Palace, 1975-9', *Transactions of the London and Middlesex Archaeological Society*, vol. xxxiii (1982), pp.217-18.
5. *VCH, Kent*, vol. iii (1932), p.223.
6. *Ibid*.
7. Lysons, D., *The Environs of London*, vol. iv (1796), p.394.
Ekwall, E., *Studies on English Place and Personal Names* (1931), p.23.
Ekwall, E., *Concise Oxford Dictionary of English Place Names* (1960), pp.xiv, 163, 165.
Wallenberg, J.K., *Kentish Place Names* (1931), p.361; *The Place Names of Kent* (1934), p.2.
8. Ekwall, E. *op. cit.* (1931), p.23.
Ekwall, E., *op. cit.* (1960), pp.xiv, 163, 165.
Wallenberg, J.K., *op. cit.* (1931), p.361; *op. cit.* (1934), p.2.
9. *VCH, Kent*, vol. iii (1932), p.223.
Finn, R.A.W., *Domesday Book* (1973), pp.25, 38, 65-7, 78.
10. Darby, H.C. and Campbell, E.M.J. (eds), *Domesday Geography of South East England* (1962), pp.502-13, 524, 596-7.
Finn, R.A.W., *op. cit.* (1973), pp.2, 4.
Postan, M.M. (ed.), *Cambridge Economic History of Europe*, vol. i, 'The Agrarian Life of the Middle Ages' (1966), pp.548-9, 551.
11. *VCH, Kent*, vol. iii (1932), p.223.
12. Cockayne, G.E., *et al* (eds), *The Complete Peerage*, vol. vii (1929), pp.124-9.
DNB, vol. xiv (1909), pp.869-71.
13. Douglas, D.C. (ed.), *The Domesday Monachorum of Christchurch, Canterbury* (1944), pp.55, 103.
14. Cockayne, G.E., *op. cit.*, vol. v (1926), pp.683-6.
DNB, vol. xvi (1929), pp.1242-4.
Drake, H.H. (ed.), *Hasted's History of Kent Corrected*, part 1, 'The Hundred of Blackheath' (1886), pp.171-2.
15. *DNB*, vol. xvi (1929), pp.1242-4.
Cockayne, G.E., *op. cit.*, vol. v (1926), pp.682-6.
Whitelock, D., with Douglas, D.C. (eds), *The Anglo-Saxon Chronicles* (1961), p.199.
Slocombe, G., *Sons of the Conqueror* (1960), pp.167-82.
Davis, R.C.H., *King Stephen* (1967), pp.14-15, 36-7, 39-40, 52-3, 64-5, 96.
16. Cockayne, G.E., *op. cit.*, vol. v (1926), pp.687-9.
Calendar of Patent Rolls 1367-70 (1913), 287-88.
Drake, H.H. (ed.), *op. cit.*, p.172.
Playford, H. (ed.), *Rot. Orig. in Curia ... Hen. III, Edw. I et Edw. II.*, vol. ii, Record Commission (1810), p.304.
17. Warren, W.L., *King John* (1961), pp.66-76.
Cockayne, G.E., *op. cit.*, vol. v (1926), pp.689-92.
18. Cockayne, G.E., *op. cit.*, vol. v (1926), pp.689-92.
Drake, H.H. (ed.), *op. cit.*, p.172.
19. S.C. 6/890/19.
20. Woods, H., *op. cit.* (1982), p.218.
21. Cockayne, G.E., *op. cit.*, vol. v (1926), p.694-6.
DNB, vol. iv (1908), p.378.
22. Cockayne, G.E., *op. cit.*, vol. v (1926), p.696-702.
DNB, vol. iv (1908), pp.395-6.
23. Illingworth, W. (ed.), *Placita de Quo Warrento ... Edw. I, II et III*, Record Commission (1818), p.341.
24. Cockayne, G.E., *op. cit.*, vol. v (1926), p.696-702.
DNB, vol. iv (1908), pp.395-6.
25. C. 132/27/5 m 34.
26. Cockayne, G.E., *op. cit.*, vol. v (1926), pp.702-8.
DNB, vol. iv (1908), pp.378-92.
Beamish, T., *Battle Royal* (1965), pp.151, 155, 223-4, 231.
27. C. 133/54/7 m 8.

28. *Cal. Fine Rolls 1272-1307* (1911), 135-6, 259.
Cal. Close Rolls 1279-88 (1902), 67.
29. *Cal. Charter Rolls*, vol. ii, 1257-1300 (1906), 246.
30. Cockayne, G.E., *op. cit.*, vol. xii, part 2 (1959), pp.278-80.
DNB, vol. xx (1909), p.287.
31. *Cal. Charter Rolls*, vol. ii, 1257-1300 (1906), 279.
32. C.P. 25(1)/99/65 No. 244.
C. 133/54/7 m 8.
33. *Cal. Inquisitions Post Mortem*, vol. ii, Edward I (1906), 446.
34. *Cal. Fine Rolls 1272-1307*, 259.
35. *Ibid*.
36. Cockayne, G.E., *op. cit.*, vol. xii, part 2 (1959), pp.281-3.
DNB, vol. xx (1909), pp.288-9.
37. *Cal. Inq. Post Mortem*, vol. ii, Edward I (1906), 446.
38. BL MSS Dept Harl. Ch. 43.1.48.
39. Fraser, C.M., *A History of Antony Bek, Bishop of Durham 1283-1311* (1957).
40. *Ibid.*, pp.248-9.
41. Raine, J. (ed.), Robertus de Graystanes, *Historia Dunelmensis*, Surtees Society (1839), p.91.
42. Woods, H., *op. cit.* (1982), pp.218-27, 234-6, 238-44.
43. Flenley, R. (ed.), *Six Town Chronicles of England* (1911), p.128.
Trinity College, Dublin, MS E.5.10. f 166r.
44. BL MSS Dept. Harl. Ch. 43.D.12.
Palgrave, Sir F. (ed.), *The Antient Kalendars and Inventories of the Treasury of Exchequer*, vol. i (1836), p.59.
45. Fraser, C.M., *op. cit.*, p.228.
46. *Ibid.*, pp.229-32, 243, 246, 248-9.
47. C. 134/21/8 m 6.
48. *Cal. Fine Rolls 1272-1307*, 136.
Cal. Close Rolls 1279-88, 67.
Cal. Charter Rolls, vol. ii, 1257-1300, 246.
C. 132/27/5 m 34.
Palgrave, Sir F. (ed.), *op. cit.*, p.62.
49. C. 134/21/8 m 6.
50. CPR 1307-13 (1894), 172.
51. *Cal. Treaty Rolls 1234-1325*, vol. i (1955), 132-3, 185-6.
Hardy, Sir T.D. (ed.), *Syllabus Rymer's Foedera*, vol. i, Edward I, II (1869), pp.125-6.

52. Cockayne, G.E., *op. cit.*, vol. v (1926), pp.708-12.
53. Cal. Fine Rolls 1272-1307, 388-91.
54. *Syllabus Rymer's Foedera*, vol. i (1955), p.127.
55. *Ibid.*
56. Cal. Close Rolls 1296-1302, 71-2.
57. *Ibid.*
58. *Ibid.*, 72.
59. CPR 1292-1301 314.
60. Cal. Close Rolls 1296-1302, 71.
    CPR 1292-1301 314-15.
61. Cal. Charter Rolls, vol. ii, 1257-1300, 470.
62. CPR 1292-1301 313-14.
63. *Ibid.* 314.
64. Cal. Close Rolls 1296-1302, 71-2.

2. THE EARLY YEARS OF ROYAL ELTHAM

1. Johnstone, H. (ed.), *Letters of Edward, Prince of Wales, 1304-05* (1931), p.126.
2. *Ibid.*, p.xxxvi.
   BL MSS Dept, Cotton Nero c. viii f 54v.
   Cal. Inq. Misc., vol. ii, 1308-48 (1916), 1-2, 5.
   Cal. Chancery Rolls, 1277-1326 (1912), 145.
   Cal. Charter Rolls, Edward I, Edward II, vol. iii, 1300-26 (1908), 109.
   CPR 1307-13 (1894), 45-6, 48, 85.
   Cal. Close Rolls, 1307-13 (1892), 19-20, 23, 52.
   Cal. Fine Rolls, 1307-19 (1912), 14-15.
   Communications made to the British Archaeological Association, *Collectanea Archaeologica*, vol. i (1861), p.114.
3. Johnstone, H. (ed.), *op. cit.*, p.xxxvi.
4. *Collectanea Archaeologica*, p.114.
5. *Ibid.*, p.121.
6. Cal. Close Rolls, 1307-13 (1892), 380.
7. Cotton Nero c. viii ff 124-124v.
8. *Ibid.* f 125.
9. *Ibid.* f 126.
10. *Ibid.* f 126v.
11. *Ibid.* f 127.
12. *Ibid.* f 135.
13. *Ibid.* f 140.
14. *Ibid.* f 135.
15. *Ibid.* f 128.
16. *Ibid.* f 140.
17. *Ibid.* f 137d.
    Tout, T.F., *Chapters in the Administrative History of Medieval England*, vol. v (1920-33), p.241.
18. Cotton Nero c. viii f 152v.
19. 'Chronicle of the Reigns of Edward I and Edward II', Annales Londonienses, rolls series, vol. i (1862), p.45.
    Thompson, E.M. (ed.), *Chronicon Galfridi le Baker de Synbroke* (1889), p.6.
20. 'Chronicle of the Reigns of Edward I and Edward II', vol. i (1862), p.221.
21. E 101/375/9 ff 3, 5, 7-11, 13, 17, 22v, 33v.
22. *Ibid.* f 7.
23. *Ibid.* ff 1, 33v.
24. *Ibid.* f 3.
25. *Ibid.* f 13.
26. *Ibid.* f 17.
27. *Ibid.* f 13.
28. *Ibid.* f 22v.
29. Stapleton, T. (ed.), 'Wardrobe Accounts of 10th, 11th and 14th Edward II', *Archaeologia*, vol. xxvi (1836), pp.320, 336.
30. *Ibid.*, p.336.
31. *Ibid.*, p.320.
32. *Ibid.*, p.342.
33. Cal. Close Rolls, 1346-9 (1905), 26, 107, 326.
34. 'Chronicle of the Reigns of Edward I and

Edward II', vol. i (1862), p.128.
    Cockayne, G.E., *The Complete Peerage*, vol. iii (1913), pp.434-5.
35. E 101/375/9 f 33v.
36. E 101/375/8.
37. BL MSS Dept, Add. MSS 17362 f 32.
38. *Ibid.* f 4.
39. Cal. Fine Rolls, 1319-27 (1912), 390.
    Collectanea Archaeologica, vol. i (1861), p.142.
    CPR 1324-27 276.
    Cal. Close Rolls, 1323-27 (1898), 572.
40. K.B. 27/268, Rex m 4d.
41. K.B. 27/269, Rex m 6d.
42. K.B. 27/268, Rex m 4d, 11.
43. K.B. 27/269, Rex m 8.
44. K.B. 27/268, Rex m 11.
45. CPR 1324-27 294
46. 'Chronicle of the Reigns of Edward I and Edward II', vol. i (1862), pp.313-38.
    Thompson, E.M. (ed.), *op. cit.*, pp.20-34.
    Hutchison, H.F., *Edward II* (1971), pp.127-42.
    Packe, M., *Edward III* (1983), pp.22-31.
47. K.B. 27/268, Rex m 4d.
48. *Ibid.*
    K.B. 27/270, Rex m 14d.
49. K.B. 27/269, Rex mm 6d, 8.
50. *Ibid.* Rex m 6d.
51. CPR 1327-30 110-12.
52. K.B. 27/270, Rex mm 3d, 14d.
    CPR 1324-27 348.
53. CPR 1327-30 56-7.
54. *Ibid.* 37-9, 58.
55. Packe, M., *op. cit.*, pp.32-3, 40-1, 43, 45-6.
    Hutchison, H.F., *op. cit.*, pp.132, 136, 141, 143.
56. Froissart, J. (ed. de Lettenhove, K.), *Oeuvres*, vol. ii (1870), pp.93-5.
57. 'Chronicle of the Reigns of Edward I and Edward II', vol. i (1862), pp.338-9; vol. ii, p.99.
    Froissart, J., *op. cit.* (1870), p.196.
58. E 101/384/1 ff 17v-18.
    CPR 1327-30 37-9, 58, 364-5, 368-74, 376-7, 381, 383, 385-93, 395, 402-9, 422-3, 425-31, 468-70, 474, 481-6, 488-9, 491, 496, 501.
    Cal. Charter Rolls, vol. iv, 1327-41 (1912), 101, 118, 120.
    Cal. Close Rolls 1327-30 429-30, 432, 435, 439-42, 445-6, 451-2, 454-65, 471-4, 503-4, 514-16, 518-20, 522, 532, 537-44, 546-7, 552-4, 593-4.
    Wylie, J.H. and J. (eds), 'Report on the Records of the City of Exeter', Royal Commission on Historical MSS (1916), p.3.
    Cal. Fine Rolls 1327-37 (1913), 120-5, 130-5, 138-9, 144, 150, 161-3, 168.
    Cal. Inq. Misc. 1308-48, 263-4, 267-8, 270-2, 274, 277-8, 282, 289.
    Hutchison, H.F., *op. cit.*, pp.126-52, 169-70.
    Packe, M., *op. cit.*, pp.23, 25-31, 38-9.
59. *Ibid.*, pp.40-2, 44-53.
60. Froissart, J., *op. cit.* (1870), p.254.
61. Froissart, J., *op. cit.* (1870), pp.234-6.
    Longman, W., *Life of Edward III*, vol. i (1869), p.45.
    Cal. Close Rolls 1330-33 130.
62. Packe, M., *op. cit.*, pp.46-53.
63. S.C. 8/297 no. 14837.
64. As no. 58 above.
65. CPR 1327-30 363-4.
66. CPR 1327-30 386.
    Cal. Close Rolls 1327-30 456, 459, 474.
    Syllabus Rymer's Foedera, vol. i (1869), p.251.
67. *Ibid.*
68. *Ibid.*, pp.253-4.
69. *Ibid.*, p.254.
70. Froissart, J., *op. cit.* (1870), pp.234-6.
    Tout, T.F., *The Political History of England*,

vol. iii (1930), p.328.
    Syllabus Rymer's Foedera, vol. i (1869), p.260.
    CPR 1330-34 90-5.
71. Cal. Close Rolls 1330-33 199.
    CPR 1330-34 96, 98, 117.
72. Packe, M., *op. cit.*, pp.103-4.
73. *Syllabus Rymer's Foedera*, vol. i. (1869), p.260.
74. CPR 1330-34 99-105.
75. Froissart, J., *op. cit.* (1870), pp.323, 437-8, 441.
76. Packe, M., *op. cit.*, pp.89-93.
    Vale, Juliet, *Edward III and Chivalry* (1982), pp.82, 150-1.
77. Cal. Close Rolls 1341-43 501-2.
    Thompson, E.M. (ed.), *Adam Murimuth. Continuatio Chronicarum Robert de Avesbury. de Gestis Mirabilibus Regis Edwardi Tertii*, rolls series (1889), pp.124, 223-4.
78. Scattergood, V.J. and Sherborne, J.W. (eds), *English Court Culture in the Later Middle Ages* (1983), p.192.
79. CPR 1343-45 263, 445.
80. E 372/163 rot. 14d m 2.
    Cal. Close Rolls 1313-18 502.
81. Cal. Close Rolls 1327-30 335.
82. Colvin, H.M. (ed.), *op. cit.*, vol. ii (1963), pp.930-1.
    Salzman, L.F., *Building in England down to 1540* (1952), pp.27-8, 422-4.
    Pleas of the Exchequer 10 Edw. II m 16.
83. Charlton, J., 'Eltham Palace Anniversary Address 1986', *Transactions of the Ancient Monuments Society*, vol. xxxi (N.S.) (1987), pp.10-11.
    E 372/200 rot. 41.
84. E 101/494/7 m 3.
85. Drake, H.H. (ed.), *Hasted's History of Kent Corrected* (1886), pp.173-4, 176.
    CPR 1307-13 398.
86. CPR 1307-13 398.
    CPR 1313-17 490-1.
87. CPR 1327-30 66-9, 96, 401.
    CPR 1330-34 367.
88. CPR 1313-17 206, 490-1.
89. *Ibid.*
    CPR 1317-21 159.
90. *Arch. Aeliana*, 3rd series, vol. ix (1913), p.209.
    BL MSS Dept, Harl. Ch. 43 D. 12.
91. C. 134/21/8 m 6.
    Playford, H. (ed.), *Cal. Inq. P.M. Temp. Regum Hen. III, Edw. I, Edw. II* (1810). Vol. I, Record Commission (1806), 242.
92. Ashe, T. (ed.), Cal. Rot. Pat. in *Turri Londiniensi*, Record Commission (1802), p.83.
    Lysons, D., *The Environs of London*, vol. iv (1796), p.396.
93. Lysons, D., *op. cit.*, p.396.
94. *Ibid.*, pp.395-6.
    Dugdale, W., *Baronage*, vol. i (1675), p.95.
95. Stones, E.L.G., 'Sir Geoffrey le Scrope', *English Historical Review*, vol. lxix (1954), pp.1-17.
96. Cal. Charter Rolls, vol. iv, 1327-41, 196-7.
97. *Ibid.*
98. *Ibid.*
    E 352/152 rot. 11.
99. Tout, *op. cit.* (1930), vol. v, p.276.
100. E 372/190 rot. 39.
     E 372/200 rot. 41d.
101. S.C. 6/1090/10 m 6.
     Westminster Abbey MSS 27852-61.
     Cal. Fine Rolls 1327-37 215, 299.
102. Westminster Abbey MSS 27847mm 1, 2d, 27848, 27850, 27850d, 27851 mm 1-2, 27853 m 1, 27854d, 27855, 27856, 27857, 27858, 27859, 27862, 27876, 27877.
     Priestley, E.J., 'The Manor and Palace of Eltham 1086-1663', unpublished MPhil thesis, University of London (1973), p.382.

103. Westminster Abbey MSS 27846, 27847 mm 3, 3d, 27854d, 27855 mm 1, 2d, 27858, 27862, 27863d, 27868B, 27877.
104. *Ibid.* MSS 27858, 27861.
105. *Ibid.* MSS 27847 m 3.
Priestley, *op. cit.*, p.417.
106. *Ibid.*, pp.329-32.
107. Westminster Abbey MSS 27857d, 27861d.
108. *Ibid.* MSS 27854, 27859d.
109. *Ibid.* MSS 27856.
110. *Ibid.* MSS 27854d, 27859, 27861, 27862.
111. *Ibid.* MSS 27847 m 3d.
112. Priestley, E.J., *op. cit.*, pp.334-5, 337, 340-2, 344-5, 347, 349-50, 352-5.
113. *Ibid.*, pp.329-32.
114. *Ibid.*, pp.334-58.
115. *Ibid.*, pp.329-32.
116. *Ibid.*, pp.327-8.
117. Westminster Abbey MSS 27847 mm 2, 2d, 27848, 27848d, 27849d, 27850d.
118. *Ibid.* MSS 27847 mm 2, 2d, 27848, 27848d, 27849, 27849d, 27850, 27850d.
119. *Ibid.* MSS 27847 m 2d.
120. *Ibid.* MSS 27850.
121. *Ibid.* MSS 27848, 27849d.
122. *Ibid.* MSS 27851 m 1, 27852, 27853 m 1, 27854d, 27855, 27855 m 1, 27856, 27857, 27861, 27862, 27863.
123. *Ibid.* MSS 27854, 27855 m 1d, 27861d.
124. *Ibid.* 27853 m 1, 27860, 27861, 27876.
125. *Ibid.* MSS 27851 m 1, 27853 m 1, 27854d, 27859, 27860, 27861, 27861d, 27862.
126. *Ibid.* MSS 27861, 27862.
127. *Ibid.* MSS 27859.
128. *Ibid.* MSS 27860.
129. *Ibid.* ES 27865.
130. *Ibid.* MSS 27853 m 2, 27855 mm 1d, 2d, 27857d, 27860d, 27861d, 27864 m 2d.
131. *Ibid.* MSS 27853 m 2, 27854, 27854d, 27855 m 1d, 27856, 27856d, 27857d, 27859d, 27860d, 27861d, 27863d.
132. *Ibid.* MSS 27854, 27855 m 1d, 27856d, 27857d.
133. *Ibid.* MSS 27853 m 2.
134. *Ibid.* MSS 27853 m 2, 27854.
135. *Ibid.* MSS 27853 mm 1d, 2, 27854, 27868Bd.
136. *Ibid.* MSS 27851 m 2d, 27853 mm 1d, 2, 27854, 27855 mm 1d, 2d, 27856, 27856d, 27859, 27861d, 27862d, 27863d, 27868Bd.
137. *Ibid.* MSS 27859.
138. *Ibid.* MSS 27851 mm 1d, 2, 2d, 27852, 27853 mm 1, 1d, 27854d, 27855 mm 1, 1d, 27856, 27856d, 27857, 27857d, 27859, 27859d, 27860, 27860d, 27861d, 27862, 27862d.
139. *Ibid.* MSS 27876.
140. *Ibid.* MSS 27855 m 1
141. *Ibid.* MSS 27851 m 1, 27853 m 1, 27854d, 27855, 27857, 27859, 27860, 27862, 27863, 27864 m 1.
142. *Ibid.* MSS 27859, 27860, 27861, 27862.
143. *Ibid.* MSS 27861.
144. *Ibid.* MSS 27862.
145. *Ibid.* MSS 27854, 27854d.
146. *Ibid.* MSS 27853 m 1, 27863.
147. *Ibid.* MSS 27851 m 1, 27853 m 1, 27855 m 1, 27857, 27859, 27860, 27861, 27862, 27863.
148. *Ibid.* MSS 27862, 27863.
149. *Ibid.* MSS 27854d, 27855 m 1, 27859, 27860.
150. *Ibid.* MSS 27857, 27859, 27859d, 27860.
151. *Ibid.* MSS 27859, 27859d, 27860, 27860d.
152. *Ibid.* HSS 27854d.
153. *Ibid.* MSS 27855 m 1, 27856, 27856d, 27857d.

154. *Ibid.* MSS 27877.
155. E 403/163 m 4; /164 m 10.
E 372/163 rot. 14d m 2; /165 rot. 29d m 2.
Cal. Close Rolls, 1313-18 502.
Westminster Abbey MSS 27850, 27850d, 27865.
CPR 1324-27 323.
CPR 1327-30 110-12.
K.B. 27/268. Rex mm 4d, 11; /269. Rex mm 6d, 8; /270. Rex mm 3d, 14d.
156. Cal. Close Rolls, 1323-27 439.
157. CPR 1330-34 122.
158. CPR 1324-27 323.
Cal. Close Rolls, 1343-46 541.
E 372/190 rot. 39.
Cal. Fine Rolls, 1327-37 215.
159. CPR 1343-45 445.
160. Cal. Fine Rolls, 1327-37 299.

3. BUILDING A ROYAL PALACE.

1. CPR 1345-48 195, 217, 242.
Cal. Inq. Misc., vol. ii, 1308-48, 491, 495, 504, 512, 514-16.
Drake, H.H. (ed.), *Hasted's History of Kent: Hundred of Blackheath* (1886), p.177.
Froissart, J. (ed. de Lettenhove, K.), *Oeuvres*, vol. iv (1870), p.383.
2. Cal. Inq. Misc., vol. ii, 1308-48, p.491.
3. CPR 1345-48 211.
4. CPR 1345-48 225.
Syllabus of Rymer's Foedera, vol. v, 1346-7 (1869), pp.352-3.
5. *Syllabus of Rymer's Foedera*, vol. v, 1346-7 (1869), p.352.
6. CPR 1345-48 226.
CPR 1361-64 454.
Cal. Fine Rolls, 1337-47 494.
Syllabus of Rymer's Foedera, vol. i, 1346-7, pp.352-3.
7. Vale, J., *Edward III and Chivalry* (1982), pp.82, 150-1.
Syllabus of Rymer's Foedera, vol. i, 1346-7, pp.352-3.
Cal. Close Rolls, 1346-49 133.
8. CPR 1345-48 391.
9. Ramsay, J.H., *The Genesis of Lancaster*, vol. i (1913), pp.353-4.
Nicolas, Sir N.E., *History of the Orders of Knighthood*, vol. i (1842), pp.lxxiii, lxxxi, 11-14.
Beltz, G.F., *Memorials of the Order of the Garter* (1841), pp.xxxi, 379-81.
E 101/391/15 mm 1, 10.
10. Froissart, J., *op. cit.* (1870), vol. v, p.233.
Cal. Close Rolls, 1346-49, 458.
11. Zeigler, P., *The Black Death* (1969), pp.157-62.
12. CPR 1348-50 352, 355-7, 360, 376.
Cal. Close Rolls, 1349-54 48, 52-3, 95, 101.
Cal. Fine Rolls, 1347-56 117, 120, 123, 149.
13. E 101/392/12 ff 7v-8v, 27-29.
Tout, T.F., *Chapters in the Administrative History of Medieval England*, vol. iv (1920-33), p.179.
14. E 101/392/12 f 34.
15. E 101/392/12 ff 34v, 44.
16. Register of Edward the Black Prince preserved in the Public Record Office, vol. iv (1933), pp.123-4.
17. Froissart (ed. Jolliffe, J.), *Chronicles* (1967), pp.165-75.
18. *Ibid.*, pp.214-16.
19. Cockayne, G.E., *Complete Peerage*, vol. iii, p.258.
Cal. Inq. Misc., vol. ii, 1308-48, 491.
20. Cockayne, G.E., *op. cit.*, vol. iii, pp.257-8.
21. Cal. Inq. Post Mortem, vol. xii (1938), 370-1.
Cockayne, G.E., *op. cit.*, vol. x, pp.231-2; vol. xii, part 2, p.180.
CPR 1396-99 583.

21. Fourth Report of the Deputy Keeper of the Public Records, appx ii (1843), p.135.
22. Cockayne, G.E., *op. cit.*, vol. iii, p.258.
23. E 101/493/4 m 5d.
24. *DNB*, vol. x (1887), p.156.
25. Crow, M.M., and Olsen, C.C. (eds), *Chaucer Life Records* (1966), pp.13-15, 18.
26. E 101/493/4 mm 1-6.
27. E 372/202; /203; /204.
28. Pauli, R., *Geshichte von England*, vol. iv (1855), p.452.
Viard, J., and Deprez, E. (eds), *Chronique de Jean le Bel*, vol. ii (1904), pp.318-19.
Douet-d'Arcq, L. (ed.), *Comptes de l'Argenterie des Rois de France, Journal de la Depense du Roi Jean en Angleterre* (1851), pp.270-1.
29. Rymer, T., *Foedera*, vol. iii, part 2, pp.3-7, Viard, J., and Deprez, E., *op. cit.*, pp.319-20.
30. Froissart, J. (ed. Johnes, T.), *Chronicle*, vol. i (1849), p.305.
31. Froissart, J., *Oeuvres*, vol. vi, pp.388-9, 391-3.
Delachenel, R. (ed.), *Chronique des Regnes de Jean II et de Charles V*, vol. i (1910), p.340.
Kingsford, C.L., 'The Feast of the Five Kings', *Archaeologia*, vol. lxvii (1916), pp.119-26.
CPR 1361-64 433, 436, 439-42, 455-6, 470.
32. Cockayne, G.E., *op. cit.*, vol. ii (1912), pp.69-70.
Green, M.A.E., *Lives of the Princesses of England*, vol. iii (1851), pp.201-2, 205-6.
33. Froissart, J., *op. cit.*, pp.388, 391; *Poesies*, vol. ii, pp.308-10.
Gregory, R.R.C., *The Story of Royal Eltham* (1909), pp.128-30.
Delachenel, R., *op. cit.*, vol. ii, p.340.
34. Cal. Rot. Pat. in *Turri Londinensi* (1802), p.240.
35. Green, M.A.E., *op. cit.*, pp.206-7.
36. Cal. Rot. Pat. in *Turri Londinensi* (1802), p.240.
Green, M.A.E., *op. cit.*, pp.210, 221-2.
Cockayne, G.E., *op. cit.*, vol. x, pp.231-2.
37. Cal. Fine Rolls, 1369-77 147.
E 101/397/5 ff 18-28, 34-34v, 45v, 46v, 52v-53, 62-65, 77, 81, 86.
Cal. Close Rolls, 1369-74 271, 427-8.
CPR 1370-74 164.
38. E 101/397/5 ff 34-34v.
39. *Ibid.* f 86.
40. Armitage-Smith, S. (ed.), *John of Gaunt's Register 1372-76*, part I, vol. 2 (1911), p.298-9.
41. E 101/397/12 mm 1, 2.
42. *Archaeologia*, vol. xix (1821), pp.411-12.
43. Devon, F. (ed.), 'Issues of the Exchequer Henry III-Henry VI', *Pell Records*, p.201.
44. CPR 1374-77 91-6, 98, 105, 107, 129.
Cal. Close Rolls, 1374-77 218-19, 253.
Tout, T.F., *op. cit.*, vol. iii, p.287.
45. Rot. Parl., vol. ii, Edward III (1783), 330, 360.
Kay, F.G., *Lady of the Sun* (1966), p.146.
Holmes, G., *The Good Parliament* (1975), pp.159-61, 165, 178-98.
46. E 101/397/12 m 2.
47. Tout, T.F., *op. cit.*, vol. iii, p.304.
Kay, F.G., *op. cit.*, p.149.
48. McKisack, M., *The Fourteenth Century 1307-1399* (1959), pp.384-95.
49. CPR 1348-50 588.
50. E 372/197 rot. 44d.
51. E 372/200 rots. 41, 41d.
52. E 101 /493/4 mm 2-6.
E 101/493/30 mm 1-2.
53. *Ibid.*
54. E 101/493/12 m 8.
E 101 /493/18 m 11.
E 101/494/28 mm 1, 2d, 8, 9.
E 101/494/29 m 2.

55. E 101/494/28 m 9.
 E 101/494/19 m 1.
 E 101/545/40.
56. E 101/545/38 mm 4, 5.
 E 101/494/7 m 3.
 E 101/494/19 mm 1, 2.
 E 101/494/29 mm 1-3.
57. E 101/545/38 m 4.
 E 101/493/4 m 6.
 E 372/200 rot. 41.
58. *Country Life*, vol. lxxxi, 22 May 1937, p.573.
 Clapham, A.W., and Godfrey, W.H., *Some Famous Buildings and Their Story* (1913), pp.54-5.
 E 101/497/1 ff 4-4v.
59. E 101/545/38 m 4.
60. E 101/473/2 m 12.
 E 372/200 rot. 41d.
61. E 101/493/4 m 5d.
62. E 101/493/4 m 5.
 E 101/493/8.
63. E 101/494/18 m 2.
64. E 101/493/4 mm 3, 4, 5d.
 E 101/502/15 m 4.
65. E 101/493/4 m 6.
 E 101/493/8.
 E 101/493/12 m 9.
 E 101/493/18 mm 11, 12.
 E 101/493/30 m 2.
 E 101/494/7 mm 3, 4.
 E 101/545/37 m 3.
 E 101/494/15 m 2.
 E 101/494/22 m 5.
 E 101/545/38 mm 4, 5.
 E 364/6 rots. Dd, Ed.
 E 101/495/23 m 2.
66. E 101/493/4 m 5.
 E 101/494/7 m 3.
 E 101/494/28 m 9.
 E 101/493/4 m 5.
67. E 101/493/30 m 2.
 E 101/493/12 m 9.
 E 101/493/18 m 12.
68. E 101/493/18 m 11.
 E 101/473/2 m 12.
 E 101/502/31 m 1.
69. E 101/494/22 m 5.
 E 101/493/4 m 3.
70. E 101/493/12 m 8.
 E 101/493/30 m 1.
 E 101/494/7 m 3.
 E 101/494/18 m 2.
 E 101/494/19 m 1.
 E 101/493/4 m 5.
71. E 101/493/4 m 5.
 E 101/473/2 m 12.
 E 101/502/15 m 4.
 E 101/502/21 m 4.
72. E 101/502/31 m 1.
 E 101/502/21 m 4.
73. E 101/493/18 m 11.
 E 101/494/18 m 2.
 E 101/494/22 m 5.
 E 101/493/12 m 8.
 E 101/493/30 m 2.
 E 101/473/3 m 8.
 E 101/473/2 mm 12, 21.
 E 101/502/31 m 2.
74. E 101/545/38 m 4.
 E 101/494/28 m 9.
 E 101/494/29 mm 1, 3.
 E 101/493/4 m 3.
 E 101/495/23 m 4.
75. E 101/493/30 m 1.
76. E 101/495/23 mm 1, 4.
 E 101/502/15 m 4.

77. E 101/502/31 m 1.
 E 101/493/30 m 1.
 E 101/493/18 m 11.
 E 101/473/2 m 12.
78. E 101/473/3 m 8.
 E 101/502/15 m 4.
 E 101/502/21 m 4.
79. E 101/473/2 m 21.
 E 101/502/15 m 4.
 E 101/502/21 m 4.
 E 101/502/31 m 1.
80. E 101/493/30 m 2.
 E 101/494/7 m 3.
81. E 101/493/4 m 5.
82. E 101/493/30 m 2.
83. E 364/6 rot. Dd.
 E 101/494/7 m 3.
84. E 372/197 rot. 44d.
 E 372/200 rot. 41.
85. E 101/502/31 mm 1, 2.
86. E 101/493/4 m 6.
 E 372/200 rot. 41.
87. E 101/493/30 mm 1, 2.
88. E 101/493/18 m 11.
 E 101/493/12 m 8.
89. E 101/493/30 m 1.
90. E 101/493/4 mm 3, 5.
91. E 372/200 rots. 41-41d.
92. CPR 1343-45 445.
93. E 101/493/4 m 5d.
94. E 101/545/38 m 4.
95. E 372/200 rot. 41.
96. E 101/493/8.
 E 101/494/18 m 2.
 E 101 /494/22 m 5.
97. E 101/494/19 m 1.
98. E 101/494/15 m 2.
99. E 101/493/4 mm 5-5d.
 E 101/493/8.
100. E 101/494/18 m 2.
 E 101/493/4 m 5d.
101. E 101/493/18 m 3.
102. E 101/494/7 m 3.
103. E 101/493/4 m 5.
104. E 101/494/7 m 3.
 E 101/493/30 m 2.
105. E 101/494/18 m 2.
106. Godfrey, W.H., 'Eltham Hall', *Architectural Review*, vol. lxxx (October 1936), p.152.
 Seely and Paget, File 16, Notes on inspection by Sir Charles Peers, 18 January 1934.
107. E 101/494/28 m 8.
108. E 101/493/4 m 5.
109. Clapham, A.W. and Godfrey, W.H., *op. cit.*, pp.54-5.
110. King, D., and Clayton, A.B., *Subterranean Passages at Eltham Palace Lately Discovered and Explored* (1834), illns 3-8.
111. Brook, R., *The Story of Eltham Palace* (1960), p.40.
112. Godfrey, W.H., *op. cit.*, p.152.
113. E 101/497/1 f 6.
114. Clapham, A.W. and Godfrey, W.H., *op. cit.*, pp.54-5.
 Hatfield MSS. BM Maps, Cecil Papers, Maps 1/5.
115. Woods, H., 'Excavations at Eltham Palace, 1975-9', *Transactions of the London and Middlesex Archaeological Society*, vol. 32 (1982), pp.215-65.
116. E 101/493/4 mm 2, 3, 5-5d.
 E 101/494/7 m 3.
117. E 101/493/30 m 2.
118. *Ibid.* m 1.
119. E 372/190 rot. 39.

120. E 101/397/5 f 45v.
 E 101/403/10 f 41.
 E 101/404/21 f 41.
 E 101/406/21 f 22.
 E 101/409/9 ff 34-34v.
 E 101/409/16 f 29v.
 E 101/410/3 f 27.
 E 101/410/9 ff 39-39v.
121. E 101/409/9 f 34v.
 E 101/410/3 f 27.
 E 101/410/9 f 39.
122. E 101/409/9 f 34.
 E 101/409/16 f 29v.
123. E 101/397/5 f 45v.
 E 101/403/10 f 41.
 E 101/404/21 f 41.
 E 101/406/21 f 22.
 E 101/409/9 ff 34-34v.
 E 101/409/16 f 29v.
 E 101/410/3 f 27.
 E 101/410/9 ff 39-39v.
124. E 372/190 rot. 39.
 E 101/406/21 f 22.
125. E 101/403/10 ff 41-41v.
126. *Ibid.* f 41.
 E 101/406/21 ff 22-22v.
127. E 101/493/30 m 1.
128. E 101/494/7 m 3.
129. E 101/493/12 m 8.
 E 101/545/37 m 3.
130. E 101/502/15 mm 5-6.
 E 101/494/15 m 2.
131. E 372/197 rot. 44d.
132. Cal. Close Rolls, 1377-81 157, 161, 398.
 CPR 1367-70 220.
 CPR 1377-81 143.
 E 364/16 rot. Hd.
133. E 101/494/7 m 3.
134. E 101/494/27 m 1.
 E 101/494/28 mm 1, 9.
 E 101/494/29 mm 1, 3.
 E 101/545/40.
135. E 101/493/4 mm 2-4, 6.
136. *Ibid.* m 4.
137. *Ibid.* mm 2, 3.
138. *Ibid.* m 6.
139. *Ibid.* mm 2-4.
140. *Ibid.* mm 2-3.
 Priestley, E.J., 'The Manor and Palace of Eltham, Kent 1086-1663', unpublished MPhil thesis, University of London (1973), pp.243-6.
141. *Ibid.*, pp.246-7.
142. *Ibid.*, pp.261-2.
143. *Ibid.*, pp.246-7.
144. E 101/494/28 m 9.
145. E 101/493/30 m 2.
 E 101/494/7 m 4.
146. E 101/493/4 m 6.
147. *Ibid.* mm 4-6.
 E 101/493/30 m 1.
 E 101/494/7 mm 3, 4.
148. E 101/493/4 mm 5, 6.
149. E 101/494/7 m 3.
150. E 101/493/30 m 1.
151. E 101/493/4 m 6.
152. *Ibid.*
153. *Ibid.*
154. E 101/494/7 m 4.
 E 101/493/30 mm 1, 2.
155. E 101/493/4 m 6.
156. E 101/493/4 m 6.
157. E 101/493/30 mm 1, 2.
 E 101/494/7 m 4.
 E 101/493/4 m 6.
158. E 101/494/18 m 2.
159. E 101/494/28 mm 8, 9.

160. Colvin, H.M. (ed.), *The King's Works*, vol. ii, p.931, note 5.
161. *Ibid.*, note 3.
  Drake, H.H. (ed.), *op. cit.*, p.176.
162. E 372/190 rots. 39, 39d.
163. CPR 1345–48 254.
  Cal. Close Rolls, 1346–49 465–6.
  Rot. Orig., in *Curia Scaccarii Abbreviato Temp. Edw. III*, vol. ii (1810), p.187.
164. Cat. Ancient Deeds, vol. iii (1900), p.128.
  Drake, H.H. (ed.), *op. cit.*, p.176.
165. Rot. Orig., in *Curia Scaccarii Abbreviato Temp. Edw. III*, vol. ii (1810), p.196.
166. Cal. Charter Rolls, vol. v, 1341-1417, 95.
  Cat. Ancient Deeds, vol. iii (1900), p.225.
  Palgrave, F. (ed.), *Antient Kalendars*, vol. i (1836), p.54.
167. CPR 1367-70 6.
  Hall, H. (ed.), *The Red Book of the Exchequer*, part 1 (1896), pp.cxlvii–cxlviii.
  Drake, H.H. (ed.), *op. cit.*, p.123.
168. Drake, H.H. (ed.), *op. cit.*, p.187.
  E 101/494/7 m 3.
  Cal. Fine Rolls,1369-77 41.
  Rot. Orig., in *Curia Scaccarii Abbreviato Temp. Edw. III*, vol. ii, p.303.
  E 101/545/37 m 3.
169. CPR 1367-70 247, 287-8.
  E 164/44 f 8.
170. CPR 1307-13 172.
  C 134/21/8 m 6.
  Drake, H.H. (ed.), *op. cit.*, p.184.
171. E 101/473/18 f 18v.
  CPR 1476-85 240.
172. CPR 1385-89 187.
  Mandy, W.H., 'Eltham A.D. 1271', *Greenwich Antiquarian Society Transactions*, vol. i (1911), p.285.
  Drake, H.H. (ed.), *op. cit.*, p.201.
  Johnson, C. (ed.), *Diocesis Roffensis 1319-1352*, Canterbury and York Society, vol. xvi (1914), pp.37-8.
173. Rivers, E., *Some Records of Eltham* (1904), pp.53-4.
  Gregory, R.R.C., *op. cit.*, p.60.
174. CPR 1367-70 287-8.
175. E 372/200 rot. 41.
176. E 372/211 rot. 50; /212 rot. 36.
177. E 364/2 rot. F; /3 rot. H.
178. S.C. 6/1285/1 (1) (2) (4) (5) mm 2, 6.
179. CPR 1367-70 6.
180. E 101/493/30 m 1.
181. Cal. Close Rolls, 1323-27 439.
182. *Letters and Papers of Henry VIII*, vol. xxi, part 1 p.404.
183. C 134/2/8 m 6.
184. E 101/493/30 m 1.
185. E 101/494/7 m 3.
  E 101/545/37 m 3.
  E 101/494/18 m 2.
  E 101/494/19 m 1.
  E 101/494/22 m 5.
  E 101/545/38 m 4.
  E 101/494/28 m 8.
186. E 372/200 rot. 41.
187. E 101/493/12 m 8.
  E 101/493/18 m 11.
  E 101/493/30 m 1.
  E 101/494/7 m 3.
  E 101/545/37 m 3.
  E 101/494/15 m 2.
  E 101/494/18 m 2.
  E 101/494/22 m 5.
  E 101/545/38 m 4.
  E 101/494/28 m 8.
188. E 101/493/12 m 10.

E 101/493/18 m 12.
E 101/493/30 mm 2, 3.
E 101/494/7 m 4.
E 101/545/37 m 4.
E 101/494/15 m 2.
E 101/494/18 m 3.
E 101/545/38 m 5.
E 101/494/28 m 8.
E 101/495/1 m 1.
189. Priestley, E.J., *op. cit.*, pp.307-64.
190. E 101/473/2 m 12.
191. Priestley, E.J., *op. cit.*, pp.313-18.
192. *Ibid.*, pp.313-14, 317.
193. *Ibid.*, pp.313-14, 317-18, 363-4.
194. *Ibid.*, p.324.
195. *Ibid.*, pp.320-2.
196. *Ibid.*, pp.320-2.
197. *Ibid.*, pp.332-61.
198. *Ibid.*, pp.333-61.
199. *Ibid.*, pp.327-8.
200. *Ibid.*, p.362.
201. *Ibid.*, p.363.
202. *Ibid.*, pp.359-61.
203. CPR 1364-67 230, 334, 379.
  CPR 1367-70 97, 164.
  CPR 1370-74 42, 253-54.
  CPR 1374-77 238.
204. Given-Wilson, C.J., 'Purveyance for the Royal Household 1362-1413', *Bulletin of the Institute for Historical Research*, vol. lvi (1983), pp.145-63.
  Maddicott, J.R., 'The English Peasantry and the Demands of the Crown 1294-1341', *Past and Present*, vol. lxvi (1975), supplement no. 1, pp.1-75.
  Boyle, L.E., 'William of Pagula and the Speculum Regis Edwardi III', *Medieval Studies*, vol. xxxii (1970), pp.329-36.
205. Given-Wilson, C.J., *The Royal Household and the King's Affinity 1377-1413* (1986), p.28.
206. Cal. Close Rolls, 1346-49 465-6.
207. Cal. Close Rolls, 1374-77 36.
208. E 1401-05 492.
  Drake, H.H. (ed.), *op. cit.*, p.185.
209. Cal. Fine Rolls, 1327-37 215.
  CPR 1343-45 445.
210. CPR 1340-43 335.
  CPR 1343-45 556.
211. CPR 1354-58 350.
212. Cal. Close Rolls, 1374-77 502.
213. CPR 1381-85 204.
214. E 364/18 rot. Cd. No. 75.
215. E 101/493/18 m 12.
216. E 372/212 rot. 36 No. 68.
217. Cal. Close Rolls, 1374-77 2, 15, 485, 502.
  Cal. Close Rolls, 1377-81 153, 398.
  Cal. Close Rolls, 1381-85 18, 265.
  Cal. Close Rolls, 1385-89 585.
  Cal. Close Rolls, 1389-92 22.
  Cal. Close Rolls, 1402-05 63, 327, 389, 391.
  Cal. Close Rolls, 1435-41 413.
  Cal. Close Rolls, 1447-54 81, 309, 459.
  Cal. Close Rolls, 1461-68 9, 26-7.
  Cal. Close Rolls, 1476-85 376.
  Cal. Close Rolls, 1485-1500 68.
218. Cal. Fine Rolls, 1369-77 170.
219. CPR 1358-61 28, 243.
  CPR 1364-67 414, 417, 426-7.
  CPR 1377-81 186, 197.
  CPR 1385-89 377-78.
220. E 101/493/4 mm 1, 4.
221. CPR 1348-50 551, 588.
  CPR 1350-54 515, 522.
  CPR 1364-67 414, 417, 426-7.
  CPR 1370-74 270.
  CPR 1377-81 271, 326.

E 352/152 rot. 11d.
E 101/395/2 No. 195.

4. RICHARD II AND ELTHAM.

1. Cal. Close Rolls, 1377-81 251.
  CPR 1377-81 8, 337, 342, 454, 456.
2. Hilton, R.H., and Fagan, H., *The English Rising of 1381* (1950), p.114.
3. Pardon Roll of Richard II, 6 Feb, 27 Mar 1382. CP 40/490 m 230, CP 40/491 m 230 (Courtesy of Professor A.L. Brown, Glasgow University).
4. E 364/16 rot. Hd.
  Reville, A., *Le Soulevement des Travailleurs d'Angleterre en 1381* (1898), appx ii, pp.231-3, 281.
5. Pardon Roll ... CP 40/490 m 230, CP 40/491 m 230.
6. Reville, A., *op. cit.*, pp.231-3, 281.
7. Hutchison, H.F., *The Hollow Crown* (1961), pp.59-75.
8. *Ibid.*, p.77.
9. CPR 1381-85 36-8, 41-2, 77-8.
  Cal. Inq. Misc., vol. iv, 1377-88, 1957, 96.
  Cal. Close Rolls, 1381-85 79-81, 83.
10. Cal. Close Rolls, 1381-85 7-8.
11. Hutchison, H.F., *op. cit.*, p.77.
12. CPR 1381-85 564.
13. Saul, N., *Richard II* (1997), pp.337-8, 468-73.
  Cheney, C.R. (ed.), *Handbook of Dates* (1961), p.158.
14. CPR 1381-85 131, 151, 179, 183, 316, 345, 384, 440, 449, 476, 483-4, 488, 532-3, 537, 539-40, 542, 545-54, 560, 562, 564, 567, 572-3, 575, 577, 580, 593-4.
  Cal. Close Rolls, 1381-85 530, 555, 625, 632.
15. E 101/401/4 m 2.
  CPR 1381-85 359-60, 363, 366-7, 370.
  Cal. Close Rolls, 1381-85 353.
  Higden, R., *Polychronicon* (ed. Lumby, J.R.), rolls series, vol. ix (1886), p.27.
  Stow, J., *Annales* (1615), p.296.
  Walsingham, T., *Historia Anglicana* (ed. Riley, H.T.), rolls series, vol. ii (1864), p.110.
16. E 101/401/2 f 37.
  Charlton, J., 'Eltham Palace', *Transactions of the Ancient Monuments Society*, vol. xxxi (N.S.) (1987), p.17.
17. Saul, N., *op. cit.*, p.116.
  Hector, L.C. and Harvey, B.A. (ed. and trans.), *The Westminster Chronicle 1381-94* (1982), pp.55-9.
18. Higden, R., *op. cit.*, p.28.
19. *Westminster Chronicle* lv, p.155.
  Rymer, T. (ed.), *Foedera*, vol. vii (1709), p.494.
  Higden, R., *op. cit.*, pp.76-7.
  Walsingham, T., *op. cit.*, p.142.
  Stow, J., *op. cit.*, pp.298-9.
  Davies, J.S. (ed.), *Chronicle of the Reigns of Richard II, Henry IV, Henry V and Henry VI*, Camden Society (1856), p.3.
  Holinshed, R., *Chronicles*, vol. ii (1807), p.768.
  Brie, F.W.D. (ed.), *The Brut*, E.E.T.S. (Original Series), no. 136, part 2 (1908), p.339-40.
20. Lumby, J.R. (ed.), *Chronicon Henrici Knighton Monarchi Leycestrensis*, rolls series, vol. ii (1895), pp.215-20.
  Hutchison, H.F., *op. cit.*, pp.84-6, 94-6, 100-7.
  Steel, A., *Richard II* (1941), pp.121-3.
  Cockayne, G.E., *Complete Peerage*, vol. vii (1929), p.70.
  Tout, T.F., *Chapters in the Administrative History of Medieval England*, vol. iii, 1920-33, p.412.
  Wright, H.G., 'Career of Thomas, Duke of Gloucester', Unpublished MA Thesis, London University (1930), p.143.

E 101/473/2 m 13.

Saul, N., *op. cit.*, pp.157-8, 166.

Daviot, G., 'Richard of Bordeaux', *Famous Plays of 1933* (1933), pp.176-90.

21. Hutchison, H.F., *op. cit.*, pp.111-12, 115-20.

22. Higden, R., *op. cit.*, pp.201-2.
CPR 1385-89 536-8, 540.
Ibid. 1-3.
Westminster Chronicle, 375.

23. Steel, A., *op.cit.*, p.173.
Hutchison, H.F., *op. cit.*, pp.122-8.

24. Hutchison, H.F., *op. cit.*, pp.129-64.

25. Skeat, W.W. (ed.), *Complete Works of Geoffrey Chaucer*, vol. iii (1894).

26. CPR 1388-92 82.
E 101/502/10 m 4.
Selby, W.D. (ed.), *Life Records of Chaucer*, Chaucer Society (1900), pp.xxxvi-vii.
Chaucer Life Records, 402-4, 406-8, 413-14, 418, 450-8, 460-2, 464-7.
E 364/22 rots. K, Kd.

27. E 364/25 rot. C.
Selby, W.D. (ed.), *op. cit.*, p.xliii.

28. Higden, R., *op. cit.*, p.215.
Walsingham, T., *op. cit.*, pp.184, 197.

29. Chaucer Life Records, 472, 489.
Selby, W.D. (ed.), *op. cit.*, pp.xl-xliii, The Robberies of Chaucer (1875), pp.6-38.

30. Selby, W.D. (ed.), *op. cit.*, pp.xxxix-xl.
Chaucer Life Records, 494-99.

31. Chaucer Life Records, 62-4, 120, 514-15.

32. BL MSS Dept. Add. MS 17362 f 4.

33. E 101/419/5 f 30.
E 101/422/10 f 31.

34. E 101/402/5 ff 14v-16, 26-26v.

35. E 101/402/10 ff 12-13, 33-33v.
BL MSS Dept. Add. 35115 ff 33-33v.

36. E 101/392/12 f 34.
E 101/397/5 f 34.

37. E 101/402/5 f 26.
E 101/402/10 f 33v.

38. BL MSS Dept. Harl. 319 ff 39-39v.

39. E 101/402/5 f 26.

40. E 101/402/10 f 33v.

41. BL MSS Dept. Harl. 319 f 39.

42. E 101/392/12 f 34.

43. E 101/397/5 ff 34-34v.

44. BL MSS Dept. Harl. 319 f 39.

45. E 101/404/21 ff 22, 36v.

46. BL MSS Dept. Add. 35115 f 33v.
E 101/402/5 f 26v.

47. E 1.01/402/10 f 33v.

48. Brown, I.D., 'The King's Evil', *Seaby's Coin and Medal Bulletin* (November 1956), p.434.

49. Hutchison, H.F., *op. cit.*, pp.138-9.
Tout, T.F., *op. cit.*, vol. iv, 1920-33, p.18.

50. Higden, R., *op. cit.*, p.278.
Tout, T.F., *op. cit.*, p.221.
du Boulay, F.R.H. and Barrow, C.M. (eds), 'The Reign of Richard II', *Essays Presented to May McKisack* (1971), p.195.
Westminster Chronicle, p.511.
Reikert, E. (compiler), Olsen, C.C. and Crow, M.M. (eds), *Chaucer's World* (1948), p.189.

51. Tout, T.F., *op. cit.*, vol. iii, 1920-33, p.485.
Palmer, J.J.N., 'The Anglo-French Peace Negotiations 1390-96', *Transactions of the Royal Historical Society*, vol. xvi (1966), pp.85-94.
Palmer, J.J.N., *England, France and Christendom* (1972), pp.142-50, 152, 163.
Syllabus of Rymer's Foedera, vol. ii (1873), p.526.
Westminster Chronicle, pp.400, 479.

52. Hutchison, H.F., *op. cit.*, pp.143-4.

53. Hutchison, H.F., *op. cit.*, pp.159-60.
Tuck, A., *Richard II and the English Nobility*

(1973), pp.205-6.

54. *Ibid.*, p.178.
Rymer's Foedera, vol. vii, p.813.

55. Hutchison, H.F., *op. cit.*, pp.163-4.
Froissart, J., *Oeuvres* (ed. de Lettenhove, K.), vol. xv (1871), pp.306-7.
CPR 1396-99 49-50, 60, 69.

56. Froissart, J., *Chronycles* (trans. Bourchier, Sir John, Lord Berners), vol. ii, part 4, (1927-8), pp.1034-42.
Froissart, J., *Les Chroniques de Sire Jean Froissart* (ed. Buchon, J.A.C.), vol. iii (1835), p.540.
Froissart, J., *op. cit.* (1871), pp.148, 156-82.

57. Froissart, J., *Chronicles* (ed. Brereton, G.) (1968), pp.10-15.
Galway, M., 'Froissart in England', *University of Birmingham Historical Journal*, vol. vii, no. 1, 1959-60, pp.18, 35.
Saul, N., *op. cit.*, p.447.

58. Froissart, J., *op. cit.* (1871), pp.157-66.
Froissart, J., *op. cit.*, (1927-8), pp.1030-50.
E 101/403/10 ff lv, 27-29, 30v-31, 41.
CPR 1391-96 606-13, 615-16, 642, 652, 663.
Goodman, A., *The Loyal Conspiracy* (1971), pp.63, 155.
Galway, M., *op. cit.*, p.35.
Syllabus of Rymer's Foedera, vol. ii, p.528.
Palmer, J.J.N., *Froissart: Historian* (1981), p.62.
Baldwin, J.F., *The King's Council* (1913), pp.107, 135-7, 391, 504-5.
Hutchison, H.F., *op. cit.*, pp.158-60.
McGregor, R.R. (ed.), 'The Lyric Poems of Jehan Froissart: A Critical Edition', *North Carolina Studies in the Romance Languages and Literatures* (1975), pp.16-21.
Goodman, A., *John of Gaunt* (1992), p.197.

59. Mathew, G., *The Court of Richard II* (1968), pp.22-3, 32-7, 40, 47-9, 199.

60. Scheler, M.A. (ed.), *Oeuvres de Froissart: Poesies*, vol. iii (1872), pp.421, 432.
Fourrire, A. (ed.), *Froissart's 'L'Espinette Amoureuse'* (1963), pp.7-11.

61. Wylie, J.H., *History of England under Henry IV*, vol. ii (1894), p.147.

62. CPR 1391-96 621.
Cal. Close Rolls, 1392-96 482.
Froissart, J., *op. cit.* (1927-8), p.1050.

63. Froissart, J., *op. cit.* (1835), p.540.
McGregor, R.R. (ed.), *op. cit.*, p.16.

64. E 101/495/23 mm 1-4.

65. Williams, B. (ed.), *Chronique de la Traison et Mort de Richart Deux Roy Dengleterre* (1846), p.110.
Douet D'Arcq, L. (ed.), *Choix de Pieces Inedites Relatives au Regne de Charles VI* (1864), pp.273, 275, 277.

66. Froissart, J., *op. cit.* (1927-8), pp.1151-7, 1160-3, 1184-90.
Steel, A., *op. cit.*, p.231.
Froissart, J., *op. cit.* (1968), pp.16-17.

67. CPR 1396-99 109-110, 112, 114-15, 118, 120, 123.
Cal. Close Rolls, 1396-99 102, 118.

68. *Syllabus of Rymer's Foedera*, vol. ii, p.530.

69. Tait, J., 'Did Richard II Murder the Duke of Gloucester?', *Historical Essays ... Jubilee, the Owens College, Manchester* (1907), pp.193-216.
CPR 1401-05 381, 385.
Chronique de la Traison, pp.xviii-xxii, p.127.
Froissart, J., *op. cit.* (1927-8), pp.1160-3.

70. Froissart, J., *op. cit.* (1871), vol. xvi, p.73, p.80.

71. Froissart, J., *op. cit.* (1927-8), pp.1194-1206.
Hutchison, H.F., *op. cit.*, pp.190-8, 205-9.
Le Beau, J., 'Chronique de Richard II' (ed. Buchon, J.A.C.), *Collection des Chroniques*

Francaises, vol. xxv, suppt 1 (1826), p.11.
Oman, C., *Political History of England*, vol. iv (1930), pp.141-3.
McKisack, M., *The Fourteenth Century* (1959), pp.485-8.
Steel, A., *op. cit.*, p.244-53.

72. Froissart, J., *op. cit.* (1871), vol. xvi, pp.92-3, 106-7.

73. Williams, B. (ed.), *op. cit.*, p.159.
Froissart, J., *op. cit.* (1871), p.109-10.

74. Legge, M.D. (ed.), 'Anglo-Norman Letters', *Anglo-Norman Text Society* (1941), pp.69-70.

75. Saul, N., *op. cit.*, pp.473-4.

76. Froissart, J., *op. cit.* (1968), p.17.
Steel, A., *op. cit.*, pp.231, 238.

77. Hutchison, H.F., *op. cit.*, p.207.
Steel, A., *op. cit.*, p.249.

78. Steel, A., *op. cit.*, p.249.
Hutchison, H.F., *op. cit.*, p.207.

79. Hutchison, H.F., *op. cit.*, pp.215-16.

80. *Ibid.*, p.217.

81. *Ibid.*, p.218.

82. *Ibid.*, p.219-20.

83. *Ibid.*, p.221.

84. *Ibid.*, p.222-32.
Saul, N., *op. cit.*, pp.405-24.

85. E 101/473/2 mm 12-13, 21, 4d.
Ibid., mm 2, 5, 8-9.
E 101/495/23 mm 1-4.
E 101/502/31 mm 1-2.

86. E 101/495/23 m 4.

87. E 101/502/31 m 1.

88. E 101/495/23 mm 1, 4.

89. E 101/473/18 f 18v.

90. E 101/502/31 m 1.
E 101/473/2 mm 12, 13.
E 101/473/3 m 8.

91. E 101/494/15 m 2.
E 101/545/40 No. 1.
E 101/494/29 m 1.
E 101/493/4 m 2.

92. E 101/473/2 mm 12-13, 21.
E101/473/3 mm 2, 5, 8-9.

93. Devon, F. (ed.), 'Issues of the Exchequer Henry III—Henry VI', *Pell Records* (1837), p.247.
E 101/473/2 m 12.

94. E 101/502/21 mm 4, 5.

95. E 101/473/2 mm 12, 13.
E 101/473/3 m 8.

96. Woods, H., 'Excavations at Eltham Palace', *Transactions of London and Middlesex Archaeological Society*, vol. xxxii (1982), pp.218-22, 230-2, 234-5.
E 101/545/15 mm 4-5.

97. E 101/502/31 m 1.

98. E 101/473/3(1) mm 2-3.

99. E 101/473/2 m 13.

100. E 101/502/31 m 1.
E 101/473/3(1) m 2.

101. E 101/473/3 m 9.

102. E 101/473/2 m 12.

103. *Ibid.* mm 12-13.

104. *Ibid.*
E 101/502/31 m 1.

105. E 101/473/2 m 12.

106. E 101/495/23 mm 1-2.

107. E 101/502/31 m 1.

108. E 101/502/15 m 5.
E 101/495/23 mm 1, 4.

109. E 101/473/3 m 8.

110. E 101/473/2 mm 12, 13.

111. *Ibid.* m 12.

112. *Ibid.* mm 12, 13.
E 101/473/3 m 8.

113. E 101/502/31 mm 1, 2.

114. E 101/502/15 mm 5, 6.
    E 101/495/23 m 4.
115. E 101/473/2 m 13.
116. E 101/502/15 mm 4-6.
    E 101/502/31 mm 1-2.
    E 101/473/2 mm 12, 13.
    E 101/473/3 mm 5, 9.
117. E 101/502/15 mm 4-5.
118. E 101/502/31 m 2.
119. *Ibid.* m 1.
120. E 101/473/3 mm 2, 9.
    E 101/473/2 m 13.
    E 101/502/15 m 5.
    Saul, N., *op. cit.*, pp.332, 450.
121. E 101/473/2 mm 13, 21.
122. *Ibid.* m 12.
    E 101/473/3 m 9.
    E 101/502/31 m 1.
123. E 101/502/31 m 1.
124. E 101/502/15 m 5.
125. E 101/473/2 m 12.
126. *Ibid.* mm 12-13.
    E 101/473/3 m 8.
127. E 101/473/2 mm 12, 13.
128. E 101/501/25 m 42.
    E 101/502/31 m 1.
    E 101/473/2 m 13.
129. E 101/502/31 mm 1-2.
130. E 101/473/2 mm 12-13.
131. *Ibid.* m 13.
132. *Ibid.*
133. *Ibid.*
134. *Ibid.*
135. E 101/495/23 m 1.
136. E 101/473/2 mm 12, 13.
137. E 101/473/3(1) m 2.
138. E 101/473/2 m 12.
    E 101/473/3(1) m 2.
139. E 101/473/2 m 13.
140. *Ibid.* m 8.
141. *Ibid.* m 12.
142. *Ibid.* m 13.
143. *Ibid.*
144. *Ibid.*
145. *Ibid.*
146. E 101/473/3(1) m 2.
147. *Ibid.* m 3.
    E 101/473/3 m 8.
148. CPR 1377-81 177.
149. E 101/473/2 mm 12-13, 21.
    E 101/473/3 mm 8, 9.
150. E 101/502/31 m 1.
151. Cal. Close Rolls, 1392-96 510.
    CPR 1396-99 3.
    CPR 1399-1401 139.
    CPR 1374-77 358.
152. CPR 1396-99 294.
    CPR 1413-16 58.
    CPR 1429-36 193.
    CPR 1436-41 445.
153. CPR 1374-77 484.
154. CPR 1381-85 464.
155. *Ibid.* 238.
    CPR 1385-89 35.
156. CPR 1381-85 266.
    CPR 1385-89 440.
157. CPR 1385-89 437.
158. CPR 1396-99 495.
159. CPR 1413-16 385.
160. CPR 1461-67 457, 521.
161. E 364/2 rot. F; /3 rot. H.
    E 372/212 rot. 36.
162. Cal. Fine Rolls, 1369-77 170.
163. Cal. Fine Rolls, 1377-83 281.
    E 364/2 rot. F; /21 rot. Ed; /22 rot. D; /23
    rot. Bd; /24 rot. D.

164. Cal. Fine Rolls, 1383-91 348.
165. Cal. Fine Rolls, 1391-99 158.
166. Cal. Fine Rolls, 1383-91 355.
    Cal. Fine Rolls, 1396-99 159.
167. CPR 1399-1401 459.
168. CPR 1354-58 293.
169. CPR 1401-05 192, 273.

5. ELTHAM AND THE EARLY
LANCASTRIAN KINGS.
    1. Wylie, J.H., *History of England under Henry IV*,
       vol. iv (1898), pp.288, 293, 295, 301-2.
       Kirby, J.L., *Henry IV* (1970), pp.108, 131-2,
       177, 183, 190, 206-7, 219-20, 224, 242, 247.
       CPR 1401-05 9, 25, 31-4, 53, 66, 84, 107.
       Cal. Close Rolls, 1399-1402 446.
    2. E 101/502/23 mm 3-6.
       E 101/502/24 mm 1-3.
       E 101/502/25 m 4.
       E 101/502/26 mm 6-8.
    3. CPR 1399-1401 140.
    4. *Ibid.* 222-3, 226-8, 232, 239, 252, 255-6, 258-
       61, 310.
       CPR 1401-05 50.
       CPR 1422-29 47, 88.
       Syllabus of Rymer's Foedera, vol. ii (1873),
       p.538.
       Cal. Close Rolls, 1399-1402 122.
       Kirby, J.L., *op. cit.*, pp.53-4, 66, 68-70, 72, 78.
       Nicolas, Sir H. (ed.), *Proceedings and Ordinances
       of the Privy Council*, vol. i (1834), p.117.
    5. Kirby, J.L., *op. cit.*, pp.86-90, 93-5.
       Hutchison, H.F., *The Hollow Crown* (1961),
       pp.233-7.
       Wylie, J.H., *op. cit.*, vol. i, pp.111-18.
       Saul, N., *Richard II* (1997), pp.425-6.
    6. De Wavrin, J., *Chronicles* (trans. Hardy,
       Sir W. and Hardy, E.C.L.P), 1399-1422,
       rolls series (1887), pp.17-18.
       Froissart, J., *Chronycles* (1927-28 edn), vol. ii,
       part 4, pp.1271-2.
       Strickland, A., *Lives of the Queens of England*,
       vol. ii (1890), p.30.
    7. Kirby, J.L., *op. cit.*, pp.119-22.
       Wylie, J.H., *op. cit.*, vol. i, pp.205-11.
    8. Wylie, J.H. and Waugh, W.T., *The Reign of
       Henry V*, vol. iii (1929), p.268.
       Kirby, J.L., *op. cit.*, p.122.
    9. Wylie, J.H., *op. cit.*, vol. i, pp.161-4.
       Adam of Usk, *Chronicon Adae de Usk* (ed.
       Thompson, Sir E.M.) (1904), pp.219-20.
       Kirby, J.L., *op. cit.*, p.109.
       Nicol, D.M., 'A Byzantine Emperor in
       England', *University of Birmingham Historical
       Journal*, vol. xii, no. 2 (1971), pp.204-25.
       Lambeth Palace Library, MS no. 78 f 25lr.
       Nicolas, Sir N.H. and Tyrrell, E. (eds), *A
       Chronicle of London from 1089 to 1483* (1827),
       p.87.
       BL. MSS Dept. Harl. 565 f 66; Cotton Titus
       D.xv f 49v.
       Hearne, T. (ed.), *Duo Rerum Anglicarum*
       (Otterbourne's Chronicle) (1732), p.231.
       Riley, H.T. (ed.), *Chronica et Annales
       Johannis de Trokelowe et Henrici de Blaneforde*,
       rolls series (1866), pp.335-7.
    10. Wylie, J.H., *op. cit.*, vol. i, pp.158-65.
    11. Nicolas, Sir N.H. and Tyrrell, E. (eds), *op.
        cit.*, p.87.
    12. Sussman, S.A., 'Anglo-Byzantine relations
        during the Middle Ages', Unpublished PhD
        Thesis, University of Pennsylvania (1966)
        (Courtesy of Reference Librarian, The Charles
        Van Pelt Library, University of Pennsylvania),
        p.249.
    13. E 101/502/21 mm 4, 5.

    Wylie, J.H., *op. cit.* vol. iv. pp.220, 222, 288.
    14. Wylie, J.H., *op. cit.* vol. iv., p.129.
        College of Arms, Arundel xxvi ff 33-40v;
        MS L.6 ff 145v-50v.
        Bodleian Library, MS Douce 271 ff 40r-47r.
        BL MSS Dept. Cotton Nero D. ii ff 260r-
        262r; Add. MSS 34801 ff 36-42v.
    15. Wylie, J.H., *op. cit.*, vol. ii, pp.436-7; vol.
        iii, pp.248-53.
        Wood, M.A.E., *Lives of the Princesses of
        England*, vol. iii (1851), pp.313-15.
        Kirby, J.L., *op. cit.*, pp.18, 117, 129, 132,
        138-9, 179.
    16. Alexander, J. and Binski, B. (eds), *Age of
        Chivalry* (1987) p.178, pp.202-3.
    17. Bodleian MS Douce 271, letters 1, 4-6, 8.
    18. *Ibid.* 2, 3, 7, 9.
    19. *Ibid.* 6, 13.
    20. *Ibid.* 4, 6.
    21. *Ibid.* 4.
    22. *Ibid.* 3.
    23. *Ibid.* 4.
    24. *Ibid.* 10.
    25. *Ibid.*
    26. *Ibid.*
    27. *Ibid.* 7.
    28. *Ibid.* 4.
    29. *Ibid.* 1.
    30. *Ibid.* 5.
    31. *Ibid.* 6.
    32. *Ibid.* 6, 7.
    33. *Ibid.* 3, 5, 7, 8, 10-12.
    34. *Ibid.* 8.
    35. *Ibid.* 10.
    36. *Ibid.*
    37. *Ibid.* 1.
    38. *Ibid.* 9.
    39. *Ibid.* 5.
    40. *Ibid.* 6.
    41. *Ibid.* 1.
    42. *Ibid.* 4.
    43. *Ibid.*
    44. *Ibid.* 7.
    45. *Ibid.* 9.
    46. *Ibid.* 11.
    47. *Ibid.* 3.
    48. *Ibid.* 2-5, 7, 8, 10, 12.
    49. *Ibid.* 1, 5, 9.
    50. *Ibid.* 1, 4, 5, 7, 9, 10, 12, 13.
    51. *Ibid.* 1, 5, 7, 8, 10, 12, 13.
    52. *Ibid.* 1-5, 7-13.
    53. *Ibid.* 2.
    54. *Ibid.* 7.
    55. *Ibid.* 4.
    56. Kirby, J.L., *op. cit.*, p.109.
        Wylie, J.H., *op. cit.*, vol. i, p.163.
    57. Kirby, J.L., *op. cit.*, p.109.
        Wylie, J.H., *op. cit.* vol. i, pp.163-4.
    58. *Ibid.*, vol. iv, pp.287-302.
    59. E 28/12 No. 52, numbered 40.
    60. E 101/405/13 m 3.
        E 101/405/14 f 14v.
    61. E 101/405/13 m 3.
        E 101/405/14 f 14v.
    62. E 101/502/26 mm 7-8.
    63. E 101/397/12 mm 1-2.
    64. E 101/405/9 m 13.
    65. E 101/405/2.
    66. *Ibid.*
        E 101/409/2 f 19v.
        E 101 /404/21 f 40v.
    67. E 101/405/25 m 2.
    68. Bodleian, Rawl. D. 776 ff 94-104.
    69. Kirby, J.L., *op. cit.*, p.42.
    70. *Ibid.*, pp.7, 135-8.
        Wylie, J.H., *op. cit.* vol. i, pp.262-3, 289.

71. *Ibid.*, pp.205–11, 307.
Kirby, J.L., *op. cit.*, pp.149–50.
72. *Ibid.*, pp.150–1.
Wylie, J.H., *op. cit.* vol. i, p.310.
73. *Ibid.*, vol. iv, p.290.
E 101/404/21 ff 18v–19v, 20–22v, 35–36v, 40–41.
74. CPR 1401–05 213.
Wylie, J.H., *op. cit.*, vol. i, p.311; vol. iv, p.290.
Kirby, J.L., *op. cit.*, p.151.
75. *Ibid.*, pp.55, 58–9, 61, 68, 71–2, 135, 144–5, 147–8, 152–8, 165, 169–70, 185–8, 195, 218–20, 222.
Wylie, J.H., *op. cit.* vol. i, pp.357–65.
76. *Ibid.*, vol. iv, pp.290, 295, 298.
Cheney, C.R. (ed.), *Handbook of Dates* (1961), pp.132, 159.
BL MSS Dept. Harl. 319 ff 39–39v.
E 101 /404/21 ff 21v–22.
77. CPR 1401–05 379, 381, 385.
78. CPR 1401–05 379.
79. E 101/405/9 m 13.
80. Hearne, T. (ed.), *op. cit.*, p.250.
Wylie, J.H., *op. cit.* vol. ii, pp.40–1; vol. iv, p.293.
Kirby, J.L., *op. cit.*, pp.177, 182–3.
81. *Syllabus of Rymer's Foedera*, vol. i (1869), p.556.
82. E 101/502/26 m 8.
Kirby, J.L., *op. cit.*, pp.206–7.
83. Wylie, J.H., *op. cit.*, vol. ii, p.478.
84. Kirby, J.L., *op. cit.*, pp.222–3.
Wylie, J.H., *op. cit.*, vol. iii, pp.159, 233; vol. iv, p.298.
85. *Ibid.*, pp.283–4; vol. iv, p.299.
86. *Ibid.*, vol. i, pp.5, 88; vol. iii, pp.283–4; vol. iv, pp.8–9, 14–16.
Kirby, J.L., *op. cit.*, pp.29–36.
CPR 1408–13 156, 229–35.
Galbraith, V.H. (ed.), *The St Albans Chronicle 1406–20* (1937), p.44.
Cal. Close Rolls, 1409–13 72.
87. Kirby, J.L., *op. cit.*, pp.242–3.
Wylie, J.H., *op. cit.*, vol. iv, pp.3–30, 66–8.
De Wavrin, J., *Chronicles* (trans. Hardy, Sir W. and Hardy, E.C.L.P), 1399–1422, rolls series (1887), pp.152.
88. Kirby, J.L., *op. cit.*, pp.244–5.
Walsingham, T., *Ypodigma Neustriae* (ed. Riley, H.T.) (1876), pp.436–7.
Walsingham, T., *Historia Anglicana* (ed. Riley, H.T.) (1863), pp.288–9.
89. CPR 1408–13 476.
Wylie, J.H., *op. cit.*, vol. iv, p.38.
90. Wylie, J.H., *op. cit.*, vol. iv, pp.100–1, 301–2.
Galbraith, V.H. (ed.), *op. cit.*, p.68.
Kirby, J.L., *op. cit.*, pp.242, 247–9.
Walsingham, T., *op. cit.* (1876), p.437.
Walsingham, T., *op. cit.* (1863), p.289.
91. Kirby, J.L., *op. cit.*, p.245.
92. Wylie, J.H. and Waugh, W.T., *op. cit.*, vol. i, p.162.
93. *Ibid.*, pp.51, 261–80.
Gairdner, J. (ed.), *Collections of a London Citizen* (Gregory's Chronicle), Camden Society (1876), p.108.
Williams, E.C., *My Lord of Bedford* (1963), pp.42–3.
Hearne, T. (ed.), *op. cit.*, pp.272, 274.
Devon, F. (ed.), 'Henry III–Henry VI', *Pell Records* (1837), p.330.
Brie, F.W.D. (ed.), *Brut*, part 2, Early English Text Society (1908), p.551.
Walsingham, T., *op. cit.* (1876), pp.446–7.
de Elmham, T., *Vita et Gesta Henrici Quinti* (ed. Hearne, T.) (1727), p.31.
Cole, C.A. (ed.), 'Memorials of Henry V',

Redmanni Historia, rolls series (1858), pp.22–3.
Capgrave, J., *Chronicle* (ed. Hingeston, F.C.), rolls series (1858), pp.306–7.
Galbraith, V.H. (ed.), *op. cit.*, p.77.
Williams, B. (ed.), *Henrici Quinti Angliae Regis Gesta* (1850), p.4.
Gesta Henrici Quinti (trans. & notes Taylor, F. and Roskell, J.S.) (1975), pp.xlvii, 6–7.
Kingsford, C.L. (ed.), *The First English Life of Henry V* (1911), p.23.
Drake, H.H., *Hundred of Blackheath* (1886), p.185.
Williams, N., *The Royal Residences of Great Britain* (1960), p.63.
94. Wylie, J.H. and Waugh, W.T., *op. cit.*, vol. ii, p.256.
Nicolas, Sir N.H. (ed.), *The History of the Battle of Agincourt* (1827), pp.165, 278.
95. Wylie, J.H. and Waugh, W.T., *op. cit.*, vol. ii, p.257.
Nicolas, Sir N.H. (ed.), *op. cit.*, pp.291–5.
96. Nicolas, Sir N.H. (ed.), *op. cit.*, pp.cccxciii, 356, Appx 76.
Schirmer, W.F., *John Lydgate* (1961), pp.275, 279.
97. CPR 1416–22 44.
Wylie, J.H. and Waugh, W.T., *op. cit.*, vol. iii, pp.18–19.
Nicolas, Sir N.H. and Tyrrell, E. (eds), *op. cit.*, p.104.
Drake, H.H., *op. cit.*, p.185.
98. Devon, F. (ed.), *op. cit.*, p.348.
99. Wylie, J.H. and Waugh, W.T., *op. cit.*, vol. ii, pp.322, 355–6, 365; vol. iii, pp.6–21.
100. *Syllabus of Rymer's Foedera*, vol. ii, p.591.
Drake, H.H., *op. cit.*, p.185.
Wylie, J.H. and Waugh, W.T., *op. cit.*, vol. iii, p.39.
101. *Ibid.*, pp.53–206.
102. *Ibid.*, pp.268–70.
de Elmham, T., *op. cit.*, p.296.
Taylor, F. (ed.), 'The Chronicle of John Strecche for the Reign of Henry V', *Bulletin of the John Rylands Library*, vol. xvi, no. 1, Jan. 1932, pp.183–4, reprint 49.
Thomas, A.H. and Thornley, I.D. (eds), *Great Chronicle of London* (1938), p.115.
103. E 364/58 rot. E.
104. Wylie, J.H. and Waugh, W.T., *op. cit.*, vol. iii (1929), pp.318, 393, 402, 406–7.
105. CPR 1416–22 401.
106. Wylie, J.H. and Waugh, W.T., *op. cit.*, vol. iii (1929), pp.198, 203–4, 207–357, 418.
107. E 101/502/23 mm 3, 5.
Colvin, H.M. (ed.), *The History of the King's Works*, vol. ii, pp.935–6.
108. E 101/502/23 m 5.
109. E 101/502/24 m 1.
E 101/502/23 mm 3, 5.
110. *Ibid.*
111. *Ibid.* m 5.
112. *Ibid.* mm 3, 5.
113. *Ibid.* mm 3, 5.
114. *Ibid.* m 3.
115. *Ibid.* m 4.
116. *Ibid.* m 5.
117. *Ibid.* 3.
118. *Ibid.*
119. *Ibid.* mm 4–5.
120. *Ibid.* m 3.
121. *Ibid.* mm 4, 6.
122. *Ibid.*
123. E 101/502/24 m 1.
124. E 101/502/23 mm 3–4.
125. *Ibid.* m 4.
126. *Ibid.* mm 3–4.

E 101/502/24 m 1.
127. E 101/502/23 m 4.
128. *Ibid*
129. E 101/502/24 m 1.
130. E 101/502/23 m 4.
131. *Ibid.* mm 3–4.
132. *Ibid.* m 4.
133. *Ibid.*
134. *Ibid.*
135. *Ibid.*
136. *Ibid.*
137. *Ibid.*
138. E 101/502/24 m 1.
139. *Ibid.*
140. *Ibid.*
141. *Ibid.*
142. E 101/502/23 m 4.
E 101/502/24 m 1.
143. E 101/502/23 mm 4–5.
144. *Ibid.* m 5.
145. *Ibid.* m 4.
146. *Ibid.*
147. *Ibid.*
148. *Ibid.*
E 101/502/15 m 5.
149. CPR 1401–05 426.
150. E 101/496/7 mm 1–2.
151. E 101/502/26 m 7.
152. E 101/502/25 m 4.
153. E 101/502/26 mm 6–7.
E 101/496/7 m 2.
154. E 101/502/26 mm 7–8.
155. E 101/496/7 m 2.
156. *Ibid.*
157. E 101/502/26 m 8.
158. *Ibid.*
159. E 101/502/23 m 4–5.
160. E 101/502/24 m 2.
161. *Ibid.*
162. *Ibid*
163. *Ibid.*
164. *Ibid.*
165. E 101/502/23 mm 1–2.
166. *Ibid.* m 2.
167. *Ibid.*
168. *Ibid.*
169. *Ibid.*
170. E 101/502/15 m 5.
171. *Ibid.*
172. *Ibid.*
173. *Ibid.*
174. E 101/502/26 m 8.
175. E 101/502/15 m 5.
176. *Ibid.*
177. E 101/496/7 m 1.
178. Priestley, E.J., 'The Palace and Manor of Eltham 1086–1663', Unpublished MPhil thesis (1973), University of London, pp.177–9.
179. E 101/502/15 m 5.
E 101/502/21 m 4.
E 101/502/23 m 6.
E 101/502/25 m 4.
180. *Ibid.*
181. *Ibid.*
182. *Ibid.*
183. E 101/502/23 m 5.
184. E 101/502/15 mm 4, 6.
185. E 101/502/23 m 5.
186. E 101/502/21 m 4.
187. *Ibid.*
188. *Ibid.*
189. E 101/502/23 mm 4–5.
190. *Ibid.* m 5.
191. Kirby, J.L., *op. cit.*, pp.16, 30, 258–9.
192. Devon, F. (ed.), *op. cit.*, p.330.
193. E 101/502/15 mm 4–5.

E 101/502/21 m 4.
194. *Ibid.* mm 4-5.
195. E 101/502/23 m 5.
196. E 101/502/21 m 4.
197. E 101/502/23 m 3.
198. E 101/502/15 m 5.
199. E 101/502/24 m 2.
200. E 101/502/26 m 6.
201. E 101/502/23 m 3.
202. E 101/502/21 m 4.
203. *Ibid.*
204. E 101/502/21 m 4.
205. E 101/502/15 mm 4-5.
E 101/502/25 m 2d.
206. E 101/502/26 m 6.
E 101/502/15 m 5.
207. *Ibid.*
208. E 101/502/24 m 3.
E 101/502/25 m 4.
E 101/496/7 m 1.
E 101/502/23 m 5.
E 101/502/21 mm 4-5.
Ibid.
209. E 101/496/21 f 2.
210. E 101/502/24 m 2.
211. E 101/502/15 m 5.
M.P.F. 228.
212. E 101/502/15 m 5.
213. *Ibid.*
214. E 101/502/26 m 7.
215. E 101/502/23 mm 3-6.
E 101/502/24 m 2.
E 101/502/26 m 7.
216. *Ibid.*
217. E 101/502/26 m 8.
218. E 101/502/15 mm 4-6.
219. E 101/502/21 m 4.
220. E 101/502/24 m 1.
E 101/502/15 mm 4-6.
E 101/502/21 m 4.
E 101/502/23 mm 3-5.
221. E 101/502/24 m 1.
222. *Ibid.* mm 1-2.
223. E 101/502/15 mm 5-6.
E 101/502/23 m 6.
224. E 351/3238 m 9.
225. E 101/502/15 m 6.
226. *Ibid.*
E 101/502/21 m 5.
E 101/502/26 m 8.
227. E 101/502/21 m 5.
E 101/502/23 m 6.
228. E 101/502/29 m 3.
229. E 101/502/15 m 6.
230. *Ibid.*
231. E 101/502/23 m 6.
232. Somerset House, 5 Marche f 37, William Reynewelle.
233. E 101/473/18 f 18v.
E 101/502/24 m 2.
234. E 101/502/15 m 6.
E 101/502/21 mm 4-5.
E 101/502/23 m 5-6.
E 101/502/24 m 2.
E 101/502/25 m 3.
E 101/502/26 mm 7-8.
235. E 101/502/15 m 6.
E 101/502/25 m 5.
E 101/502/26 m 8.
236. E 101/502/15 m 6.
237. CPR 1396-99 3.
CPR 1399-1401 139.
CPR 1408-13 235.
238. E 364/41 rot. D.
239. CPR 1401-05 457.
240. CPR 1413-16 383.

241. S.C. 6/1285/2(4) mm 2-5. No. 38.
242. CPR 1401-05 32.
CPR 1405-08 162.
S.C. 6/1285/2(4) No. 39.
243. CPR 1396-99 294.
E 101/502/21 m 5.
CPR 1399-1401 339.
CPR 1413-16 58.
E 101/502/15 m 6.
244. S.C. 12/27/7.
E 317/Kent/18 mm 3, 6.
245. CPR 1436-41 255.
246. CPR 1370-74 456.
247. E 101/402/5 ff 26-26v.
E 101/404/21 ff 35-36.
BL MSS Dept. Harl. 319 ff 39-39v.
248. CPR 1405-08 226.
249. CPR 1377-81 197.
250. E 101/502/15 m 6.
251. Somerset House, William Reynewelle, 16 July 1403, 5 Marche ff 37-38v.

6. LANCASTRIANS AND YORKISTS.

1. Brie, E.W.D. (ed.), *The Brut*, part ii, Early English Text Society, vol. cxxxvi (1908), pp.567-8.
Christie, M.E., *Henry VI* (1922), pp.44-5, 375.
Gairdner, J. (ed.), *Gregory's Chronicle*, Camden Society, vol. cix (1876), pp.159-60.
Vickers, K.H., *Humphrey, Duke of Gloucester* (1907), pp.170-87, 192.
Williams, E.C., *My Lord of Bedford* (1963), pp.137-43.
Kingford, C.L. (ed.), *Chronicles of London*, Julius B ii, Cleopatra C iv, Vitellius A xvi (1905), p.77.
Thomas, A.H. and Thornley, I.D. (eds), *Great Chronicle of London* (1938), pp.136-49, 416.
Nicolas, Sir N.H. (ed.), *Proceedings and Ordinances of the Privy Council*, vol. iii (1834), p.285.
Wolffe, B., *Henry VI* (1981), pp.40-2.
Griffiths, R.A., *The Reign of King Henry VI*, (1981), pp.76, 91.
2. Shakespeare, W., *Henry VI Part I*, act 1, scenes I, III, act 3, scene I.
Shakespeare, W., *Henry VI Part I* (Arden edn) (1962), pp.xlv-xlvi.
3. Schirmer, W.F., *John Lydgate* (1961), pp.100-2.
Pearsall, D., *John Lydgate* (1970), p.184.
Brotanek, R., *Die Englischen Maskenspiele* (1902), pp.305-8.
MacCracken, H.N. (ed.), *Minor Poems of John Lydgate: Part ii*, Early English Text Society, vol. lxxvi (1934), pp.672-4.
Brown, C. and Robbins, R.H., *The Index of Middle English Verse* (1943), p.75.
Griffiths, R.A., *op. cit.*, pp.44, 56, 64, 375.
4. Wolffe, B., *Henry VI* (1981), p.37.
5. *Ibid.*
'John Benet's Chronicle', *Camden Miscellany*, vol. xxiv, 4th series, vol. ix (1972), pp.161, 181.
Trinity College, Dublin, MS E.5.10 f 158r.
6. Christie, M.E., *op. cit.*, p.375.
7. Gairdner, J. (ed.), *op. cit.*, p.163.
8. Rymer, T., *Foedera*, vol. x (1710), pp.387-8.
9. Wolffe, B., *op. cit.*, pp.361-2, 369.
Griffiths, R.A., *op. cit.*, p.257.
10. Thomas, A.H. and Thornley, I.D. (eds), *op. cit.*, p.154.
Gairdner, J. (ed.), *op. cit.*, p.171.
Christie, M.E., *op. cit.*, p.376.
11. Riley, H.T. (ed.), *Munimenta Gildhallae Londoniensis*, vol. iii (1862), pp.457-8.
Wolffe, B., *op. cit.*, p.63.
12. Christie, M.E., *op. cit.*, p.377.
Wolffe, B., *op. cit.*, p.361.

13. E 101/409/9 ff iv, 7, 8v-10, 11v-13v, 15-15v, 23v-24, 33-34v.
CPR 1436-41 31-4, 39, 41, 47, 121-2, 124, 126-31, 135-6, 142-4, 151, 153, 156-8, 162-3, 192-3, 197, 219-27, 229-31, 233, 238-9, 245, 251-2, 255-6, 265, 284, 291, 301, 303, 308-9, 349, 382, 384, 393, 409-10, 417, 468, 471.
Raine, J. (ed.), *Hist. Dunelm Scriptores Tres*, Surtees Society (1839), p.cclii.
CPR 1441-46 32-3, 35, 38, 126-8, 133-4, 141-3, 145, 149, 153, 158, 177, 197.
Syllabus of Rymer's Foedera, vol. ii, pp.664-5, 671, p.683.
Cal. Close Rolls, 1435-41 148-9, 169-70, 197-8, 206-8, 249-50.
Christie, M.E., *op. cit.*, pp.378, 380-7.
Wolffe, B., *op. cit.*, pp.81, 88, 93, 361-71.
Storey, R.L., *The End of the House of Lancaster* (1966), p.35.
Cal. Fine Rolls, 1437-45 84-5.
CPR 1452-61 36, 93-102.
E 101/409/2 f 19v.
14. Nicolas, Sir N.H. (ed.), *op. cit.*, vol. v, 1436-43, pp.136-8, 210-22, 249-54, 264-6.
Kingford, C.L. (ed.), *op. cit.*, p.145.
E 101/409/9 f 7.
Christie, M.E., *op. cit.*, p.380.
CPR 1441-46 128, 133, 158, 177, 197.
Syllabus of Rymer's Foedera, vol. ii, p.671.
15. Cal. Charter Rolls, vol. vi, 1427-1516 7.
16. Cal. Charter Rolls, vol. ii, 1257-1300 279.
17. Cal. Close Rolls, 1307-13 380.
18. Cal. Rot. Parl., vol. v (1783), pp.174-5.
19. Nicolas, Sir N.H. (ed.), *op. cit.*, vol. v, 1436-43, pp.136-8, 212, 214-15, 249, 251.
20. Blacman, J., *Henry the Sixth* (ed. James, M.R.) (1919), pp.37-8.
Wolffe, B., *op. cit.*, p.8.
Storey, R.L., *op. cit.*, p.35.
21. Stevenson, J. (ed.), *Letters and Papers Illustrative of the Wars of the English in France during the Reign of Henry VI*, rolls series, vol. ii, part 2 (1864), pp.434-6.
22. Bannister, A.T. (ed.), 'Diocesis Herefordensis', *Registrum Thome Spofford*, Canterbury and York Society (1919), pp.252-4.
23. Arnold, R. (ed.), *Memorials of St. Edmund's Abbey*, rolls series, vol. iii (1896), p.246.
Colvin, H.M. (ed.), *The History of the King's Works*, vol. i (1963), pp.271-4.
24. Nicolas, Sir N.H. (ed.), *op. cit.*, vol. vi (1837), pp.31-2.
Griffiths, R.A., *op. cit.*, pp.312, 448.
25. E 404/63/121.
26. Weir, A., *Lancaster and York: The Wars of the Roses* (1995), p.123.
Bagley, J.J., *Margaret of Anjou, Queen of England* (1948), p.46.
'John Benet's Chronicle', *Camden Miscellany*, vol. xxiv, 4th series, vol. ix (1972), p.191.
27. Cal. of State Papers (Venetian), vol. vi, 1557-58 and Appendix (1884), pp.1580-1.
28. *Ibid.*
29. Monro, C. (ed.), *Letters of Queen Margaret of Anjou*, Camden Society, 1863-64, pp.96-8.
30. Flenley, R. (ed.), *Six Town Chronicles of England* (Bale's Chronicle) (1911), p.128.
Trinity College, Dublin. MS E.5.10 f 166r.
'John Benet's Chronicle', *Camden Miscellany*, p.162, p.197.
31. Woods, H., 'Excavations at Eltham Palace, 1975-9', *Transactions of the London and Middlesex Archaeological Society*, vol. xxxii (1982), pp.225, 228-9, fig. 5.
32. E 364/87 rot. K; /89 rot. Ed; /92 rot O.
33. *Syllabus of Rymer's Foedera*, vol. ii (1873), p.683.

Wolffe, B., *op. cit.*, pp.368-71.
E 101/410/3 ff 3-6v, 11v, 21-23, 24-24v, 26.
E 101/410/6 ff 9-10v, 29v-31v, 34, 36.
E 101/410/9 ff 13-13v, 16v-17, 18-18v, 29-30, 35v-37v, 38v.
CPR 1452-61 36, 93-102.
'John Benet's Chronicle', *Camden Miscellany*, p.205.
34. Christie, M.E., *op. cit.*, p.306-7.
Gairdner, J. (ed.), *Paston Letters*, vol. i (1904), p.116; vol. iii, pp.233-4.
35. E 364/87 rots. I, Id, K; /89 rot. Ed; /93 rot. A; /97 rot. Cd.
E 101/503/13 m 6.
36. CPR 1461-67 96-97.
37. E 364/104 rot. B.
38. Wyrcester, W., *Annales* (ed. Hearne, T.) (1728), p.501.
39. MacGibbon, D., *Elizabeth Woodville* (1938), p.45.
40. Hudson Turner, T. (ed.), *Manners and Household Expenses of England*, Roxburghe Club (1841), pp.483-4.
41. Strickland, A., *Queens of England*, vol. ii (1851), p.334.
42. Gairdner, J. (ed.), *op. cit.*, vol. iv (1904), pp.275-7.
43. Thomas, A.H. and Thornley, I.D. (eds), *Great Chronicle of London* (1938), p.204.
44. E 101/412/6 mm 1, 3.
45. E 101/412/10 ff 1v, 10-18.
Scofield, C.J., *Life and Reign of Edward IV*, vol. ii (1923), p.238.
46. Nicolas, Sir N.H. (ed.), *Privy Purse Expenses of Elizabeth of York, Wardrobe Expenses of Edward the Fourth* (1830), pp.xxiv, 122.
Davies, K., *The First Queen Elizabeth* (1937), pp.173-4.
BL MSS Dept. Harl. 4780 f 20v.
MacGibbon, D., *op. cit.*, pp.130-1.
47. Nicolas, Sir N.H. (ed.), *op. cit.*, p.125-6.
48. *Ibid.*, p.xxix-xxx.
MacGibbon, D., *op. cit.*, pp.130-1.
BL MSS Dept. Add. MSS 6113 f 49v.
49. Davies, K., *op. cit.*, pp.174-5.
BL MSS Dept. Add. MSS 6113 ff 74-74v.
50. Malden, H.E. (ed.), *Cely Papers, 1475-1488*, Camden Society (1900), p.46.
51. Weir, A., *Britain's Royal Families* (1989), p.140.
52. BL MSS Dept. Add. MSS 6113 ff 49v, 74-74v.
53. Malden, H.E. (ed.), *op. cit.*, p.91.
54. BL MSS Dept. Add. MSS 6113 f 111v.
Davies, K., *op. cit.*, p.179.
MacGibbon, D., *op. cit.*, p.135.
Stow, J., *Annales* (1615), p.434.
55. Seward, D., *Richard III* (1997), pp.132-5, 143-55.
Weir, A., *The Princes in the Tower* (1992), pp.143-52, 156-78.
Williamson, A., *The Mystery of the Princes* (1987), pp.87-199.
56. Cockayne, G.E. (ed.), *Complete Peerage*, vol. vi, pp.370-4.
57. *Ibid.*, vol. iv, pp.8-9.
58. *DNB*, vol. xliv (1895), pp.3-5.
59. *Ibid.*, vol. xliii (1895), pp.366-7.
60. Cockayne, G.E. (ed.), *op. cit.*, vol. ix, pp.611-12.
61. *Ibid.*, pp.717-19.
62. *Ibid.*, vol. iv, pp.205-7; vol. xii, part 1, p.251.
63. *Ibid.*, vol. iv, pp.418-19.
64. *Ibid.*, vol. ii, p.133.
65. *Ibid.*, vol. v, pp.429-30.
66. *Ibid.*, vol. xii, part 2, pp.447-9.
67. *Ibid.*, vol. I, pp.249-50.
Shaw, W.G., *Knights of England*, vol. i (1906), p.134.

68. *Ibid.*, p.138.
69. Cockayne, G.E. (ed.), *op. cit.*, vol. vii, pp.688-90.
70. *Ibid.*, vol. viii, pp.223-5.
71. *Ibid.*, vol. iv, pp.223-5.
72. Pollet, M., *John Skelton* (1971), p.258.
73. Bell, W.G., Cottrill, F., Spon, C., *London Wall* (1937), pp.49-50.
74. Colvin, H.M. (ed.), *op. cit.*, vol. ii, p.729.
75. Tipping, H.A., *Marquess Curzon of Kedleston, Tattershall Castle* (1929), p.114.
76. Colvin, H.M. (ed.), *op. cit.*, vol. ii, pp.640-1.
Thurley, S., *The Royal Palaces of Tudor England* (1993), p.19.
77. Colvin, H.M. (ed.), *op. cit.*, vol. ii, pp.764-5.
Thurley, S., *op. cit.*, p.18.
78. Colvin, H.M. (ed.), *op. cit.*, vol. ii, pp.884-8.
Thurley, S., *op. cit.*, p.19.
79. Skelton, J., *Complete Poems* (ed. Henderson, P.) (1948), pp.1-3.
Colvin, H.M. (ed.), *op. cit.*, vol. ii, pp.936-7.
Thurley, S., *op. cit.*, pp.19-21.
80. E 364/70 rot. H; /74 rot. H.
Colvin, H.M. (ed.), *op. cit.*, vol. ii, p.936.
CPR 1429-36 2, 602.
CPR 1436-41 89.
81. E 101/503/9 ff 1, 9-10v, 23-24.
82. E 404/61/128.
Griffiths, R.A., *op. cit.*, pp.312, 488.
83. E 404/63/121.
84. Flenley, R. (ed.), *op. cit.*, p.128.
Trinity College, Dublin. MS E.5.10 f 166r.
85. E 364/87 rot. K.
E 101/503/13 m 5.
86. CPR 1461-67 96-97.
E 101/503/9 f 9v.
87. E 101/496/21 ff 1-2.
E 28/92, 92v.
E 403/847 m 10; /848 m 2, 6-7, 11; /850 mm 1-7.
Colvin, H.M. (ed.), *op. cit.*, vol. ii, pp.936-7.
E 405/66 mm 2d-3, 4; /67 mm 1, 3d-4d; /68 mm 1d, 2, 3-5; /69 mm 4d-5; /70 mm 2-3, 5, 7d; /71 mm 1, 3, 6; /80 m 28.
E 101/329/2.
E 101/496/23 mm 1, 4.
88. E 364/87 rot. K ; /89 rot. Ed; /93 rot. A, /97 rots. C, Cd; /100 rots. B, C; /104 rot. B; /106 rots. D, Dd.
89. E 101/503/13 m 5.
90. E 364/104 rot. B.
91. Royal Commission on Historical Monuments (England), East London (1930), p.104.
92. Charlton, J., 'Eltham Palace', *Transactions of the Ancient Monuments Society*, vol. xxxi (1987), p.21.
93. Colvin, H.M. (ed.), *op. cit.*, vol. ii, p.937.
94. E 101/497/1 f 1.
Colvin, H.M. (ed.), *op. cit.*, vol. iv, part 2 (1982), p.78.
95. CPR 1467-77 555.
E 405/80 m 28.
E 403/847 m 10.
E 101/329/2.
E 405/66 mm 2d-3, 4.
E 403/848 mm 2, 6-7, 11.
E 403/850 mm 1-3, 6-7.
E 405/67 mm 1, 3d-4d.
E 101/496/21 ff 1-2.
E 405/68 mm ld-5.
E 29/92.
E 405/69 mm 4d-5.
96. Hussey, C., 'Eltham Hall I', *Country Life*, 15 May 1937, p.536.
Crown Estates Office, file 121, Thomas Gayfree to Robert J. Saunders, 2 May 1823.

97. CPR 1467-77 555.
98. E 403/850 mm 2-3, 7.
99. Simons, E.N., *The Reign of Edward IV* (1966), pp.270-1, 273-7.
100. E 101/496/21 f 2.
101. *Ibid.* f 1.
Pevsner, N., *London 2: South* (1983), p.301.
102. E 101/496/21 f 1.
103. Drake, H.H. (ed.), *Hasted's History of Kent: Hundred of Blackheath* (1886), p.279.
104. Harvey, J., *Tudor Architecture* (1949), pp.16-17, 55.
Harvey, J., *English Medieval Architecture* (1954), p.118.
105. Harvey, J., *op. cit.* (1949), p.17.
Harvey, J., *Gothic England* (1948), p.116.
Harvey, J., *The King's Chief Carpenters* (1948), p.28.
Harvey, J., *op. cit.* (1954), p.118.
106. CPR 1467-77 555.
E 405/80 m 28.
E 403/847 m 10.
E 101/329/2.
E 405/66 mm 2d-4.
E 403/848 mm 2, 6-7, 11.
E 403/850 mm 1-3, 6-7.
E 405/67 mm 1, 3d-4d.
E 101/496/21 ff 1-2.
E 405/68 mm 1d-5.
E 28/92.
E 405/69 mm 4d-5.
107. E 701/496/21 ff 1-2.
Drake, H.H. (ed.), *op. cit.*, p.279.
CPR 1476-85 103.
108. Colvin, H.M. (ed.), *op. cit.*, vol. ii, pp.936-7.
RCHM(E). East London. 107.
Spurgeon, J.W., 'Royal Eltham', *Bygone Kent* (ed. Stead, R.) (1892), p.165.
Harris, J., *History of Kent* (1719), p.116.
Historic MSS Commission, MSS of the Earl of Egmont, Diary of the First Viscount Percival, 1730-33, vol. i (1920), p.198.
Dunnage, H. and Laver, C., *Plans ... of the Great Hall of ... Eltham* (1828), pp.10-22.
Buckler, J.C., *An ... Account of the Royal Palace at Eltham* (1828), pp.69, 71-2, 75-8, 80, 82, 103.
Pugin, A., *Examples of Gothic Architecture* (1831), pp.36-7.
Fletcher, B., *Royal Homes near London* (1930), pp.61-2.
Hussey, C., *op. cit.*, p.539.
Scott, G., *Medieval Architecture*, vol. ii (1879), p.213.
Pevsner, N., *Kent* (1983), p.301.
109. Harvey, J., *op. cit.* (1948), p.28.
Ibid., p.116.
110. Nairn, I., *Nairn's England* (1966), p.208.
111. Fawcett, R., *Stirling Castle* (1995), pp.39, 41.
Campbell, W. (ed.), *Materials Illustrative of the Reign of Henry VII*, vol. i (1873), p.229.
Nichols, F.M. (ed.), *The Epistles of Erasmus*, vol. i (1901), pp.xix, 201-2, 245.
112. E 101/503/13 m 5.
E 364/97 rot. Cd.
113. E 101/503/9 f 9.
114. E 317/Kent/18 m 2.
115. E 405/70 mm 2, 3, 5, 7d.
116. E 101/493/12 m 8.
E 101/545/37 m 3.
E 101/494/15 m 2.
E 101/495/23 mm 2, 4.
E 101/502/15 m 5.
E 101/502/23 m 4.
E 101/502/26 mm 6, 7.
117. E 101/502/15 m 6.

REFERENCES

159

E 101/Kent/18 m 2.

118. Strong, D.E., *Eltham Palace* (1958), pp.11-13, 21.
119. *Ibid.*, p.12.
  Bodleian. M.S. Top. Gen. d. 14 f 15v.
120. *Eltham and Kentish Times*, 22 Aug. 1952, p.1.
121. Hussey, C., *op. cit.*, p.536.
  Strong, D.E., *op. cit.*, p.12.
122. E 101/496/21 ff 1-2.
  E 317/Kent/18 m 2.
123. Clapham, A.W. and Godfrey, W.H., *op. cit.*, ill. opp. p.49.
  'Eltham Palace', *Country Life*, 18 November 1933, p.534.
124. Crown Estate Office, file Eltham, 911.
  Eltham and Kentish Times, 28 July 1911, p.5; 5 Jan. 1912, p.7.
125. Dunnage and Laver plates 1, 8.
  Gregory, R.R.C., *The Story of Eltham Palace* (1909), 3 illns opp. p.24.
126. Buck print of Eltham Palace in 1735.
  Buckler, J.C., *op. cit.*, frontispiece.
127. Hussey, C., *op. cit.*, p.538.
128. *Ibid.*, p.128.
129. E 317/Kent/18 f 2.
130. Hussey, C., *op. cit.*, p.538.
131. Buckler, J.C., *op. cit.*, pp.104-7.
132. Hussey, C., *op. cit.*, p.538.
133. *Ibid.*, p.538.
  Seely and Paget, file 98, estimate; file 23, estimate 26 March 1935; file 29, instructions for hall screen 12 March 1936; file 44, model of screen 5 July 1935; file 30, bill 30 January 1936.
134. E 317/Kent/18 f 2.
135. Hussey, C., *op. cit.*, p.538.
136. Dunnage and Laver 16, plate 8.
137. Pevsner, N., *op. cit.*, p.301.
  Pugin, A.C., *op. cit.*, p.37.
  Wood, M., *The English Medieval House* (1965), pp.319-20.
138. Wood, M., *The English Medieval House* (1965), pp.319-20.
139. Emery, A., 'Eltham Palace', *Archaeologia Cantiana*, vol. lxxix (1960), pp.106, 140.
  Fawcett, R., *op. cit.*, p.39.
  Emery, A., *op. cit.*, p.112.
141. Cal. Inq. P.M. vol. iv, Temp. Hen. V, Hen. VI, Edw. IV et Ric. III (1828), 232.
142. E 101/473/18 f 18v.
143. CPR 1476-85 240.
144. CPR 1401-05 32.
  CPR 1422-29 21.
  CPR 1446-52 60.
145. Collier, J.P. (ed.), Trevelyan papers, Camden Society, 1856-57, 33-34.
146. Cal. Fine Rolls, 1471-85 26.
  Cal. Fine Roll, 1485-1509 13-14.
147. E 364/117 rot. B.
148. E 364/97 rot. C.
149. CPR 1446-52 76.
150. CPR 1330-34 414.
151. CPR 1401-05 28.
152. Cal. Fine Rolls, 1461-71 26-7.
  Cal. Close Rolls, 1476-85 376.
153. Cal. Fine Rolls, 1471-85 26.
154. Cal. Fine Rolls, 1485-1509 13-14.
155. CPR 1485-94 97.
156. CPR 1461-67 43, 110.
157. Cal. Close Rolls, 1461-68 26.
  CPR 1461-67 43, 110.
158. S.C. 6/Henry VII/339 No. 39.
  Campbell, W. (ed.), *op. cit.*, vol. i, pp.34, 72, 96, 320; vol. ii, pp.55, 59-60, 187.
159. CPR 1485-94 177.
160. Campbell, W. (ed.), *op. cit.*, vol. i, p.67.

161. *Ibid.*, p.305.
  CPR 1485-94 109.
  CPR 1476-85 119, 250.
162. CPR 1494-1509 453.
163. Cal. Close Rolls, 1461-68 26.
  CPR 1485-94 65.
164. Kent County Archives. DRb/Pwr I(f 77a) 83b-84a William Wydemer ;/Pwr 1 f 110b (119b) John Cheseman; /Pwr 2 f 44 Robert Cheseman; /Pwr 2 ff 83-83v Robert Rande; / PW 2 f 91b Philip Bird; /Pwr 2 f 175a Robert Howman; /Pwr 2 f 208b Thomas Myrfyn; /Pwr 2 ff 356v-358 John Hooman; /Pwr 3 f 10v Richard Tottnam; /Pwr 3 ff 10v-11 William Gosse; /Pwr 3 f 10a Robert Dauson; /Pwr 3 ff 61-62b Margaret Forneux; /Pwr 4 f 161b Richard Skull; /Pwr 3 ff 203a-b, 204-204v John Frauncis; /Pwr 6 ff 157b-158a John a Dene.
  Somerset House. 16 Stokton (f 121) William Wetynhale.
165. Kent Archives Office. /Pwr 2 ff 356v-358 John Hooman.
166. Kent Archives Office. /Pwr 3 ff 203a-b, 204-204v John Frauncis.

7. THE EARLY TUDORS AND ELTHAM PALACE.

1. Campbell, W. (ed.), *Materials Illustrative of the Reign of Henry VII*, vol. i (1873), p.229.
  Cal. Letters between England and Spain, vol. i, 1485-1509 (1862), p.32.
  Macdougall, N., *James III* (1982), p.217.
  Conway, A., *Henry VII's Relations between England and Scotland 1485-1498* (1932), p.9.
2. Gairdner, J. (ed.), *Letters and Papers Illustrative of the Reigns of Richard III and Henry VII*, rolls series, vol. i (1863), pp.388-9.
  Thomas, A.H. and Thornley, I.D. (eds), *The Great Chronicle of London* (1938), p.440.
3. Thomas, A.H. and Thornley, I.D. (eds), *op. cit.*, pp.260, 440.
  Kingsford, C.L. (ed.), *Chronicles of London* (1905), p.207.
4. Chambers, R.W., *Thomas More* (1935), pp.70-1.
  Huizinga, J., *Erasmus of Rotterdam* (1952), p.30.
  Froude, J.A., *Life and Letters of Erasmus* (1984), pp.49-51.
  Routh, E.M.G., *Sir Thomas More and his Friends: 1477-1535* (1934), pp.18-19.
  Cecil, A., *A Portrait of Thomas More* (1937), p.29.
  Allen, P.S. (ed.), *Opus Epistolarum Des Erasmi Roterdami*, vol. i (1906), pp.239-41.
  Miller, C.H., Bradner, L., Lynch, C.A. and Oliver, R.P. (eds), *Complete works of St Thomas More*, vol. iii, part 2 (1984), pp.42, 44-6.
  Nichols, F.M. (ed.), *The Epistles of Erasmus*, vol. i (1901), pp.xix, 201-2, 245.
5. Nichols, F.M. (ed.), *op. cit.*, p.200.
  Cockayne, G.E. (ed.), *The Complete Peerage*, vol. ix (1936), p.338.
  Moreana, *Thomas More Gazette*, no. 2 (1980) p.15.
6. BL MSS Add. MSS 26787.
  Sellers, M. (ed.), *The York Mercers and Merchant Adventurers 1356-1917*, Surtees Society (1918), p.109.
7. Miller, C.H. *et al* (eds), *op. cit.*, pp.44-6.
  Reedijk, C. (ed.), *The Poems of Desiderius Erasmus* (1956), pp.68, 248-54.
  Burke's Guide to the Royal Family (1973), pp.204-5.
8. Nichols, F.M. (ed.), *op. cit.*, p.201.
9. Smith, P., *Erasmus* (1923), pp.61-2.

10. *Eltham and District Times*, 30 September 1910.
  Charlton, J., 'Eltham Palace: Anniversary Address', *Transactions of the Ancient Monuments Society*, vol. xxxi (N.S.) (1987), p.13.
11. Jobson, A., *Suffolk Miscellany* (1975), p.28.
12. E 101/413/13 ff 46-54.
  E 101/414/3 ff 3, 11-14,17-18, 20.
  Sellers, M. (ed.), *op. cit.*, p.109.
13. Bentley, S. (ed.), *Excerpta Historica* (1831), p.116.
  E 101/414/14 f 15v.
14. E 101/415/3 ff 23v, 48.
  E 101/415/4 ff 17-18, 26v, 31.
  CPR 1494-1509 245, 249.
15. *Cal. Letters between England and Spain*, vol. i, 1485-1509 (1862), p.401.
16. Gairdner, J. (ed.), *Memorials of Henry VII*, rolls series (1858), pp.115-19, 127-8.
17. *Ibid.*, pp.127-8.
18. Drake, H.H. (ed.), *Hasted's History of Kent ... Hundred of Blackheath* (1886), p.197 and note 14.
19. Lambarde, W., *A Perambulation of Kent* (1576), p.386.
20. Byrne, M. St C. (ed.), *Letters of Henry VIII* (1936), pp.5-11.
21. *Letters and Papers of Henry VIII*, vol. i, part 1, pp.69-70, 76, 118, 126, 135, 165, 426, 429-30, 432, 434-5, 441, 447, 486, 497, 509, 655, 664, 667-9, 787; vol. i, part 2, pp.1044, 1556; vol. ii, part 2, pp.1447, 1451, 1453, 1457-9, 1464-6, 1469, 1474-6, 1480, 1505-6, 1526, 1545; vol. iii, part 1, pp.50-1; vol. iii, part 2, pp.1158, 1176, 1180, 1542; vol. iv, part 1, pp.434, 843-4, 860-72, 1259.
  E 101/416/15 ff 18-23, 51-55, 60-64.
  E 101/417/4.
  E 101/418/4.
  E 101/418/16 ff 4-5, 8v-9v.
  E 101/419/2 p 2.
  E 101/419/5 ff 4v-5, 10v, 19v-20, 30.
22. *Letters and Papers of Henry VIII*, vol. i, part 2, p.1556.
23. *Ibid.*, vol. ii, part 2, p.1447.
24. *Ibid.*, vol. i, part 1, p.664.
25. E 101/418/4.
  Letters and Papers of Henry VIII, vol. i, part 2, pp.1145, 1251-3, 1263, 1266-7, 1272, 1275, 1280-5, 1287, 1292, 1301, 1303, 1305, 1309-13, 1317-18, 1321, 1329-30, 1365-7, 1373, 1380-1.
26. *Ibid.*, pp.1266-7.
27. *Ibid.*
28. *Complete Peerage*, vol. ix (1936), p.114, appendix F 44.
  Letters and Papers of Henry VIII, vol. i, part 2, p.1267.
29. *Letters and Papers of Henry VIII*, vol. i, part 2, p.1145; vol. ii, part 1, p.532; vol. iv, p.2580.
  Cockayne, G.E. (ed.), *op. cit.*, vol. ix, pp.338-9.
30. Cruikshank, C.G., *The English Occupation of Tournai* (1971), pp.1-290.
  Letters and Papers of Henry VIII, vol. ii, part 2, p.1374.
  Cockayne, G.E. (ed.), *op. cit.*, vol. ix, p.338.
31. *Letters and Papers of Henry VIII*, vol. i, part 2, p.1400.
32. *Ibid.*, p.1429.
33. *Ibid.*, p.1318.
34. *Ibid.*, pp.1301, 1380.
35. *Ibid.*, p.1301.
36. Nichols, F.M. (ed.), *op. cit.*, vol. ii (1904), pp.136, 145.
  Letters and Papers of Henry VIII, vol. i, part 2, pp.1292, 1313, 1315.
37. *Gentleman's Magazine*, June 1837, p.592.

38. *Letters and Papers of Henry VIII*, vol. ii, part 2, p.1466.
39. E 101/497/1 f 5.
    Letters and Papers of Henry VIII, vol. iv, part 3, p.2440; vol. v, pp.304, 308–10, 313, 316, 319, 323.
40. *Ibid.*, vol. i, part 2, p.1380.
41. *Ibid.*, vol. ii, part 1, p.1421.
    Ridley, J., *Henry VIII* (1984), pp.75, 77.
42. *Letters and Papers of Henry VIII*, vol. ii, part 1, pp.6–7, 74.
    Ridley, J., *op. cit.*, pp.73, 77.
43. *Letters and Papers of Henry VIII*, vol. ii, part 1, pp.74–5.
    Ridley, J., *op. cit.*, pp.79–80.
44. *Letters and Papers of Henry VIII*, vol. ii, part 1, pp.75–6.
    Ridley, J., *op. cit.*, p.80.
    Richardson, W.C., *Mary Tudor: The White Queen* (1970), pp.174–7.
45. Richardson, W.C., *op. cit.*, pp.177–85.
    Ridley, J., *op. cit.*, pp.81–2.
46. Richardson, W.C., *op. cit.*, pp.166–74.
    Ridley, J., *op. cit.*, p.84.
47. *Letters and Papers of Henry VIII*, vol. ii, part 1, p.359.
48. Halle, E., *Chronicle* (ed. Ellis, Sir H.) (1809), p.583.
    Letters and Papers of Henry VIII, vol. ii, part 2, pp.1505–6.
    Anglo, S., *Spectacle, Pageantry and Early Tudor Policy* (1969), pp.119–20.
    Geoffrey of Monmouth, *The History of the Kings of Britain* (ed. Thorpe, L.) (1966), pp.54–5, 71–2.
    Hillebrand, E.N. (ed.), *The Child Actors* (1926), pp.55–6, 324–5.
49. *Letters and Papers of Henry VIII*, vol. ii, part 1, pp.499, 506.
    Anstis, J., *The Order of the Garter*, vol. ii (1724), p.277.
50. *Letters and Papers of Henry VIII*, vol. ii, part 2, p.1475.
51. *Ibid.*, vol. iii, part 1, pp.49–51.
52. *Ibid.*, vol. ii, part 2, pp.1363–4; vol. iii, part 1, p.334.
    Cal. State Papers (Venetian), 1509–19, vol. ii, 457–58.
    E 101/418/16 ff 4–5, 8v–9v.
53. *Ibid.*, vol. iii, part 1, pp.331–2.
54. Halle, E., *op. cit.*, pp.651, 707.
    Gwyn, P., *The King's Cardinal: The Rise and Fall of Thomas Wolsey* (1990), pp.368–9.
55. *Ibid.*, pp.366, 368.
56. *Ibid.*, pp.366–7, 563–4.
    Pollard, A.F., 'The Council under the Tudors', *English Historical Review*, vol. xxxvii, no. cxlvii, July 1922, pp.358–60.
    Halle, E., *op. cit.*, p.707.
    Letters and Papers of Henry VIII, vol. iv, part 1, pp.860–72.
57. Gwyn, P., *op. cit.*, pp.367, 549, 561–64.
    Reese, M.M., *Master of the Horse* (1976), p.134.
    Ives, E.W., *Anne Boleyn* (1986), p.15.
58. *Letters and Papers of Henry VIII*, vol. iv, part 1, pp.860–72.
    Gwyn, P., *op. cit.*, p.366.
59. Reese, M.M., *op. cit.*, p.134.
    Gwyn, P., *op. cit.*, pp.549–55, 560–4.
60. Reese, M.M., *op. cit.*, p.134.
    Gwyn, P., *op. cit.*, p.368.
61. *Letters and Papers of Henry VIII*, vol. iv, part 1, p.434.
62. Thompson, H.L., *Christ Church* (1900), pp.10–12.

63. Halle, E., *op. cit.*, p.707.
64. *Letters and Papers of Henry VIII*, vol. iv, part 1, pp.845–6.
65. *Ibid.*, part 2, p.1905.
66. *Ibid.*, pp.1259, 1905.
67. *Ibid.*, part 3, p.2440; vol. v, pp.304, 308–10, 313, 316, 319, 323–4.
    E 101/420/11 ff 5v, 18v, 22v, 30, 33, 36v, 43, 44, 47, 51v, 57–58, 61v, 65, 70, 77, 91, 96v–97, 101, 113v, 116, 128, 131v, 139v, 154.
68. *Letters and Papers of Henry VIII*, vol. v, pp.323–4.
69. E 101/497/1 ff 4–7.
    Colvin, H.M. (ed.), *King's Works*, vol. iv, part 2, pp.80–2.
    Thurley, S., *The Royal Palaces of Tudor England* (1993), pp.45–6, 196.
    Woods, H., 'Excavations at Eltham Palace 1975–9', *Transactions of London & Middlesex Archaeological Society*, vol. xxxiii (1982), pp.230–2.
70. *Letters and Papers of Henry VIII*, vol. v, pp.486, 502, 507–9, 527–8, 736, 758–9; vol. vi, pp.87, 142, 260.
    Nicolas, Sir H. (ed.), *Privy Purse Expenses of Henry VIII* (1827), pp.218, 220–1, 223–7, 229–30.
    E 101/421/3 ff 13v–14, 16, 17, 26, 27.
71. *Letters and Papers of Henry VIII*, vol. v, pp.659–62, 760–1.
    Nicolas, Sir H. (ed.), *op. cit.*, pp.258, 265, 275.
72. *Ibid.*, pp.94, 218, 220–1, 223–7, 229–30, 258, 265, 275.
73. *Letters and Papers of Henry VIII*, vol. v, p.759.
74. *Ibid.*, p.758.
75. *Ibid.*
    Nicolas, Sir H. (ed.), *op. cit.*, p.220.
76. *Letters and Papers of Henry VIII*, vol. v, p.758.
    Nicolas, Sir H. (ed.), *op. cit.*, pp.218, 229.
77. *Letters and Papers of Henry VIII*, vol. v, p.758.
    Nicolas, Sir H. (ed.), *op. cit.*, pp.220, 227.
78. *Letters and Papers of Henry VIII*, vol. v, pp.758, 760.
    Nicolas, Sir H. (ed.), *op. cit.*, pp.94, 230, 258, 265.
79. *Letters and Papers of Henry VIII*, vol. v, pp.599, 660–2.
    Cal. Letters between England and Spain, vol. iv, part 2, pp.556–61.
80. *Letters and Papers of Henry VIII*, vol. v, p.659.
81. *Ibid.*, p.660.
82. Ives, E.W., *op.cit.*, p.201.
    Letters and Papers of Henry VIII, vol. v, p.761.
83. Nicolas, Sir H. (ed.), *op. cit.*, p.218.
84. *Ibid.*, pp.221, 224.
85. *Ibid.*, p.220.
86. *Letters and Papers of Henry VIII*, vol. v, p.758.
    Nicolas, Sir H. (ed.), *op. cit.*, pp.218, 220.
87. *Letters and Papers of Henry VIII*, vol. v, p.758.
    Nicolas, Sir H. (ed.), *op. cit.*, pp.223–4.
88. *Letters and Papers of Henry VIII*, vol. v, p.758.
    Nicolas, Sir H. (ed.), *op. cit.*, p.221.
89. *Letters and Papers of Henry VIII*, vol. v, p.759.
    Nicolas, Sir H. (ed.), *op. cit.*, p.226.
90. *Letters and Papers of Henry VIII*, vol. v, pp.758, 761.
    Nicolas, Sir H. (ed.), *op. cit.*, p.275.
91. *Letters and Papers of Henry VIII*, vol. v, p.758.
    Nicolas, Sir H. (ed.), *op. cit.*, p.224.
92. As for note 91.
93. As for note 89.
94. Nicolas, Sir H. (ed.), *op. cit.*, p.220.
95. *Letters and Papers of Henry VIII*, vol. v, p.761.
    Nicolas, Sir H. (ed.), *op. cit.*, p.275.
96. *Letters and Papers of Henry VIII*, vol. v, p.758.
    Nicolas, Sir H. (ed.), *op. cit.*, p.218.

97. Ridley, J., *op. cit.*, pp.217–21.
98. *Ibid.*, pp.214–15.
99. *Ibid.*, p.221.
100. *Ibid.*, pp.226–7.
     Strickland, A., *The Lives of the Queens of England*, vol. iv (1888), p.5.
101. *Letters and Papers of Henry VIII*, vol. vii, part 1, p.204.
     Byrne, M. St G. (ed.), *The Lisle Letters*, vol. ii (1981), p.128.
     Mumby, F.A., *The Girlhood of Queen Elizabeth* (1909), p.13.
102. Ives, E.W., *op. cit.*, p.248.
     Bodleian. Rawl. D. 776. 96, 102.
103. *Ibid.* 94.
104. *Ibid.* 97v–100; D. 777. ff 90v–91v.
105. Byrne, M. St G. (ed.), *op. cit.*, p.220.
     Cal. Letters between England and Spain, vol. v, part 1, pp.219–24.
106. Ives, E.W., *op. cit.*, p.248.
     Clifford, H., *The Life of Jane Dormer* (1887), pp.xiii, 15, 62–3, 81–2, 104, 110.
107. Bodleian. Rawl. D. 777 ff 88–88v.
108. *Ibid.* f 88v.
109. *Ibid.* ff 88–88v.
110. *Ibid.* ff 90v–91v, 102v.
111. Friedmann, P., *Anne Boleyn*, vol. ii (1884), pp.122–4.
     Bodleian. Rawl. D. 777 f 90v.
112. Friedmann, P., *op. cit.*, pp.122–4.
113. Cal. Letters between England and Spain, vol. v, part 1, p.595.
     Letters and Papers of Henry VIII, vol. ix, pp.300, 356, 359–60; vol. x, pp.3, 5, 10, 79, 362–3.
     Byrne, M. St G. (ed.), *op. cit.*, p.637.
114. Ridley, J., *op. cit.*, pp.253–6, 264–71, 281, 285–9, 291–7, 310–12.
115. *Letters and Papers of Henry VIII*, vol. x, pp.361–2.
116. *Ibid.*, p.364.
117. Ridley, J., *op. cit.*, pp.271, 296, 303.
118. *Letters and Papers of Henry VIII*, vol. xiii, part 1, pp.435, 455; vol. xiii, part 2, pp.531; vol. addenda, vol. i, part 1, p.451.
     E 101/422/10 ff 22v, 31.
119. *Letters and Papers of Henry VIII*, vol. xiv, part 2, p.336.
120. *Ibid.*, vol. xvi, p.324.
121. *Ibid.*, vol. xix, part 2, pp.169, 173–4, 193–5, 311, 406–7.
122. Ridley, J., *op. cit.*, pp.383–5.
123. *Letters and Papers of Henry VIII*, vol. xix, part 2, pp.404–7.
124. E 101/424/1 ff 23, 33, 44, 49.
125. *Letters and Papers of Henry VIII*, vol. xix, part 2, pp.169, 173–4, 193–5, 311, 406–7.
126. *Acts of the Privy Council of England* (New Series), vol. iii, 1550–2 (1891), p.347.
     E 351/3326 mm 5d, 9.
127. Priestley, E.J., 'The Palace and Manor of Eltham 1086–1663', Unpublished MPhil thesis, University of London, vol. ii (1973), p.199.
128. Erickson, C., *Bloody Mary: The Life of Mary Tudor* (1978), pp.289–97, 307–8, 357–8.
129. CPR 1547–53, vol. v, 234–5, 248.
     CPR 1553–54 404–5.
     Strype, J., *Ecclesiastical Memorials*, vol. iii (1721), p.304.
130. E 351/3326 m 5d.
131. Nichols, J.G. (ed.), *Diary of Henry Machyn 1550–63*, Camden Society (1848), p.110.
     CSP (Venetian) 1555–56 534–36.
     E 101/428/4.
132. *Acts of the Privy Council of England* (New Series), vol. v, 1554–56, p.311–30.
133. CPR 1555–57 265–6, 277, 346–7.

134. *Ibid.* 500, 502, 504.
135. *Ibid.* 274–6.
136. *Ibid.* 516.
137. *Ibid.* 280–1, 547.
138. *Ibid.* 270–4, 280, 470.
139. *Ibid.* 278–9, 516, 547.
140. Mumby, F.A., *op. cit.*, pp.212–13.
Pepys Library, Cambridge, no. 2870 f 315.
141. Loades, D.M., *Two Tudor Conspiracies* (1965), pp.15–127, 177–237.
MacCaffrey, W., *Elizabeth I* (1993), p.12–26.
142. CPR 1555–57 274.
143. Neale, J.E., *Queen Elizabeth* (1945), pp.48, 93–5.
CPR 1557–58 210–12.
E 101/428/8.
144. E 101/428/15.
145. CSP (Foreign) 1558–59 449.
146. Royal Commission on Historical MSS, 15th report, MSS of Charles Haliday, appx. iii, p.73.
147. Bodleian. Rawl. D. 776 ff 98v–99v; D. 777 ff 88, 90v–91v, 99; D. 781 ff 37, 39.
148. *Ibid.* 776 ff 97v–99v, 103; D. 777 ff 88, 90v, 91v, 99.
E 101/497/1 ff 4–4v, 5v.
149. Bodleian. Rawl. D. 776 f 98v.
150. *Ibid.* ff 98, 99; D. 777 f 91.
151. *Ibid.* 776 ff 98–99; D. 777 ff 90, 91; D. 781 f 37.
152. *Ibid.* 776 ff 94, 97v–98; D. 777 ff 90v, 91v, 97.
E 101/497/1 f 5v.
153. *Ibid.* 776 ff 98, 103–03v; D. 777 ff 98–98v, 99.
E 101/497/1 f 4.
154. *Ibid.* f 5v.
155. *Ibid.* f 5v.
156. Bodleian. Rawl. D. 776 f 98v.
157. E 101/497/1 f 4.
158. Bodleian. Rawl. D. 777 f 99.
159. E 101/497/1 f 4.
Bodleian. Rawl. D. 777 f 98v.
160. *Ibid.* ff 96, 99v, 103.
161. *Ibid.* ff 88, 92, 99–99v.
162. E 101/497/1 f 4.
163. Bodleian. Rawl. D. 777 f 98v.
164. *Ibid.* f 99v.
165. *Ibid.* f 98v.
166. *Ibid.* f 98; D. 777 f 90.
E 101/497/1 f 4v.
167. *Ibid.* f 4v.
168. *Ibid.* f 5v.
169. Thurley, S., *op. cit.*, pp.117–20, 125, 139–41, plans 4, 8, 13–14.
170. E 101/497/1 f 4v.
171. *Ibid.* f 5.
172. Bodleian. Rawl. D. 776 f 97v.
173. *Ibid.* f 95.
174. *Ibid.* 777 f 88.
175. E 101/497/1 f 4.
176. Bodleian. Rawl. D. 781 f 36; D. 779 f 65.
177. *Ibid.* 776 ff 94, 97.
178. *Ibid.* 781 f 36.
179. *Ibid.* 777 f 97.
180. E 351/3218 mm 11–11d.
181. Drake, H.H. (ed.), *op. cit.*, p.186, note 15.
182. *ibid.*, p.186, note 15.
183. Bodleian. Rawl. D. 776 ff 95, 96v; D. 777 ff 99v, 103, 104v, 105v, 107v, 108v, 109v.
Drake, H.H. (ed.), *op. cit.*, p.186, note 15.
184. Bodleian. Rawl. D. 776 ff 96, 103–03v.
185. *Ibid.* 777 f 92; D. 776 f 94.
186. *Ibid.* 777 f 92; D. 776 ff 99v–100.
187. *Ibid.* 777 f 92.
188. *Ibid.* 776 ff 96, 103.
189. *Ibid.* 781 f 39.
190. Colvin, H.M. (ed.), *op. cit.*, vol. iv, part 2

(1982), pp.78–9.
191. Lambarde, W., *op. cit.*, p.386.
Historical Monuments Commission, *East London* (1930), pp.104–6.
192. CPR 1485–94 220.
193. Campbell, W. (ed.), *op. cit.*, vol. ii, p.298.
BL MSS Dept. Eg. 2358 f 50.
E 101/503/22.
E 101/474/19.
CPR 1494–1509 516.
E 101/414/16 f 57.
Colvin, H.M. (ed.), *op. cit.*, pp.78–9.
194. E 101/497/1 ff 1–2, 4–4v.
195. Colvin, H.M. (ed.), *op. cit.*, pp.79–81.
Letters and Papers of Henry VIII, vol. iv, part i, p.696.
196. E 101/497/1 ff 1–2.
Colvin, H.M. (ed.), *op. cit.*, p.78.
197. BM Maps 186 h.i. No. 5.
198. Colvin, H.M. (ed.), *op. cit.*, pp.79–81.
Letters and Papers of Henry VIII, vol. ii, part 2, pp.1453–4, 1457–8, 1475–7; vol. iii, part 1, p.169; vol. iii, part 2, pp.1156–7, 1534–5, 1538–9, 1541, 1543–4.
199. E 164/44 ff 5–7.
200. *Letters and Papers of Henry VIII*, vol. ii, part 2, pp.1474–5.
201. Colvin, H.M. (ed.), *op. cit.*, pp.79–81.
Letters and Papers of Henry VIII, vol. iv, part 1, p.696.
202. Colvin, H.M. (ed.), *op. cit.*, pp.80–2.
E 101/497/1 f 4–7v.
Thurley, S., *op. cit.*, pp.45–6, 196.
203. E 101/497/1 f 4–4v.
204. E 101/420/11 ff 18v, 22v, 30, 33, 36v, 43, 44, 47, 51, 57v–58, 61v, 65, 70v, 77, 96v–97, 101, 113v, 116, 128, 131v, 139v, 154.
Letters and Papers of Henry VIII, vol. v, pp.304, 308–10, 313, 316, 323–4, 759.
205. E 101/420/11 f 139v.
E 101/497/1 f 5.
Letters and Papers of Henry VIII, vol. v, p.323.
Colvin, H.M. (ed.), *op. cit.*, pp.79–81.
206. Woolwich and District Archaeological Society, vol. xxxiv (1973), p.6.
207. E 317/Kent/18 m 2.
208. A. Wells-Cole, Temple Newsam to E.J. Priestley, 27 March 2003.
Woolwich and District Archaeological Society, vol. xxxiv (1973), p.6.
209. *Letters and Papers of Henry VIII*, vol. v, p.323.
E 101/420/11 f 139v.
Colvin, H.M. (ed.), *op. cit.*, vol. iv, part 2 (1982), pp.81–2.
210. E 101/497/1 f 6.
211. Brook, R., *The Story of Eltham Palace* (1960), pp.40–1.
King, D. and Clayton, A.B., *Subterranean Passages at Eltham Palace* (1834), p.6.
212. *Letters and Papers of Henry VIII*, vol. x, p.275.
213. *Ibid.*, vol. ii, part 2, p.1474.
Pevsner, N., *London 2: South* (1983), p.302.
Royal Commission on Historical Monuments, *East London* (1930), p.108, plate 8.
214. *Letters and Papers of Henry VIII*, vol. ii, part 2, p.1474.
215. Pevsner, N., *op. cit.*, p.302.
Royal Commission on Historical Monuments, *East London* (1930), p.108, plate 8.
216. Colvin, H.M. (ed.), *op. cit.*, pp.80–1.
E 101/497/1 ff 6–6v.
217. E 101/497/1 f 5.
218. *Letters and Papers of Henry VIII*, vol. i, part 1, p.536; vol. ii, part 2, pp.1453–4, 1457–8.

219. Colvin, H.M. (ed.), *op. cit.*, p.79.
E 164/44 ff 5–7.
220. *Letters and Papers of Henry VIII*, vol. ii, part 2, pp.1474–5.
221. Thurley, S., *op. cit.*, pp.70–2.
222. E 317/Kent/18 mm 4, 8.
223. *Letters and Papers of Henry VIII*, vol. xiii, part 1, pp.435, 455; vol. xiii, part 2, p.531; vol. xiv, part 2, p.336; vol. xvi, p.324; vol. addenda, vol. i, part 1, p.451.
E 101/422/10 ff 22–22v, 31.
224. Bodleian. Rawl. D. 777 ff 87–113; D. 779 ff 64v–65v; D. 781 ff 36–39v.
E 101/504/2 ff 39–40v.
Drake, H.H. (ed.), *op. cit.*, pp.186–7.
225. E 164/44 ff 8v–9.
226. *Ibid.* 9, 16v–17, 26, 58–58v.
227. *Letters and Papers of Henry VIII*, vol. i, part 1, p.536.
E 164/44 ff 5–7.
228. *Letters and Papers of Henry VIII*, vol. v, p.558; vol. vi, pp.138–9; vol vii, part 1, p.342; vol. x, p.513.
Cat. Ancient Deeds, vol. iii (1900), p.159.
229. Erickson, C., *op. cit.*, p.237.
CSP (Spanish), vol. ix, p.405.
230. *Letters and Papers of Henry VIII*, vol. i, part 2, p.336; vol. iv, part 3, p.2976.
231. CPR 1485–94 177, 193.
S.C. 6/Henry V11/330 No. 39.
CPR 1547–53, vol. v, 234–35, 248.
Close Rolls 1485–1500, vol. i, 68.
Campbell, W. (ed.), *op. cit.*, vol. i, p.96; vol. ii, pp.55, 187.
232. *Letters and Papers of Henry VIII*, vol. iv, part 2, p.1773.
CPR 1547–53, vol. v, 235.
CPR 1553–54, 405.
233. *Letters and Papers of Henry VIII*, vol. vii, part 2, p.559.
234. Drake, H.H. (ed.), *op. cit.*, p.178.
235. Loades, D.M., *Mary I* (1979), pp.71–2.
Strype, J., *op. cit.*, vol. iii (1721), p.29.
Prescott, H.E.M., *Spanish Mary* (1940), p.229.
236. CPR 1547–53 404–6.
CPR 1547–53, vol. v, 234–5, 248.
CSP(D) 1553–58, 1998. 359.
237. CSP(D) 1547–53. 1992. 4, 55, 125–6, 198, 215–16, 233, 239, 268, 270, 279–80, 284, 294, 356.
238. Loades, D.M., *op. cit.*, pp.89, 98–9.
CPR 1553–54 24, 36, 57, 182–83, 233–34, 392, 404–06.
CPR 1555–57 103, 222, 229.
CPR 1557–58 66, 142.
239. Kent Archives Office, DRb/PW 1. Christopher Segryg.
240. KCA. DRb/PW 7 f 309a–v. Thomas Parkar.
241. KCA. DRb/Pwr 9 f 77v. Willyam Atkynson.
242. KCA. DRb/Pwr 9 f 177b–178. John Rolte.
243. KCA. DRb/Pwr 9 f 178. John Rolte; /Pwr 9 ff 176–177v. John Colenson.
244. *Letters and Papers of Henry VIII*, vol. iii, part 1, pp.866, 1492; vol. vii, part 1, p.233.
245. KCA. DRb/Pwr 9 ff 176b–177v. John Colenson.
246. *Letters and Papers of Henry VIII*, vol. iv, part 3, p.2440; vol. v, pp.304–5, 308, 310, 316, 319, 324, 523–4, 759.
247. KCA. DRb/Pwr 9 ff 175b–176v. John Plom.
248. Somerset House. 3 Alen. John Wyllesdon.
249. SH. 44 Alen, 8 Populwell. John Plume.
250. SH. 51 Alen. Robert Hordron.
251. KCA. DRb/PW 1. Christopher Segryg; /Pwr 7 f 372. Thomas Sybson.
252. KCA. DRb/Pwr 7 ff 372–72v. Thomas Sybson.

253. SH. Hogen 25. John Browne.
254. KCA. DRb/PW 1. John Passey.
Rivers, E., *Some Records of Eltham* (1904), pp.109, 112.
255. KCA. DRb/Pwr 8 f 60a-v. Henry Skylman.
Letters and Papers of Henry VIII, vol. iii, part 2, pp.866, 1492.
256. KCA. DRb/Pwr 8 f 234. Agnys Passey.
257. KCA. DRb/PW 1. Rauffe Wotton; /PW 1. Herre Kyghley.
258. KCA. DRb/Pwr 7 f 273a-b. Henry Olde Castell.
259. Drake, H.H. (ed.), *op. cit.*, p.189.
Rivers, E., *op. cit.*, p.109.
260. KCA. DRb/Pwr 5 f 389v. Roger Ottley; /Pwr 6 f 167a. Thomas Birde; /Pwr 6 ff 77b-78. Richard Homan; /PW 1. Jhon Nedum; John Passey; Roberte Herte; Luce Dosyng; /Pwr 8 f 235v. Agnys Passey; /Pwr 7 f 273a-b. Henry Olde Castell; 73a-b. John Downe; ff 87b-88. Roger Leche; /PW 1. Rauffe Wotton; Elesabeth Hogson; Herre Kyghley; /PW 5. Willyam Carlell; f 215. William Lytylman; f 220v. Johan Wilshawe or Oldeshaw; f 223. William Byrde; f 232v. Richard Pemberton; f 300b. Kateryn Cheseman; /PW 1. Christopher Segryg; Robert Robson; /Pwr 7. Thomas Parkar; f 346v. Thomas Fynlaye; /PW 2. John Downer; /Pwr 8 f 60a-v. Henry Skylman; f 117a-v. John A Dene; ff 124b-125. Philip Carrok; /Pwr 9 f 177-177v. John Colenson; f 178. John Rolte; /Pwr 8 f 211a.
Nicholas Priour; /Pwr 9 f 382v. Lettys Collynson; /Pwr 10 f 218b. Roger Grenwodd; /Pwr 12 ff 360a-361v. Margret Breckett; /Pwr 8 f 179-179v. Robert Ducker; ff 223b-224b. Roger Ewgham; f 77v. Willyam Atkynson; /Pwr 9 f 175b. John Plom.
SH. 12 Vox. William Dygon; 24 Adeane. Thomas Barett; 38 Bennet. Richard Olde Castell; 44 Alen, 8 Populwell. John Plume; 17 Tashe. John Leyke.
261. KCA. DRb/PW 5. Willyam Carlell; Thomas Deyne; Richard Maynard; Thomas Huxley.
SH. 48 Wrastley. Christopher Wymyngton; 28 Wrastley. Roger Leche.
262. KCA. DRb/PW 5. Thomas Huxley.
263. SH. 48 Wrastley. Christopher Wymyngton.
264. KCA. DRb/PW 5. Richard Maynard.
265. SH. 12 Vox. William Dygon.
266. KCA. DRb/PW 5. Thomas Huxley.
267. SH. 48 Wrastley. Christopher Wymyngton.
268. SH. 5 Marche f 38v. William Reynewell.
KCA. DRb/PW 1. Roberte Herte.
269. KCA. DRb/Pwr 8 ff 223-224b. Roger Ewgham.
270. KCA. DRb/Pwr 9 f 177. John Colenson.
271. *Ibid.* f 383. Lettys Collynson.
272. KCA. DRb/PW 5. Richard Maynard.
273. KCA. DRb/PW 1. John Passey.
274. KCA. DRb/Pwr 8 ff 233b-234v. Agnys Passey.
275. SH Hogen 25. John Browne.
276. KCA. DRb/PW 5. Thomas Deyne; John Stobbese; Richard Maynard.
277. *Ibid.* Thomas Huxley.
278. KCA. DRb/Pwr 11 ff 102b-103v. Henry Stewunson.
279. KCA. DRb/PW 1. Elesabeth Hogson.
SH. Hogen 25. John Browne.
280. SH. 24 Adeane. Thomas Barett.
KCA. DRb/PW 1. Luce Dosyng; /Pwr 9 f 392. Christopher Nicholson.
281. KCA. DRb/PW 1. Luce Dosyng; /Pwr 7 f 273v. Henry Olde Castell.

282. KCA. DRb/Pwr 7 f 273a-b. Henry Olde Castell; /PW 1. Robert Robson; /Pwr 8 f 60a-v. Henry Skylman.
283. SH. 44 Alen, 8 Populwell. John Plume.
284. *Ibid.*
285. *Ibid.*
286. KCA. DRb/PW 7. Katheryne Halle.
287. KCA. DRb/PW 5. Thomas Huxley.
288. KCA. DRb/PW 1. Robert Robson.
289. SH. 17 Tashe. John Leyke.
KCA. DRb/PW 4. Henrye Underwod; /PW 5. Thomas Huxley.
290. KCA. DRb/Pwr 8 ff 124b-125. Philip Carrok.
291. KCA. DRb/PW 5. Thomas Huxley.
292. KCA. DRb/Pwr 7 275a-b, v. Henry Olde Castell; /PW 1. Elesabeth Hogson; /Pwr 8 ff 124b-125. Philip Carrok; /Pwr 11 ff 102b-103v. Henry Stewunson; /PW 4. Henrye Underwod; /PW 7. Katheryne Halle.
SH. 44 Alen, 8 Populwell. John Plume; 17 Tashe. John Leyke.
293. KCA. DRb/Pwr 7 f 273a-b, v. Henry Olde Castell; /Pwr 9 f 77v. Willyam Atkynson; /Pwr 11 ff 102b-103v. Christopher Nicholson; Henry Stewunson.
SH. Hogen 25. John Browne; 48 Wrastley. Christopher Wymyngton.
294. KCA. DRb/Pwr 7 f 273a-b, v. Henry Olde Castell; /PW 1. Elesabeth Hogson; /Pwr 8 ff 124b-125. Philip Carrok; /PW 5. Thomas Deyne.
SH. 12 Vox. William Dygon; 24 Adeane. Thomas Barett; 44 Alen, 8 Populwell. John Plume; 17 Tashe. John Leyke.
295. SH. 51 Alen. Robert Hordron.
KCA. DRb/Pwr 11 f 102b. Henry Stewunson; /Pwr 7 f 273v. Henry Olde Castell; /Pwr 8 f 60a-v. Henry Skylman; /Pwr 9 f 176. John Plom; /Pwr 10 ff 218-19. Roger Grenwodd.
296. SH. 44 Alen, 8 Populwell. John Plume; 51 Alen. Robert Hordron; 48 Wrastley. Christopher Wymyngton; 17 Tashe. John Leyke.
KCA. DRb/Pwr 7 f 273v. Henry Olde Castell; /Pwr 11 f 103. Henry Stewunson; /PW 4. Henrye Underwod.
297. KCA. DRb/Pwr 11 ff 102b-103v. Henry Stewunson.
298. KCA. DRb/Pwr 9 f 392. Christopher Nicholson.
299. KCA. DRb/Pwr 5 f 300b. Kateryn Chesman; /PW 1. Luce Dosyng.
300. KCA. DRb/PW 1. Luce Dosyng.
301. *Ibid.* Elesabeth Hogson.
302. KCA. DRb/Pwr 5 f 300b. Kateryn Chesman; /PW 1. Luce Dosyng; Elesabeth Hogson.
303. KCA. DRb/PW 1. Luce Dosyng.
304. *Ibid.* Jhon Nedum; Luce Dosyng; /PW 7. Katheryne Halle.
305. SH. 44 Alen, 8 Populwell. John Plume.
306. SH. 12 Vox. William Dygon.
307. KCA. DRb/Pwr 12 f 360a. Margret Breckett.
308. SH. 12 Vox. William Dygon.
309. KCA. DRb/Pwr 12 f 360a. Margret Breckett.
310. KCA. DRb/PW1. Luce Dosyng; /Pwr 7 f 273a-b. Henry Olde Castell; /Pwr 5 f 215. William Lytylman; /Pwr 9 f 176. John Plom.
SH. 12 Vox. William Dygon.
311. KCA. DRb/Pwr 9 f 177b. John Rolte; /Pwr 9 f 176. John Plom; /Pwr 8 f 211a. Nicholas Priour; /PW 1. Luce Dosyng; /Pwr 7 f 273a-b. Henry Olde Castell; /PW 1. Elesabeth Hogson; /Pwr 8 f 179-179v. Robert Ducker.
SH. 12 Vox. William Dygon.
312. *Ibid.*
KCA. DRb/Pwr 7 f 273a-b. Henry Olde

· Castell.
313. KCA. DRb/PW 6. John Harvy; /Pwr 7 f 273a-b. Henry Olde Castell; /Pwr 6 f 300b. Kateryn Chesman; /PW 1. Elesabeth Hogson; /Pwr 9 f 176. John Plom; 211a. Nicholas Priour.
SH. 12 Vox. William Dygon.
314. KCA. DRb/Pwr 7f 273a-b. Henry Olde Castell; /Pwr 5 f 215. William Lytylman; /Pwr 9 f 176. John Plom; /Pwr 12 f 360a. Margret Breckett.
SH. 12. William Dygon.
315. KCA. DRb/PW 1. Luce Dosyng; /Pwr 7 f 273a-b. Henry Olde Castell; /Pwr 9 f 211a. Nicholas Priour.
SH. 12 Vox. William Dygon.
316. KCA. DRb/Pwr 9 f 211a. Nicholas Priour; /Pwr 9 f 176. John Plom; /Pwr 11 f 102b. Henry Stewunson; /Pwr 12 f 361. Margret Breckett; /Pwr 9, f 382v. Lettys Collynson; /PW 1. Jhon Nedum; Luce Dosyng; /Pwr 7 f 273a-b. Henry Olde Castell; /Pwr 5 f 215. William Lytylman; f 300b. Kateryn Chesman; /Pwr 8 ff 124b-125. Philip Carrok.
SH. 17 Tashe. John Leyke; 12 Vox. William Dygon.
317. KCA. DRb/PW 1. Luce Dosyng; /Pwr 8 f 179-179a. Robert Ducker; /Pwr 8 ff 223b-224b. Roger Ewgham; /Pwr 9 f 177b. John Rolte; f 211a. Nicholas Priour; f 176. John Plom; /Pwr 11 f 103. Henry Stewunson; /PW 4. Henry Underwod.
SH. 17 Tashe. John Leyke; Hogen 25. John Browne.
318. KCA. DRb/Pwr 9 f 211a. Nicholas Priour.
319. KCA. DRb/Pwr 12 f 360v. Margret Breckett; /Pwr 7 f 273a-b, v. Henry Olde Castell.
320. KCA. DRb/Pwr 5 f 300b. Kateryn Chesman; /PW 1. Luce Dosyng; /Pwr 7 f 273a-b. Henry Olde Castell; /Pwr 8 f 179-179v. Robert Ducker; /Pwr 12 f 360v. Margret Breckett.
321. KCA. DRb/Pwr 9 f 211a. Nicholas Priour; /Pwr 12 f 360v. Margret Breckett.
322. KCA. DRb/PW 1. Luce Dosyng; /Pwr 7 f 273a-b. Henry Olde Castell; /Pwr 5 f 215. William Lytylman; /Pwr 8 ff 223-224b. Roger Ewgham; /Pwr 9 f 176. John Plom; /Pwr 12 f 361. Margret Breckett; /PW 6. John Harvy; /PW 8. John Poll.
SH. 12 Vox. William Dygon.
323. SH. 12 Vox. William Dygon.
324. KCA. DRb/Pwr 12 f 360v. Margret Breckett.
325. KCA. DRb/Pwr 9 f 176. John Plom; /Pwr 5 f 300b. Kateryn Chesman; /Pwr 7 f 273a-b. Henry Olde Castell; /Pwr 12 f 360v. Margret Breckett; /PW 7. Katheryne Halle.
SH. 12 Vox. William Dygon.
326. KCA. DRb/Pwr 12 f 361. Margret Breckett.
SH. 12-Vox. William Dygon.
327. *Ibid.*
328. KCA. DRb/PW 1. Luce Dosyng; /PW 8. John Poll.
329. KCA. DRb/Pwr 5 f 300b. Kateryn Chesman.
330. *Ibid.*; /Pwr 12 ff 360a-361. Margret Breckett.
331. KCA. DRb/Pwr 5 f 300b. Kateryn Chesman.
332. KCA. DRb/Pwr 7 f 273a-b. Henry Olde Castell.
333. SH. 12 Vox. William Dygon.
KCA. DRb/Pwr 7 f 273a-b. Henry Olde Castell; /Pwr 9 f 176. John Plom; f 211a. Nicholas Priour; /PW 6. John Harvy.
334. KCA. DRb/Pwr 7 f 273a-b. Henry Olde Castell; /Pwr 9 f 176. John Plom; f 211a. Nicholas Priour.
SH. 12 Vox. William Dygon.

335. KCA. DRb/Pwr 7 f 273a-b. Henry Olde Castell; /Pwr 9 f 176. John Plom; f 211a. Nicholas Priour. SH. 12 Vox. William Dygon.

336. KCA. DRb/Pwr 7 f 273a-b. Henry Olde Castell; /PW 4. Henry Underwod; /Pwr 12 ff 360-361. Margret Breckett.

337. KCA. DRb/Pwr 7 f 273a. Henry Olde Castell; /Pwr 9 f 176. John Plom.

338. KCA. DRb/PW 1. Luce Dosyng; /Pwr 5 f 300b. Kateryn Chesman; /Pwr 9 f 382v. Lettys Collynson; /Pwr 12 f 360v. Margret Breckett.
SH. 24 Adeane. Thomas Barett.

339. KCA. DRb/PW 1. Luce Dosyng; /Pwr 9 ff 382-83. Lettys Collynson; /Pwr 11 f 103. Henry Stewunson; /Pwr 12 ff 360v-361. Margret Breckett.

340. SH. 12 Vox. William Dygon; Hogen 25. John Browne.

341. KCA. DRb/Pwr 10 f 218b. Roger Grenwodd.

342. SH. 12 Vox. William Dygon.

343. KCA. DRb/Pwr 9 f 382v. Lettys Collynson; /Pwr 10 f 218a. Roger Grenwodd; /Pwr 7 f 273v. Henry Olde Castell.
SH. 12 Vox. William Dygon; 24 Adeane. Thomas Barett.

344. KCA. DRb/Pwr 10 f 218b. Roger Grenwodd.

345. SH. 12 Vox. William Dygon; 24 Adeane. Thomas Barett.

346. SH. 12 Vox. William Dygon.

347. SH. 51 Alen. Robert Hordron. KCA. DRb/Pwr 5 f 300b. Kateryn Chesman.

348. SH. Hogen 25. John Browne.

349. SH. 12 Vox. William Dygon. KCA. DRb/PW 1. Luce Dosyng; /PW 5. Thomas Huxley.

350. KCA. DRb/PW 4. Henrye Underwod; /PW 5. Thomas Huxley; /Pwr 12 f 361. Margret Breckett.

351. KCA. DRb/Pwr 12 f 360v. Margret Breckett.

352. SH. 12 Vox. William Dygon.

353. SH. 12 Vox. DRb/Pwr 5 f 300b. Kateryn Chesman; /Pwr 7 f 273a-b. Henry Olde Castell; /Pwr 9 f 176. John Plom; /Pwr 12 f 360v. Margret Breckett.

354. KCA. DRb/Pwr 11 ff 102b-103v. Henry Stewunson.

355. SH. 12 Vox. William Dygon.

356. KCA. DRb/Pwr 11 f 103. Henry Stewunson.

357. SH. 24 Adeane. Thomas Barett.

358. SH. 51 Alen. Robert Hordron.

359. SH. 12 Vox. William Dygon.

360. KCA. DRb/Pwr 12 ff 360-361v. Margret Breckett.

8. DECLINE AND CIVIL WAR.

1. Drake, H.H. (ed.), Hasted's History of Kent ... Part I: The Hundred of Blackheath (1886), pp.187, 206.
RCHMSS, Calendar at Hatfield House, vol. xii (1910), p.226.
Chambers, R.K., The Elizabethan Stage, vol. i (1923), p.11; vol. iv (1923), pp.76-9, 92, 98, 110-13, 115.
Calendar of Letters and State Papers relating to English Affairs preserved principally in the archives of Simancas, vol. iii, Elizabeth 1580-96 (1896) pp.140, 142.
E 101/429/8.
E 101/429/13.

2. Drake, H.H. (ed.), op. cit., pp.187, 206.
Rivers, E., Some Records of Eltham (1904), p.75.
Corner, G.R., 'Extracts from the Churchwardens' Accounts of the Parish of Eltham in Kent', Archaeologia, vol. xxxiv (1851), pp.57, 61, 65.

3. Strype, J., Annals of the Reformation (1709), p.191.
Strickland, A., Lives of the Queens of England, vol. iv (1888), p.171.
Spurgeon, J.W., 'Royal Eltham', Bygone Kent (ed. Stead, R.) (1892), pp.161-2.

4. Yorke, P. (ed.), Miscellaneous State Papers from 1501 to 1726, vol. i (1778), p.163.
Household Accounts ... Robert Dudley, Earl of Leicester, 1558-61, 1584-6, Camden 5th Series, vol. vi (1995), pp.145-6.

5. Corner, G.R., op. cit., p.61.

6. Calendar of Letters and State Papers relating to English Affairs preserved principally in the archives of Simancas, vol. iii, Elizabeth 1580-96 (1896) p.140.
E 351/3237 m 17.

7. Chambers, R.K., op. cit., vol. iv (1923), p.115.

8. E 101/429/8.
E 351/3237 m 17.
E 101/429/13.

9. E. 351/3200 mm 3-5, 6, 7d, 8d-9d, 12-14d; /3202 mm 7d-8; /3203 mm 16-16d; /3204 m 18d; /3209 mm 8-8d; /3211 mm 5d-6; /3216 mm 15d-16; /3218 m 11; /3219 m 14d; /3220 mm 6d-7; /3221 mm 6-10; /3222 mm 8d-9d; /3224 m 11d; /3225 mm 10-10d; /3227 mm 10-10d; /3228 mm 11-11d; /3231 m 6; /3233 m 10; /3235 m 5; /3236 m 8d; /3237 mm 17-18d; /3238 m 9.

10. E 406/2561 f 11v.

11. DNB, vol. xxv (1891), pp.159-62.
Brooks, E. St J., Sir Christopher Hatton (1946), pp.83-103, 332-44.

12. Woolwich Reference Library, Letters Patent to Sir Christopher Hatton, 27 July 1568.

13. Segar, Sir William, Honour, Military and Civil (1602), p.200.

14. Calendar of Letters and State Papers relating to English Affairs preserved principally in the archives of Simancas, vol. iii, Elizabeth 1580-96 (1896) p.140.

15. Gregory, R.R.C., The Story of Royal Eltham (1909), p.188.

16. Ibid., illns between pp.24-5, pp.32-3 and p.89.

17. E 351/3224 m 11d; /3239 m 28d.
DNB, vol. xxv (1891), p.161.

18. E 351/3209 m 8.

19. E 351/3221 mm 9-10; /3222 m 9.

20. MPF, 228.

21. Corner, G.R., op. cit., pp.59-60.

22. Ibid.
Rivers, E., op. cit., pp.75-6.

23. Lambarde, W., A Perambulation of Kent (1576), pp.384-6.
Lambarde, W., Alphabetical Description of the Chief Places in England and Wales (1730), p.109.

24. Camden, W., Britannia (1590), p.243.

25. Habington, W., The Historie of Edward the Fourth, King of England (1640), p.229.

26. Philipot, T., Villare Cantianum (1659), pp.134-5.

27. E 403/2561 f 11v.

28. E 351/3238 m 1, 9-9d; /3239 m 1, 25d-30; /3240 mm 1, 9d-10d.

29. Corner, G.R., op. cit., p.65.
CSP(D) 1611-18 135.
CSP(D) 1619-23 46, 390.
RCHMSS, 12th Report and Appendix i, MSS of the Earl Cowper, vol. i, p.163.
Chambers, R.K., op. cit., vol. iv (1923), p.126.

30. Akrigg, G.F., 'England in 1609', The Huntingdon Library Quarterly, vol. xiv (1950-1), pp.92-3.

31. Nichols, J., Progresses of James I, vol. ii (1828), pp.61-2.

32. Jonson, B., Epicoene or The Silent Woman (eds Percy, H. & Simpson, P.), act v, scene iii, vol. v (1609), p.258; vol. viii (1947); 'On the New Motion', Epigrammes xcvii (1616), p.62.
Peacham, H., 'Panegyricke Verses' preceding text of Coryat, T., Coryat's Crudities (1611).
Harris, L.E., The Two Netherlanders (1961), pp.140-1.
Akrigg, G.F., op. cit., pp.92-3.

33. Rye, W.B., England as Seen by Foreigners (1865), p.61.

34. Jonson, B., op. cit.

35. Harris, L.E., op. cit., pp.140-1.

36. Peacham, H., op. cit.

37. Akrigg, G.F., op. cit., pp.92-3.

38. Rye, W.B., op. cit., p.61.

39. Tymme, T., A Dialogue Philosophicall (1612), pp.60-1.
Harris, L.E., op. cit., pp.132, 140-8.

40. Tierie, G., Cornelis Drebbel (1932), pp.5, 10, 37-43, 45, 59-75.
Harris, L.E., op. cit., pp.141-5, 166-70, 182-4, 194-6.

41. Ibid., p.145.

42. Ibid., pp.162-84, 194-6.

43. CSP(D) 1611-18 135.
CSP(D) 1619-23 46, 53, 390.
RCHMSS, 12th Report and Appendix i, MSS of the Earl Cowper, vol. i (1888), p.163.
Chambers, R.K., op. cit., vol. iv (1923), p.126.

44. CSP(D) 1619-23 53.
Gregory, R.R.C., op. cit., pp.197-8.

45. CSP(D) 1629-31 95.

46. BL. MSS Dept. Add. MSS. 34741 f 95.

47. BL. MSS Dept. Harl. MS 7000 f 349. Mr Pory to Sir Thomas Puckering, 3 Jan. 1632/3.
Oman, C., Elizabeth of Bohemia (1938), p.328.

48. Walpole Society, Vertue i (1929-30), p.101.

49. Firth, C.H. and Rait, R.S. (eds), Acts and Ordinances of the Interregnum 1642-1660, vol. i (1911), pp.299-303.

50. CSP(D) 1644 66.

51. Devereux, W.B., Lives and Letters of the Devereux, Earls of Essex, vol. ii (1853), pp.465-6, p.473.

52. Wood, A., Athenae Oxoniensis, vol. ii (1691), cols 94-5.

53. The True Manner of the ... Funerall of ... Robert, Earl of Essex (1646), title page.

54. Drake, H.H. (ed.), op. cit., pp.181-2.
Rivers, E., op. cit., p.87.

55. Ibid.

56. L.R. 3/31/6 m 1.

57. E 317/Kent/18 mm 1, 4, 7, 9.
A Perfect Diurnall, 3-10 September 1649.
The Moderate Intelligencer, 30 August-6 September 1649 (September 5).

58. CSP(D) 1649, 1650 221.

59. A Modest Narrative, 1-8 September 1649 (September 6).

60. E 317/Kent/18 mm 1, 4, 7, 9.

61. The Moderate Intelligencer, 4-11 September 1649.

62. Firth, C.H. and Rait, R.S. (eds), Acts and Ordinances of the Interregnum 1642-1660, vol. ii (1911), pp.168-91.
E 317/Kent/18 mm 1-38.

63. E 317/Kent/18 mm 1-38.
CSP(D) 1649, 1650 221.

64. Cambridge University Library. Dd 13.20 140 Nos. 571, 573-75.
C 54/3740 mm 23-26 No. 13; /3740 mm 30-31 No. 10; /3745 mm 4-5 No. 29; /3850 mm 9-10 No. 29; /3855 mm 32-33 No. 11; /3775 mm 22-23 No. 15; /3776 mm 23-24 No. 20; /3882 m 1.

65. E 121/2/11 No. 19. ff 1-2.
BL. MSS Dept. Add. MSS 30208 ff 61v-62.

66. L.R. 3/31/6 mm 1-7.
67. C 54/3745 m 1 No.33; /3745 mm 3-4 No.30; /3778 m 43 No.1; /3960 mm 10-12 No.26.
68. E 320/ZZ 18 mm 2-19, 48-50.
    CSP(D) 1653-54 559.
    C 54/3745 mm 5-6 No.28.
69. L.R. 3/31/7 m 1.
70. C 54/3745 mm 5, 6 No.28; /3850 mm 9-10 No.29.
71. C 54/3850 m 10.
72. Evelyn, J., *Diary* (ed. de Beer, E.S.), vol. iii (1956), entry for 26 April 1656.
73. Bentley, J., *A List of Woods … Sold Out of the King and Queen their … Lands* (1648), pp.2-5.
    CSP(D) 1657-58 397.
    Greenwich Local History Library, Information with plan dated 4 December 1741 of Eltham Palace by Samuel Robinson. Col. Panton's name given in error for Col. Rich.
    CSP(D) 1649-50 11, 129, 526-27.
    CSP(D) 1653-54 426.
    CSP(D) 1655 119.
74. *DNB*, vol. xlviii (1896), p.119.
    Firth, Sir Charles and Davies, G., *The Regimental History of Cromwell's Army*, vol. i (1940), pp.7, 36, 41-2, 143-7; vol. ii, pp.407, 519-20.
75. *DNB*, vol. xlviii, pp.119-20.
    Firth, Sir Charles and Davies, G., *op. cit.*, pp.146-9.
76. Hyde, E. Earl of Clarendon, *The History of the Great Rebellion* (ed. Lockyer, R.) (1967), p.412.
77. CSP(D) 1656-57 130.
    DNB, vol. xlviii (1896), p.120.
78. CSP(D) 1658-59 377, 387-88.
    DNB, vol. xlviii (1896), p.120.
    Firth, Sir Charles and Davies, G., *op. cit.*, pp.154-8.
79. Firth, Sir Charles and Davies, G., *op. cit.*, pp.154-8.
80. *Ibid.*
81. *DNB*, vol. xlviii (1896), p.120.
82. *Ibid.*
83. CSP(D) 1660 1237.
84. CSP(D) 1664-65 483, 517.
85. Firth, Sir Charles and Davies, G., *op. cit.*, p.162.
86. CSP(D) 1660-61 237, 293.
87. *Ibid.* 576.
88. CSP(D) 1670 Addenda 1660-70 623.
89. L.R. 1/115 ff 29-32.
90. E 351/3238 mm 1, 9-9d; /3239 mm 1, 25d-30; /3240 mm 1, 9d-10d.
91. MPF 228.
    BL. Maps 186 h.1, No. 5.
    CSP(D) 1581-90 706.
92. Hussey, C., 'Eltham Hall–II Kent', *Country Life*, 22 May 1937, p.573.
93. E 164/44 ff I-58v.
94. E 317/Kent/18 mm 1-39.
95. E 164/44 f 2v.
96. *Ibid.* ff 2v-3.
97. MPF 228.
98. E 351/3221 mm 9-10.
99. MPF 228.
100. Historic Monuments Commission, *East London* (1930), p.106.
101. MPF 228.
102. E 101/494/15 m 1.
     E 101/473/3 mm 5, 9.
     Ibid. (1) m 2.
     E 372/197 rot. 44d.
     E 101/493/4 m 2.

E 101/493/8.
E 101/494/7 m 3.
E 101/473/2 m 12.
E 101/502/25 m 4.
E 101/502/26 mm 7-8.
E 101/502/21 m 5.
E 164/44 f 5.
E 317/Kent/18 mm 3-4, 8, 18-20, 22d-23d.
Letters and Papers of Henry VIII, vol. i, part i, p.536.
E 351/3253 mm 8; /3238 m 9.
103. E 351/3238 m 9.
104. E 101/504/2 f 39v.
     E 164/44 f 10.
     E 317/Kent/18 mm 3-4, 8, 18-20, 22d-23d.
     E 351/3253 m 8.
105. E 351/3227 m 10; /3240 m 9d; /3253 m 8.
     Historic Monuments Commission, *East London* (1930), p.107.
106. E 317/Kent/18 mm 3-4, 6, 8.
107. E 351/3239 m 26.
108. MPF 228.
109. Clapham, A.W. and Godfrey, W.H., *Some Famous Buildings and Their Story* (1913), pp.49-66.
110. RCHMSS, MSS of Marquess of Salisbury, vol. xiv (1923), p.48.
     CSP(D) 1581-90 706.
111. Courtauld, S.L., *Eltham Palace* (1937), cover.
     Hussey, C., *op. cit.*, p.573.
     Bodleian Library, Gough Maps 46 ff 159-60.
     Priestley, E.J., 'The 'Stent' View of Eltham Palace', *Torch*, vol. xx, no. 1, Spring 1986, pp.37, 39.
112. Globe, A., *Peter Stent London Printseller circa 1642-1665* (1985), pp.105-6, plate 142.
113. Colvin, H.M. (ed.), *The King's Works*, vol. iv, 1485-1660 (part ii) (1982), p.216.
114. *Ibid.*, p.216.
115. Courtauld, S.L., *op. cit.*, cover.
     Hussey, C., *op. cit.*, p.573.
     Bodleian Library. Gough Maps 46 ff 159-60.
     Priestley, E.J., *op. cit.*, pp.37, 39.
116. Bodleian Library. Rawl. A 195c f 225, 230.
     E 351/3239 m 26.
117. As for note 115.
118. E 101/497/1 ff 6-7.
119. BL Maps Dept. Hatfield MSS. Cecil Papers. Maps I/5.
120. E 317/Kent/18 m 2.
     Courtauld, S.L., *op. cit.*, cover.
121. As for note 115.
122. As for note 115.
123. Colvin, H.M. (ed.), *op. cit.*, p.83.
     E 351/3218 m 11; /3219 m 14d; /3221 m 9.
124. E 101/493/30 m 1.
     E 101/502/24 m 1.
125. E 101/497/1 f 6.
126. Hussey, C., *op. cit.*, p.573.
127. E 101/497/1 f 6.
128. Hussey, C., *op. cit.*, pp.571, 573.
129. E 164/44 f 8.
130. E 317/Kent/18 m 2.
131. *Ibid.*
132. *Ibid.*
133. Dent, J., *The Quest for Nonsuch* (1962), p.294.
134. E 317/Kent/18 m 2.
135. Bodleian Library. Rawl. D. 777 ff 98-98v, 99v.
136. E 351/3240 m 10.
137. E 101/497/1 f 4.
138. *Ibid.*
139. *Ibid.*
     Bodleian. Rawl. D. 781 f 39; D. 776 f 98v.
140. E 101/497/1 f 4.
     Bodleian. Rawl. D. 776 f 98v.
141. E 101/497/1 f 5.

Bodleian. Rawl. D. 776 f 98v.
E 351/3239 mm 25d-26d, 28d, 29d-30.
142. Bodleian. Rawl. D. 776 f 98v.
143. *Ibid.* 777 ff 90v, 91v, 97.
     E 351/3240 m 10.
144. Bodleian. Rawl. D. 781 f 39.
145. *Ibid.* 777 f 91.
     E 351/3240 m 9d.
147. Bodleian. Rawl. D. 776 f 98v.
148. E 317/Kent/18 m 2.
149. E 101/497/1 f 4v.
     E 351/3239 mm 25d, 26, 28d, 29d-30.
     Bodleian. Rawl. D. 776 f 98.
150. *Ibid.* 777 f 88.
151. *Ibid.* 776 f 98.
152. *Ibid.* 776 f 97v; /D. 781 f 39.
     E 351/3239 m 30d.
153. Bodleian. Rawl. D. 776 f 98.
154. E 101/497/1 f 4v.
155. Bodleian. Rawl. D. 776 ff 98-98v, 103.
156. E 317/Kent/18 m 2.
157. Bodleian. Rawl. D. 776 f 99.
158. E 101/497/1 f 5v.
     E 351/3239 m 30.
     Bodleian. Rawl. D. 776 f 99.
159. E 101/497/1 f 5v.
     Bodleian. Rawl. D. 776 f 99.
160. *Ibid.* 776 ff 98v-99.
     E 351/3239 m 30.
161. *Ibid.* mm 26d, 30.
162. E 101/497/1 f 5v,
     E 351/3239 m 26d.
     Bodleian. Rawl. D. 776 f 94.
163. E 101/497/1 f 5v.
     E 351/3239 m 30.
164. *Ibid.*
165. E 351/3200 mm 3-5, 6, 7d, 8d-9d, 12-14d; /3202 mm 7d-8; /3203 mm 16-16d; /3204 m 18d; /3209 mm 8-8d; /3211 m 5d; /3216 mm 15d-16; /3218 mm 11-11d; /3219 m 14d; /3220 mm 6d-7; /3221 mm 9-10; /3222 mm 8d-9d; /3224 m 11d; /3225 mm 10-10d; /3227 mm 10-10d; /3228 mm 10d-11d; /3231 m 6; /3233 m 10; /3235 m 5; /3236 m 8d; /3237 mm 17-18; /3238 mm 9-9d; /3239 mm 25d-30d; /3240 mm 9d-10d; /3241 m 35; /3242 m 13; /3243 mm 25d-26d; /3244 mm 15-15d; /3245 m 18; /3246 m 15d; /3247 m 11; /3248 m 9d; /3249 m 12; /3252 mm 2d, 9d-10; /3253 mm 8-8d; /3255 m 10; /3256 mm 10d-11; /3257 mm 2d, 13-15; /3258 2d, 10; /3259 m 23; /3261 mm 2d, 11d-12; /3265 mm 12-13; /3266 m 11d; /3267 mm 2d, 11; /3268 mm 2d, 6d; /3269 m 9; /3270 m 5d; /3272 m 8d.
     A.O. 1/2429/71 m 16d.
166. E 351/3239 mm 25d-30d; /3240 m 13.
     Colvin, H.M. (ed.), *op. cit.*, pp.84-5.
167. E 351/3203 mm 16-16d; /3204 m 18d; /3209 mm 8-8d.
168. E 351/3221 mm 9-10.
169. E 351/3256 mm 10d-11; /3257 mm 2d, 13-15; /3258 mm 2d, 10.
170. E 351/3261 mm 2d, 11d-12.
171. E 351/3265 mm 12-13; /3266 m 11d.
172. E 351/3209 mm 8-8d.
173. E 351/3221 mm 9-10.
174. E 351/3239 mm 29-30.
175. E 351/3221 m 10.
176. E 351/3216 m 15d; /3218 m 11; /3233 m 10.
177. E 351/3218 m 11; /3219 m 14d.
178. E 351/3221 mm 9-10.
179. E 351/3218 m 11.
180. E 351/3245 m 18; /3252 m 9; /3265 m 12.
     Colvin, H.M. (ed.), *op. cit.*, p.86.
181. E 351/3221 mm 9-10; /3224 m 11d.
182. E 351/3235 m 5.

183. E 351/3236 m 8d; /3237 m 17; /3238 m 9; /3239 m 28d; /3243 m 25d; /3245 m 18; /3252 m 9d.
184. E 351/3265 m 12.
185. E 351/3243 m 26.
186. E 351/3257 m 13; /3258 m 10; /3259 m 23. Colvin, H.M. (ed.), *op. cit.*, p.86.
187. E 164/44 ff 8-8v.
188. E 317/Kent/18 mm 3-10. E 164/44 ff 8-8v.
189. E 317/Kent/18 mm 3, 6, 8.
190. CPR 1555-57 114. Hughes, P.L., and Larkin, J.F. (ed.), *Tudor Royal Proclamations*, 1964-9, vol. ii, nos. 425-64.
191. RCHMSS, MSS of the Marquess of Bath, vol. ii (1907), p.16.
192. CSP(D) 1603-10 221.
193. *Ibid.* 454.
194. *Acts of the Privy Council 1619-21*, pp.186-7, 278.
195. Hughes, P.L. and Larkin, J.F. (ed.), *Stuart Royal Proclamations*, vol. ii (1973), p.554.
196. CSP(D) 1638-39 148.
197. *Ibid.* 294.
198. CSP(D) 1603-10 160, 217, 402, 422.
199. *Calendar of Letters and State Papers relating to English Affairs preserved principally in the archives of Simancas*, vol. ii, pp.140-5.
200. Nichols, J., *Progresses of James I*, vol. ii (1828), pp.61-2. CSP(D) 1619-23 46, 53. RCHMSS, Cowper, vol. i, p.163. Drake, H.H. (ed.), *op. cit.*, p.179.
201. CSP(D) 1547-80 590. SP 15/25 No. 130.
202. Kent Archives Office. QM/SB 706.
203. RCHMSS, Cowper, vol. iii, p.151.
204. *Acts of the Privy Council 1619-21*, pp.186-7.
205. *Ibid.*, p.278.
206. Bentley, J., *A List of Woods ... Sold Out of the King and Queen their ... Lands* (1648), p.2.
207. *Acts of the Privy Council 1619-21*, pp.186-7.
208. Bentley, J., *op. cit.*, pp.2-4.
209. Evelyn, J., *op. cit.*, vol. iii (1955), p.170.
210. Fry, C. and S., *A Draught of Eltham Court Described in a South View Taken the 4th Day of December 1741 by Samuel Robinson*, copy, Greenwich Local History Library.
211. RCHMSS, MSS of the Earl of Egmont, Diary of the First Viscount Percival, vol. i, 1730-33 (1920), p.198.
212. E 317/Kent/18 mm 4, 6, 7, 9, 10. CSP(D) 1649, 1650 11, 129, 526-27. CSP(D) 1653-54 426. CSP(D) 1655 119-20. CSP(D) 1657-58 397. CSP(D) Addenda 1660-85 432.
213. Woolwich Reference Library, Letters Patent to Sir Christopher Hatton, 27 July 1568.
214. CSP(D) 1595-97 450.
215. E 317/Kent/18 m 36.
216. *Ibid.* m 5.
217. *Ibid.* m 9.
218. *Ibid.* m 6.
219. *Ibid.* m 10.
220. *Cal. of Committee for Advance of Money*, vol. ii (1888) p.695.
221. *Cal. of Committee for Compounding 1643-60*, p.1070.
222. *Ibid.*
223. *Cal. of Committee for Advance of Money*, vol. ii (1888), p.695.
224. *Cal. of Committee for Compounding 1643-60*, p.1070.
225. L.R. 3/31/5 mm 1-6d.
226. L.R. 3/31/7 m 1d.
227. L.R. 3/31/5 mm 1-6d.

L.R. 3/31/6 mm 1-7.
L.R. 3/31/7 mm 1-3.
L.R. 3/31/8 mm 1-6d.
L.R. 3/31/9 mm 1-22d.
L.R. 3/32 1-43.
228. L.R. 3/31/5 m 1. L.R. 3/31/8 mm 1d, 3d.
229. *Ibid.* mm 2d, 4, 5d.
230. L.R. 3/31/6 m 6. L.R. 3/31/8 m 6d.
231. L.R. 3/31/6 m 1d. L.R. 3/31/7 mm 2, 3. L.R. 3/31/8 mm 2, 3-3d, 6d.
232. L.R. 3/31/5 m 1. L.R. 3/31/7 m 2.
233. *Ibid.*
234. L.R. 3/31/5 m 1. L.R. 3/31/7 m 2. L.R. 3/31/8 m 2.
235. *Ibid.* mm 3, 5, 6.
236. L.R. 3/31/6 m 5.
237. L.R. 3/31/6 m 1.
238. L.R. 3/31/7 m 2.
239. CSP(D) 1636-37 130. Priestley, E.J., *op. cit.*, pp.121-3.
240. Somerset House. Hughe Tenche Jan 1562 (7 Chayre).
241. SH. John Reston 21 Sep 1599 (90 Kidd).
242. Kent County Archives. DRb/ Thomas Reston (23 Apr 1601) PW 18.
243. KCA. John Phillips (9 May 1609) PW 20.
244. SH. William Bull 3 Jul 1618 (103 Meade).
245. SH. John Philipott 15 Nov 1645 (54 Fines).
246. SH. Katherine Flower 21 Dec 1598 (2 Kidd).
247. SH. John Goodall alias Goodgame 6 Apr 1612 (31 Fenner).
248. Drake, H.H. (ed.), *op. cit.*, p.212. Brooks, E. St J., *op. cit.*, pp.16, 69-70, 131, 141-2, 280, 347, 349, 354-5, 368, 389.
249. *Ibid.*, pp.272-3, 280.
250. SH. John Smithson alias Taylor, 22 Jul 1585 (107 Windebanck) & 29 Dec 1588 (74 Wingfield).
251. *Ibid.*
252. C 66/1559 m 38.
253. KCA. DRb/Hughe Miller (1615) PW 23. Eltham Church. Legatt Charity Documents (No. 33). Hugh Miller of Eltham. 1615.
254. Drake, H.H. (ed.), *op. cit.*, pp.207, 209.
255. *Ibid.*, p.212.
256. *Ibid.*, p.212. SH. Cornelius Ortson 22 Apr 1621 (100 Dale).
257. SH. Anne Twist 21 May 1624 (57 Byrde).
258. Drake, H.H. (ed.), *op. cit.*, pp.207, 209.
259. *Ibid.*, p.212.
260. *Ibid.*
261. *Cal. of Assise Records, Kent, Indictments, Elizabeth I* (1979), p.495.
262. SH. Elisabeth Smithson 28 May 1593 (2 Dixy).
263. SH. John Goodall alias Goodgame 6 Apr 1612 (31 Fenner).
264. SH. Richard Slynn 6 Oct 1642 (121 Cambell).
265. KCA. DRb/John Mertyndall (13 Oct 1572) PW 10. SH. Johan Busshe 30 Mar 1566 (24 Crymes); William Roper 10 Jan 1576 (27 Langley); Antony Leckener 13 Aug 1579 (37 Bakon); Elisabeth Smithson 28 May 1593 (2 Dixy); William Plumbe 20 Jul 1593 (24 Dixy); James Twyst 10 Oct 1597 (Lewyn 17-18); Katherine Flower 21 Dec 1598 (2 Kidd); Willian Baker 3 Sep 1603 (24 Harte); Sir William Rooper 6 Apr 1628 (105 Barrington).

KCA. DRb/Cristofor Clarke (12 Oct 1565) PW 8; Edwarde Kinge (4 Feb 1565) PW 8; Thomas Starkey (27 Jun 1566?) Pwr 13 f 259a; Tomas Mombe (25 Oct 1570) PW 12; Rycharde Smythe (27 Nov 1570) PW 10; Jhone Carlyll (28 Jan 1570) PW 9; John Mertyndall (13 Oct 1572) PW 10; John Rolte (9 Aug 1575) PW 12; John Dyer (7 Dec 1577) PW 12; Robart (A L)eyghe (20 Jul 1579?) PW 12; Edwarde Elyot (16 Oct 1579) PW 13; Rycchard Fellton (9 Nov 1582) PW 13; John Haryson (14 Aug 1585) PW 14; Robert Stubbes (31 Dec 1594) PW 17; Walter Parye (13 Aug 1616) PW 25.
266. KCA. DRb/Emme Castlemane (12 Nov 1561) PW 6; John Cowlard (26 May 1625) PW 27; Margery Harryson (14 Jun 1588) PW 15; Katheryne Haight (25 Jan 1590) PW 16; Robert Stubbes (31 Dec 1594) PW 17; SH. Philipp Potts 26 Jan 1597 (Lewyn 23).
267. KCA. DRb/Herry Stwbes (14 Dec 1569) PW 10.
268. SH. Sir Nicholas Stoddard 29 Feb 1635 (72 Pile).
269. KCA. DRb/Elizabethe Baker (26 Feb 1613) PW 23.
270. SH. Bridgitt Clarke 22 Nov 1608 (107 Windebanck).
271. SH. Philipp Potts 26 Jan 1597 (Lewyn 23). KCA. DRb/William Swallow (21 Mar 1615) PW 23.
272. SH. Thomas Blonck 11 Sep 1624 (102 Byrde).
273. *Ibid.* KCA. DRb/John Haryson (14 Aug 1585) PW 14.
274. SH. William Bull 3 Jul 1618 (103 Meade).
275. SH. Philipp Potts 26 Jan 1597 (Lewyn 23); Bridgitt Clarke 22 Nov 1608 (107 Windebanck); James Twyst 10 Oct 1597 (Lewyn 17-18); William Bull 3 Jul 1618 (103 Meade). KCA. DRb/Katheryne Haight (25 Jan 1590) PW 16; Elizabethe Baker (26 Feb 1613) PW 23; William Swallow (21 Mar 1615) PW 23.
276. SH. Bridgitt Clarke 22 Nov 1608 (107 Windebanck); Phillipp Potts 26 Jan 1597 (Lewyn 23). KCA. DRb/Elizabethe Baker (26 Feb 1613) PW 23.
277. SH. Bridgitt Clarke 22 Nov 1608 (107 Windebanck). KCA. DRb/Elizabethe Baker (26 Feb 1613) PW 23.
278. SH. James Twyst 10 Oct 1597 (Lewyn 17-18). KCA. DRb/Elizabethe Baker (26 Feb 1613) PW 23; Margery Harryson (14 Jun 1588) PW 15.
279. KCA. DRb/Elizabethe Baker (26 Feb 1613) PW 23.
280. *Ibid.*
281. *Ibid.*
282. SH. Lucy Rooper 30 Jan 1607 (8 Windebanck); Bridgitt Clarke 22 Nov 1608 (107 Windebanck); Elizabethe Jenney 11 Mar 1622 (93 Swann). KCA. DRb/Elizabethe Baker (26 Feb 1613) PW 23.
283. KCA. William Bremington (6 Apr 1609) PW 19.
284. SH. Lucy Rooper 30 Jan 1607 (8 Windebanck).
285. SH. Bridgitt Clarke 22 Nov 1608 (107 indebanck).
286. KCA. DRb/Walter Parye (13 Aug 1616) PW 25.

287. SH. Lucy Rooper 30 Jan 1607 (8 Windebanck).

288. *Ibid.*; Bridgitt Clarke 22 Nov 1608 (107 Windebanck).

289. SH. Lucy Rooper 30 Jan 1607 (8 Windebanck).

290. SH. Sir William Rooper 12 Nov 1628 (105 Barrington).

291. KCA. DRb/John Forde (30 Jun 1628) PW 27.

292. KCA. DRb/Hugh Edwardes (l7 Feb 1627) PW 29.

293. SH. Ingram Friser 30 Oct 1627 (99 Skynner).
Norman, C., *The Muses' Darling: Christopher Marlowe* (1960), pp.202-10.

294. St. John's Church, Eltham. Legatt Charity Documents No. 33. Inventory of Hugh Miller of Eltham. 1615.

295. KCA. DRb/Hughe Miller (1615) PW 23.

296. E 164/44 ff 9-9v, 34-35, 39v.

297. Trevor Roper, H., *Europe's Physician: The Various Life of Sir Theodore de Mayerne* (2006), pp.217-18, 337, 405.
E 317/Kent/18 mm 8-9.

9. ELTHAM AND THE SHAW CROWN TENANCY.

1. Evelyn, J., *Diary* (ed. de Beer, E.S.), vol. iii (1955), p.170, entry for 26 April 1656.

2. L.R. 1/115 ff 29v-30v, 32.

3. Crest 6/21 76-77.

4. Bodleian Library. M.S. Top. gen. d. 14 f 15v. W. Stukeley. 1724.

5. Hussey, C., 'Eltham Hall I', *Country Life*, 15 May 1937, p.536.

6. E 320/ZZ 18 mm 2-19, 48-50.
CSP(D) 1653-54 559.
C 54/3745 mm 5-6 No. 28.

7. L.R. 1/115 ff 29-32,

8. *Ibid.*

9. Sandby, P., *The Great Hall at Eltham from the North* (1785), E.J. Priestley.

10. 'Mr King's Sequel to the Observations on Ancient Castles', *Archaeologia*, vol. vi (1782), figs lxxii, lxxiii.

11. Bodleian Library. W. Stukeley, 1724.

12. Buck, S. and N., *View of Eltham Palace* (1735).

13. Royal Commission on Historical Monuments (England), *East London*, vol. v (1930), p.108.

14. RCHM(E). Vol. v. 108.

15. Buck, S. and N., *op. cit.* (1735).
Robinson, S., 'A draught of Eltham Court ... 1741'.

16. Buck, S. and N., *op. cit.* (1735).

17. Robinson, S., *op. cit.*

18. Bodleian Library. W. Stukeley. 1724.

19. L.R. 3/31/8 mm 2d, 6d.

20. L.R. 1/115 ff 29-32.

21. L.R. 3/31/9 m 2.

22. *Ibid.*

23. L.R. 9/120 No. 54. m 1d.

24. *Thurloe's State Papers*, vol. vii, 1658-59 (1742), pp.222, 866.
Henning, B.D. (ed.), *The History of Parliament: The House of Commons 1660-1690*, vol. iii, members M-Y (1983), pp.429-30.

25. Routledge, F.J. (ed.), *Cal. of the Clarendon State Papers*, vol. iv, 1657-1660 (1932), p.575.

26. S.P. 44/46 119.
L.R. 2/141 f 28.

27. Henning, B.D. (ed.), *op. cit.*, p.429.

28. *Ibid.*

29. L.R. 1/115 ff 30v-31v.

30. Evelyn, J., *op. cit.*, pp.375-6, entry for 14 July 1664.
Tipping, H.A., 'Eltham Lodge – I: Kent', *Country Life*, 9 August 1919, p.168; 16 August 1919, p.210.

31. Brook, R., *The Story of Eltham Palace* (1960), pp.50-2.
Tipping, H.A., *op. cit.*, p.169.

32. Crest 6/21 74-80.
L.R. 1/121 ff 345-47v.
Crest 6/59 239, 242-3, 297-305.
Crest 6/67 11-16, 220-31.
Crest 2/73 72-7, 106-27.
Crest 2/355. Letters dated 1805-09. Cotton to Land Revenue Board 23 March 1810, Parkinson and Marriott to J. Fordyce 27 September 1808.

33. Crest 2/355. E. Driver to Woods & Forests 29 January 1838: Cotton to Land Revenue Board 23 March 1810.

34. *Sidcup & District Times*, 1 April, 13 May, 27 May, 4 December 1892; 5 May 1893.

35. *Eltham & Kentish Times*, 30 March 1956.

36. Henning, B.D. (ed.), *op. cit.*, p.429.
Cockayne, G.E. (ed.), *Complete Baronetage*, vol. iv, 1665-1707 (1904), p.12.

37. *Ibid.*, pp.12-13.

38. *Ibid.*

39. Rivers, E., *Some Records of Eltham*, N.D. (1910), pp.98-102, p.107.

40. Henning, B.D. (ed.), *op. cit.*, p.429.

41. Latham, R. and Matthews, W. (eds), *The Diary of Samuel Pepys*, 1970-83, vol. iii, p.188; vol. v, pp.218-19; vol. vi, pp.126, 258; vol. ix, p.214.

42. *Ibid.*, vol. viii, p.398.

43. Cockayne, G.E. (ed.), *op. cit.*, pp.12-13.

44. Crest 2/355. Cotton to Land Revenue Board 23 March 1810.

45. Gregory, R.R.C., *The Story of Royal Eltham* (1909), pp.45-51, 268-73; illustrations between pp.48-9, 272-3.

46. Crest 2/355. Cotton to Land Revenue Board 23 March 1810.

47. Crest 2/355. E. Leake to G. Harrison 25 August 1810.
Fourth Report of the Commissioners of Woods (1823), pp.12-13, appx. 107-8.
Fifteenth Report of the Commissioners of Woods (1838), p.6.
Crown Estate Office. File Eltham 1948.

48. L.R. 3/31/8 mm 1d, 2d-6d;. 3/31/9 mm 1-22d; 3/32 1-144; 3/33 1-269.
Crest 5/281 1-194.

49. Robinson, S., *op. cit.*

50. Bodleian Library. M.S. Top. gen. d. 14 f l5v.
Buck, S. and N., *op. cit.*
Aquatint, '(South West) View of the Remains of King John's Palace at Eltham in Kent', P. Sandby, 1782.
Aquatint, 'South East View of the Remains of King John's Palace at Eltham in Kent, London, Westminster & in the Distance,' P. Sandby, 1787.
Watercolour, 'North West View of Eltham Palace', P. Sandby. Mappin Art Gallery, Sheffield.

51. Robinson, S., *op. cit.*
Buck, S. and N., *op. cit.*

52. Crest 2/1643.

53. 'North West View of Eltham Palace', P. Sandby, Mappin Art Gallery, Sheffield.
'North East View of Eltham Palace, 1787', P. Sandby, illn *Country Life*, 3 June 1965, p.1343, E.J. Priestley and in catalogue

Parke-Bernet Galleries, New York, 13 April 1963, no. 86. Larger copy in Christie's catalogue, 14 December 1971.
No. 87. Aquatint of this view, dated 1787, in Prints & Drawings Dept., British Library.
Watercolours, 'North and South Views of East end of Hall, with West end of Eltham Court Farm', E.J. Priestley, Copy of South View in Tate Gallery, no. 1855, previously no. 155 in 1884 Nottingham exhibition of work of Paul Sandby. A copy of 1884 Nottingham exhibition catalogue in Victoria and Albert Museum library. Five drawings of Eltham Palace by Paul Sandby in Prints & Drawings Dept., British Library.

54. Anon., *Summer Excursions in the County of Kent* (1847), pp.93-4.

55. Robinson, S., *op. cit.*

56. Aquatint, 'South East View of King John's Palace at Eltham', P. Sandby, 1787.

57. 'Mr King's Sequel to the Observations on Ancient Castles', *Archaeologia*, vol. vi (1782), pp.367-811.

58. Crown Estate Office. File Eltham 121. 1822-29.

59. Buckler, J.C., *An Historical and Descriptive Account of the Royal Palace at Eltham* (1828), p.96.
Anderson, E., *Eltham in Past Times* (1910), illn opp. p.22.

60. 'Mr King's Sequel to the Observations on Ancient Castles', *Archaeologia*, vol. vi (1782), illns. lxxii-iii.
Original watercolours by S.H. Grimm, 1779, E.J. Priestley.

61. Girtin, T. and Loshak, D., *The Art of Thomas Girtin* (1954), p.138.
Brook, R., *op. cit.*, frontispiece.
Mayne, J., *Thomas Girtin* (1949), pp.99, 107, 110.
Finberg, A.J., *The Life of J.M.W. Turner R.A* (1961), p.457 (no. 2).
Anderson, E., *op. cit.*, illn (upper) opp. 12.

62. Crown Estates Office. File Eltham 121. Driver to Milne 4 March 1828.

63. Aquatint, 'South West View of Eltham Palace', P. Sandby, 1782 and 1812.
Watercolour, 'North West View', P. Sandby, Mappin Art Gallery, Sheffield.

64. Drawing, formerly in RIBA library drawings collection, Joseph Nash, 1827, illustrated in Priestley, E.J., *op. cit.*

65. Pugin, A.C., *A Series of Views Illustrative of the Examples of Gothic Architecture* (1830), 'North West View of the Great Hall'.

66. Buck, S. and N., *op. cit.*
Robinson, S., *op. cit.*
Buckler, J.C., *op. cit.*, frontispiece.
Pencil, 'View of Eltham Palace from the North', P. Sandby, Prints & Drawings Dept., British Library.
Gentleman's Magazine, January 1812, p.13.

67. Buck, S. and N., *op. cit.*
Robinson, S., *op. cit.*

68. Harris, J., *History of Kent*, vol. i (1719), pp.115-16.
Bodleian Library. MSS Dept. of Printed Books, 'The Hall and Ruins of the King's Palace at Eltham 17 Oct 1724'. William Stukeley. M.S. Top. gen. d. 14 f 15ᵛ.

69. Hearne, T., *op. cit.*, p.362.

70. Gregory, R.R.C., *op. cit.*, p.291.

71. Defoe, D., *A Tour through the Whole Island of Great Britain*, vol. i, letter ii (1724), p.11.

72. Harris, J., *op. cit.*, pp.115-16.

73. Cox, T., *Magna Britannia*, vol. ii (1720), p.1079.

74. Bodleian Library. MSS Dept. of Printed Books, 'The Hall and Ruins of the King's Palace at Eltham 17 Oct 1724'. William Stukeley. M.S. Top. gen. d. 14 f 15ᵛ.

75. MSS Dept., British Library, 'The Hall belonging to the Royal Palace of Eltham in Kent Built by Anthony Beck Bp of Durham about the Year MCCLXX' (1727), W. Mellecant. Add. MSS 32363 f 38.

76. MSS Dept., British Library, Lens, A.B., 'The North Prospect of King John's Hall at Eltham in Kent' (1733), Add. MSS 32363 f 53, copy in Map Library, British Library, Royal XVI 52 f b; Lens, A.B., 'A View taken in the Moat at King John's Palace at Eltham in Kent' (1733), Add. MSS 32363 f 81 top. Copy in Map Library, British Library, Royal XVI 52 f a.

77. Buck, S. and N., op. cit.

78. Robinson, S., op. cit.

79. Jackson, T. (ed.), Journal of the Rev. Charles Wesley, vol. ii (1849), pp.240-1.

80. Cockayne, G.E. (ed.), op. cit., vol. v (1926), pp.6-7, 62.

81. Ibid., vol. xiii (1940), p.257.

82. The Times, 22 April 1981, pp.14, 23.

83. Harris, J., op. cit., pp.115-16.
Cox, T., op. cit., p.1079.

84. RCHMSS. MSS of the Earl of Egmont, Diary of the First Viscount Percival, vol. i, 1730-33 (1920), 198.

85. Robinson, S., op. cit.
Crest 2/1643.

86. Ibid.

87. Markham, S., John Loveday of Caversham (1984), p.364.
Markham, F., Loveday MSS, tour no. 102, 28 April 1746.

88. 'Mr King's Sequel to the Observations on Ancient Castles', Archaeologia, vol. vi (1782), pp.367-8.

89. Seymour, C., History of Kent (1776), pp.349-51.
'Mr King's Sequel to the Observations on Ancient Castles', Archaeologia, vol. vi (1782), pp.367-8.

90. Hasted, E., History of Kent, vol. i (1778), pp.48-54, illn between pp.52-3.

91. Graves, A. (ed.), The Royal Academy Contributors 1769-1904, vol. iii, p.95, no. 107.

92. Works Exhibited at the Royal Society of British Artists 1824-1893 (1975), 53 (no. 199), 56 (no. 653), 146 (no. 702).
Royal Academy Contributors, vol. i, 38 (nos 501, 529), 150 (no. 848), 295 (no. 198), 390 (no. 597); vol. ii, 170 (no. 1156); vol. iii, 95 (no. 107); vol. iv, 387 (no. 453); vol. v, 35 (no. 1184); vol. vii, 214 (nos 490, 1090), 216 (no. 703); vol. viii, 33 (no. 494), 306 (no. 1053), 323 (no. 882), 364 (no. 432).
Graves, A. (ed.), The British Institution 1806-1867 (1908), 462 (no. 209), 517 (no. 161).

93. 'Mr King's Sequel to the Observations on Ancient Castles', Archaeologia, vol. vi (1782). Two watercolours, signed by S.H. Grimm and dated 1779, are the original views copied by Basire to illustrate two of the three illustrations to King's article. E.J. Priestley.

94. Christie's, 17 June 1817, nos 76, 85, 105, 107; 27 June 1833, no. 63; 2 July 1833, no. 89.

95. Christie's, 2 May 1811, nos 19, 37-8; 16 April 1817, no. 115; 2 April 1818, no. 24; 2 March 1971, no. 82; 14 December 1971, nos 86-7).
Aquatint, '(South West) View of the Remains of King John's Palace at Eltham in Kent', P. Sandby (1782). Watercolour version Smith College Museum of Art, Northampton, Conn, U.S.A.

Aquatint, 'South East View of the Remains of King John's Palace at Eltham in Kent', P. Sandby (1787). Watercolour version National Gallery of Ireland.
Watercolour, 'North West View of Eltham Palace', P. Sandby, Kent Life, April 1966, 37. Original Mappin Art Gallery, Sheffield.
'North East View of Eltham Palace (1787)', Watercolour, Country Life, 3 June 1965, 1343 and Parke-Bernet Galleries catalogue, New York, 13 April 1963 (no. 86). E.J. Priestley. Larger copy Christie's 14 December 1971 (no. 87), Aquatint, British Library, Dept. Prints & Drawings. Pen copy Kent County Museum, Maidstone. Christie's 15 April 1916 (no. 1273).
Watercolours, 'North and South Views', 'East end Eltham Hall', 'West end Eltham Court Farm', P. Sandby. E.J. Priestley. Copy South View Tate Gallery (no. 1855) and Paul Sandby exhibition, Nottingham 1884 (no. 155). Catalogue of exhibition in Victoria and Albert Museum library.
Five drawings Eltham Palace. P. Sandby (from South East, South West, North East, North West and from bridge) British Library, Prints & Drawings Dept.

96. Girtin, T. and Loshak, D., op. cit., p.152.
Mayne, J., op. cit., p.110.
Finberg, A.J., op. cit., p.457.
Graves, A. (ed.), Royal Academy Exhibitions, vol. viii, p.33 (no. 494).

97. Lysons, D., The Environs of London, vol. iv (1796), pp.394-421.

98. Gentleman's Magazine, January 1812, pp.13-14; February 1812, pp.110-11; November 1816, pp.407-8, 446-7; January 1822, pp.9-10; May 1823, p.424; May 1828, pp.403-4; September 1828, pp.217-22; November 1828, pp.424-7; February 1830, pp.103-4; January 1831, pp.24-5; December 1834, pp.594-5; March 1835, pp.226; June 1837, p.592.
Aiken, J., England Described (1818), p.375.
The Ambulator (1782), p.82.
Excursions in the County of Kent (1822), p.161.
Antiquarian and Topographical Cabinet. N.D.
Brayley, E.W., The Graphic and Historical Illustrator (1834), pp.320-8.
Capper, B.P., Topographical Dictionary of the UK (1826), p.300.
Cooke, G.A., Topographical and Statistical Description of the County of Kent (1818), p.268.
Cruttwell, C., Tour through the Whole Island of Great Britain, vol. ii (1801), p.61.
Dugdale, T., Curiosities of Great Britain. England and Wales Delineated, vol. ii (c.1830), p.731.
Ferrey, B., Recollections of A.W.N. Pugin and his father Augustus Pugin (1861), pp.53-4.
Hone, W., The Year Book (1832), cols. 462-7.
Ireland, S., History of the County of Kent (c.1830), pp.644-54.
The Literary Times, 12 December 1835, no. ix, p.1.
Luckombe, P., England's Gazetteer, vol. i (1790).
The Mirror, vol. viii, no. 222, 11 November 1826, pp.289-90.
The Mirror of Parliament: House of Lords, 15 July 1828, p.2351.
The Monthly Register of Literature or Magazin des Savans, vol. i (1792), pp.420-2.
Penny Magazine, September 1832, p.263.
The Saturday Magazine, 10 January 1835, pp.15-16.
Select Views of London and its Environs, vol. i (1804), Eltham Palace, Kent.

Tymms, S., The Family Topographer, vol. i (1832), pp.58, 76, 82-6, 91, 103.
Virtue, G., Picturesque Beauties of Great Britain: Kent (1828), p.19.
Walpoole, G.A., The New British Traveller (1780), p.23.

99. Ferrey, B., Recollections of A.W.N. Pugin and his father Augustus Pugin (1861), pp.53-4.
Crown Estate Office. File Eltham 121.
Saunders to King 15 November 1827.
Crest 2/359.

100. Crown Estate Office. File Eltham 121.
Chawner & Rhodes report 10 June 1823.
Crest 2/359.

101. Crown Estate Office. File Eltham 121.
Smirke to King 12 November 1827.
Saunders to King 15 November 1827.
Crest 9/22 151, 236, 251, 266, 270.
T 25/14 108.

102. Crest 9/22 272, 280, 288, 308, 317, 364.
T 25/14 108.
Crown Estate Office. File Eltham 121.
Treasury to Commissioners of Woods. 31 December 1827.
Crest 25/32 14, 19, 26 February 1828.

103. Crown Estate Office. File Eltham 121.
Driver to Milne 4 March 1828.

104. The Evening Standard, 11 April 1828.
Crown Estate Office. File Eltham 121.
Smirke to King 12 November 1827.
Priestley, E.J., 'First Campaign to Preserve a Building?', Country Life, 26 May 1977, pp.1412, 1414.
Gentleman's Magazine, May 1828, pp.403-4; September 1828, pp.217-18; November 1828, p.424.
Literary Gazette (1828), p.460.
Mirror of Parliament, 15-16 July 1828, pp.2506, 2531, 2558.
Kent and Essex Mercury, 15 April 1828.
Penny Magazine, September 1832, p.263.
Morning Advertiser, 16 July 1828, p.2.

105. Crown Estate Office. File Eltham 121, 1822-9.
Saunders to King, 23 February 1828.

106. Morning Advertiser, 16 July 1828, p.2.
The Standard, 15-16 July 1828.
St James Chronicle, 15-17 July 1828, p.2.
The Times, 16 July 1828.

107. Crest 9/22 474-75; /23 28, 126.

108. Crest 9/23 455.
T 29/285 257.
T 25/15 18 September 1828, 11 April 1829.
Crest 25/32 12, 29 August, 2, 23 September 1828.
Buckler, J.C., op. cit., pp.104-7.

109. Anderson, E., op. cit., illn opp. 14.
Dunnage, H. and Laver, C., Plans ... of the Great Hall of ... Eltham (1828), plates 1, 8.
Baynes, T.M., and Watkins, W., Eltham Palace, Kent, print (1831).
Summer Excursions in the County of Kent (1847), p.94.

110. Ion Elton, P., 'Eltham Palace', The Architect and Contract Reporter, 6 March 1903, p.161.

111. Hone, W., The Year Book (1832), p.466.
Beattie, W., Castles and Abbeys of England, vol. i (1842), pp.111, 125.
Summer Excursions in the County of Kent (1847), p.96.

112. Buckler, J.C., op. cit., pp.1-107.
Bl. MSS Dept. Add. MSS 32363 ff 225-26, 244-50.

113. Dunnage, H., and Laver, C., op. cit.

114. Pugin, A.C., Examples of Gothic Architecture (1831), pp.31-42, plates i-vii.

115. Pugin, A.C., op. cit. (1830).

116. Pugin, A.C., *Specimens of Gothic Architecture* (1821), vol. i, pp.19-20; vol. ii, pp.5, 17.
Pugin, A.C., *Gothic Ornaments* (1831), plate 2.
Pugin, A.C., *Ornamental Gables* (1839), p.14, plates xxiv-v.

117. Crown Estate Office. File Eltham 121.
T. Gayfree to Saunders 2 May 1823.

118. Hunt, J., *Designs for Parsonage Houses* (1827), pp.17-18, plate xii.

119. King, D. and Clayton, A.B., *Subterranean Passages at Eltham Palace lately Discovered and Explored*, N.D. (1834), pp.1-8 and plate.
The Saturday Magazine, 10 January 1835, pp.15-16.

120. *Gentleman's Magazine*, December 1834, pp.594-5.

121. *Ibid.*, November 1816, pp.446-7.
Rivers, E., *op. cit.*, pp.18-19,

122. Anon.,'To Eltham Palace', *All the Year Round*, 8 October 1892, p.347.
Brayley, E.W., *op. cit.*, p.320.
Buckler, J.C., *op. cit.*, p.107.
Anderson, E., *op. cit.*, pp.27-8.

10. REPAIR AND RESTORATION.

1. Anon., *The Journey Book of England: Kent* (1842), p.45.
Beattie, W., *Castles and Abbeys of England*, vol. 1 (1842), pp.111, 126.
Anon., *Summer Excursions in the County of Kent* (1847), pp.95-6, 98.

2. Corner, G.R., 'On the Existing Remains of Eltham Palace', *Transactions of the British Archaeological Association*, second annual congress, Winchester, August 1845 (1846), p.331.

3. Bagshaw, S., *History, Gazetteer & Directory of Kent*, vol. i (1847), p.611.

4. *Eltham and District Times*, 14 September 1923.
Anon., 'A Visit to an Old Hall at Eltham', *Once a Week*, 6 October 1860, p.402.

5. Bodleian Library, Oxford. Rawl. D. 777 f 88v.

6. *Illustrated London News*, 30 December 1893, p.827.

7. Personal observation.

8. Anon., 'To Eltham Palace', *All the Year Round*, 8 October 1892, p.347.
Butts, R., *Historical Guide to Lewisham, Ladywell, Lee, Blackheath and Eltham* (1878), p.39.

9. Anon., *Suburban Homes of London* (1881), p.328.

10. Gregory, R.R.C., *The Story of Royal Eltham* (1909), pp.278, 315.

11. Crown Estate Office. Files Eltham 121A, 122.
Illustrated Sporting and Dramatic News, 8 December 1888, p.333.

12. Gregory, R.R.C., *op. cit.*, p.278.
Crown Estate Office. File Eltham 73.

13. Gregory, R.R.C., *op. cit.*, p.278.
Crown Estate Office. File Eltham 1948.
Illustrated Sporting and Dramatic News, 8 December 1888, p.333.

14. Crown Estate Office. File Eltham 1948.

15. Greenwich Local History Library. 1863 census RG 9/412.

16. *Once a Week*, 6 October 1860, p.402.

17. *Kentish Mercury*, 16 August 1862.

18. *Eltham and District Times*, 25 September, 2 October 1908, 19 March 1909.
The Builder, 20 March 1880, p.359.
Besant, W., *South London* (1899), p.97.
Thorne, J., *The Environs of London* (1885), p.171.

19. *Eltham and District Times*, 10 February 1911.

20. Gregory, R.R.C., *op. cit.*, p.316.
Kentish Mercury, 16 August 1862.

21. Butts, R., *op. cit.*, p.39.

22. Gregory, R.R.C., *op. cit.*, illn no. 12 between pp.8-9.

23. Graves, A. (ed.), *Royal Academy Exhibitions 1769-1904*, 1905-6, vol. v, p.35; vol. viii, p.306.
Works Exhibited at the Royal Society of British Artists 1824-1893, including New English Art Club 1888-1917 (1975), p.53.

24. See Chapter 9 references 90-3.

25. Turner, J.H., *Some Account of Domestic Architecture in England*, vol. ii, part 2 (1859), p.303.
Architectural Association Sketch-Books, 1869-70, 1886-7.
Rickman, T., *Styles of Architecture in England*, 7th edn (1881), p.218.
Scott, G., *Medieval Architecture*, vol. i (1879), pp.31, 277, 314; vol. ii, pp.213, 324.
Brandon, R. and J.A., *The Open Timber Roofs of the Middle Ages* (1849), pp.31-2.
The Builder, 4 April 1885, p.479.
Fletcher, Sir Banister, *A History of Architecture on the Comparative Method* (1896), p.156.
Allport, D.H., *A Short History of Wilson's Grammar School* (1951), p.122.

26. Jefferies, R., *The Open Air* (1948), p.182.

27. Cull, M., *Poems* (1854), pp.22-4.

28. Personal information from the late Lady Elliott (*née* Gillian Bloxam), 10 December 1960.

29. *Archaeologia Cantiana*, vol. xii (1878), p.xliii.

30. *Sidcup and District Times*, 6, 13 August 1886, 2, 9 June 1893, 27 September 1895, 28 July 1899.
Eltham and District Times, 15, 22 June 1906, 21 June 1907, 21 May 1909, 25 June 1909, 2 July 1909, 26 August 1910, 2 September 1910, 31 March 1911, 21 July 1911, 6 November 1914, 1 October 1920, 1 August 1922, 9 December 1927.
Eltham and Kentish Times, 28 July 1928, 21 September 1928, 27 May 1932, 4 August 1933, 27 January 1950, 21 October 1960, 27 April 1962, 11 May 1962, 26 August 1966, 2 June 1967, 17 November 1967.
Archaeologia Cantiana, vol. xii, p.xliii; vol. xxiv, p.xlii; vol. xxviii, p.lxxii; vol. xxx, p.xliii; vol. xli, p.xlvi; vol. lxiv, p.xli; vol. lxx, p.xlvi.
Greenwich Antiquarian Society Transactions, vol. i, p.112; vol. iii, pp.11, 147; vol. iv, p.263.
Woolwich & District Antiquarian Society, vol. i, p.32; vol. xiii, p.36; vol. xv, p.74; vol. xxiv, pp.15, 18; vol. xxviii, p.18; vol. xxxi, p.xi; vol. xxxii, p.xi.
Journal of the London Society, August 1928; June 1936.
Meetings of the Upper Norwood Athenaeum, vol. xxxiv, p.109.
Transactions of the Ancient Monuments Society, vol. xxxi (NS), pp.6-8.

31. *Sidcup and District Times*, 14 July 1883, 10 July 1885, 9 July 1886, 20 July 1888, 19 July 1889, 4 July 1890, 17 July 1891, 8 July 1892, 16 June 1893, 29 June 1894, 12 July 1895, 10 July 1896, 9 July 1897, 22 July 1898, 14 July 1899, 13 July 1900, 12 July 1901, 18 July 1902, 17 July 1903, 22 July 1904.
Eltham and District Times, 14 July 1905, 13 July 1906, 12 July 1907, 17 July 1908, 9 July 1909, 15 July 1910, 14 July 1911, 12 July 1912, 11 July 1913.
Eltham Parish Magazine, August 1889, April 1890, July 1890, March 1891, August 1891, April 1892.
Lieut-Col J.B. Gladstone to E.J. Priestley, 16 November 1966.

Smith, A., *Eltham's Village Days: Recollections since 1857* (1940), p.28,

32. *Sidcup and District Times*, 17 July 1885, 25 June 1886, 15 July 1887, 5 July 1889.

33. *Eltham and District Times*, 7 July 1911.
Smith, A., *Eltham's Village Days: Recollections since 1857* (1940), p.28.

34. *Sidcup and District Times*, 9 August 1895, 10 April 1896, 23 April 1897, 3 June 1898, 5 August 1898, 7 April 1899, 8 June 1900, 31 May 1901, 9 August 1901, 23 May 1902, 17 April 1903.

35. *Sidcup and District Times*, 5 July 1884.

36. *Ibid.*, 26 June 1903.

37. *Ibid.*, 11 August 1883, 7 August 1891, 28 July 1899.
Eltham Parish Magazine, August 1889, August 1890, September 1890, September 1891.

38. *Sidcup and District Times*, 7 August 1891.

39. *Eltham and District Times*, 5 July 1907.

40. *Ladies Pictorial*, 14 August 1897, p.228.

41. *Motor Car Journal*, 15 August 1908, p.522.

42. Drake, H.H. (ed.), *Hasted's History of Kent Corrected: Part 1: The Hundred of Blackheath* (1886), pp.171-213, 279.

43. Milne, A.G., *Eltham Palace* (1886), N.D. (1900), 2nd edn (1921), pp.1-19.
Sidcup and District Times, 30 November 1900.

44. I.A.J. Baker, A.G. Milne letter to H.H. Drake, 26 December 1881.
Milne letter to Drake, 1881.
Courtauld, S., *Eltham Palace* (1936)

45. Gregory, R.R.C., *op. cit.*, pp.315-16, plates between pp.272-3.
Crown Estate Office File, 1948.

46. Gregory, R.R.C., *op. cit.*, pp.315-16, plates between pp.272-3.
Crown Estate Office File, 1948.

47. *The Times*, 29 February 1896.
Sidcup and District Times, 28 February 1896, 2 October 1899.
Estates Gazette, 19 November 1899.
Solicitors Journal, vol. xl, 29 February 1896, p.292.

48. Crown Estate Office File, 1948.
Gregory, R.R.C., *op. cit.*, p.278.

49. *Ibid.*, p.278.

50. Seely & Paget File 16. Letters of Mrs E.L. Parnell, 6, 9 February 1934.
Hussey, C., 'Eltham Hall II', *Country Life*, 22 May 1937, p.573.

51. Gregory, R.R.C., *op. cit.*, p.278.
Crown Estate Office File 911.
Personal information.

52. Gregory, R.R.C., *op. cit.*, p.278.
Eltham and District Times, 21 May 1909.
Crown Estates Office File 911.

53. *Eltham and District Times*, 22 September 1916.

54. Crown Estates Office File 1948.
Eltham and Kentish Times, 28 April 1933.

55. *Ibid.*, 5 June 1942, 2 February 1945.

56. Crown Estates Office File Eltham 911.
Victoria and Albert Museum, Prints and Drawings Dept., 'Water colour of great hall from the South', A.E. Perkins.
Illustrated Sporting and Dramatic News, 8 December 1888, p.333.

57. Crown Estates Office File Eltham 911.
Transactions of Woolwich Antiquarian Society, vol. i (1896), p.33.

58. *Sidcup and District Times*, 20 June 1902.
Ion Elton, P., 'Eltham Palace', *The Architect & Contract Reporter*, 6 March 1903, pp.161-2.

59. Crown Estates Office File Eltham 911.
Eltham and District Times, 13 January, 3 February, 21, 28 July, 24 November 1911, 5 January, 13 September 1912, 28 February, 25 April, 13 June, 29 August, 19 September 1913, 10 April, 12 June, 28 August 1914.

The Times, 19 April 1913.
Parliamentary Debates Official Report, 5th Series, Commons 1914, vol. ix, March 23 to April 8, col. 367, 25 March 1914.

60. Eltham Society, Newsletters nos 101, August 1980; 103, February 1991, 112. May 1993.
61. Rivers, E., *Some Records of Eltham*, N.D. (1904).
62. Gregory, R.R.C., *op. cit.*, appendix II, 1910.
    Eltham and District Times, 6 May 1910.
63. Anderson, E., *Eltham in Past Times* (1910). Personal information.
64. *Eltham and District Times*, 17 May 1907-4 December 1908, 10 December 1909, 22 April, 6 May 1910, 10 November 1911, 28 November 1913.
65. Gregory, R.R.C., *op. cit.*, appendix II, 1910.
66. Godfrey, W.H., 'An Unpublished Plan of Eltham Palace', *Architectural Review*, April 1910, pp.218-20.
67. Godfrey, W.H., 'New Light on Old Subjects' - VI - 'The Royal Palace of Eltham', *Architectural Review*, August 1911, pp.81-6.
68. Clapham, A.W. and Godfrey, W.H., *Some Famous Buildings and Their Story*, N.D. (1913), chapter iv, pp.47-66.
    Eltham and District Times, 28 November 1913.
69. *Ibid.*, 10 November 1911.
70. Royal Commission on Historic Monuments, *East London* (1930), pp.103-8.
71. Pevsner, N., *Buildings of England: London (except the Cities of London and Westminster)* (1952), pp.458-9; revised edition, *Buildings of England: London – 2: South* (1983), pp.300-2.
72. Colvin, H.M. (ed.), *The History of the King's Works*, vol. ii (1963), pp.930-7; vol. iv (1982) pp.78-86.
73. Strong, D.E., *Eltham Palace* (1958); later edns 1963, 1983, 1986.
74. Brook, R., *The Story of Eltham Palace* (1960).
75. Woods, H., 'Excavations at Eltham Palace, 1975-9', *Transactions of London and Middlesex Archaeological Society*, vol. xxxiii (1982), pp.215-65.
76. *Eltham and District Times*, 28 April 1933.
77. *Ibid.*, 23 July 1915, 13 July 1917, 28 June, 5 July 1918.
78. *Ibid.*, 5, 12 July, 27 September, 11, 18 October, 1 November 1918.
79. *Ibid.*, 25 July 1919, 16 July, 6 August 1920, 21 July 1922, 10 July 1925, 23 September 1927.
    Eltham and Kentish Times, 15 June 1928, 12, 26 July 1929, 1, 22 August 1930, 10 April, 10 July 1931, 22 July 1932, 27 June 1933.
80. *Eltham and District Times*, 1 August 1919.
81. *Ibid.*, 20 June 1924.
    Sphere, 21 June 1924, pp.318-19.
    Illustrated London News, 14 June 1924, p.1123.
    Daily Mirror, 9 June 1924.
    Kentish Mercury, 20 June 1924.
    'Ye Olde Eltham Fayre. Eltham Palace, 13 and 14 June 1924', programme.
82. Aslet, C., 'An Interview with the late Paul Paget', *The Thirties Society Journal*, no. 6 (1987), p.19.
    Eltham and Kentish Times, 8 December 1933.
    Turner, M., *Eltham Palace* (1999), pp.1-5, 36-7, 40.
83. Crown Estates Office. File Eltham 2126, letter, 26 June 1933.
    Seely and Paget File 16.
84. *Ibid.* Seely and Paget to Courtauld, 30 June 1933.
85. Crown Estates Office. Files Eltham 2126, 1948.
    Seely and Paget File 9.

86. Butts, R., *Historical Guide to Lewisham, Ladywell, Lee, Blackheath and Eltham* (1878), pp.39-40.
    Illustrated Sporting and Dramatic News, 8 December 1888, p.333.
    Anon., 'A Visit to an Old Hall at Eltham', *Once a Week*, 6 October 1860, p.401.
    Seely and Paget Files 9, 16.
    Crown Estates Office. File Eltham 2126A.
87. RCHM(E), *London East*, vol. v (1930), p.106.
    Seely and Paget File 9. Plans, 15 December 1933.
    Crown Estates Office. File Eltham 2126.
88. Seely and Paget Files 9, 16, 22-3, 26-7, 29-30, 44, 98, 129.
89. Hussey, C., 'Eltham Hall I', *Country Life*, 15 May 1937, pp.534-9.
90. Seely and Paget File 26. Seely and Paget to J. Hopkins, 24 October 1935.
    P. Paget to A. Mawson, 4 May 1935.
    Hussey, C., *op. cit.*, 22 May 1937, pp.571-3; 'Eltham Hall III', *Country Life*, 29 May 1937, p.594.
91. Estate Plan. Eltham Palace.
    RCHM(E), *London East*, vol. v (1930), p.106.
    Daily Telegraph, 7 August 1936.
92. Hussey, C., *op. cit.*, 22 May 1937, pp.571, 573.
93. Seely and Paget File 30. December 1933-May 1937; Files Eltham Hall.
    Aslet, C., *The Last Country Houses* (1982), p.34.
94. *Ibid.*, pp.315-16.
    Hussey, C., *op. cit.*, 22 May 1937, pp.568-9, 571-2; *op. cit.*, 29 May 1937, pp.594-9.
    Aslet, C., *The Last Country Houses* (1982), interview 17.
    Pevsner, N., *op. cit.* (1983), pp.300-1.
    Godfrey, W.B., 'Eltham Hall', *Architectural Review*, October 1936, pp.152-3.
95. *Ibid.*, p.153.
    Hussey, C., *op. cit.*, 22 May 1937, p.572.
    Brook, R., *op.cit.*, p.62.
    Seely and Paget. Letters to H. Attwood 3 April 1935-5 October 1936.
    Seely and Paget File 26. G. Ledward to J. Seely, 19 September 1935.
96. Godfrey, W.B., *op. cit.*, p.152.
    Hussey, C., *op. cit.*, 22 May 1937, pp.568-73; *op. cit.*, 29 May 1937, pp.594-9.
97. Aslet, C., *op. cit.*, interview 17-21.
    Godfrey, W.B., *op. cit.*, p.152.
    Turner, M., *op. cit.*, pp.32-3.
98. Godfrey, W.B., *op. cit.*, p.153.
    Aslet, C., *op. cit.*, pp.81, 109, 283.
    Hussey, C., *op. cit.*, 29 May 1937, pp.595-8.
99. Seely and Paget File 30. Letters September 1935-7, December 1936.
    Aslet, C., *op. cit.*, p.88.
    Hussey, C., *op. cit.*, 29 May 1937, pp.595, 597-8.
    R. Engstromer letter to E.J. Priestley, 6 May 1959.
    Aslet, C., *op. cit.*, interview 17.
100. Aslet, C., *op. cit.*, interview 20.
     Seely and Paget File 44; File 98. Paul Paget to Marchese Malacrida, 14 May 1934.
     Turner, M., *op. cit.*, pp.5-10, 13-19, 35-6.
101. Hussey, C., *op. cit.*, 15 May 1937, pp.534-9; *op. cit.*, 29 May 1937, pp.594-9.
     Brook, R., *op. cit.*, p.61.
102. Seely and Paget File 27. Sir Charles Peers to Paul Paget, 12 January 1936.
     Turner, M., *op. cit.*, pp.31-2.
     Hussey, C., *op. cit.*, 15 May 1937, p.538.
103. *Eltham and District Times*, 21 July 1911.
104. Hussey, C., *op. cit.*, 15 May 1937, p.538.
105. *Ibid.*

106. *Ibid.*, p.539.
     The Times, 21 July 1936, p.13.
107. *Ibid.*
     Godfrey, W.B., *op. cit.*, p.152.
108. Hussey, C., *op. cit.*, 15 May 1937, p.534, p.536.
109. *Ibid.*, p.539.
110. *Ibid.*
111. *Ibid.*, p.536.
     Brook, R., *op. cit.*, p.61.
112. Personal information.
113. Hussey, C., *op. cit.*, 15 May 1937, pp.535, 538.
114. *Ibid.*, p.538.
115. *Ibid.*, pp.537-8.
     Turner, M., *op. cit.*, p.12.
     Seely and Paget File 29. Paul Paget to *Kentish Times*, 2 June 1936.
116. Hussey, C., *op. cit.*, 15 May 1937, p.538.
     Seely and Paget File 23. Seely & Paget to Graham & Groves 28 May 1935.
117. Seely and Paget File 26. J. Seely to Sir Charles Peers 15 November 1935.
     Brook, R., *op. cit.*, p.62.
118. Seely and Paget File 27; Files Eltham Hall.
119. Brook, R., *op. cit.*, p.62,
120. Hussey, C., *op. cit.*, 15 May 1937, p.539.
     Seely and Paget File 29. Seely & Paget to Cluttons, 14 May 1936; File 22. Paul Paget to J. Hopkins, 4 February 1935.
     Godfrey, W.B., *op. cit.*, p.152.
121. Seely and Paget File 22. Paul Paget to Sir Eric Maclagan, Victoria and Albert Museum, 4 February 1935.
122. Seely and Paget File 98. Letter, 26 July 1934; File 29. Seely and Paget to Cluttons, 14 May 1936.
123. RCHM(E), *London East*, vol. v (1930), p.104.
124. Woods, H., *op. cit.*, pp.218-21, 228-30, 234-5.
125. Hussey, C., *op. cit.*, 15 May 1937, pp.535-7.
     Turner, M., *op. cit.*, pp.12-13, 43.
126. Young, G.M., *Victorian Essays* (1962), p.74.
     The Times, 23 July 1936, Letter G.M. Young.
127. *Ibid.*, 25 July 1936, Letters Sir Herbert Baker, Francis Howard; 6 August, Sir Herbert Baker; 15 August, Francis Howard.
128. Brook, R., *op. cit.*, p.65.
     The Times, 23 July 1936, Letter Sir Herbert Baker.
129. *Ibid.*, 25 July 1936, Letter Sir Herbert Baker.
130. *Country Life*, 15 August 1936, p.183.
     The Times, 25 July 1936. Letter Paul Paget, John Seely; 4 August, Gilbert Ledward; 13 August, Paul Paget.
     The Observer, 16 August 1936.
     Anon., 'Romance Dies at Eltham', *Architect and Building News*, 7 August 1936.
131. Brook, R., *op. cit.*, p.65.
     The Times, 4 August 1936. Letter Paul Paget.
132. Anon., 'Romance Dies at Eltham', *Architect and Building News*, 7 August 1936.
     Kentish Independent, 14 August 1936.
     Kentish Mercury, 23 February 1934.
134. *The Observer*, 16 August 1936.
     Daily Mail, 6, 7 April 1936.
     Daily Telegraph, 7 August 1936.
     Evening Standard, 6 April, 3 October 1936.
     Illustrated London News, 25 July 1936, p.159.
     Hussey, C., *op. cit.*, 15 May 1937, pp.534-9; *op. cit.*, 22 May 1937, pp.568-73; *op. cit.*, 29 May 1937, pp.594-9.
     Sphere, 9 December 1933, p.404; 27 July 1935, p.145.
135. *The Builder*, 22 June 1934, pp.1069-71.
     Building, May 1934, p.164.
     Anon., 'Romance Dies at Eltham', *Architect and Building News*, 7 August 1936; 17 November 1933, frontispiece.

Parthenon, August 1934, p.387.
The Gas Times, 5 December 1936, pp.28-9.
Architects Journal, 23 November 1933, p.651.
Godfrey, W.B., *op. cit.*, pp.151-2.
Seely and Paget Files 23, 98.
136. *Royal Academy Exhibitions 1905-70*, vol. v (1973), pp.11-12, 103, 467.
Turner, M., *op. cit.*, pp.19-24.
Seely and Paget File 23. P. Paget to A. Mawson, 4 May 1935.
137. Hussey, C., *op. cit.*, 15 May 1937, pp.534-9; *op. cit.*, 22 May 1937, pp.568-73; *op. cit.*, 29 May 1937, pp.594-9.
138. Courtauld, S., *Eltham Palace* (1936).
Hussey, C., 22 May 1937, p.573.
139. Information from Mr P.H. Pierano.
Turner, M., *op. cit.*, pp.37-9.
140. *Eltham and Kentish Times*, 16 July 1937.
Evening Standard, 8 July 1937.
The Observer, 11 July 1937.
Butler, M., *August and Rab: A Memoir* (1987), pp.61-2.
141. *Eltham and Kentish Times*, 29 July 1938.
142. *Ibid.*, 27 May 1938, 28 April 1939, 17 July 1942.
143. *Ibid.*, 27 March 1931.
144. *Ibid.*, 12 July 1935.
Seely and Paget File 44. 1, 14 July 1935.
145. *Eltham and Kentish Times*, 10 June 1938.
146. *Ibid.*, 10 July 1936.
147. *R.A.E.C. Gazette*, November 1970, p.1, pp.16-20.
148. *Torch*, Winter 1977, p.1; Summer 1978, pp.1, 30; Winter 1978, pp.2, 5; Summer 1984, p.5.
149. Towey, J., 'A Mess at the Palace', *Eltham Palace and Eltham People* (2003), p.35.
150. *News Shopper*, 15 November 1995.
151. *Eltham and Kentish Times*, 15 September 1939.
152. *Ibid.*, 1 December 1939; 5 September 1941; 24 April 1942.
153. Crown Estates Office. File 3551. S. Courtauld 14, 25 September 1940.
Eltham and Kentish Times, 20, 27 September 1940.
Illustrated London News, 27 September 1940, p.410.
154. Crown Estates Office. File 3551. S. Courtauld 21 April 1941.
155. *Eltham and Kentish Times*, 22 August, 12 September 1952, 29 January 1954.
156. *Ibid.*, 22 August 1952, 13 August 1954.
157. Seely and Paget File 29. P. Paget to Sir Charles Peers 8, 11 May 1936.
158. Strong, D.E., *op. cit.*, reverse of cover; (1986), reverse of cover.
159. *Eltham and Kentish Times*, 9 July, 24 September 1943.
160. *Ibid.*, 9, 16, 23, 30 May 1941.
161. Turner, M., *op. cit.*, pp.39-40.
Seely and Paget File 129. Letter to P. Paget, 10 September 1944.
162. Information from Mr P.H. Pierano.
163. *Ibid.*
164. Turner, M., *op. cit.*, p.39.
Information from Mr P.H. Pierano.
Godfrey, W.B., *op. cit.*, p.152.

165. Petro, W., *Triple Commission* (1968), p.206.
166. Seely and Paget File 129. Letter to P. Paget 10 September 1944.
167. Turner, M., *op. cit.*, p.41.
Seely and Paget File 129.
Eltham and Kentish Times, 26 January, 2 February 1945.
Brook, R., *op. cit.*, p.67.
168. *Ibid.*, p.68.
169. Aslet, C., *op. cit.*, interview 21.
Turner, M., *op. cit.*, pp.40-1.
170. *The Times*, 1 January 1958, p.4.
171. Butler, M., *August and Rab: A Memoir* (1987), p.62.
Daily Telegraph, 1 April 1969, p.27.
Eltham and Kentish Times, 3 January 1958.
The Times, 11, 13, 17, 18 October 1967.
172. *Ibid.*, 4 January 1971.
173. *Soldier*, 5 January 1946.
Turner, M., *op. cit.*, p.42.
Eltham and Kentish Times, 25 January 1946.
White, A.C.T., *The Story of Army Education* (1963), pp.197-201, illustration between pp.192-3.
174. Brook, R., *op. cit.*, pp.69-70.
Borden, J., 'Eltham Revisited', *Torch*, vol. xi, no. 2, Winter 1977, pp.43-4.
175. Brook, R., *op. cit.*, p.69.
176. *Torch*, vol. v, no. 3, May 1963.
177. *Ibid.*, vol. i, no. 1, Summer 1992, p.55.
178. *Ibid.*
179. *The Times*, 15 May 1990.
Daily Telegraph, 15 May 1990.
180. *Torch*, vol. i, no. 2, Winter 1992; vol. ii, no. 1, Spring 1993.
181. *Torch, Army Education, R.A.E.C. Gazette* September 1947 onwards.
182. *Eltham and Kentish Times*, 7 July 1950, 29 June 1951, 16 July 1954, 13 July 1956, 5 July 1957, 14 July 1961, 5 July 1963, 10 July 1964, 15 July 1966.
Torch, Army Education, R.A.E.C. Gazette September 1947 onwards.
183. *Eltham and Kentish Times*, 5 July 1946, 15 July 1955, 6 July 1956.
184. *Ibid.* 7 July 1950, 29 June 1951, 16 July 1954, 6 July 1956, 5, 12 July 1957, 14 July 1961.
185. Personal information.
186. *Ibid.*
187. Brook, R., *op. cit.*.
Torch (ETS (Army) and R.A.E.C. Assn), vol. ii, no. 2, Winter 1993, p.22.
188. *Eltham and Kentish Times*, 14 June 1946.
189. *Ibid.*, 22, 29 May, 5 June 1953.
190. *Ibid.* 29 May, 12 June 1953.
191. *Ibid.*, 14 June, 13, 20 September, 4, 25 October, 8, 15 November 1946, 19 September 1952, 11 June 1954, 17 December 1965, 13 June 1969.
192. *Ibid.*, 4 July 1947, 13, 20 July 1951, 8, 15 June 1953, 5 July 1957, 14 December 1962, 3, 10 December 1965, 17 June 1966, 20 January, 28 April 1967, 12, 19 January, 5 April 1968, 4 April, 1 August, 19 December 1969.
193. *Ibid.*, 13 December 1946, 8 July 1955, 10 August 1962, 8 December 1967, 13 June 1969.

194. *Ibid.*, 16, 23 September 1966.
195. *Ibid.*, 3, 24 September, 8 October 1954, 5 July 1957, 11 May 1962, 17 November, 22 December 1967.
196. *Ibid.*, 19 September 1947.
Towey, J., 'Mastermind at Eltham', *Eltham Palace and Eltham People* (2003), pp.26-8.
197. Towey, J., 'Any Questions?', *Eltham Palace and Eltham People* (2003), pp.40-2.
198. *Eltham and Kentish Times*, 27 August 1954, 24 May 1957, 20 May, 5 August 1966, 26 January, 21 June 1968.
199. *Ibid.*, 18 April 1969.
200. *Ibid.*, 26 August, 16 September 1960.
201. *Ibid.*, 1 June, 5, 12, 19 September 1947, 27 August, 3 September 1948.
202. *Ibid.*, 28 June, 4 August 1946, 28 November 1952, 12 January 1954, 3 May, 28 June 1957, 20 October 1961, 2 November 1962.
203. Middleton, P.A., *Chaos; Happy and Glorious; Faces and Places; Eltham (Around and About)*; 1960s.
204. *News Shopper*, 20, 27 September 1995.
The Independent, 22 September 1995.
Heritage Today, September 1995, p.7.
Evening Standard, 20 September 1995.
Sunday Telegraph, 10 September 1995.
Kentish Times, 28 September 1995.
English Heritage News Release, 21 September 1995.
Powers, A., 'Eltham Palace, London', *Country Life*, 9 November 1995, pp.68-71.
The Scotsman, 28 December 1995.
The Times, 10 April 1996.
Sunday Times, 31 March 1996.
Priestley, F.J., 'Return to Eltham', *Torch*, vol. v, no. 1, Summer 1996, pp.29-30.
205. *Sunday Times*, 16 March 1996.
206. *Sunday Telegraph*, 4 April 1999.
Turner, M., *op. cit.*, pp.43-4.
'Eltham Palace', *The World of Interiors*, June 1999, pp.116-25.
Herdman, S., 'Tale of the Unexpected', *BBC Homes and Antiques*, June 1999, pp.55-60.
Pitman, J., 'Another Time, Another Place', *The Times Magazine*, 12 June 1999, pp.28-32.
Worsley, G., 'Homage to Hollywood', *Daily Telegraph*, 14 June 1999.
'Big Day Out', *Metro*, 15 June 1999.
Silvester-Carr, D., 'Art Deco Renaissance', *History Today*, July 1999, pp.5-6.
Musson, J., 'Eltham Palace, London', *Country Life*, 17 June 1999, pp.86-91.
Campbell Dixon, A., 'Hollywood Meets the Tudors', *Daily Telegraph Travel Section*, 3 July 1999, p.13.
Grant, L., 'The Revival of Eltham Palace', *The Lady*, 13-19 July 1999, pp.32-3.
King, M., 'Playpen of the Rich', *Heritage*, April/May 2000, pp.48-9.
Abitare, G.C., '1933 Eltham Palace', September 2001, pp.128-33.

Select Bibliography

Brook, R., *The Story of Eltham Palace* (1960)

Buckler, J.C., *An Historical and Descriptive Account of the Royal Palace at Eltham* (1828)

Clapham, A.W. and Godfrey, W.H., *Some Famous Buildings and Their Story* (1913)

Colvin, H.M. (ed.), *The King's Works*, vols. i, ii (1963), iv (1982)

Drake, H.H. (ed.), *Hasted's History of Kent Corrected: Part i: The Hundred of Blackheath* (1886)

Dunnage, H. and Laver, C., *Plans, Elevations, Sections, Details and Views of the Great Hall of the Royal Palace of Eltham in Kent, with an Essay Historical and Descriptive* (1828)

Fraser, C.M., *A History of Antony Bek* (1957)

Gregory, R.R.C., *The Story of Royal Eltham* (1909)

Salzman, L.F., *Building in England down to 1540* (1952)

Strong, D.E., *Eltham Palace* (1958, 1963, 1983, 1986 edns)

Turner, M., *Eltham Palace* (1999)

ARTICLES

Aslet, C., 'An Interview with the late Paul Paget', *The Thirties Society Journal*, no. 6 (1987), pp.16–23

Emery, A., 'Eltham Palace', *Archaeologia Cantiana*, vol. 74 (1960), pp.99–112

Hussey, C., 'Eltham Hall I, II, III', *Country Life*, vol. 81, 15, 22, 29 May 1937, pp.534–9, 568–73, 594–9

Pragnell, H.J., 'Eltham Palace: Its Chapels and Chaplains', *Archaeologia Cantiana*, vol. 83 (1968), pp.205–16

Priestley, E.J., 'Artists' Views of a Kentish Palace'; 'First Canpaign to Preserve a Building?', *Country Life*, vols 127, 3 June 1965, pp.1342–3; 161, 26 May 1977, pp.1412, 1414

Woods, H., 'Excavations at Eltham Palace, 1975–9', *Transactions of London and Middlesex Archaeological Society*, vol. 33 (1982), pp.215–65

UNPUBLISHED THESIS

Priestley, E.J., 'The Manor and Palace of Eltham 1086–1663' (M.Phil, London University, 1973).

MSS

Bodleian Library, Oxford; British Library (MSS Dept.); Cambridge University Library; College of Arms; Crown Estates Office; Trinity College, Dublin; Edinburgh University Library; St John's Church, Eltham; Kent Archives Office; Lambeth Palace Library; National Archives; Principal Probate Registry; Westminster Abbey Archives; Woolwich Reference Library.

INDEX